PYTHON AND PYGAME
FUNDAMENTALS AND APPLICATIONS

Kruger Brentt
Publishers

PYTHON AND PYGAME
FUNDAMENTALS AND APPLICATIONS

Gustavo Ponce
Daniel Roberto

Kruger Brentt
Publishers

2025

Kruger Brentt Publishers UK. LTD.
Company Number 9728962

Regd. Office: 68 St Margarets Road, Edgware, Middlesex HA8 9UU

ISBN: 978-1-78715-379-0

For information on all our publications visit our website at http://krugerbrentt.com/

PREFACE

Python, with its simplicity, versatility, and robust ecosystem of libraries, has become one of the most popular programming languages for a wide range of applications, from web development and data science to artificial intelligence and game development. Pygame, a set of Python modules designed for creating video games, extends the capabilities of Python into the realm of interactive multimedia applications, providing developers with a powerful platform for building games and simulations. Understanding the fundamentals of Python and Pygame is essential for aspiring game developers, educators, and enthusiasts seeking to create interactive experiences and unleash their creativity in the digital realm.

This handbook, titled **"Python and Pygame: Fundamentals and Applications**" is a comprehensive exploration of the principles, techniques, and applications of Python programming and Pygame development. Drawing upon the expertise of software engineers, game developers, and educators, this volume offers theoretical insights, practical guidance, and hands-on examples for understanding and utilizing Python and Pygame in various projects and applications.

From the basic syntax and data structures of Python to the advanced features and libraries of Pygame, "Python and Pygame" covers a wide range of topics essential for mastering the fundamentals of game development. Through clear explanations, code snippets, and interactive exercises, readers will gain a deep understanding of the principles and techniques used to create interactive multimedia applications using Python and Pygame.

Moreover, this handbook explores the applications of Python and Pygame across different domains and projects, including game development, interactive simulations, educational tools, and multimedia presentations. By examining case studies, project tutorials, and creative examples, we highlight the diverse ways in which Python and Pygame can be used to bring ideas to life and engage audiences in interactive experiences.

As we continue to explore new frontiers in digital creativity and interactive media, the importance of Python and Pygame in enabling game development and multimedia applications has never been greater. It is our hope that "Python and Pygame: Fundamentals and Applications" will serve as a valuable resource for developers, educators, and hobbyists in the field of game development and interactive media. Whether you are creating your first game, teaching programming concepts, or exploring the possibilities of interactive multimedia, this handbook invites you to dive into the world of Python and Pygame and unleash your creativity in the digital domain.

Gustavo Ponce
Daniel Roberto

CONTENTS

1 Chapter

INSTALLING PYTHON AND PYGAME

WHAT YOU SHOULD KNOW BEFORE YOU BEGIN

It might help if you know a bit about Python programming (or how to program in another language besides Python) before you read through this book; however even if you haven't you can still read this book anyway. Programming isn't nearly as hard as people think it is.

You don't need to know how to use the Pygame library before reading this book. The next chapter is a brief tutorial on all of Pygame's major features and functions.

Just in case you haven't read the first book and already installed Python and Pygame on your computer, the installation instructions are in this chapter. If you already have installed both of these then you can skip this chapter.

DOWNLOADING AND INSTALLING PYTHON

Before we can begin programming you'll need to install software called the Python interpreter on your computer. (You may need to ask an adult for help here.) The **interpreter** is a program that understands the instructions that you'll write (or rather, type out) in the Python language. Without the interpreter, your computer won't be able to run your Python programs. We'll just refer to "the Python interpreter" as "Python" from now on.

Windows Instructions

When you get to http://python.org, you should see a list of links on the left (such as "About", "News", "Documentation", "Download", and so on). Click on the **Download** link to go to the download page, then look for the file called "Python 3.2 Windows Installer (Windows binary -- does not include source)" and click on its link to download Python for Windows.

Double-click on the *python-3.2.msi* file that you've just downloaded to start the Python installer. (If it doesn't start, try right-clicking the file and choosing **Install**.) Once the installer starts up, just keep clicking the **Next** button and just accept the choices in the installer as you go (no need to make any changes). When the install is finished, click **Finish**.

Mac OS X Instructions

Mac OS X 10.5 comes with Python 2.5.1 pre-installed by Apple. Currently, Pygame only supports Python 2 and not Python 3. However, the programs in this book work with both Python 2 and 3.

The Python website also has some additional information about using Python on a Mac at http://docs.python.org/dev/using/mac.html.

UBUNTU AND LINUX INSTRUCTIONS

Pygame for Linux also only supports Python 2, not Python 3. If your operating system is Ubuntu, you can install Python by opening a terminal window (from the desktop click on **Applications > Accessories > Terminal**) and entering "sudo apt-get install python2.7" then pressing Enter. You will need to enter the root password to install Python, so ask the person who owns the computer to type in this password if you do not know it.

You also need to install the IDLE software. From the terminal, type in "sudo apt-get install idle". The root password is also needed to install IDLE (ask the owner of your computer to type in this password for you).

STARTING PYTHON

We will be using the IDLE software to type in our programs and run them. IDLE stands for **I**nteractive **D**eve**L**opment **E**nvironment. The development environment is software that makes it easy to write Python programs, just like word processor software makes it easy to write books.

If your operating system is Windows XP, you should be able to run Python by clicking the Start button, then selecting Programs, Python 3.1, IDLE (Python GUI). For Windows Vista or Windows 7, just click the Windows button in the lower left corner, type "IDLE" and select "IDLE (Python GUI)".

If your operating system is Max OS X, start IDLE by opening the Finder window and click on Applications, then click Python 3.2, then click the IDLE icon.

If your operating system is Ubuntu or Linux, start IDLE by opening a terminal window and then type "idle3" and press Enter. You may also be able to click on Applications at the top of the screen, and then select Programming, then IDLE 3.

The window that appears when you first run IDLE is called the **interactive shell.** A **shell** is a program that lets you type instructions into the computer. The Python shell lets you type Python instructions, and the shell sends these instructions to the Python interpreter to perform.

INSTALLING PYGAME

Pygame does not come with Python. Like Python, Pygame is available for free. You will have to download and install Pygame, which is as easy as downloading and installing the Python interpreter. In a web browser, go to the URL http://pygame.org and click on the "Downloads" link on the left side of the web site. This book assumes you have the Windows operating system, but Pygame works the same for every operating system. You need to download the Pygame installer for your operating system and the version of Python you have installed.

You do not want to download the "source" for Pygame, but rather the Pygame "binary" for your operating system. For Windows, download the pygame-1.9.1.win32-py3.2.msi file. (This is Pygame for Python 3.2 on Windows. If you installed a different version of Python (such as 2.7 or 2.6) download the .msi file for your version of Python.) The current version of Pygame at the time this book was written is 1.9.1. If you see a newer version on the website, download and install the newer Pygame.

For Mac OS X, download the .zip or .dmg file for the version of Python you have and run it.

For Linux, open a terminal and run “sudo apt-get install python-pygame”.

On Windows, double click on the downloaded file to install Pygame. To check that Pygame is install correctly, type the following into the interactive shell:

```
>>> import pygame
```

If nothing appears after you hit the Enter key, then you know Pygame has successfully been installed. If the error ImportError: No module named pygame appears, then try to install Pygame again (and make sure you typed import pygame correctly).

This chapter has five small programs that demonstrate how to use the different features that Pygame provides. In the last chapter, you will use these features for a complete game written in Python with Pygame.

HOW TO USE THIS BOOK

“Python and Pygame: Fundamentals and Applications” is different from other programming books because it focuses on the complete source code for several game programs. Instead of teaching you programming concepts and leaving it up to you to figure out how to make programs with those concepts, this book shows you some programs and then explains how they are put together.

In general, you should read these chapters in order. There are many concepts that are used over and over in these games, and they are only explained in detail in the first game they appear in. But if there is a game you think is interesting, go ahead and jump to that chapter. You can always read the previous chapters later if you got ahead of yourself.

THE FEATURED PROGRAMS

Each chapter focuses on a single game program and explain how different parts of the code work. It is very helpful to copy these programs by typing in the code line by line from this book.

LINE NUMBERS AND SPACES

When entering the source code yourself, do not type the line numbers that appear at the beginning of each line. For example, if you see this in the book:

```
1. number = random.randint(1, 20)

2. spam = 42

3. print('Hello world!')
```

You do not need to type the “1.” on the left side, or the space that immediately follows it. Just type it like this:

```
number = random.randint(1, 20)
```

```
spam = 42
print('Hello world!')
```

Those numbers are only used so that this book can refer to specific lines in the code. They are not a part of the actual program.

Aside from the line numbers, be sure to enter the code exactly as it appears. Notice that some of the lines don't begin at the leftmost edge of the page, but are indented by four or eight or more spaces. Be sure to put in the correct number of spaces at the start of each line. (Since each character in IDLE is the same width, you can count the number of spaces by counting the number of characters above or below the line you're looking at.)

For example in the code below, you can see that the second line is indented by four spaces because the four characters ("whil") on the line above are over the indented space. The third line is indented by another four spaces (the four characters, "if n" are above the third line's indented space):

```
while spam < 10:
    if number == 42:
        print('Hello')
```

TEXT WRAPPING IN THIS BOOK

Some lines of code are too long to fit on one line on the pages in this book, and the text of the code will wrap around to the next line. When you type these lines into the file editor, enter the code all on one line without pressing Enter.

You can tell when a new line starts by looking at the line numbers on the left side of the code. For example, the code below has only two lines of code, even though the first line wraps around:

```
1. print('This is the first line! xxxxxxxxxxxxxxxxxxxxxxxxxxxxxxxxxxxxxxxx
xxx')
2. print('This is the second line, not the third line.')
```

CHECKING YOUR CODE ONLINE

Some of the programs in this book are a little long. Although it is very helpful to learn Python by typing out the source code for these programs, you may accidentally make typos that cause your programs to crash. It may not be obvious where the typo is.

You can copy and paste the text of your source code to the online diff tool on the book's website. The diff tool will show any differences between the source code in the book and the source code you've typed. This is an easy way of finding any typos in your program.

2 Chapter PYGAME BASICS

Just like how Python comes with several modules like random, math, or time that provide additional functions for your programs, the Pygame framework includes several modules with functions for drawing graphics, playing sounds, handling mouse input, and other things.

This chapter will cover the basic modules and functions that Pygame provides and assumes you already know basic Python programming.

GUI VS. CLI

The Python programs that you can write with Python's built-in functions only deal with text through the print() and input() functions. Your program can display text on the screen and let the user type in text from the keyboard. This type of program has a **command line interface**, or **CLI** (which is pronounced like the first part of "climb" and rhymes with "sky"). These programs are somewhat limited because they can't display graphics, have colors, or use the mouse. These CLI programs only get input from the keyboard with the input() function and even then user must press Enter before the program can respond to the input. This means **real-time** (that is, continuing to run code without waiting for the user) action games are impossible to make.

Pygame provides functions for creating programs with a **graphical user interface**, or **GUI** (pronounced, "gooey"). Instead of a text-based CLI, programs with a graphics-based GUI can show a window with images and colors.

SOURCE CODE FOR HELLO WORLD WITH PYGAME

Our first program made with Pygame is a small program that makes a window that says "Hello World!" appear on the screen. Open a new file editor window by clicking on IDLE's **File** menu, then **New Window**. Type in the following code into IDLE's file editor and save it as *blankpygame.py*. Then run the program by pressing **F5** or selecting **Run > Run Module** from the menu at the top of the file editor.

Remember, do not type the numbers or the periods at the beginning of each line (that's just for reference in this book).

```
import pygame, sys
from pygame.locals import *

pygame.init()
DISPLAYSURF = pygame.display.set_mode((400, 300))
pygame.display.set_caption('Hello World!')
while True: # main game loop
    for event in pygame.event.get():
        if event.type == QUIT:
            pygame.quit()
            sys.exit()
    pygame.display.update()
```

When you run this program, a black window like this will appear:

Yay! You've just made the world's most boring video game! It's just a blank window with "Hello World!" at the top of the window (in what is called the window's **title bar**, which holds the **caption** text). But creating a window is the first step to making graphical games. When you click on the X button in the corner of the window, the program will end and the window will disappear.

Calling the print() function to make text appear in the window won't work because print() is a function for CLI programs. The same goes for input() to get keyboard input from the user. Pygame uses other functions for input and output which are explained later in this chapter. For now, let's look at each line in our "Hello World" program in more detail.

SETTING UP A PYGAME PROGRAM

The first few lines of code in the Hello World program are lines that will begin almost every program you write that uses Pygame.

```
1. import pygame, sys
```

Line 1 is a simple import statement that imports the pygame and sys modules so that our program can use the functions in them. All of the Pygame functions dealing with graphics, sound, and other features that Pygame provides are in the pygame module.

Note that when you import the pygame module you automatically import all the modules that are in the pygame module as well, such as pygame.images and pygame.mixer.music. There's no need to import these modules-inside-modules with additional import statements.

```
2. from pygame.locals import *
```

Line 2 is also an import statement. However, instead of the import modulename format, it uses the from modulename import * format. Normally if you want to call a function that is in a module, you must use the modulename.functionname() format after importing the module. However, with from modulename import *, you can skip the modulename. portion and simply use functionname() (just like Python's built-in functions).

The reason we use this form of import statement for pygame.locals is because pygame.locals contains several constant variables that are easy to identify as being in the pygame.locals module without pygame.locals. in front of them. For all other modules, you generally want to use the regular import modulename format.

```
4. pygame.init()
```

Line 4 is the pygame.init() function call, which always needs to be called after importing the pygame module and before calling any other Pygame function. You don't need to know what this function does, you just need to know that it needs to be called first in order for many Pygame functions to work. If you ever see an error message like pygame.error: font not initialized, check to see if you forgot to call pygame.init() at the start of your program.

```
5. DISPLAYSURF = pygame.display.set_mode((400, 300))
```

Line 5 is a call to the pygame.display.set_mode() function, which returns the pygame.Surface object for the window. (Surface objects are described later in this chapter.) Notice that we pass a tuple value of two integers to the function: (400, 300). This tuple tells the set_mode() function how wide and how high to make the window in pixels. (400, 300) will make a window with a width of 400 pixels and height of 300 pixels.

Remember to pass a tuple of two integers to set_mode(), not just two integers themselves. The correct way to call the function is like this: pygame.display.set_mode((400, 300)). A function call like pygame.display.set_mode(400, 300) will cause an error that looks like this: TypeError: argument 1 must be 2-item sequence, not int.

The pygame.Surface object (we will just call them Surface objects for short) returned is stored in a variable named DISPLAYSURF.

```
6. pygame.display.set_caption('Hello World!')
```

Line 6 sets the caption text that will appear at the top of the window by calling the pygame.display.set_caption() function. The string value 'Hello World!' is passed in this function call to make that text appear as the caption:

GAME LOOPS AND GAME STATES

```
7. while True: # main game loop
8.     for event in pygame.event.get():
```

Line 7 is a while loop that has a condition of simply the value True. This means that it never exits due to its condition evaluating to False. The only way the program execution will ever exit the loop is if a break statement is executed (which moves execution to the first line after the loop) or sys.exit() (which terminates the program). If a loop like this was inside a function, a return statement will also move execution out of the loop (as well as the function too).

The games in this book all have these while True loops in them along with a comment calling it the "main game loop". A **game loop** (also called a **main loop**) is a loop where the code does three things:

1. Handles events.
2. Updates the game state.
3. Draws the game state to the screen.

The **game state** is simply a way of referring to a set of values for all the variables in a game program. In many games, the game state includes the values in the variables that tracks the player's health and position, the health and position of any enemies, which marks have been made on a board, the score, or whose turn it is. Whenever something happens like the player taking damage (which lowers their health value), or an enemy moves somewhere, or something happens in the game world we say that the game state has changed.

If you've ever played a game that let you saved, the "save state" is the game state at the point that you've saved it. In most games, pausing the game will prevent the game state from changing.

Since the game state is usually updated in response to events (such as mouse clicks or keyboard presses) or the passage of time, the game loop is constantly checking and re-checking many times a second for any new events that have happened. Inside the main loop is code that looks at which events have been created (with Pygame, this is done by calling the pygame.event.get() function). The main loop also has code that updates the game state based on which events have been created. This is usually called **event handling.**

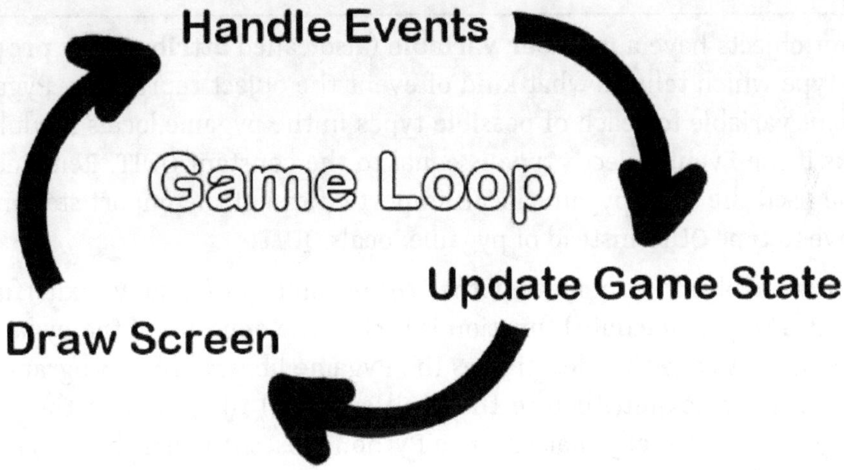

pygame.event.Event Objects

Any time the user does one of several actions (they are listed later in this chapter) such as pressing a keyboard key or moving the mouse on the program's window, a pygame.event.Event object is created by the Pygame library to record this "event". (This is a type of object called Event that exists in the event module, which itself is in the pygame module.) We can find out which events have happened by calling the pygame.event.get() function, which returns a list of pygame.event. Event objects (which we will just call Event objects for short).

The list of Event objects will be for each event that has happened since the last time the pygame.event.get() function was called. (Or, if pygame.event.get() has never been called, the events that have happened since the start of the program.)

```
7. while True: # main game loop
8.     for event in pygame.event.get():
```

Line 8 is a for loop that will iterate over the list of Event objects that was returned by pygame.event.get(). On each iteration through the for loop, a variable named event will be assigned the value of the next event object in this list. The list of Event objects returned from pygame.event.get() will be in the order that the events happened. If the user clicked the mouse and then pressed a keyboard key, the Event object for the mouse click would be the first item in the list and the Event object for the keyboard press would be second. If no events have happened, then pygame.event.get() will return a blank list.

THE QUIT EVENT AND PYGAME.QUIT() FUNCTION

```
9.          if event.type == QUIT:
10.             pygame.quit()
11.             sys.exit()
```

Event objects have a **member variable** (also called **attributes** or **properties**) named type which tells us what kind of event the object represents. Pygame has a constant variable for each of possible types in the pygame.locals modules. Line 9 checks if the Event object's type is equal to the constant QUIT. Remember that since we used the from pygame.locals import * form of the import statement, we only have to type QUIT instead of pygame.locals.QUIT.

If the Event object is a quit event, then the pygame.quit() and sys.exit() functions are called. The pygame.quit() function is sort of the opposite of the pygame.init() function: it runs code that deactivates the Pygame library. Your programs should always call pygame.quit() before they call sys.exit() to terminate the program. Normally it doesn't really matter since Python closes it when the program exits anyway. But there is a bug in IDLE that causes IDLE to hang if a Pygame program terminates before pygame.quit() is called.

Since we have no if statements that run code for other types of Event object, there is no event-handling code for when the user clicks the mouse, presses keyboard keys, or causes any other type of Event objects to be created. The user can do things to create these Event objects but it doesn't change anything in the program because the program does not have any event-handling code for these types of Event objects. After the for loop on line 8 is done handling all the Event objects that have been returned by pygame.event.get(), the program execution continues to line 12.

```
12.     pygame.display.update()
```

Line 12 calls the pygame.display.update() function, which draws the Surface object returned by pygame.display.set_mode() to the screen (remember we stored this object in the DISPLAYSURF variable). Since the Surface object hasn't changed (for example, by some of the drawing functions that are explained later in this chapter), the same black image is redrawn to the screen each time pygame.display.update() is called.

That is the entire program. After line 12 is done, the infinite while loop starts again from the beginning. This program does nothing besides make a black window appear on the screen, constantly check for a QUIT event, and then redraws the unchanged black window to the screen over and over again. Let's learn how to make interesting things appear on this window instead of just blackness by learning about pixels, Surface objects, Color objects, Rect objects, and the Pygame drawing functions.

PIXEL COORDINATES

The window that the "Hello World" program creates is just composed of little square dots on your screen called **pixels**. Each pixel starts off as black but can be set to a different color. Imagine that instead of a Surface object that is 400 pixels wide and 300 pixels tall, we just had a Surface object that was 8 pixels by 8 pixels. If that tiny 8x8 Surface was enlarged so that each pixel looks like a square in a grid, and we added numbers for the X and Y axis, then a good representation of it could look something like this:

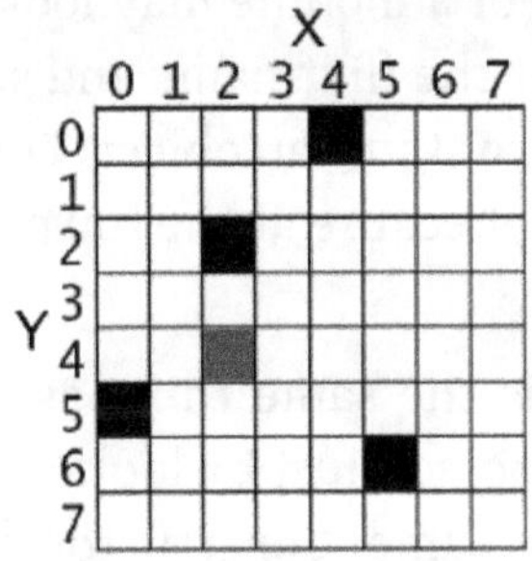

We can refer to a specific pixel by using a Cartesian Coordinate system. Each column of the **X-axis** and each row of the **Y-axis** will have an "address" that is an integer from 0 to 7 so that we can locate any pixel by specifying the X and Y axis integers.

For example, in the above 8x8 image, we can see that the pixels at the XY coordinates (4, 0), (2, 2), (0, 5), and (5, 6) have been painted black, the pixel at (2, 4) has been painted gray, while all the other pixels are painted white. XY coordinates are also called **points**. If you've taken a math class and learned about Cartesian Coordinates, you might notice that the Y-axis starts at 0 at the *top* and then increases going *down*, rather than increasing as it goes up. This is just how Cartesian Coordinates work in Pygame (and almost every programming language).

The Pygame framework often represents Cartesian Coordinates as a tuple of two integers, such as (4, 0) or (2, 2). The first integer is the X coordinate and the second is the Y coordinate.

A REMINDER ABOUT FUNCTIONS, METHODS, CONSTRUCTOR FUNCTIONS, AND FUNCTIONS IN MODULES (AND THE DIFFERENCE BETWEEN THEM)

Functions and methods are almost the same thing. They can both be called to execute the code in them. The difference between a function and a method is that a method will always be attached to an object. Usually methods change something about that particular object (you can think of the attached object as a sort of permanent argument passed to the method).

This is a function call of a function named foo():

```
foo()
```

This is a method call of a method also named foo(), which is attached to an object stored in a variable named duckie:

```
duckie.foo()
```

A call to a function inside of a module may look like a method call. To tell the difference, you need to look at the first name and see if it is the name of a module or the name of a variable that contains an object. You can tell that sys.exit() is a call to function inside of a module, because at the top of the program will be an import statement like import sys.

A **constructor function** is the same thing as a normal function call, except that its return value is a new object. Just by looking at source code, a function and constructor function look the same. Constructor functions (also called simply a "constructor" or sometimes "ctor" ("see-tor") for short) are just a name given to functions that return a new object. But usually ctors start with a capital letter. This is why when you write your own programs, your function names should only begin with a lowercase letter.

For example, pygame.Rect() and pygame.Surface() are both constructor functions inside the pygame module that return new Rect and Surface objects. (These objects are described later.)

Here's an example of a function call, a method call, and a call to a function inside a module:

```
import whammy
fizzy()
```

```
egg = Wombat()
egg.bluhbluh()
whammy.spam()
```

Even though these names are all made up, you can tell which is a function call, a method call, and a call to a function inside a method. The name whammy refers to a module, since you can see it is being imported on the first line. The fizzy name has nothing before it and parentheses after it, so you know it is a function call.

Wombat() is also a function call, in this case it is a constructor function that returns an object. (The capital letter that it starts with isn't a guarantee that it's a constructor function rather than a regular function, but it is a safe bet.) The object is stored in a variable named egg. The egg.bluhbluh() call is a method call, which you can tell because bluhbluh is attached to a variable with an object in it.

Meanwhile, whammy.spam() is a function call, not a method call. You can tell it is not a method because the name whammy was imported as a module earlier.

SURFACE OBJECTS AND THE WINDOW

Surface objects are objects that represent a rectangular 2D image. The pixels of the Surface object can be changed by calling the Pygame drawing functions (described later in this chapter) and then displayed on the screen. The window border, title bar, and buttons are not part of the display Surface object.

In particular, the Surface object returned by pygame.display.set_mode() is called the **display Surface**. Anything that is drawn on the display Surface object will be displayed on the window when the pygame.display.update() function is called. It is a lot faster to draw on a Surface object (which only exists in the computer's memory) than it is to draw a Surface object to the computer screen. Computer memory is much faster to change than pixels on a monitor.

Often your program will draw several different things to a Surface object. Once you are done drawing everything on the display Surface object for this iteration of the game loop (called a **frame**, just like a still image on a paused DVD is called) on a Surface object, it can be drawn to the screen. The computer can draw frames very quickly, and our programs will often run around 30 frames per second (that is, 30 FPS). This is called the "frame rate" and is explained later in this chapter.

Drawing on Surface objects will be covered in the "Primitive Drawing Functions" and "Drawing Images" sections later this chapter.

COLORS

There are three primary colors of light: red, green and blue. (Red, blue, and yellow are the primary colors for paints and pigments, but the computer monitor uses light, not paint.) By combining different amounts of these three colors you can form any other color. In Pygame, we represent colors with tuples of three integers. The first value in the tuple is how much red is in the color. An integer value of 0 means there is no red in this color, and a value of 255 means there is the maximum amount of red in the color. The second value is for green and the third value is for blue. These tuples of three integers used to represent a color are often called **RGB values.**

Because you can use any combination of 0 to 255 for each of the three primary colors, this means Pygame can draw 16,777,216 different colors (that is, 256 x 256 x 256 colors). However, if try to use a number larger than 255 or a negative number, you will get an error that looks like "ValueError: invalid color argument".

For example, we will create the tuple (0, 0, 0) and store it in a variable named BLACK. With no amount of red, green, or blue, the resulting color is completely black. The color black is the absence of any color. The tuple (255, 255, 255) for a maximum amount of red, green, and blue to result in white. The color white is the full combination of red, green, and blue. The tuple (255, 0, 0) represents the maximum amount of red but no amount of green and blue, so the resulting color is red. Similarly, (0, 255, 0) is green and (0, 0, 255) is blue.

You can mix the amount of red, green, and blue to form other colors. Here are the RGB values for a few common colors:

Color	RGB Values
Aqua	(0, 255, 255)
Black	(0, 0, 0)
Blue	(0, 0, 255)
Fuchsia	(255, 0, 255)
Gray	(128, 128, 128)
Green	(0, 128, 0)
Lime	(0, 255, 0)
Maroon	(128, 0, 0)
Navy Blue	(0, 0, 128)
Olive	(128, 128, 0)
Purple	(128, 0, 128)
Red	(255, 0, 0)
Silver	(192, 192, 192)
Teal	(0, 128, 128)
White	(255, 255, 255)
Yellow	(255, 255, 0)

TRANSPARENT COLORS

When you look through a glass window that has a deep red tint, all of the colors behind it have a red shade added to them. You can mimic this effect by adding a fourth 0 to 255 integer value to your color values.

This value is known as the **alpha value**. It is a measure of how opaque (that is, not transparent) a color is. Normally when you draw a pixel onto a surface object, the new color completely replaces whatever color was already there. But with colors that have an alpha value, you can instead just add a colored tint to the color that is already there.

For example, this tuple of three integers is for the color green: (0, 255, 0). But if we add a fourth integer for the alpha value, we can make this a half transparent green color: (0, 255, 0, 128). An alpha value of 255 is completely opaque (that is, not transparency at all). The colors (0, 255, 0) and (0, 255, 0, 255) look exactly the same. An alpha value of 0 means the color is completely transparent. If you draw any color that has an alpha value of 0 to a surface object, it will have no effect, because this color is completely transparent and invisible.

In order to draw using transparent colors, you must create a Surface object with the convert_alpha() method. For example, the following code creates a Surface object that transparent colors can be drawn on:

```
anotherSurface = DISPLAYSURF.convert_alpha()
```

Once things have been drawn on the Surface object stored in anotherSurface, then anotherSurface can be "blitted" (that is, copied) to DISPLAYSURF so it will appear on the screen. (See the "Drawing Images with pygame.image.load() and blit()" section later in this chapter.)

It's important to note that you cannot use transparent colors on Surface objects not returned from a convert_alpha() call, including the display Surface that was returned from pygame.display.set_mode().

If we were to create a color tuple to draw the legendary Invisible Pink Unicorn, we would use (255, 192, 192, 0), which ends up looking completely invisible just like any other color that has a 0 for its alpha value. It is, after all, invisible.

(Above is a screenshot of a drawing of the Invisible Pink Unicorn.)

PYGAME.COLOR OBJECTS

You need to know how to represent a color because Pygame's drawing functions need a way to know what color you want to draw with. A tuple of three or four integers is one way. Another way is as a pygame.Color object. You can create Color objects by calling the pygame.Color() constructor function and passing either three or four integers. You can store this Color object in variables just like you can store tuples in variables. Try typing the following into the interactive shell:

```
>>> import pygame
>>> pygame.Color(255, 0, 0)
(255, 0, 0, 255)
>>> myColor = pygame.Color(255, 0, 0, 128)
>>> myColor == (255, 0, 0, 128)
True
>>>
```

Any drawing function in Pygame (which we will learn about in a bit) that has a parameter for color can have either the tuple form or Color object form of a color passed for it. Even though they are different data types, a Color object is equal to a tuple of four integers if they both represent the same color (just like how 42 == 42.0 will evaluate to True).

Now that you know how to represent colors (as a pygame.Color object or a tuple of three or four integers for red, green, blue, and optionally alpha) and coordinates (as a tuple of two integers for X and Y), let's learn about pygame.Rect objects so we can start using Pygame's drawing functions.

RECT OBJECTS

Pygame has two ways to represent rectangular areas (just like there are two ways to represent colors). The first is a tuple of four integers:

1. The X coordinate of the top left corner.
2. The Y coordinate of the top left corner.
3. The width (in pixels) of the rectangle.
4. Then height (in pixels) of the rectangle.

The second way is as a pygame.Rect object, which we will call Rect objects for short. For example, the code below creates a Rect object with a top left corner at (10, 20) that is 200 pixels wide and 300 pixels tall:

```
>>> import pygame
>>> spamRect = pygame.Rect(10, 20, 200, 300)
>>> spamRect == (10, 20, 200, 300)
True
```

The handy thing about this is that the Rect object automatically calculates the coordinates for other features of the rectangle. For example, if you need to know the X coordinate of the right edge of the pygame.Rect object we stored in the spamRect variable, you can just access the Rect object's right attribute:

```
>>> spamRect.right
210
```

The Pygame code for the Rect object automatically calculated that if the left edge is at the X coordinate 10 and the rectangle is 200 pixels wide, then the right edge must be at the X coordinate 210. If you reassign the right attribute, all the other attributes are automatically recalculated:

```
>>> spam.right = 350
>>> spam.left
150
```

Here's a list of all the attributes that pygame.Rect objects provide (in our example, the variable where the Rect object is stored in a variable named spamRect):

Attribute Name	Description
myRect.left	The int value of the X-coordinate of the left side of the rectangle.
myRect.right	The int value of the X-coordinate of the right side of the rectangle.
myRect.top	The int value of the Y-coordinate of the top side of the rectangle.
myRect.bottom	The int value of the Y-coordinate of the bottom side.
myRect.centerx	The int value of the X-coordinate of the center of the rectangle.
myRect.centery	The int value of the Y-coordinate of the center of the rectangle.
myRect.width	The int value of the width of the rectangle.
myRect.height	The int value of the height of the rectangle.
myRect.size	A tuple of two ints: (width, height)
myRect.topleft	A tuple of two ints: (left, top)
myRect.topright	A tuple of two ints: (right, top)
myRect. bottomleft	A tuple of two ints: (left, bottom)
myRect. bottomright	A tuple of two ints: (right, bottom)
myRect.midleft	A tuple of two ints: (left, centery)
myRect.midright	A tuple of two ints: (right, centery)
myRect.midtop	A tuple of two ints: (centerx, top)
myRect. midbottom	A tuple of two ints: (centerx, bottom)

PRIMITIVE DRAWING FUNCTIONS

Pygame provides several different functions for drawing different shapes onto a surface object. These shapes such as rectangles, circles, ellipses, lines, or individual pixels are often called **drawing primitives.** Open IDLE's file editor and type in the following program, and save it as *drawing.py*.

```
import pygame, sys
from pygame.locals import *
```

```

pygame.init()

# set up the window
DISPLAYSURF = pygame.display.set_mode((500, 400), 0, 32)
pygame.display.set_caption('Drawing')

# set up the colors
BLACK = (  0,   0,   0)
WHITE = (255, 255, 255)
RED   = (255,   0,   0)
GREEN = (  0, 255,   0)
BLUE  = (  0,   0, 255)

# draw on the surface object
DISPLAYSURF.fill(WHITE)
pygame.draw.polygon(DISPLAYSURF, GREEN, ((146, 0), (291, 106), (236, 277), (56, 277), (0, 106)))
pygame.draw.line(DISPLAYSURF, BLUE, (60, 60), (120, 60), 4)
pygame.draw.line(DISPLAYSURF, BLUE, (120, 60), (60, 120))
pygame.draw.line(DISPLAYSURF, BLUE, (60, 120), (120, 120), 4)
pygame.draw.circle(DISPLAYSURF, BLUE, (300, 50), 20, 0)
pygame.draw.ellipse(DISPLAYSURF, RED, (300, 250, 40, 80), 1)
pygame.draw.rect(DISPLAYSURF, RED, (200, 150, 100, 50))

pixObj = pygame.PixelArray(DISPLAYSURF)
pixObj[480][380] = BLACK
pixObj[482][382] = BLACK
pixObj[484][384] = BLACK
pixObj[486][386] = BLACK
pixObj[488][388] = BLACK
del pixObj

# run the game loop
while True:
    for event in pygame.event.get():
        if event.type == QUIT:
            pygame.quit()
            sys.exit()
    pygame.display.update()
```

When this program is run, the following window is displayed until the user closes the window:

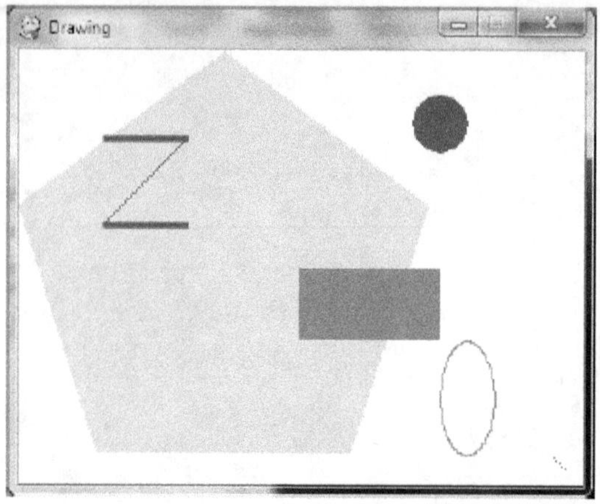

Notice how we make constant variables for each of the colors. Doing this makes our code more readable, because seeing GREEN in the source code is much easier to understand as representing the color green than (0, 255, 0) is.

The drawing functions are named after the shapes they draw. The parameters you pass these functions tell them which Surface object to draw on, where to draw the shape (and what size), in what color, and how wide to make the lines. You can see how these functions are called in the *drawing.py* program, but here is a short description of each function:

- **fill(color)** – The fill() method is not a function but a method of pygame. Surface objects. It will completely fill in the entire Surface object with whatever color value you pass as for the color parameter.
- **pygame.draw.polygon(surface, color, pointlist, width)** – A polygon is shape made up of only flat sides. The surface and color parameters tell the function on what surface to draw the polygon, and what color to make it.

The pointlist parameter is a tuple or list of points (that is, tuple or list of two-integer tuples for XY coordinates). The polygon is drawn by drawing lines between each point and the point that comes after it in the tuple. Then a line is drawn from the last point to the first point. You can also pass a list of points instead of a tuple of points.

The width parameter is optional. If you leave it out, the polygon that is drawn will be filled in, just like our green polygon on the screen is filled in with color. If you do pass an integer value for the width parameter, only the outline of the polygon will be drawn. The integer represents how many pixels width the polygon's outline will be. Passing 1 for the width parameter will make a skinny polygon, while passing 4 or 10 or 20 will make thicker polygons. If you pass the integer 0 for the width parameter, the polygon will be filled in (just like if you left the width parameter out entirely).

All of the pygame.draw drawing functions have optional width parameters at the end, and they work the same way as pygame.draw.polygon()'s width parameter. Probably a better name for the width parameter would have been thickness, since that parameter controls how thick the lines you draw are.

- **pygame.draw.line(surface, color, start_point, end_point, width)** - This function draws a line between the start_point and end_point parameters.
- **pygame.draw.lines(surface, color, closed, pointlist, width)** - This function draws a series of lines from one point to the next, much like pygame.draw.polygon(). The only difference is that if you pass False for the closed parameter, there will not be a line from the last point in the pointlist parameter to the first point. If you pass True, then it will draw a line from the last point to the first.
- **pygame.draw.circle(surface, color, center_point, radius, width)** - This function draws a circle. The center of the circle is at the center_point parameter. The integer passed for the radius parameter sets the size of the circle.
- The radius of a circle is the distance from the center to the edge. (The radius of a circle is always half of the diameter.) Passing 20 for the radius parameter will draw a circle that has a radius of 20 pixels.
- **pygame.draw.ellipse(surface, color, bounding_rectangle, width)** - This function draws an ellipse (which is like a squashed or stretched circle). This function has all the usual parameters, but in order to tell the function how large and where to draw the ellipse, you must specify the bounding rectangle of the ellipse. A **bounding rectangle** is the smallest rectangle that can be drawn around a shape. Here's an example of an ellipse and its bounding rectangle:

  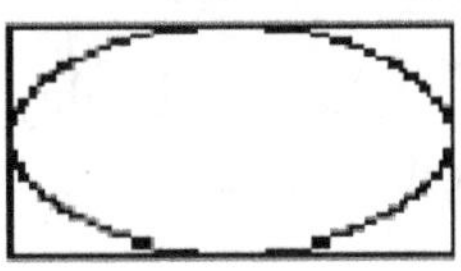

  The bounding_rectangle parameter can be a pygame.Rect object or a tuple of four integers. Note that you do not specify the center point for the ellipse like you do for the pygame.draw.circle() function.
- **pygame.draw.rect(surface, color, rectangle_tuple, width)** - This function draws a rectangle. The rectangle_tuple is either a tuple of four integers (for the XY coordinates of the top left corner, and the width and height) or a pygame.Rect object can be passed instead. If the rectangle_tuple has the same size for the width and height, a square will be drawn.

PYGAME.PIXELARRAY OBJECTS

Unfortunately, there isn't a single function you can call that will set a single pixel to a color (unless you call pygame.draw.line() with the same start and end point). The Pygame framework needs to run some code behind the scenes before and after drawing to a Surface object. If it had to do this for every single pixel you wanted to set, your program would run much slower. (By my quick testing, drawing pixels this way is two or three times slower.)

Instead, you should create a pygame.PixelArray object (we'll call them PixelArray objects for short) of a Surface object and then set individual pixels. Creating a PixelArray object of a Surface object will "lock" the Surface object. While a Surface object is locked, the drawing functions can still be called on it, but it cannot have images like PNG or JPG images drawn on it with the blit() method. (The blit() method is explained later in this chapter.)

If you want to see if a Surface object is locked, the get_locked() Surface method will return True if it is locked and False if it is not.

The PixelArray object that is returned from pygame.PixelArray() can have individual pixels set by accessing them with two indexes. For example, line 28's pixObj[480][380] = BLACK will set the pixel at X coordinate 480 and Y coordinate 380 to be black (remember that the BLACK variable stores the color tuple (0, 0, 0)).

To tell Pygame that you are finished drawing individual pixels, delete the PixelArray object with a del statement. This is what line 33 does. Deleting the PixelArray object will "unlock" the Surface object so that you can once again draw images on it. If you forget to delete the PixelArray object, the next time you try to blit (that is, draw) an image to the Surface the program will raise an error that says, "pygame.error: Surfaces must not be locked during blit".

THE PYGAME.DISPLAY.UPDATE() FUNCTION

After you are done calling the drawing functions to make the display Surface object look the way you want, you must call pygame.display.update() to make the display Surface actually appear on the user's monitor.

The one thing that you must remember is that pygame.display.update() will only make the display Surface (that is, the Surface object that was returned from the call to pygame.display.set_mode()) appear on the screen. If you want the images on other Surface objects to appear on the screen, you must "blit" them (that is, copy them) to the display Surface object with the blit() method (which is explained next in the "Drawing Images" section).

ANIMATION

Now that we know how to get the Pygame framework to draw to the screen, let's learn how to make animated pictures. A game with only still, unmoving images would be fairly dull. (Sales of my game "Look At This Rock" have been disappointing.) Animated images are the result of drawing an image on the screen, then a split second later drawing a slightly different image on the screen. Imagine the program's window was 6 pixels wide and 1 pixel tall, with all the pixels white except for a black pixel at 4, 0. It would look like this:

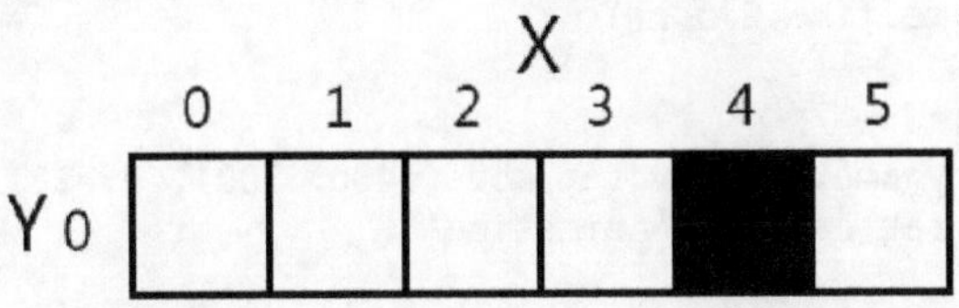

If you changed the window so that 3, 0 was black and 4, 0 was white, it would look like this:

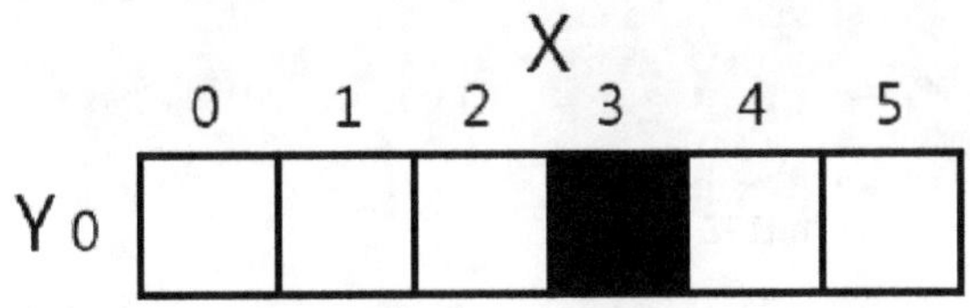

To the user, it looks like the black pixel has "moved" over to the left. If you redrew the window to have the black pixel at 2, 0, it would continue to look like the black pixel is moving left:

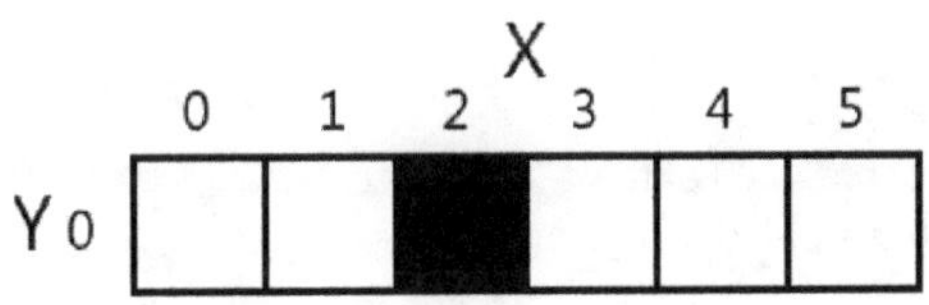

It may look like the black pixel is moving, but this is just an illusion. To the computer, it is just showing three different images that each just happen to have one black pixel. Consider if the three following images were rapidly shown on the screen:

To the user, it would look like the cat is moving towards the squirrel. But to the computer, they're just a bunch of pixels. The trick to making believable looking animation is to have your program draw a picture to the window, wait a fraction of a second, and then draw a *slightly* different picture.

Here is an example program demonstrating a simple animation. Type this code into IDLE's file editor and save it as *catanimation.py*. It will also require the image file cat.png to be in the same folder as the *catanimation.py* file.

```
import pygame, sys
from pygame.locals import *

pygame.init()

FPS = 30 # frames per second setting
fpsClock = pygame.time.Clock()

# set up the window
DISPLAYSURF = pygame.display.set_mode((400, 300), 0, 32)
pygame.display.set_caption('Animation')

WHITE = (255, 255, 255)
catImg = pygame.image.load('cat.png')
catx = 10
caty = 10
direction = 'right'

while True: # the main game loop
    DISPLAYSURF.fill(WHITE)

    if direction == 'right':
        catx += 5
        if catx == 280:
            direction = 'down'
    elif direction == 'down':
        caty += 5
        if caty == 220:
            direction = 'left'
    elif direction == 'left':
        catx -= 5
        if catx == 10:
            direction = 'up'
    elif direction == 'up':
        caty -= 5
        if caty == 10:
            direction = 'right'

    DISPLAYSURF.blit(catImg, (catx, caty))

    for event in pygame.event.get():
        if event.type == QUIT:
            pygame.quit()
            sys.exit()

    pygame.display.update()
```

```
47.     fpsClock.tick(FPS)
```

Look at that animated cat go! This program will be much more of a commercial success than my game, "Look At This Rock 2: A Different Rock".

FRAMES PER SECOND AND PYGAME.TIME.CLOCK OBJECTS

The **frame rate** or **refresh rate** is the number of pictures that the program draws per second, and is measured in **FPS** or **frames per second**. (On computer monitors, the common name for FPS is hertz. Many monitors have a frame rate of 60 hertz, or 60 frames per second.) A low frame rate in video games can make the game look choppy or jumpy. If the program has too much code to run to draw to the screen frequently enough, then the FPS goes down. But the games in this book are simple enough that this won't be issue even on old computers.

A pygame.time.Clock object can help us make sure our program runs at a certain maximum FPS. This Clock object will ensure that our game programs don't run too fast by putting in small pauses on each iteration of the game loop. If we didn't have these pauses, our game program would run as fast as the computer could run it. This is often too fast for the player, and as computers get faster they would run the game faster too. A call to the tick() method of a Clock object in the game loop can make sure the game runs at the same speed no matter how fast of a computer it runs on. The Clock object is created on line 7 of the *catanimation.py* program.

```
7. fpsClock = pygame.time.Clock()
```

The Clock object's tick() method should be called at the very end of the game loop, after the call to pygame.display.update(). The length of the pause is calculated based on how long it has been since the previous call to tick(), which would have taken place at the end of the previous iteration of the game loop. (The first time the tick() method is called, it doesn't pause at all.) In the animation program, is it run on line 47 as the last instruction in the game loop.

All you need to know is that you should call the tick() method once per iteration through the game loop at the end of the loop. Usually this is right after the call to pygame.display.update().

```
47.     fpsClock.tick(FPS)
```

Try modifying the FPS constant variable to run the same program at different frame rates. Setting it to a lower value would make the program run slower. Setting it to a higher value would make the program run faster.

DRAWING IMAGES WITH PYGAME.IMAGE.LOAD() AND BLIT()

The drawing functions are fine if you want to draw simple shapes on the screen, but many games have images (also called **sprites**). Pygame is able to load images onto Surface objects from PNG, JPG, GIF, and BMP image files.

The image of the cat was stored in a file named *cat.png*. To load this file's image, the string 'cat.png' is passed to the pygame.image.load() function. The pygame.image.load() function call will return a Surface object that has the image drawn on it. This Surface object will be a separate Surface object from the display Surface object, so we must blit (that is, copy) the image's Surface object to the display Surface object. **Blitting** is drawing the contents of one Surface onto another. It is done with the blit() Surface object method.

If you get an error message like "pygame.error: Couldn't open cat.png" when calling pygame.image.load(), then make sure the *cat.png* file is in the same folder as the *catanimation.py* file before you run the program.

```
39.     DISPLAYSURF.blit(catImg, (catx, caty))
```

Line 39 of the animation program uses the blit() method to copy catImg to DISPLAYSURF. There are two parameters for blit(). The first is the source Surface object, which is what will be copied onto the DISPLAYSURF Surface object. The second parameter is a two-integer tuple for the X and Y values of the topleft corner where the image should be blitted to.

If catx and caty were set to 100 and 200 and the width of catImg was 125 and the height was 79, this blit() call would copy this image onto DISPLAYSURF so that the top left corner of the catImg was at the XY coordinate (100, 200) and the bottom right corner's XY coordinate was at (225, 279).

Note that you cannot blit to a Surface that is currently "locked" (such as when a PixelArray object has been made from it and not yet been deleted.)

The rest of the game loop is just changing the catx, caty, and direction variables so that the cat moves around the window. There is also a call to pygame.event.get() to handle the QUIT event.

FONTS

If you want to draw text to the screen, you *could* write several calls to pygame.draw.line() to draw out the lines of each letter. This would be a headache to type out all those pygame.draw.line() calls and figure out all the XY coordinates, and probably wouldn't look very good.

The above message would take forty one calls to the pygame.draw.line() function to make. Instead, Pygame provides some much simpler functions for fonts and creating text. Here is a small Hello World program using Pygame's font functions. Type it into IDLE's file editor and save it as *fonttext.py*:

```
1. import pygame, sys
2. from pygame.locals import *
3.
4. pygame.init()
5. DISPLAYSURF = pygame.display.set_mode((400, 300))
6. pygame.display.set_caption('Hello World!')
7.
8. WHITE = (255, 255, 255)
9. GREEN = (0, 255, 0)
10. BLUE = (0, 0, 128)
11.
12. fontObj = pygame.font.Font('freesansbold.ttf', 32)
13. textSurfaceObj = fontObj.render('Hello world!', True, GREEN, BLUE)
14. textRectObj = textSurfaceObj.get_rect()
15. textRectObj.center = (200, 150)
16.
17. while True: # main game loop
18.     DISPLAYSURF.fill(WHITE)
19.     DISPLAYSURF.blit(textSurfaceObj, textRectObj)
20.     for event in pygame.event.get():
21.         if event.type == QUIT:
22.             pygame.quit()
23.             sys.exit()
24.     pygame.display.update()
```

There are six steps to making text appear on the screen:

1. Create a pygame.font.Font object. (Like on line 12)
2. Create a Surface object with the text drawn on it by calling the Font object's render() method. (Line 13)
3. Create a Rect object from the Surface object by calling the Surface object's get_rect() method. (Line 14) This Rect object will have the width and height correctly set for the text that was rendered, but the top and left attributes will be 0.
4. Set the position of the Rect object by changing one of its attributes. On line 15, we set the center of the Rect object to be at 200, 150.
5. Blit the Surface object with the text onto the Surface object returned by pygame.display.set_mode(). (Line 19)
6. Call pygame.display.update() to make the display Surface appear on the screen. (Line 24)

The parameters to the pygame.font.Font() constructor function is a string of the font file to use, and an integer of the size of the font (in points, like how word processors measure font size). On line 12, we pass 'freesansbold.ttf' (this is a font that comes with Pygame) and the integer 32 (for a 32-point sized font).

The parameters to the render() method call are a string of the text to render, a Boolean value to specify if we want anti-aliasing (explained later in this chapter), the color of the text, and the color of the background. If you want a transparent background, then simply leave off the background color parameter in the method call.

ANTI-ALIASING

Anti-aliasing is a graphics technique for making text and shapes look less blocky by adding a little bit of blur to their edges. It takes a little more computation time to draw with anti-aliasing, so although the graphics may look better, your program may run slower (but only just a little).

If you zoom in on an aliased line and an anti-aliased line, they look like this:

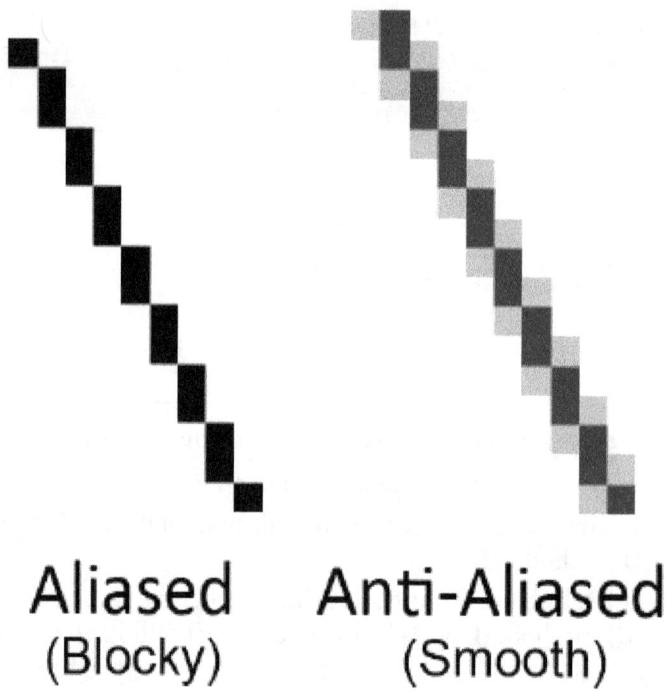

To make Pygame's text use anti-aliasing, just pass True for the second parameter of the render() method. The pygame.draw.aaline() and pygame.draw.aalines() functions have the same parameters as pygame.draw.line() and pygame.draw.lines(), except they will draw anti-aliased (smooth) lines instead of aliased (blocky) lines.

PLAYING SOUNDS

Playing sounds that are stored in sound files is even simpler than displaying images from image files. First, you must create a pygame.mixer.Sound object (which we will call Sound objects for short) by calling the pygame.mixer.Sound() constructor function. It takes one string parameter, which is the filename of the sound file. Pygame can load WAV, MP3, or OGG files.

To play this sound, call the Sound object's play() method. If you want to immediately stop the Sound object from playing call the stop() method. The stop() method has no arguments. Here is some sample code:

```
soundObj = pygame.mixer.Sound('beeps.wav')
soundObj.play()
import time
time.sleep(1) # wait and let the sound play for 1 second
soundObj.stop()
```

The program execution continues immediately after play() is called; it does not wait for the sound to finish playing before moving on to the next line of code.

The Sound objects are good for sound effects to play when the player takes damage, slashes a sword, or collects a coin. But your games might also be better if they had background music playing regardless of what was going on in the game. Pygame can only load one music file to play in the background at a time. To load a background music file, call the pygame.mixer.music.load() function and pass it a string argument of the sound file to load. This file can be WAV, MP3, or MIDI format.

To begin playing the loaded sound file as the background music, call the pygame.mixer.music.play(-1, 0.0) function. The -1 argument makes the background music forever loop when it reaches the end of the sound file. If you set it to an integer 0 or larger, then the music will only loop that number of times instead of looping forever. The 0.0 means to start playing the sound file from the beginning. If you pass a larger integer or float, the music will begin playing that many seconds into the sound file. For example, if you pass 13.5 for the second parameter, the sound file with begin playing at the point 13.5 seconds in from the beginning.

To stop playing the background music immediately, call the pygame.mixer.music.stop() function. This function has no arguments.

Here is some example code of the sound methods and functions:

```
# Loading and playing a sound effect:
soundObj = pygame.mixer.Sound('beepingsound.wav')
soundObj.play()

# Loading and playing background music:
pygame.mixer.music.load(backgroundmusic.mp3')
pygame.mixer.music.play(-1, 0.0)
# ...some more of your code goes here...
pygame.mixer.music.stop()
```

SUMMARY

This covers the basics of making graphical games with the Pygame framework. Of course, just reading about these functions probably isn't enough to help you learn how to make games using these functions. The rest of the chapters in this book each focus on the source code for a small, complete game. This will give you an idea of what complete game programs "look like", so you can then get some ideas for how to code your own game programs.

3 Chapter

MEMORY PUZZLE

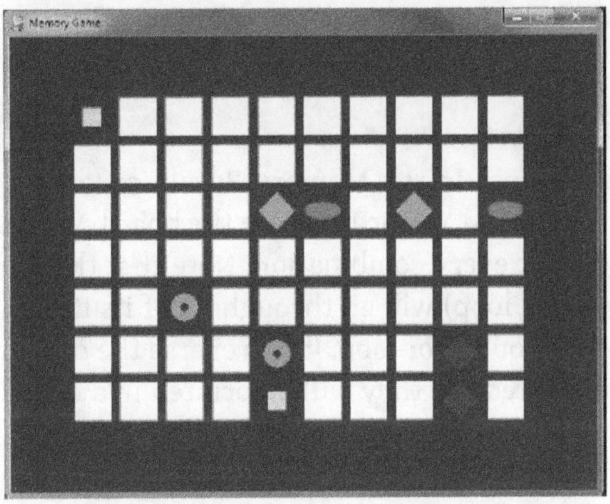

HOW TO PLAY MEMORY PUZZLE

In the Memory Puzzle game, several icons are covered up by white boxes. There are two of each icon. The player can click on two boxes to see what icon is behind them. If the icons match, then those boxes remain uncovered. The player wins when all the boxes on the board are uncovered. To give the player a hint, the boxes are quickly uncovered once at the beginning of the game.

NESTED FOR LOOPS

One concept that you will see in Memory Puzzle (and most of the games in this book) is the use of a for loop inside of another for loop. These are called nested for loops. Nested for loops are handy for going through every possible combination of two lists. Type the following into the interactive shell:

```
>>> for x in [0, 1, 2, 3, 4]:
...     for y in ['a', 'b', 'c']:
...         print(x, y)
...
0 a
0 b
0 c
1 a
1 b
1 c
2 a
```

```
2 b
2 c
3 a
3 b
3 c
4 a
4 b
4 c
>>>
```

There are several times in the Memory Puzzle code that we need to iterate through every possible X and Y coordinate on the board. We'll use nested for loops to make sure that we get every combination. Note that the inner for loop (the for loop inside the other for loop) will go through all of its iterations before going to the next iteration of the outer for loop. If we reverse the order of the for loops, the same values will be printed but they will be printed in a different order. Type the following code into the interactive shell, and compare the order it prints values to the order in the previous nested for loop example:

```
>>> for y in ['a', 'b', 'c']:
...     for x in [0, 1, 2, 3, 4]:
...         print(x, y)
...
0 a
1 a
2 a
3 a
4 a
0 b
1 b
2 b
3 b
4 b
0 c
1 c
2 c
3 c
4 c
>>>
```

SOURCE CODE OF MEMORY PUZZLE

Go ahead and first type in the entire program into IDLE's file editor, save it as *memorypuzzle.py*, and run it. If you get any error messages, look at the line number that is mentioned in the error message and check your code for any typos.

You'll probably pick up a few ideas about how the program works just by typing it in once. And when you're done typing it in, you can then play the game for yourself.

```
# Memory Puzzle
# By Al Sweigart al@inventwithpython.com
# http://inventwithpython.com/pygame
# Released under a "Simplified BSD" license

import random, pygame, sys
from pygame.locals import *

FPS = 30 # frames per second, the general speed of the program
WINDOWWIDTH = 640 # size of window's width in pixels
WINDOWHEIGHT = 480 # size of windows' height in pixels
REVEALSPEED = 8 # speed boxes' sliding reveals and covers
BOXSIZE = 40 # size of box height & width in pixels
GAPSIZE = 10 # size of gap between boxes in pixels
BOARDWIDTH = 10 # number of columns of icons
BOARDHEIGHT = 7 # number of rows of icons
assert (BOARDWIDTH * BOARDHEIGHT) % 2 == 0, 'Board needs to have an even number of boxes for pairs of matches.'
XMARGIN = int((WINDOWWIDTH - (BOARDWIDTH * (BOXSIZE + GAPSIZE))) / 2)
YMARGIN = int((WINDOWHEIGHT - (BOARDHEIGHT * (BOXSIZE + GAPSIZE))) / 2)

#            R    G    B
GRAY     = (100, 100, 100)
NAVYBLUE = ( 60,  60, 100)
WHITE    = (255, 255, 255)
RED      = (255,   0,   0)
GREEN    = (  0, 255,   0)
BLUE     = (  0,   0, 255)
YELLOW   = (255, 255,   0)
ORANGE   = (255, 128,   0)
PURPLE   = (255,   0, 255)
CYAN     = (  0, 255, 255)

BGCOLOR = NAVYBLUE
LIGHTBGCOLOR = GRAY
BOXCOLOR = WHITE
HIGHLIGHTCOLOR = BLUE

DONUT = 'donut'
```

```
SQUARE = 'square'
DIAMOND = 'diamond'
LINES = 'lines'
OVAL = 'oval'

ALLCOLORS = (RED, GREEN, BLUE, YELLOW, ORANGE, PURPLE, CYAN)
ALLSHAPES = (DONUT, SQUARE, DIAMOND, LINES, OVAL)
assert len(ALLCOLORS) * len(ALLSHAPES) * 2 >= BOARDWIDTH * BOARDHEIGHT, "Board is too big for the number of shapes/colors defined."

def main():
    global FPSCLOCK, DISPLAYSURF
    pygame.init()
    FPSCLOCK = pygame.time.Clock()
    DISPLAYSURF = pygame.display.set_mode((WINDOWWIDTH, WINDOWHEIGHT))

    mousex = 0 # used to store x coordinate of mouse event
    mousey = 0 # used to store y coordinate of mouse event
    pygame.display.set_caption('Memory Game')

    mainBoard = getRandomizedBoard()
    revealedBoxes = generateRevealedBoxesData(False)

    firstSelection = None # stores the (x, y) of the first box clicked.

    DISPLAYSURF.fill(BGCOLOR)
    startGameAnimation(mainBoard)

    while True: # main game loop
        mouseClicked = False

        DISPLAYSURF.fill(BGCOLOR) # drawing the window
        drawBoard(mainBoard, revealedBoxes)

        for event in pygame.event.get(): # event handling loop
            if event.type == QUIT or (event.type == KEYUP and event.key == K_ESCAPE):
                pygame.quit()
                sys.exit()
            elif event.type == MOUSEMOTION:
                mousex, mousey = event.pos
            elif event.type == MOUSEBUTTONUP:
                mousex, mousey = event.pos
                mouseClicked = True

        boxx, boxy = getBoxAtPixel(mousex, mousey)
```

```
        if boxx != None and boxy != None:
            # The mouse is currently over a box.
            if not revealedBoxes[boxx][boxy]:
                drawHighlightBox(boxx, boxy)
            if not revealedBoxes[boxx][boxy] and mouseClicked:
                revealBoxesAnimation(mainBoard, [(boxx, boxy)])
                revealedBoxes[boxx][boxy] = True # set the box as "revealed"
                if firstSelection == None: # the current box was the first box clicked
                    firstSelection = (boxx, boxy)
                else: # the current box was the second box clicked
                    # Check if there is a match between the two icons.
                    icon1shape, icon1color = getShapeAndColor(mainBoard, firstSelection[0], firstSelection[1])
                    icon2shape, icon2color = getShapeAndColor(mainBoard, boxx, boxy)

                    if icon1shape != icon2shape or icon1color != icon2color:
                        # Icons don't match. Re-cover up both selections.
                        pygame.time.wait(1000) # 1000 milliseconds = 1 sec
                        coverBoxesAnimation(mainBoard, [(firstSelection[0], firstSelection[1]), (boxx, boxy)])
                        revealedBoxes[firstSelection[0]][firstSelection[1]] = False
                        revealedBoxes[boxx][boxy] = False
                    elif hasWon(revealedBoxes): # check if all pairs found
                        gameWonAnimation(mainBoard)
                        pygame.time.wait(2000)

                        # Reset the board
                        mainBoard = getRandomizedBoard()
                        revealedBoxes = generateRevealedBoxesData(False)

                        # Show the fully unrevealed board for a second.
                        drawBoard(mainBoard, revealedBoxes)
                        pygame.display.update()
                        pygame.time.wait(1000)

                        # Replay the start game animation.
                        startGameAnimation(mainBoard)
                    firstSelection = None # reset firstSelection variable

        # Redraw the screen and wait a clock tick.
        pygame.display.update()
```

```
        FPSCLOCK.tick(FPS)


def generateRevealedBoxesData(val):
    revealedBoxes = []
    for i in range(BOARDWIDTH):
        revealedBoxes.append([val] * BOARDHEIGHT)
    return revealedBoxes


def getRandomizedBoard():
    # Get a list of every possible shape in every possible color.
    icons = []
    for color in ALLCOLORS:
        for shape in ALLSHAPES:
            icons.append( (shape, color) )

    random.shuffle(icons) # randomize the order of the icons list
    numIconsUsed = int(BOARDWIDTH * BOARDHEIGHT / 2) # calculate how many icons are needed
    icons = icons[:numIconsUsed] * 2 # make two of each
    random.shuffle(icons)

    # Create the board data structure, with randomly placed icons.
    board = []
    for x in range(BOARDWIDTH):
        column = []
        for y in range(BOARDHEIGHT):
            column.append(icons[0])
            del icons[0] # remove the icons as we assign them
        board.append(column)
    return board


def splitIntoGroupsOf(groupSize, theList):
    # splits a list into a list of lists, where the inner lists have at
    # most groupSize number of items.
    result = []
    for i in range(0, len(theList), groupSize):
        result.append(theList[i:i + groupSize])
    return result


def leftTopCoordsOfBox(boxx, boxy):
    # Convert board coordinates to pixel coordinates
    left = boxx * (BOXSIZE + GAPSIZE) + XMARGIN
```

```
    top = boxy * (BOXSIZE + GAPSIZE) + YMARGIN
    return (left, top)


def getBoxAtPixel(x, y):
    for boxx in range(BOARDWIDTH):
        for boxy in range(BOARDHEIGHT):
            left, top = leftTopCoordsOfBox(boxx, boxy)
            boxRect = pygame.Rect(left, top, BOXSIZE, BOXSIZE)
            if boxRect.collidepoint(x, y):
                return (boxx, boxy)
    return (None, None)


def drawIcon(shape, color, boxx, boxy):
    quarter = int(BOXSIZE * 0.25) # syntactic sugar
    half =    int(BOXSIZE * 0.5)  # syntactic sugar

    left, top = leftTopCoordsOfBox(boxx, boxy) # get pixel coords from board coords
    # Draw the shapes
    if shape == DONUT:
        pygame.draw.circle(DISPLAYSURF, color, (left + half, top + half), half - 5)
        pygame.draw.circle(DISPLAYSURF, BGCOLOR, (left + half, top + half), quarter - 5)
    elif shape == SQUARE:
        pygame.draw.rect(DISPLAYSURF, color, (left + quarter, top + quarter, BOXSIZE - half, BOXSIZE - half))
    elif shape == DIAMOND:
        pygame.draw.polygon(DISPLAYSURF, color, ((left + half, top), (left + BOXSIZE - 1, top + half), (left + half, top + BOXSIZE - 1), (left, top + half)))
    elif shape == LINES:
        for i in range(0, BOXSIZE, 4):
            pygame.draw.line(DISPLAYSURF, color, (left, top + i), (left + i, top))
            pygame.draw.line(DISPLAYSURF, color, (left + i, top + BOXSIZE - 1), (left + BOXSIZE - 1, top + i))
    elif shape == OVAL:
        pygame.draw.ellipse(DISPLAYSURF, color, (left, top + quarter, BOXSIZE, half))


def getShapeAndColor(board, boxx, boxy):
    # shape value for x, y spot is stored in board[x][y][0]
```

```
    # color value for x, y spot is stored in board[x][y][1]
    return board[boxx][boxy][0], board[boxx][boxy][1]


def drawBoxCovers(board, boxes, coverage):
    # Draws boxes being covered/revealed. "boxes" is a list
    # of two-item lists, which have the x & y spot of the box.
    for box in boxes:
        left, top = leftTopCoordsOfBox(box[0], box[1])
        pygame.draw.rect(DISPLAYSURF, BGCOLOR, (left, top, BOXSIZE, BOXSIZE))
        shape, color = getShapeAndColor(board, box[0], box[1])
        drawIcon(shape, color, box[0], box[1])
        if coverage > 0: # only draw the cover if there is an coverage
            pygame.draw.rect(DISPLAYSURF, BOXCOLOR, (left, top, coverage, BOXSIZE))
    pygame.display.update()
    FPSCLOCK.tick(FPS)


def revealBoxesAnimation(board, boxesToReveal):
    # Do the "box reveal" animation.
    for coverage in range(BOXSIZE, (-REVEALSPEED) - 1, - REVEALSPEED):
        drawBoxCovers(board, boxesToReveal, coverage)


def coverBoxesAnimation(board, boxesToCover):
    # Do the "box cover" animation.
    for coverage in range(0, BOXSIZE + REVEALSPEED, REVEALSPEED):
        drawBoxCovers(board, boxesToCover, coverage)


def drawBoard(board, revealed):
    # Draws all of the boxes in their covered or revealed state.
    for boxx in range(BOARDWIDTH):
        for boxy in range(BOARDHEIGHT):
            left, top = leftTopCoordsOfBox(boxx, boxy)
            if not revealed[boxx][boxy]:
                # Draw a covered box.
                pygame.draw.rect(DISPLAYSURF, BOXCOLOR, (left, top, BOXSIZE, BOXSIZE))
            else:
                # Draw the (revealed) icon.
                shape, color = getShapeAndColor(board, boxx, boxy)
                drawIcon(shape, color, boxx, boxy)

```

```
def drawHighlightBox(boxx, boxy):
    left, top = leftTopCoordsOfBox(boxx, boxy)
    pygame.draw.rect(DISPLAYSURF, HIGHLIGHTCOLOR, (left - 5, top - 5, BOXSIZE + 10, BOXSIZE + 10), 4)


def startGameAnimation(board):
    # Randomly reveal the boxes 8 at a time.
    coveredBoxes = generateRevealedBoxesData(False)
    boxes = []
    for x in range(BOARDWIDTH):
        for y in range(BOARDHEIGHT):
            boxes.append( (x, y) )
    random.shuffle(boxes)
    boxGroups = splitIntoGroupsOf(8, boxes)

    drawBoard(board, coveredBoxes)
    for boxGroup in boxGroups:
        revealBoxesAnimation(board, boxGroup)
        coverBoxesAnimation(board, boxGroup)


def gameWonAnimation(board):
    # flash the background color when the player has won
    coveredBoxes = generateRevealedBoxesData(True)
    color1 = LIGHTBGCOLOR
    color2 = BGCOLOR

    for i in range(13):
        color1, color2 = color2, color1 # swap colors
        DISPLAYSURF.fill(color1)
        drawBoard(board, coveredBoxes)
        pygame.display.update()
        pygame.time.wait(300)


def hasWon(revealedBoxes):
    # Returns True if all the boxes have been revealed, otherwise False
    for i in revealedBoxes:
        if False in i:
            return False # return False if any boxes are covered.
    return True


if __name__ == '__main__':
    main()
```

CREDITS AND IMPORTS

```
1. # Memory Puzzle
2. # By Al Sweigart al@inventwithpython.com
3. # http://inventwithpython.com/pygame
4. # Released under a "Simplified BSD" license
5.
6. import random, pygame, sys
7. from pygame.locals import *
```

At the top of the program are comments about what the game is, who made it, and where the user could find more information. There's also a note that the source code is freely copyable under a "Simplified BSD" license. The Simplified BSD license is more appropriate for software than the Creative Common license (which this book is released under), but they basically mean the same thing: People are free to copy and share this game.

This program makes use of many functions in other modules, so it imports those modules on line 6. Line 7 is also an import statement in the from (module name) import * format, which means you do not have to type the module name in front of it. There are no functions in the pygame.locals module, but there are several constant variables in it that we want to use such as MOUSEMOTION, KEYUP, or QUIT. Using this style of import statement, we only have to type MOUSEMOTION rather than pygame.locals.MOUSEMOTION.

MAGIC NUMBERS ARE BAD

```
 9. FPS = 30 # frames per second, the general speed of the program
10. WINDOWWIDTH = 640 # size of window's width in pixels
11. WINDOWHEIGHT = 480 # size of windows' height in pixels
12. REVEALSPEED = 8 # speed boxes' sliding reveals and covers
13. BOXSIZE = 40 # size of box height & width in pixels
14. GAPSIZE = 10 # size of gap between boxes in pixels
```

The game programs in this book use a lot of constant variables. You might not realize why they're so handy. For example, instead of using the BOXSIZE variable in our code we could just type the integer 40 directly in the code. But there are two reasons to use constant variables.

First, if we ever wanted to change the size of each box later, we would have to go through the entire program and find and replace each time we typed 40. By just using the BOXSIZE constant, we only have to change line 13 and the rest of the program is already up to date. This is much better, especially since we might use the integer value 40 for something else besides the size of the white boxes, and changing that 40 accidentally would cause bugs in our program.

Second, it makes the code more readable. Go down to the next section and look at line 18. This sets up a calculation for the XMARGIN constant, which is how many pixels are on the side of the entire board. It is a complicated looking expression, but you can carefully piece out what it means. Line 18 looks like this:

```
XMARGIN = int((WINDOWWIDTH - (BOARDWIDTH * (BOXSIZE + GAPSIZE))) / 2)
```

But if line 18 didn't use constant variables, it would look like this:

```
XMARGIN = int((640 - (10 * (40 + 10))) / 2)
```

Now it becomes impossible to remember what exactly the programmer intended to mean. These unexplained numbers in the source code are often called **magic numbers.** Whenever you find yourself entering magic numbers, you should consider replacing them with a constant variable instead. To the Python interpreter, both of the previous lines are the exact same. But to a human programmer who is reading the source code and trying to understand how it works, the second version of line 18 doesn't make much sense at all! Constants really help the readability of source code.

Of course, you can go too far replacing numbers with constant variables. Look at the following code:

```
ZERO = 0
ONE = 1
TWO = 99999999
TWOANDTHREEQUARTERS = 2.75
```

Don't write code like that. That's just silly.

SANITY CHECKS WITH ASSERT STATEMENTS

```
15. BOARDWIDTH = 10 # number of columns of icons
16. BOARDHEIGHT = 7 # number of rows of icons
17. assert (BOARDWIDTH * BOARDHEIGHT) % 2 == 0, 'Board needs to have an even number of boxes for pairs of matches.'
18. XMARGIN = int((WINDOWWIDTH - (BOARDWIDTH * (BOXSIZE + GAPSIZE))) / 2)
19. YMARGIN = int((WINDOWHEIGHT - (BOARDHEIGHT * (BOXSIZE + GAPSIZE))) / 2)
```

The assert statement on line 17 ensures that the board width and height we've selected will result in an even number of boxes (since we will have pairs of icons in this game). There are three parts to an assert statement: the assert keyword, an expression which, if False, results in crashing the program. The third part (after the comma after the expression) is a string that appears if the program crashes because of the assertion.

The assert statement with an expression basically says, "The programmer asserts that this expression must be True, otherwise crash the program." This is a good way of adding a sanity check to your program to make sure that if the execution ever passes an assertion we can at least know that that code is working as expected.

TELLING IF A NUMBER IS EVEN OR ODD

If the product of the board width and height is divided by two and has a remainder of 0 (the % **modulus operator** evaluates what the remainder is) then the number is even. Even numbers divided by two will always have a remainder of zero. Odd numbers divided by two will always have a remainder of one. This is a good trick to remember if you need your code to tell if a number is even or odd:

```
>>> isEven = someNumber % 2 == 0
>>> isOdd = someNumber % 2 != 0
```

In the above case, if the integer in someNumber was even, then isEven will be True. If it was odd, then isOdd will be True.

CRASH EARLY AND CRASH OFTEN!

Having your program crash is a bad thing. It happens when your program has some mistake in the code and cannot continue. But there are some cases where crashing a program early can avoid worse bugs later.

If the values we chose for BOARDWIDTH and BOARDHEIGHT that we chose on line 15 and 16 result in a board with an odd number of boxes (such as if the width were 3 and the height were 5), then there would always be one left over icon that would not have a pair to be matched with. This would cause a bug later on in the program, and it could take a lot of debugging work to figure out that the real source of the bug is at the very beginning of the program. In fact, just for fun, try commenting out the assertion so it doesn't run, and then setting the BOARDWIDTH and BOARDHEIGHT constants both to odd numbers. When you run the program, it will immediately show an error happening on a line 149 in *memorypuzzle.py*, which is in getRandomizedBoard() function!

Traceback (most recent call last):

```
Traceback (most recent call last):
```

```
  File "C:\book2svn\src\memorypuzzle.py", line 292, in <module>
    main()
  File "C:\book2svn\src\memorypuzzle.py", line 58, in main
    mainBoard = getRandomizedBoard()
  File "C:\book2svn\src\memorypuzzle.py", line 149, in getRandomizedBoard
    columns.append(icons[0])
IndexError: list index out of range
```

We could spend a lot of time looking at getRandomizedBoard() trying to figure out what's wrong with it before realizing that getRandomizedBoard() is perfectly fine: the real source of the bug was on line 15 and 16 where we set the BOARDWIDTH and BOARDHEIGHT constants.

The assertion makes sure that this never happens. If our code is going to crash, we want it to crash as soon as it detects something is terribly wrong, because otherwise the bug may not become apparent until much later in the program. Crash early!

You want to add assert statements whenever there is some condition in your program that must always, always, always be True. Crash often! You don't have to go overboard and put assert statements everywhere, but crashing often with asserts goes a long way in detecting the true source of a bug. Crash early and crash often!

(In your code that is. Not, say, when riding a pony.)

MAKING THE SOURCE CODE LOOK PRETTY

```
21. #             R    G    B
22. GRAY      = (100, 100, 100)
23. NAVYBLUE = ( 60,  60, 100)
24. WHITE     = (255, 255, 255)
25. RED       = (255,   0,   0)
26. GREEN     = (  0, 255,   0)
27. BLUE      = (  0,   0, 255)
28. YELLOW    = (255, 255,   0)
29. ORANGE    = (255, 128,   0)
30. PURPLE    = (255,   0, 255)
31. CYAN      = (  0, 255, 255)
32.
33. BGCOLOR = NAVYBLUE
34. LIGHTBGCOLOR = GRAY
35. BOXCOLOR = WHITE
36. HIGHLIGHTCOLOR = BLUE
```

Remember that colors in Pygame are represented by a tuple of three integers from 0 to 255. These three integers represent the amount of red, green, and blue in the color which is why these tuples are called RGB values. Notice the spacing of the tuples on lines 22 to 31 are such that the R, G, and B integers line up. In Python the indentation (that is, the space at the beginning of the line) is needs to be exact, but the spacing in the rest of the line is not so strict. By spacing the integers in the tuple out, we can clearly see how the RGB values compare to each other.

It is a nice thing to make your code more readable this way, but don't bother spending too much time doing it. Code doesn't have to be pretty to work. At a certain point, you'll just be spending more time typing spaces than you would have saved by having readable tuple values.

USING CONSTANT VARIABLES INSTEAD OF STRINGS

```
DONUT = 'donut'
SQUARE = 'square'
DIAMOND = 'diamond'
LINES = 'lines'
OVAL = 'oval'
```

The program also sets up constant variables for some strings. These constants will be used in the data structure for the board, tracking which spaces on the board have which icons. Using a constant variable instead of the string value is a good idea. Look at the following code, which comes from line 187:

```
    if shape == DONUT:
```

The shape variable will be set to one of the strings 'donut', 'square', 'diamond', 'lines', or 'oval' and then compared to the DONUT constant. If we made a typo when writing line 187, for example, something like this:

```
    if shape == DUNOT:
```

Then Python would crash, giving an error message saying that there is no variable named DUNOT. This is good. Since the program has crashed on line 187, when we check that line it will be easy to see that the bug was caused by a typo. However, if we were using strings instead of constant variables and made the same typo, line 187 would look like this:

```
    if shape == DUNOT:
```

This is perfectly acceptable Python code, so it won't crash at first when you run it. However, this will lead to weird bugs later on in our program. Because the code does not immediately crash where the problem is caused, it can be much harder to find it.

MAKING SURE WE HAVE ENOUGH ICONS

```
44. ALLCOLORS = (RED, GREEN, BLUE, YELLOW, ORANGE, PURPLE, CYAN)
45. ALLSHAPES = (DONUT, SQUARE, DIAMOND, LINES, OVAL)
46. assert len(ALLCOLORS) * len(ALLSHAPES) * 2 >= BOARDWIDTH * BOARDHEIGHT,
"Board is too big for the number of shapes/colors defined."
```

In order for our game program to be able to create icons of every possible color and shape combination, we need to make a tuple that holds all of these values. There is also another assertion on line 46 to make sure that there are enough color/shape combinations for the size of the board we have. If there isn't, then the program will crash on line 46 and we will know that we either have to add more colors and shapes, or make the board width and height smaller. With 7 colors and

5 shapes, we can make 35 (that is, 7 x 5) different icons. And because we'll have a pair of each icon, that means we can have a board with up to 70 (that is, 35 x 2, or 7 x 5 x 2) spaces.

TUPLES VS. LISTS, IMMUTABLE VS. MUTABLE

You might have noticed that the ALLCOLORS and ALLSHAPES variables are tuples instead of lists. When do we want to use tuples and when do we want to use lists? And what's the difference between them anyway?

Tuples and lists are the same in every way except two: tuples use parentheses instead of square brackets, and the items in tuples cannot be modified (but the items in lists can be modified). We often call lists **mutable** (meaning they can be changed) and tuples **immutable** (meaning they cannot be changed).

For an example of trying to change values in lists and tuples, look at the following code:

```
>>> listVal = [1, 1, 2, 3, 5, 8]
>>> tupleVal = (1, 1, 2, 3, 5, 8)
>>> listVal[4] = 'hello!'
>>> listVal
[1, 1, 2, 3, 'hello!', 8]
>>> tupleVal[4] = 'hello!'
Traceback (most recent call last):
  File "<stdin>", line 1, in <module>
TypeError: 'tuple' object does not support item assignment
>>> tupleVal
(1, 1, 2, 3, 5, 8)
>>> tupleVal[4]
5
```

Notice that when we try to change the item at index 2 in the tuple, Python gives us an error message saying that tuple objects do not support "item assignment".

There is a silly benefit and an important benefit to tuple's immutability. The silly benefit is that code that uses tuples is slightly faster than code that uses lists. (Python is able to make some optimizations knowing that the values in a tuple will never change.) But having your code run a few nanoseconds faster is not important.

The important benefit to using tuples is similar to the benefit of using constant variables: it's a sign that the value in the tuple will never change, so anyone reading the code later will be able to say, "I can expect that this tuple will always be the same. Otherwise the programmer would have used a list." This also lets a future programmer reading your code say, "If I see a list value, I know that it could be modified at some point in this program. Otherwise, the programmer who wrote this code would have used a tuple."

You can still assign a new tuple value to a variable:

```
>>> tupleVal = (1, 2, 3)
>>> tupleVal = (1, 2, 3, 4)
```

The reason this code works is because the code isn't changing the (1, 2, 3) tuple on the second line. It is assigning an entirely new tuple (1, 2, 3, 4) to the tupleVal, and overwriting the old tuple value. You cannot however, use the square brackets to modify an item in the tuple.

Strings are also an immutable data type. You can use the square brackets to read a single character in a string, but you cannot change a single character in a string:

```
>>> strVal = 'Hello'
>>> strVal[1]
'e'
>>> strVal[1] = 'X'
Traceback (most recent call last):
  File "<stdin>", line 1, in <module>
TypeError: 'str' object does not support item assignment
```

ONE ITEM TUPLES NEED A TRAILING COMMA

Also, one minor details about tuples: if you ever need to write code about a tuple that has one value in it, then it needs to have a trailing comma in it, such as this:

```
oneValueTuple = (42, )
```

If you forget this comma (and it is very easy to forget), then Python won't be able to tell the difference between this and a set of parentheses that just change the order of operations. For example, look at the following two lines of code:

```
variableA = (5 * 6)
variableB = (5 * 6, )
```

The value that is stored in variableA is just the integer 30. However, the expression for variableB's assignment statement is the single-item tuple value (30,). Blank tuple values do not need a comma in them, they can just be a set of parentheses by themselves: ().

CONVERTING BETWEEN LISTS AND TUPLES

You can convert between list and tuple values just like you can convert between string and integer values. Just pass a tuple value to the list() function and it will return a list form of that tuple value. Or, pass a list value to the tuple() function and it will return a tuple form of that list value. Try typing the following into the interactive shell:

```
>>> spam = (1, 2, 3, 4)
>>> spam = list(spam)
>>> spam
[1, 2, 3, 4]
>>> spam = tuple(spam)
>>> spam
(1, 2, 3, 4)
>>>
```

THE GLOBAL STATEMENT, AND WHY GLOBAL VARIABLES ARE EVIL

```
48. def main():
49.     global FPSCLOCK, DISPLAYSURF
50.     pygame.init()
51.     FPSCLOCK = pygame.time.Clock()
52.     DISPLAYSURF = pygame.display.set_mode((WINDOWWIDTH, WINDOWHEIGHT))
53.
54.     mousex = 0 # used to store x coordinate of mouse event
55.     mousey = 0 # used to store y coordinate of mouse event
56.     pygame.display.set_caption('Memory Game')
```

This is the start of the main() function, which is where (oddly enough) the main part of the game code is. The functions called in the main() function will be explained later in this chapter.

Line 49 is a global statement. The global statement is the global keyword followed by a comma-delimited list of variable names. These variable names are then marked as global variables. Inside the main() function, those names are not for local variables that might just happen to have the same name as global variables. They *are* the global variables. Any values assigned to them in the main() function will persist outside the main() function. We are marking the FPSCLOCK and DISPLAYSURF variables as global because they are used in several other functions in the program.

There are four simple rules to determine if a variable is local or global:

1. If there is a global statement for a variable at the beginning of the function, then the variable is global.
2. If the name of a variable in a function has the same name as a global variable and the function never assigns the variable a value, then that variable is the global variable.
3. If the name of a variable in a function has the same name as a global variable and the function does assign the variable a value, then that variable is a local variable.
4. If there isn't a global variable with the same name as the variable in the function, then that variable is obviously a local variable.

You generally want to avoid using global variables inside functions. A function is supposed to be like a mini-program inside your program with specific inputs (the parameters) and an output (the return value). But a function that reads and writes to global variables has additional inputs and output. Since the global variable could have been modified in many places before the function was called, it can be tricky to track down a bug involving a bad value set in the global variable.

Having a function as a separate mini-program that doesn't use global variables makes it easier to find bugs in your code, since the parameters of the function are clearly known. It also makes changing the code in a function easier, since if the new function works with the same parameters and gives the same return value, it will automatically work with the rest of the program just like the old function.

Basically, using global variables might make it easier to write your program but they generally make it harder to debug.

In the games in this book, global variables are mostly used for variables that would be global constants that never change, but need the pygame.init() function called first. Since this happens in the main() function, they are set in the main() function and must be global for other functions to see them. But the global variables are used as constants and don't change, so they are less likely to cause confusing bugs.

If you don't understand this, don't worry. Just write your code so that you pass in values to functions rather than have the functions read global variables as a general rule.

DATA STRUCTURES AND 2D LISTS

```
    mainBoard = getRandomizedBoard()
    revealedBoxes = generateRevealedBoxesData(False)
```

The getRandomizedBoard() function returns a data structure that represents the state of the board. The generateRevealedBoxesData() function returns a data structure that represents which boxes are covered, respectively. The return values of these functions are two dimensional (2D) lists, or lists of lists. A list of lists of lists of values would be a 3D list. Another word for two or more dimensional lists is a **multidimensional** list.

If we have a list value stored in a variable named spam, we could access a value in that list with the square brackets, such as spam[2] to retrieve the third value in the list. If the value at spam[2] is itself a list, then we could use another set of square brackets to retrieve a value *in that list.* This would look like, for example, spam[2][4], which would retrieve the fifth value in the list that is the third value in spam. Using this notation of lists of lists makes it easy to map a 2D board to a 2D list value.

Since the mainBoard variable will store icons in it, if we wanted to get the icon on the board at the position (4, 5) then we could just use the expression mainBoard[4][5]. Since the icons themselves are stored as two-item tuples with the shape and color, the complete data structure is a list of list of two-item tuples. Whew!

Here's an small example. Say the board looked like this:

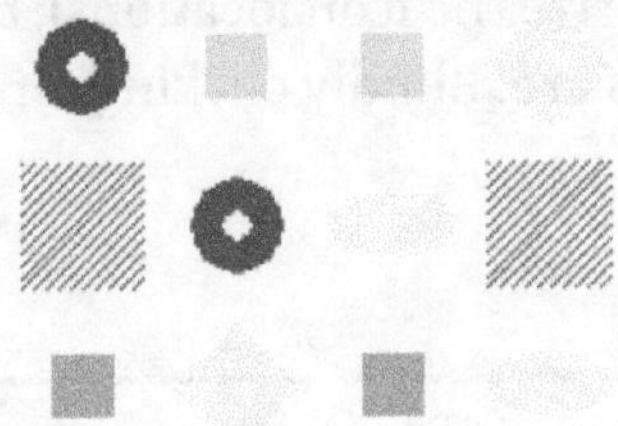

The corresponding data structure would be:

```
mainBoard = [[(DONUT, BLUE), (LINES, BLUE), (SQUARE, ORANGE)], [(SQUARE,
GREEN), (DONUT, BLUE), (DIAMOND, YELLOW)], [(SQUARE, GREEN), (OVAL, YELLOW),
(SQUARE, ORANGE)], [(DIAMOND, YELLOW), (LINES, BLUE), (OVAL, YELLOW)]]
```

You'll notice that mainBoard[x][y] will correspond to the icon at the (x, y) coordinate on the board.

Meanwhile, the "revealed boxes" data structure is also a 2D list, except instead of two-item tuples like the board data structure, it has Boolean values: True if the box at that x, y coordinate is revealed, and False if it is covered up. Passing False to the generateRevealedBoxesData() function sets all of the Boolean values to False. (This function is explained in detail later.)

These two data structures are used to keep track of the state of the game board.

THE "START GAME" ANIMATION

```
61.     firstSelection = None # stores the (x, y) of the first box clicked.
62.
63.     DISPLAYSURF.fill(BGCOLOR)
64.     startGameAnimation(mainBoard)
```

Line 61 sets up a variable called firstSelection with the value None. When the player clicks on an icon on the board, the program needs to track if this was the first icon of the pair that was clicked on or the second icon. If firstSelection is None, the click was on the first icon and we store the XY coordinates in the firstSelection variable as a tuple of two integers (one for the X value, the other for Y). On the second click the value will be this tuple and not None, which is how the program tracks that it is the second icon click. Line 63 fills the entire surface with the background color. This will also paint over anything that used to be on the surface, which gives us a clean slate to start drawing graphics on.

If you've played the Memory Puzzle game, you'll notice that at the beginning of the game, all of the boxes are quickly covered and uncovered randomly to give the player a sneak peek at which icons are under which boxes. This all happens in the startGameAnimation() function, which is explained later in this chapter.

It's important to give the player this sneak peek (but not long enough of a peek to let the player easily memorize the icon locations), because otherwise they would have no clue where any icons are. Blindly clicking on the icons isn't as much fun as having a little hint to go on.

THE GAME LOOP

```
66.     while True: # main game loop
67.         mouseClicked = False
68.
69.         DISPLAYSURF.fill(BGCOLOR) # drawing the window
70.         drawBoard(mainBoard, revealedBoxes)
```

The game loop is an infinite loop that starts on line 66 that keeps iterating for as long as the game is in progress. Remember that the game loop handles events, updates the game state, and draws the game state to the screen.

The game state for the Memory Puzzle program is stored in the following variables:

- mainBoard
- revealedBoxes
- firstSelection
- mouseClicked
- mousex
- mousey

On each iteration of the game loop in the Memory Puzzle program, the mouseClicked variable stores a Boolean value that is True if the player has clicked the mouse during this iteration through the game loop. (This is part of keeping track of the game state.)

On line 69, the surface is painted over with the background color to erase anything that was previously drawn on it. The program then calls drawBoard() to draw the current state of the board based on the board and "revealed boxes" data structures that we pass it. (These lines of code are part of drawing and updating the screen.)

Remember that our drawing functions only draw on the in-memory display Surface object. This Surface object will not actually appear on the screen until we call pygame.display.update(), which is done at the end of the game loop on line 121.

THE EVENT HANDLING LOOP

```
72.         for event in pygame.event.get(): # event handling loop
73.             if event.type == QUIT or (event.type == KEYUP and event.key == K_ESCAPE):
74.                 pygame.quit()
75.                 sys.exit()
76.             elif event.type == MOUSEMOTION:
77.                 mousex, mousey = event.pos
78.             elif event.type == MOUSEBUTTONUP:
79.                 mousex, mousey = event.pos
80.                 mouseClicked = True
```

The for loop on line 72 executes code for every event that has happened since the last iteration of the game loop. This loop is called the **event handling loop** (which is different from the game loop, although the event handling loop is inside of the game loop) and iterates over the list of pygame.Event objects returned by the pygame.event.get() call.

If the event object was a either a QUIT event or a KEYUP event for the Esc key, then the program should terminate. Otherwise, in the event of a MOUSEMOTION event (that is, the mouse cursor has moved) or MOUSEBUTTONUP event (that is, a mouse button was pressed earlier and now the button was let up), the position of the mouse cursor should be stored in the mousex and mousey variables. If this was a MOUSEBUTTONUP event, mouseClicked should also be set to True.

Once we have handled all of the events, the values stored in mousex, mousey, and mouseClicked will tell us any input that player has given us. Now we should update the game state and draw the results to the screen.

CHECKING WHICH BOX THE MOUSE CURSOR IS OVER

```
        boxx, boxy = getBoxAtPixel(mousex, mousey)
        if boxx != None and boxy != None:
            # The mouse is currently over a box.
            if not revealedBoxes[boxx][boxy]:
               drawHighlightBox(boxx, boxy)
```

The getBoxAtPixel() function will return a tuple of two integers. The integers represent the XY board coordinates of the box that the mouse coordinates are over. How getBoxAtPixel() does this is explained later. All we have to know for now is that if the mousex and mousey coordinates were over a box, a tuple of the

XY board coordinates are returned by the function and stored in boxx and boxy. If the mouse cursor was not over any box (for example, if it was off to the side of the board or in a gap in between boxes) then the tuple (None, None) is returned by the function and boxx and boxy will both have None stored in them.

We are only interested in the case where boxx and boxy do not have None in them, so the next several lines of code are in the block following the if statement on line 83 that checks for this case. If execution has come inside this block, we know the user has the mouse cursor over a box (and maybe has also clicked the mouse, depending on the value stored in mouseClicked).

The if statement on line 85 checks if the box is covered up or not by reading the value stored in revealedBoxes[boxx][boxy]. If it is False, then we know the box is covered. Whenever the mouse is over a covered up box, we want to draw a blue highlight around the box to inform the player that they can click on it. This highlighting is not done for boxes that are already uncovered. The highlight drawing is handled by our drawHighlightBox() function, which is explained later.

```
87.             if not revealedBoxes[boxx][boxy] and mouseClicked:
88.                 revealBoxesAnimation(mainBoard, [(boxx, boxy)])
```

```
89.                 revealedBoxes[boxx][boxy] = True # set the box as
"revealed"
```

On line 87, we check if the mouse cursor is not only over a covered up box but if the mouse has also been clicked. In that case, we want to play the "reveal" animation for that box by calling our revealBoxesAnimation() function (which is, as with all the other functions main() calls, explained later in this chapter). You should note that calling this function only draws the animation of the box being uncovered. It isn't until line 89 when we set revealedBoxes[boxx][boxy] = True that the data structure that tracks the game state is updated.

If you comment out line 89 and then run the program, you'll notice that after clicking on a box the reveal animation is played, but then the box immediately appears covered up again. This is because revealedBoxes[boxx][boxy] is still set to False, so on the next iteration of the game loop, the board is drawn with this box covered up. Not having line 89 would cause quite an odd bug in our program.

HANDLING THE FIRST CLICKED BOX

```
90.             if firstSelection == None: # the current box was the first box clicked
91.                 firstSelection = (boxx, boxy)
92.             else: # the current box was the second box clicked
93.                 # Check if there is a match between the two icons.
94.                 icon1shape, icon1color = getShapeAndColor(mainBoard, firstSelection[0], firstSelection[1])
95.                 icon2shape, icon2color = getShapeAndColor(mainBoard, boxx, boxy)
```

Before the execution entered the game loop, the firstSelection variable was set to None. Our program will interpret this to mean that no boxes have been clicked, so if line 90's condition is True, that means this is the first of the two possibly matching boxes that was clicked. We want to play the reveal animation for the box and then keep that box uncovered. We also set the firstSelection variable to a tuple of the box coordinates for the box that was clicked.

If this is the second box the player has clicked on, we want to play the reveal animation for that box but then check if the two icons under the boxes are matching. The getShapeAndColor() function (explained later) will retrieve the shape and color values of the icons. (These values will be one of the values in the ALLCOLORS and ALLSHAPES tuples.)

HANDLING A MISMATCHED PAIR OF ICONS

```
97.                 if icon1shape != icon2shape or icon1color != icon2color:
98.                     # Icons don't match. Re-cover up both selections.
99.                     pygame.time.wait(1000) # 1000 milliseconds = 1 sec
100.                    coverBoxesAnimation(mainBoard, [(firstSelection[0], firstSelection[1]), (boxx, boxy)])
101.                    revealedBoxes[firstSelection[0]][firstSelection[1]] = False
102.                    revealedBoxes[boxx][boxy] = False
```

The if statement on line 97 checks if either the shapes or colors of the two icons don't match. If this is the case, then we want to pause the game for 1000 milliseconds (which is the same as 1 second) by calling pygame.time.wait(1000) so that the player has a chance to see that the two icons don't match. Then the "cover up" animation plays for both boxes. We also want to update the game state to mark these boxes as not revealed (that is, covered up).

HANDLING IF THE PLAYER WON

```
103.            elif hasWon(revealedBoxes): # check if all pairs found
104.                gameWonAnimation(mainBoard)
105.                pygame.time.wait(2000)
106.
107.                # Reset the board
108.                mainBoard = getRandomizedBoard()
109.                revealedBoxes = generateRevealedBoxesData(False)
110.
111.                # Show the fully unrevealed board for a second.
112.                drawBoard(mainBoard, revealedBoxes)
113.                pygame.display.update()
114.                pygame.time.wait(1000)
115.
116.                # Replay the start game animation.
117.                startGameAnimation(mainBoard)
118.            firstSelection = None # reset firstSelection variable
```

Otherwise, if line 97's condition was False, then the two icons must be a match. The program doesn't really have to do anything else to the boxes at that point: it can just leave both boxes in the revealed state. However, the program should check if this was the last pair of icons on the board to be matched. This is done inside our hasWon() function, which returns True if the board is in a winning state (that is, all of the boxes are revealed).

If that is the case, we want to play the "game won" animation by calling gameWonAnimation(), then pause slightly to let the player revel in their victory, and then reset the data structures in mainBoard and revealedBoxes to start a new game.

Line 117 plays the "start game" animation again. After that, the program execution will just loop through the game loop as usual, and the player can continue playing until they quit the program.

No matter if the two boxes were matching or not, after the second box was clicked line 118 will set the firstSelection variable back to None so that the next box the player clicks on will be interpreted as the first clicked box of a pair of possibly matching icons.

DRAWING THE GAME STATE TO THE SCREEN

```
        # Redraw the screen and wait a clock tick.
        pygame.display.update()
        FPSCLOCK.tick(FPS)
```

At this point, the game state has been updated depending on the player's input, and the latest game state has been drawn to the DISPLAYSURF display Surface object. We've reached the end of the game loop, so we call pygame.display.update() to draw the DISPLAYSURF Surface object to the computer screen.

Line 9 set the FPS constant to the integer value 30, meaning we want the game to run (at most) at 30 frames per second. If we want the program to run faster, we can increase this number. If we want the program to run slower, we can decrease this number. It can even be set to a float value like 0.5, which will run the program at half a frame per second, that is, one frame per two seconds.

In order to run at 30 frames per second, each frame must be drawn in $1/30^{th}$ of a second. This means that pygame.display.update() and all the code in the game loop must execute in under 33.3 milliseconds. Any modern computer can do this easily with plenty of time left over. To prevent the program from running too fast, we call the tick() method of the pygame.Clock object in FPSCLOCK to have to it pause the program for the rest of the 33.3 milliseconds.

Since this is done at the very end of the game loop, it ensures that each iteration of the game loop takes (at least) 33.3 milliseconds. If for some reason the pygame.display.update() call and the code in the game loop takes longer than 33.3 milliseconds, then the tick() method will not wait at all and immediately return.

I've kept saying that the other functions would be explained later in the chapter. Now that we've gone over the main() function and you have an idea for how the general program works, let's go into the details of all the other functions that are called from main().

CREATING THE "REVEALED BOXES" DATA STRUCTURE

```
def generateRevealedBoxesData(val):
    revealedBoxes = []
    for i in range(BOARDWIDTH):
        revealedBoxes.append([val] * BOARDHEIGHT)
    return revealedBoxes
```

The generateRevealedBoxesData() function needs to create a list of lists of Boolean values. The Boolean value will just be the one that is passed to the function as the val parameter. We start the data structure as an empty list in the revealedBoxes variable.

In order to make the data structure have the revealedBoxes[x][y] structure, we need to make sure that the inner lists represent the vertical columns of the board and not the horizontal rows. Otherwise, the data structure will have a revealedBoxes[y][x] structure.

The for loop will create the columns and then append them to revealedBoxes. The columns are created using list replication, so that the column list has as many val values as the BOARDHEIGHT dictates.

CREATING THE BOARD DATA STRUCTURE

Step 1 – Get All Possible Icons

```
132. def getRandomizedBoard():
133.     # Get a list of every possible shape in every possible color.
134.     icons = []
135.     for color in ALLCOLORS:
136.         for shape in ALLSHAPES:
137.             icons.append( (shape, color) )
```

The board data structure is just a list of lists of tuples, where each tuple has a two values: one for the icon's shape and one for the icon's color. But creating this data structure is a little complicated. We need to be sure to have exactly as many icons for the number of boxes on the board and also be sure there are two and only two icons of each type.

The first step to do this is to create a list with every possible combination of shape and color. Recall that we have a list of each color and shape in ALLCOLORS and ALLSHAPES, so nested for loops on lines 135 and 136 will go through every possible shape for every possible color. These are each added to the list in the icons variable on line 137.

Step 2 – Shuffling and Truncating the List of All Icons

```
139.     random.shuffle(icons) # randomize the order of the icons list
140.     numIconsUsed = int(BOARDWIDTH * BOARDHEIGHT / 2) # calculate how many
icons are needed
141.     icons = icons[:numIconsUsed] * 2 # make two of each
142.     random.shuffle(icons)
```

But remember, there may be more possible combinations than spaces on the board. We need to calculate the number of spaces on the board by multiplying BOARDWIDTH by BOARDHEIGHT. Then we divide that number by 2 because we will have pairs of icons. On a board with 70 spaces, we'd only need 35 different icons, since there will be two of each icon. This number will be stored in numIconsUsed.

Line 141 uses list slicing to grab the first numIconsUsed number of icons in the list. This list has been shuffled on line 139, so it won't always be the same icons each game. Then this list is replicated by using the * operator so that there are two of each of the icons. This new doubled up list will overwrite the old list in the icons variable. Since the first half of this new list is identical to the last half, we call the shuffle() method again to randomly mix up the order of the icons.

Step 3 – Placing the Icons on the Board

```
144.     # Create the board data structure, with randomly placed icons.
145.     board = []
146.     for x in range(BOARDWIDTH):
147.         column = []
148.         for y in range(BOARDHEIGHT):
149.             column.append(icons[0])
150.             del icons[0] # remove the icons as we assign them
151.         board.append(column)
152.     return board
```

Now we need to create a list of lists data structure for the board. We can do this with nested for loops just like the generateRevealedBoxesData() function did. For each column on the board, we will create a list of randomly selected icons. As we add icons to the column, on line 149 we will then delete them from the front of the icons list on line 150. This way, as the icons list gets shorter and shorter, icons[0] will have a different icon to add to the columns.

To picture this better, type the following code into the interactive shell. Notice how the del statement changes the myList list.

```
>>> myList = ['cat', 'dog', 'mouse', 'lizard']
```

```
>>> del myList[0]
>>> myList
['dog', 'mouse', 'lizard']
>>> del myList[0]
>>> myList
['mouse', 'lizard']
>>> del myList[0]
>>> myList
['lizard']
>>> del myList[0]
>>> myList
[]
>>>
```

Because we are deleting the item at the front of the list, the other items shift forward so that the next item in the list becomes the new "first" item. This is the same way line 150 works.

SPLITTING A LIST INTO A LIST OF LISTS

```
155. def splitIntoGroupsOf(groupSize, theList):
156.     # splits a list into a list of lists, where the inner lists have at
157.     # most groupSize number of items.
158.     result = []
159.     for i in range(0, len(theList), groupSize):
160.         result.append(theList[i:i + groupSize])
161.     return result
```

The splitIntoGroupsOf() function (which will be called by the startGameAnimation() function) splits a list into a list of lists, where the inner lists have groupSize number of items in them. (The last list could have less if there are less than groupSize items left over.)

The call to range() on line 159 uses the three-parameter form of range(). Let's use an example. If the length of the list is 20 and the groupSize parameter is 8, then range(0, len(theList), groupSize) evaluates to range(0, 20, 8). This will give the i variable the values 0, 8, and 16 for the three iterations of the for loop.

The list slicing on line 160 with theList[i:i + groupSize] creates the lists that are added to the result list. On each iteration where i is 0, 8, and 16 (and groupSize is 8), this list slicing expression would be theList[0:8], then theList[8:16] on the second iteration, and then theList[16:24] on the third iteration.

Note that even though the largest index of theList would be 19 in our example, theList[16:24] won't raise an IndexError error even though 24 is larger than 19. It will just create a list slice with the remaining items in the list. List slicing doesn't destroy or change the original list stored in theList. It just copies a portion of it to evaluate to a new list value. This new list value is the list that is appended to the list in the result variable on line 160. So when we return result at the end of this function, we are returning a list of lists.

DIFFERENT COORDINATE SYSTEMS

```
def leftTopCoordsOfBox(boxx, boxy):
    # Convert board coordinates to pixel coordinates
    left = boxx * (BOXSIZE + GAPSIZE) + XMARGIN
    top = boxy * (BOXSIZE + GAPSIZE) + YMARGIN
    return (left, top)
```

You should be familiar with Cartesian Coordinate systems. In most of our games we will be using multiple Cartesian Coordinate systems. One system of coordinates that is used in the Memory Puzzle game is for the pixel or screen coordinates. But we will also be using another coordinate system for the boxes. This is because it will be easier to use (3, 2) to refer to the 4th box from the left and 3rd from the top (remember that the numbers start with 0, not 1) instead of using the pixel coordinate of the box's top left corner, (220, 165). However, we need a way to translate between these two coordinate systems.

Here's a picture of the game and the two different coordinate systems. Remember that the window is 640 pixels wide and 480 pixels tall, so (639, 479) is the bottom right corner (because the top left corner's pixel is (0, 0), and not (1, 1)).

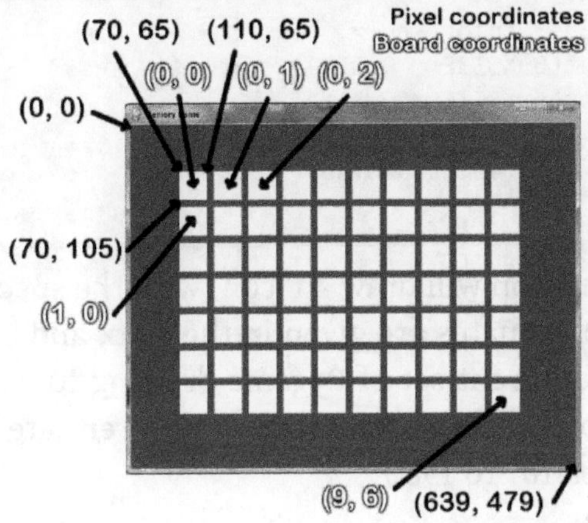

The leftTopCoordsOfBox() function will take box coordinates and return pixel coordinates. Because a box takes up multiple pixels on the screen, we will always return the single pixel at the top left corner of the box. This value will be returned as a two-integer tuple. The leftTopCoordsOfBox() function will often be used when we need pixel coordinates for drawing these boxes.

CONVERTING FROM PIXEL COORDINATES TO BOX COORDINATES

```
def getBoxAtPixel(x, y):
    for boxx in range(BOARDWIDTH):
        for boxy in range(BOARDHEIGHT):
            left, top = leftTopCoordsOfBox(boxx, boxy)
            boxRect = pygame.Rect(left, top, BOXSIZE, BOXSIZE)
            if boxRect.collidepoint(x, y):
                return (boxx, boxy)
    return (None, None)
```

We will also need a function to convert from pixel coordinates (which the mouse clicks and mouse movement events use) to box coordinates (so we can find out over which box the mouse event happened). Rect objects have a collidepoint() method that you can pass X and Y coordinates too and it will return True if the coordinates are inside (that is, collide with) the Rect object's area.

In order to find which box the mouse coordinates are over, we will go through each box's coordinates and call the collidepoint() method on a Rect object with those coordinates. When collidepoint() returns True, we know we have found the box that was clicked on or moved over and will return the box coordinates. If none of them return True, then the getBoxAtPixel() function will return the value (None, None). This tuple is returned instead of simply returning None because the caller of getBoxAtPixel() is expecting a tuple of two values to be returned.

DRAWING THE ICON, AND SYNTACTIC SUGAR

```
181. def drawIcon(shape, color, boxx, boxy):
182.     quarter = int(BOXSIZE * 0.25) # syntactic sugar
183.     half =    int(BOXSIZE * 0.5)  # syntactic sugar
184.
185.     left, top = leftTopCoordsOfBox(boxx, boxy) # get pixel coords from board coords
```

The drawIcon() function will draw an icon (with the specified shape and color) at the space whose coordinates are given in the boxx and boxy parameters. Each possible shape has a different set of Pygame drawing function calls for it, so we must have a large set of if and elif statements to differentiate between them. (These statements are on lines 187 to 198.)

The X and Y coordinates of the left and top edge of the box can be obtained by calling the leftTopCoordsOfBox() function. The width and height of the box are both set in the BOXSIZE constant. However, many of the shape drawing function calls use the midpoint and quarter-point of the box as well. We can calculate this and store it in the variables quarter and half. We could just as easily have the code int(BOXSIZE * 0.25) instead of the variable quarter, but this way the code becomes easier to read since it is more obvious what quarter means rather than int(BOXSIZE * 0.25).

Such variables are an example of syntactic sugar. **Syntactic sugar** is when we add code that could have been written in another way (probably with less actual code and variables), but does make the source code easier to read. Constant variables are one form of syntactic sugar. Pre-calculating a value and storing it in a variable is another type of syntactic sugar. (For example, in the getRandomizedBoard() function, we could have easily made the code on lines 140 and line 141 into a single line of code. But it's easier to read as two separate lines.) We don't need to have the extra quarter and half variables, but having them makes the code easier to read. Code that is easy to read is easy to debug and upgrade in the future.

```
186.     # Draw the shapes
187.     if shape == DONUT:
```

```
        pygame.draw.circle(DISPLAYSURF, color, (left + half, top + half), half - 5)
        pygame.draw.circle(DISPLAYSURF, BGCOLOR, (left + half, top + half), quarter - 5)
    elif shape == SQUARE:
        pygame.draw.rect(DISPLAYSURF, color, (left + quarter, top + quarter, BOXSIZE - half, BOXSIZE - half))
    elif shape == DIAMOND:
        pygame.draw.polygon(DISPLAYSURF, color, ((left + half, top), (left + BOXSIZE - 1, top + half), (left + half, top + BOXSIZE - 1), (left, top + half)))
    elif shape == LINES:
        for i in range(0, BOXSIZE, 4):
            pygame.draw.line(DISPLAYSURF, color, (left, top + i), (left + i, top))
            pygame.draw.line(DISPLAYSURF, color, (left + i, top + BOXSIZE - 1), (left + BOXSIZE - 1, top + i))
    elif shape == OVAL:
        pygame.draw.ellipse(DISPLAYSURF, color, (left, top + quarter, BOXSIZE, half))
```

Each of the donut, square, diamond, lines, and oval functions require different drawing primitive function calls to make.

SYNTACTIC SUGAR WITH GETTING A BOARD SPACE'S ICON'S SHAPE AND COLOR

```
def getShapeAndColor(board, boxx, boxy):
    # shape value for x, y spot is stored in board[x][y][0]
    # color value for x, y spot is stored in board[x][y][1]
    return board[boxx][boxy][0], board[boxx][boxy][1]
```

The getShapeAndColor() function only has one line. You might wonder why we would want a function instead of just typing in that one line of code whenever we need it. This is done for the same reason we use constant variables: it improves the readability of the code.

It's easy to figure out what a code like shape, color = getShapeAndColor() does. But if you looked a code like shape, color = board[boxx][boxy][0], board[boxx][boxy][1], it would be a bit more difficult to figure out.

DRAWING THE BOX COVER

```
def drawBoxCovers(board, boxes, coverage):
    # Draws boxes being covered/revealed. "boxes" is a list
    # of two-item lists, which have the x & y spot of the box.
    for box in boxes:
```

```
212.         left, top = leftTopCoordsOfBox(box[0], box[1])
213.         pygame.draw.rect(DISPLAYSURF, BGCOLOR, (left, top, BOXSIZE, BOXSIZE))
214.         shape, color = getShapeAndColor(board, box[0], box[1])
215.         drawIcon(shape, color, box[0], box[1])
216.         if coverage > 0: # only draw the cover if there is an coverage
217.             pygame.draw.rect(DISPLAYSURF, BOXCOLOR, (left, top, coverage, BOXSIZE))
218.     pygame.display.update()
219.     FPSCLOCK.tick(FPS)
```

The drawBoxCovers() function has three parameters: the board data structure, a list of (X, Y) tuples for each box that should have the cover drawn, and then the amount of coverage to draw for the boxes.

Since we want to use the same drawing code for each box in the boxes parameter, we will use a for loop on line 211 so we execute the same code on each box in the boxes list. Inside this for loop, the code should do three things: draw the background color (to paint over anything that was there before), draw the icon, then draw however much of the white box over the icon that is needed. The leftTopCoordsOfBox() function will return the pixel coordinates of the top left corner of the box. The if statement on line 216 makes sure that if the number in coverage happens to be less than 0, we won't call the pygame.draw.rect() function.

When the coverage parameter is 0, there is no coverage at all. When the coverage is set to 20, there is a 20 pixel wide white box covering the icon. The largest size we'll want the coverage set to is the number in BOXSIZE, where the entire icon is completely covered.

drawBoxCovers() is going to be called from a separate loop than the game loop. Because of this, it needs to have its own calls to pygame.display.update() and FPSCLOCK.tick(FPS) to display the animation. (This does mean that while inside this loop, there is no code being run to handle any events being generated. That's fine, since the cover and reveal animations only take a second or so to play.)

HANDLING THE REVEALING AND COVERING ANIMATION

```
def revealBoxesAnimation(board, boxesToReveal):
    # Do the "box reveal" animation.
    for coverage in range(BOXSIZE, (-REVEALSPEED) - 1, - REVEALSPEED):
        drawBoxCovers(board, boxesToReveal, coverage)


def coverBoxesAnimation(board, boxesToCover):
    # Do the "box cover" animation.
```

```
230.     for coverage in range(0, BOXSIZE + REVEALSPEED, REVEALSPEED):
231.         drawBoxCovers(board, boxesToCover, coverage)
```

Remember that an animation is simply just displaying different images for brief moments of time, and together they make it seem like things are moving on the screen. The revealBoxesAnimation() and coverBoxesAnimation() only need to draw an icon with a varying amount of coverage by the white box. We can write a single function called drawBoxCovers() which can do this, and then have our animation function call drawBoxCovers() for each frame of animation. As we saw in the last section, drawBoxCovers() makes a call to pygame.display.update() and FPSCLOCK.tick(FPS) itself.

To do this, we'll set up a for loop to make decreasing (in the case of revealBoxesAnimation()) or increasing (in the case of coverBoxesAnimation()) numbers for the converage parameter. The amount that the coverage variable will decrease/increase by is the number in the REVEALSPEED constant. On line 12 we set this constant to 8, meaning that on each call to drawBoxCovers(), the white box will decrease/increase by 8 pixels on each iteration. If we increase this number, then more pixels will be drawn on each call, meaning that the white box will decrease/increase in size faster. If we set it to 1, then the white box will only appear to decrease or increase by 1 pixel on each iteration, making the entire reveal or cover animation take longer.

Think of it like climbing stairs. If on each step you take, you climbed one stair, then it would take a normal amount of time to climb the entire staircase. But if you climbed two stairs at a time on each step (and the steps took just as long as before), you could climb the entire staircase twice as fast. If you could climb the staircase 8 stairs at a time, then you would climb the entire staircase 8 times as fast.

DRAWING THE ENTIRE BOARD

```
234. def drawBoard(board, revealed):
235.     # Draws all of the boxes in their covered or revealed state.
236.     for boxx in range(BOARDWIDTH):
237.         for boxy in range(BOARDHEIGHT):
238.             left, top = leftTopCoordsOfBox(boxx, boxy)
239.             if not revealed[boxx][boxy]:
240.                 # Draw a covered box.
241.                 pygame.draw.rect(DISPLAYSURF, BOXCOLOR, (left, top,
BOXSIZE, BOXSIZE))
242.             else:
243.                 # Draw the (revealed) icon.
244.                 shape, color = getShapeAndColor(board, boxx, boxy)
```

```
            drawIcon(shape, color, boxx, boxy)
```

The drawBoard() function makes a call to drawIcon() for each of the boxes on the board. The nested for loops on lines 236 and 237 will loop through every possible X and Y coordinate for the boxes, and will either draw the icon at that location or draw a white square instead (to represent a covered up box).

DRAWING THE HIGHLIGHT

```
def drawHighlightBox(boxx, boxy):
    left, top = leftTopCoordsOfBox(boxx, boxy)
    pygame.draw.rect(DISPLAYSURF, HIGHLIGHTCOLOR, (left - 5, top - 5, BOXSIZE + 10, BOXSIZE + 10), 4)
```

To help the player recognize that they can click on a covered box to reveal it, we will make a blue outline appear around a box to highlight it. This outline is drawn with a call to pygame.draw.rect() to make a rectangle with a width of 4 pixels.

THE "START GAME" ANIMATION

```
253. def startGameAnimation(board):
254.     # Randomly reveal the boxes 8 at a time.
255.     coveredBoxes = generateRevealedBoxesData(False)
256.     boxes = []
257.     for x in range(BOARDWIDTH):
258.         for y in range(BOARDHEIGHT):
259.             boxes.append( (x, y) )
260.     random.shuffle(boxes)
261.     boxGroups = splitIntoGroupsOf(8, boxes)
```

The animation that plays at the beginning of the game gives the player a quick hint as to where all the icons are located. In order to make this animation, we have to reveal and cover up groups of boxes one group after another. To do this, first we'll create a list of every possible space on the board. The nested for loops on lines 257 and 258 will add (X, Y) tuples to a list in the boxes variable.

We will reveal and cover up the first 8 boxes in this list, then the next 8, then the next 8 after that, and so on. However, since the order of the (X, Y) tuples in boxes would be the same each time, then the same order of boxes would be displayed. (Try commenting out line 260 and then running to program a few times to see this effect.)

To change up the boxes each time a game starts, we will call the random. shuffle() function to randomly shuffle the order of the tuples in the boxes list. Then when we reveal and cover up the first 8 boxes in this list (and each group of 8 boxes afterwards), it will be random group of 8 boxes.

To get the lists of 8 boxes, we call our splitIntoGroupsOf() function, passing 8 and the list in boxes. The list of lists that the function returns will be stored in a variable named boxGroups.

REVEALING AND COVERING THE GROUPS OF BOXES

```
    drawBoard(board, coveredBoxes)
    for boxGroup in boxGroups:
        revealBoxesAnimation(board, boxGroup)
        coverBoxesAnimation(board, boxGroup)
```

First, we draw the board. Since every value in coveredBoxes is set to False, this call to drawBoard() will end up drawing only covered up white boxes. The revealBoxesAnimation() and coverBoxesAnimation() functions will draw over the spaces of these white boxes.

The for loop will go through each of the inner lists in the boxGroups lists. We pass these to revealBoxesAnimation(), which will perform the animation of the white boxes being pulled away to reveal the icon underneath. Then the call to coverBoxesAnimation() will animate the white boxes expanding to cover up the icons. Then the for loop goes to the next iteration to animate the next set of 8 boxes.

THE "GAME WON" ANIMATION

```
269. def gameWonAnimation(board):
270.     # flash the background color when the player has won
271.     coveredBoxes = generateRevealedBoxesData(True)
272.     color1 = LIGHTBGCOLOR
273.     color2 = BGCOLOR
274.
275.     for i in range(13):
276.         color1, color2 = color2, color1 # swap colors
277.         DISPLAYSURF.fill(color1)
278.         drawBoard(board, coveredBoxes)
279.         pygame.display.update()
280.         pygame.time.wait(300)
```

When the player has uncovered all of the boxes by matching every pair on the board, we want to congratulate them by flashing the background color. The for loop will draw the color in the color1 variable for the background color and then draw the board over it. However, on each iteration of the for loop, the values in color1 and color2 will be swapped with each other on line 276. This way the program will alternate between drawing two different background colors.

Remember that this function needs to call pygame.display.update() to actually make the DISPLAYSURF surface appear on the screen.

TELLING IF THE PLAYER HAS WON

```
283. def hasWon(revealedBoxes):
284.     # Returns True if all the boxes have been revealed, otherwise False
285.     for i in revealedBoxes:
286.         if False in i:
287.             return False # return False if any boxes are covered.
288.     return True
```

The player has won the game when all of the icon pairs have been matched. Since the “revealed” data structure gets values in it set to True as icons have been matched, we can simply loop through every space in revealedBoxes looking for a False value. If even one False value is in revealedBoxes, then we know there are still unmatched icons on the board.

Note that because revealedBoxes is a list of lists, the for loop on line 285 will set the inner list as the values of i. But we can use the in operator to search for a False value in the entire inner list. This way we don’t need to write an additional line of code and have two nested for loops like this:

```
for x in revealedBoxes:
    for y in revealedBoxes[x]:
        if False == revealedBoxes[x][y]:
            return False
```

WHY BOTHER HAVING A MAIN() FUNCTION?

```
if __name__ == '__main__':
    main()
```

It may seem pointless to have a main() function, since you could just put that code in the global scope at the bottom of the program instead, and the code would run the exact same. However, there are two good reasons to put them inside of a main() function.

First, this lets you have local variables whereas otherwise the local variables in the main() function would have to become global variables. Limiting the number of global variables is a good way to keep the code simple and easier to debug. (See the “Why Global Variables are Evil” section in this chapter.)

Second, this also lets you import the program so that you can call and test individual functions. If the *memorypuzzle.py* file is in the C:\Python32 folder, then you can import it from the interactive shell. Type the following to test out the splitIntoGroupsOf() and getBoxAtPixel() functions to make sure they return the correct return values:

```
>>> import memorypuzzle
>>> memorypuzzle.splitIntoGroupsOf(3, [0,1,2,3,4,5,6,7,8,9])
[[0, 1, 2], [3, 4, 5], [6, 7, 8], [9]]
>>> memorypuzzle.getBoxAtPixel(0, 0)
(None, None)
>>> memorypuzzle.getBoxAtPixel(150, 150)
(1, 1)
```

When a module is imported, all of the code in it is run. If we didn't have the main() function, and had its code in the global scope, then the game would have automatically started as soon as we imported it, which really wouldn't let us call individual functions in it.

That's why the code is in a separate function that we have named main(). Then we check the built-in Python variable __name__ to see if we should call the main() function or not. This variable is automatically set by the Python interpreter to the string '__main__' if the program itself is being run and 'memorypuzzle' if it is being imported. This is why the main() function is not run when we executed the import memorypuzzle statement in the interactive shell.

This is a handy technique for being able to import the program you are working on from the interactive shell and make sure individual functions are returning the correct values by testing them one call at a time.

WHY BOTHER WITH READABILITY?

A lot of the suggestions in this chapter haven't been about how to write programs that computers can run so much as how to write programs that programmers can read. You might not understand why this is important. After all, as long as the code works, who cares if it is hard or easy for human programmers to read?

However, the important thing to realize about software is that it is rarely ever left alone. When you are creating your own games, you will rarely be "done" with the program. You will always get new ideas for game features you want add, or find new bugs with the program. Because of this, it is important that your program is readable so that you can look at the code and understand it. And understanding the code is the first step to changing it to add more code or fix bugs.

As an example, here is an obfuscated version of the Memory Puzzle program that was made entirely unreadable. If you type it in and run it you will find it runs exactly the same as the code at the beginning of this chapter. But if there was a bug with this code, it would be impossible to read the code and understand what's going on, much less fix the bug.

The computer doesn't mind code as unreadable as this. It's all the same to it.

```
import random, pygame, sys
from pygame.locals import *
def hhh():
    global a, b
    pygame.init()
    a = pygame.time.Clock()
    b = pygame.display.set_mode((640, 480))
    j = 0
    k = 0
    pygame.display.set_caption('Memory Game')
    i = c()
    hh = d(False)
    h = None
    b.fill((60, 60, 100))
    g(i)
    while True:
        e = False
        b.fill((60, 60, 100))
        f(i, hh)
        for eee in pygame.event.get():
            if eee.type == QUIT or (eee.type == KEYUP and eee.key == K_ESCAPE):
                pygame.quit()
                sys.exit()
            elif eee.type == MOUSEMOTION:
                j, k = eee.pos
            elif eee.type == MOUSEBUTTONUP:
                j, k = eee.pos
                e = True
        bb, ee = m(j, k)
        if bb != None and ee != None:
            if not hh[bb][ee]:
                n(bb, ee)
            if not hh[bb][ee] and e:
                o(i, [(bb, ee)])
                hh[bb][ee] = True
                if h == None:
                    h = (bb, ee)
                else:
                    q, fff = s(i, h[0], h[1])
                    r, ggg = s(i, bb, ee)
```

```
                    if q != r or fff != ggg:
                        pygame.time.wait(1000)
                        p(i, [(h[0], h[1]), (bb, ee)])
                        hh[h[0]][h[1]] = False
                        hh[bb][ee] = False
                    elif ii(hh):
                        jj(i)
                        pygame.time.wait(2000)
                        i = c()
                        hh = d(False)
                        f(i, hh)
                        pygame.display.update()
                        pygame.time.wait(1000)
                        g(i)
                    h = None
        pygame.display.update()
        a.tick(30)
def d(ccc):
    hh = []
    for i in range(10):
        hh.append([ccc] * 7)
    return hh
def c():
    rr = []
    for tt in ((255, 0, 0), (0, 255, 0), (0, 0, 255), (255, 255, 0), (255, 128,
0), (255, 0, 255), (0, 255, 255)):
        for ss in ('a', 'b', 'c', 'd', 'e'):
            rr.append( (ss, tt) )
    random.shuffle(rr)
    rr = rr[:35] * 2
    random.shuffle(rr)
    bbb = []
    for x in range(10):
        v = []
        for y in range(7):
            v.append(rr[0])
            del rr[0]
        bbb.append(v)
    return bbb
def t(vv, uu):
    ww = []
    for i in range(0, len(uu), vv):
        ww.append(uu[i:i + vv])
    return ww
def aa(bb, ee):
    return (bb * 50 + 70, ee * 50 + 65)
def m(x, y):
```

```
    for bb in range(10):
        for ee in range(7):
            oo, ddd = aa(bb, ee)
            aaa = pygame.Rect(oo, ddd, 40, 40)
            if aaa.collidepoint(x, y):
                return (bb, ee)
    return (None, None)
def w(ss, tt, bb, ee):
    oo, ddd = aa(bb, ee)
    if ss == 'a':
        pygame.draw.circle(b, tt, (oo + 20, ddd + 20), 15)
        pygame.draw.circle(b, (60, 60, 100), (oo + 20, ddd + 20), 5)
    elif ss == 'b':
        pygame.draw.rect(b, tt, (oo + 10, ddd + 10, 20, 20))
    elif ss == 'c':
        pygame.draw.polygon(b, tt, ((oo + 20, ddd), (oo + 40 - 1, ddd + 20),
(oo + 20, ddd + 40 - 1), (oo, ddd + 20)))
    elif ss == 'd':
        for i in range(0, 40, 4):
            pygame.draw.line(b, tt, (oo, ddd + i), (oo + i, ddd))
            pygame.draw.line(b, tt, (oo + i, ddd + 39), (oo + 39, ddd + i))
    elif ss == 'e':
        pygame.draw.ellipse(b, tt, (oo, ddd + 10, 40, 20))
def s(bbb, bb, ee):
    return bbb[bb][ee][0], bbb[bb][ee][1]
def dd(bbb, boxes, gg):
    for box in boxes:
        oo, ddd = aa(box[0], box[1])
        pygame.draw.rect(b, (60, 60, 100), (oo, ddd, 40, 40))
        ss, tt = s(bbb, box[0], box[1])
        w(ss, tt, box[0], box[1])
        if gg > 0:
            pygame.draw.rect(b, (255, 255, 255), (oo, ddd, gg, 40))
    pygame.display.update()
    a.tick(30)
def o(bbb, cc):
    for gg in range(40, (-8) - 1, -8):
        dd(bbb, cc, gg)
def p(bbb, ff):
    for gg in range(0, 48, 8):
        dd(bbb, ff, gg)
def f(bbb, pp):
    for bb in range(10):
        for ee in range(7):
            oo, ddd = aa(bb, ee)
            if not pp[bb][ee]:
                pygame.draw.rect(b, (255, 255, 255), (oo, ddd, 40, 40))
```

```
            else:
                ss, tt = s(bbb, bb, ee)
                w(ss, tt, bb, ee)
def n(bb, ee):
    oo, ddd = aa(bb, ee)
    pygame.draw.rect(b, (0, 0, 255), (oo - 5, ddd - 5, 50, 50), 4)
def g(bbb):
    mm = d(False)
    boxes = []
    for x in range(10):
        for y in range(7):
            boxes.append( (x, y) )
    random.shuffle(boxes)
    kk = t(8, boxes)
    f(bbb, mm)
    for nn in kk:
        o(bbb, nn)
        p(bbb, nn)
def jj(bbb):
    mm = d(True)
    tt1 = (100, 100, 100)
    tt2 = (60, 60, 100)
    for i in range(13):
        tt1, tt2 = tt2, tt1
        b.fill(tt1)
        f(bbb, mm)
        pygame.display.update()
        pygame.time.wait(300)
def ii(hh):
    for i in hh:
        if False in i:
            return False
    return True
if __name__ == '__main__':
    hhh()
```

Never write code like this. If you program like this while facing the mirror in a bathroom with the lights turned off, the ghost of Ada Lovelace will come out of the mirror and throw you into the jaws of a Jacquard loom.

SUMMARY, AND A HACKING SUGGESTION

This chapter covers the entire explanation of how the Memory Puzzle program works. Read over the chapter and the source code again to understand it better. Many of the other game programs in this book make use of the same programming concepts (like nested for loops, syntactic sugar, and different coordinate systems in the same program) so they won't be explained again to keep this book short.

One idea to try out to understand how the code works is to intentionally break it by commenting out random lines. Doing this to some of the lines will probably cause a syntactic error that will prevent the script from running at all. But commenting out other lines will result in weird bugs and other cool effects. Try doing this and then figure out why a program has the bugs it does.

This is also the first step in being able to add your own secret cheats or hacks to the program. By breaking the program from what it normally does, you can learn how to change it to do something neat effect (like secretly giving you hints on how to solve the puzzle). Feel free to experiment. You can always save a copy of the unchanged source code in a different file if you want to play the regular game again.

Chapter 4 SLIDE PUZZLE

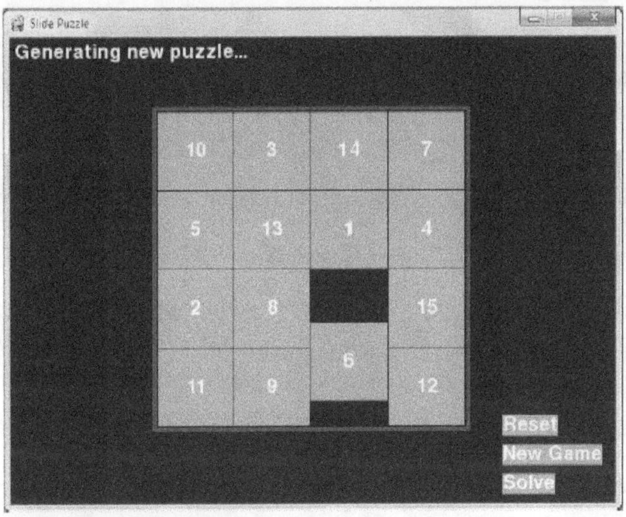

HOW TO PLAY SLIDE PUZZLE

The board is a 4x4 grid with fifteen tiles (numbered 1 through 15 going left to right) and one blank space. The tiles start out in random positions, and the player must slide tiles around until the tiles are back in their original order.

SOURCE CODE TO SLIDE PUZZLE

```
# Slide Puzzle
# By Al Sweigart al@inventwithpython.com
# http://inventwithpython.com/pygame
# Creative Commons BY-NC-SA 3.0 US

import pygame, sys, random
from pygame.locals import *

# Create the constants (go ahead and experiment with different values)
BOARDWIDTH = 4  # number of columns in the board
BOARDHEIGHT = 4 # number of rows in the board
TILESIZE = 80
```

```
WINDOWWIDTH = 640
WINDOWHEIGHT = 480
FPS = 30
BLANK = None

#                R    G    B
BLACK =         (  0,   0,   0)
WHITE =         (255, 255, 255)
BRIGHTBLUE =    (  0,  50, 255)
DARKTURQUOISE = (  3,  54,  73)
GREEN =         (  0, 204,   0)

BGCOLOR = DARKTURQUOISE
TILECOLOR = GREEN
TEXTCOLOR = WHITE
BORDERCOLOR = BRIGHTBLUE
BASICFONTSIZE = 20

BUTTONCOLOR = WHITE
BUTTONTEXTCOLOR = BLACK
MESSAGECOLOR = WHITE

XMARGIN = int((WINDOWWIDTH - (TILESIZE * BOARDWIDTH + (BOARDWIDTH - 1))) / 2)
YMARGIN = int((WINDOWHEIGHT - (TILESIZE * BOARDHEIGHT + (BOARDHEIGHT - 1))) / 2)

UP = 'up'
DOWN = 'down'
LEFT = 'left'
RIGHT = 'right'

def main():
    global FPSCLOCK, DISPLAYSURF, BASICFONT, RESET_SURF, RESET_RECT, NEW_SURF, NEW_RECT, SOLVE_SURF, SOLVE_RECT

    pygame.init()
    FPSCLOCK = pygame.time.Clock()
    DISPLAYSURF = pygame.display.set_mode((WINDOWWIDTH, WINDOWHEIGHT))
    pygame.display.set_caption('Slide Puzzle')
    BASICFONT = pygame.font.Font('freesansbold.ttf', BASICFONTSIZE)

    # Store the option buttons and their rectangles in OPTIONS.
    RESET_SURF, RESET_RECT = makeText('Reset',    TEXTCOLOR, TILECOLOR, WINDOWWIDTH - 120, WINDOWHEIGHT - 90)
```

```
    NEW_SURF,   NEW_RECT   = makeText('New Game', TEXTCOLOR, TILECOLOR, WINDOWWIDTH - 120, WINDOWHEIGHT - 60)
    SOLVE_SURF, SOLVE_RECT = makeText('Solve',    TEXTCOLOR, TILECOLOR, WINDOWWIDTH - 120, WINDOWHEIGHT - 30)

    mainBoard, solutionSeq = generateNewPuzzle(80)
    SOLVEDBOARD = getStartingBoard() # a solved board is the same as the board in a start state.
    allMoves = [] # list of moves made from the solved configuration

    while True: # main game loop
        slideTo = None # the direction, if any, a tile should slide
        msg = '' # contains the message to show in the upper left corner.
        if mainBoard == SOLVEDBOARD:
            msg = 'Solved!'

        drawBoard(mainBoard, msg)

        checkForQuit()
        for event in pygame.event.get(): # event handling loop
            if event.type == MOUSEBUTTONUP:
                spotx, spoty = getSpotClicked(mainBoard, event.pos[0], event.pos[1])

                if (spotx, spoty) == (None, None):
                    # check if the user clicked on an option button
                    if RESET_RECT.collidepoint(event.pos):
                        resetAnimation(mainBoard, allMoves) # clicked on Reset button
                        allMoves = []
                    elif NEW_RECT.collidepoint(event.pos):
                        mainBoard, solutionSeq = generateNewPuzzle(80) # clicked on New Game button
                        allMoves = []
                    elif SOLVE_RECT.collidepoint(event.pos):
                        resetAnimation(mainBoard, solutionSeq + allMoves) # clicked on Solve button
                        allMoves = []
                else:
                    # check if the clicked tile was next to the blank spot

                    blankx, blanky = getBlankPosition(mainBoard)
                    if spotx == blankx + 1 and spoty == blanky:
                        slideTo = LEFT
                    elif spotx == blankx - 1 and spoty == blanky:
```

```
                        slideTo = RIGHT
                    elif spotx == blankx and spoty == blanky + 1:
                        slideTo = UP
                    elif spotx == blankx and spoty == blanky - 1:
                        slideTo = DOWN

            elif event.type == KEYUP:
                # check if the user pressed a key to slide a tile
                if event.key in (K_LEFT, K_a) and isValidMove(mainBoard, LEFT):
                    slideTo = LEFT
                elif event.key in (K_RIGHT, K_d) and isValidMove(mainBoard, RIGHT):
                    slideTo = RIGHT
                elif event.key in (K_UP, K_w) and isValidMove(mainBoard, UP):
                    slideTo = UP
                elif event.key in (K_DOWN, K_s) and isValidMove(mainBoard, DOWN):
                    slideTo = DOWN

        if slideTo:
            slideAnimation(mainBoard, slideTo, 'Click tile or press arrow keys to slide.', 8) # show slide on screen
            makeMove(mainBoard, slideTo)
            allMoves.append(slideTo) # record the slide
        pygame.display.update()
        FPSCLOCK.tick(FPS)


def terminate():
    pygame.quit()
    sys.exit()


def checkForQuit():
    for event in pygame.event.get(QUIT): # get all the QUIT events
        terminate() # terminate if any QUIT events are present
    for event in pygame.event.get(KEYUP): # get all the KEYUP events
        if event.key == K_ESCAPE:
            terminate() # terminate if the KEYUP event was for the Esc key
        pygame.event.post(event) # put the other KEYUP event objects back


def getStartingBoard():
    # Return a board data structure with tiles in the solved state.
```

```
    # For example, if BOARDWIDTH and BOARDHEIGHT are both 3, this function
    # returns [[1, 4, 7], [2, 5, 8], [3, 6, None]]
    counter = 1
    board = []
    for x in range(BOARDWIDTH):
        column = []
        for y in range(BOARDHEIGHT):
            column.append(counter)
            counter += BOARDWIDTH
        board.append(column)
        counter -= BOARDWIDTH * (BOARDHEIGHT - 1) + BOARDWIDTH - 1

    board[BOARDWIDTH-1][BOARDHEIGHT-1] = None
    return board


def getBlankPosition(board):
    # Return the x and y of board coordinates of the blank space.
    for x in range(BOARDWIDTH)):
        for y in range(BOARDHEIGHT):
            if board[x][y] == None:
                return (x, y)


def makeMove(board, move):
    # This function does not check if the move is valid.
    blankx, blanky = getBlankPosition(board)

    if move == UP:
        board[blankx][blanky], board[blankx][blanky + 1] =
board[blankx][blanky + 1], board[blankx][blanky]
    elif move == DOWN:
        board[blankx][blanky], board[blankx][blanky - 1] =
board[blankx][blanky - 1], board[blankx][blanky]
    elif move == LEFT:
        board[blankx][blanky], board[blankx + 1][blanky] = board[blankx +
1][blanky], board[blankx][blanky]
    elif move == RIGHT:
        board[blankx][blanky], board[blankx - 1][blanky] = board[blankx -
1][blanky], board[blankx][blanky]


def isValidMove(board, move):
    blankx, blanky = getBlankPosition(board)
    return (move == UP and blanky != len(board[0]) - 1) or \
           (move == DOWN and blanky != 0) or \
```

```
            (move == LEFT and blankx != len(board) - 1) or \
            (move == RIGHT and blankx != 0)


def getRandomMove(board, lastMove=None):
    # start with a full list of all four moves
    validMoves = [UP, DOWN, LEFT, RIGHT]

    # remove moves from the list as they are disqualified
    if lastMove == UP or not isValidMove(board, DOWN):
        validMoves.remove(DOWN)
    if lastMove == DOWN or not isValidMove(board, UP):
        validMoves.remove(UP)
    if lastMove == LEFT or not isValidMove(board, RIGHT):
        validMoves.remove(RIGHT)
    if lastMove == RIGHT or not isValidMove(board, LEFT):
        validMoves.remove(LEFT)

    # return a random move from the list of remaining moves
    return random.choice(validMoves)


def getLeftTopOfTile(tileX, tileY):
    left = XMARGIN + (tileX * TILESIZE) + (tileX - 1)
    top = YMARGIN + (tileY * TILESIZE) + (tileY - 1)
    return (left, top)


def getSpotClicked(board, x, y):
    # from the x & y pixel coordinates, get the x & y board coordinates
    for tileX in range(len(board)):
        for tileY in range(len(board[0])):
            left, top = getLeftTopOfTile(tileX, tileY)
            tileRect = pygame.Rect(left, top, TILESIZE, TILESIZE)
            if tileRect.collidepoint(x, y):
                return (tileX, tileY)
    return (None, None)


def drawTile(tilex, tiley, number, adjx=0, adjy=0):
    # draw a tile at board coordinates tilex and tiley, optionally a few
    # pixels over (determined by adjx and adjy)
    left, top = getLeftTopOfTile(tilex, tiley)
    pygame.draw.rect(DISPLAYSURF, TILECOLOR, (left + adjx, top + adjy, TILESIZE, TILESIZE))
    textSurf = BASICFONT.render(str(number), True, TEXTCOLOR)
```

```
    textRect = textSurf.get_rect()
    textRect.center = left + int(TILESIZE / 2) + adjx, top + int(TILESIZE / 2) + adjy
    DISPLAYSURF.blit(textSurf, textRect)


def makeText(text, color, bgcolor, top, left):
    # create the Surface and Rect objects for some text.
    textSurf = BASICFONT.render(text, True, color, bgcolor)
    textRect = textSurf.get_rect()
    textRect.topleft = (top, left)
    return (textSurf, textRect)


def drawBoard(board, message):
    DISPLAYSURF.fill(BGCOLOR)
    if message:
        textSurf, textRect = makeText(message, MESSAGECOLOR, BGCOLOR, 5, 5)

        DISPLAYSURF.blit(textSurf, textRect)

    for tilex in range(len(board)):
        for tiley in range(len(board[0])):
            if board[tilex][tiley]:
                drawTile(tilex, tiley, board[tilex][tiley])

    left, top = getLeftTopOfTile(0, 0)
    width = BOARDWIDTH * TILESIZE
    height = BOARDHEIGHT * TILESIZE
    pygame.draw.rect(DISPLAYSURF, BORDERCOLOR, (left - 5, top - 5, width + 11, height + 11), 4)

    DISPLAYSURF.blit(RESET_SURF, RESET_RECT)
    DISPLAYSURF.blit(NEW_SURF, NEW_RECT)
    DISPLAYSURF.blit(SOLVE_SURF, SOLVE_RECT)


def slideAnimation(board, direction, message, animationSpeed):
    # Note: This function does not check if the move is valid.

    blankx, blanky = getBlankPosition(board)
    if direction == UP:
        movex = blankx
        movey = blanky + 1
    elif direction == DOWN:
        movex = blankx
```

```
        movey = blanky - 1
    elif direction == LEFT:
        movex = blankx + 1
        movey = blanky
    elif direction == RIGHT:
        movex = blankx - 1
        movey = blanky

    # prepare the base surface
    drawBoard(board, message)
    baseSurf = DISPLAYSURF.copy()
    # draw a blank space over the moving tile on the baseSurf Surface.
    moveLeft, moveTop = getLeftTopOfTile(movex, movey)
    pygame.draw.rect(baseSurf, BGCOLOR, (moveLeft, moveTop, TILESIZE,
TILESIZE))

    for i in range(0, TILESIZE, animationSpeed):
        # animate the tile sliding over
        checkForQuit()
        DISPLAYSURF.blit(baseSurf, (0, 0))
        if direction == UP:
            drawTile(movex, movey, board[movex][movey], 0, -i)
        if direction == DOWN:
            drawTile(movex, movey, board[movex][movey], 0, i)
        if direction == LEFT:
            drawTile(movex, movey, board[movex][movey], -i, 0)
        if direction == RIGHT:
            drawTile(movex, movey, board[movex][movey], i, 0)

        pygame.display.update()
        FPSCLOCK.tick(FPS)


def generateNewPuzzle(numSlides):
    # From a starting configuration, make numSlides number of moves (and
    # animate these moves).
    sequence = []
    board = getStartingBoard()
    drawBoard(board, '')
    pygame.display.update()
    pygame.time.wait(500) # pause 500 milliseconds for effect
    lastMove = None
    for i in range(numSlides):
        move = getRandomMove(board, lastMove)
        slideAnimation(board, move, 'Generating new puzzle...',
int(TILESIZE / 3))
```

```
            makeMove(board, move)
            sequence.append(move)
            lastMove = move
    return (board, sequence)


def resetAnimation(board, allMoves):
    # make all of the moves in allMoves in reverse.
    revAllMoves = allMoves[:] # gets a copy of the list
    revAllMoves.reverse()

    for move in revAllMoves:
        if move == UP:
            oppositeMove = DOWN
        elif move == DOWN:
            oppositeMove = UP
        elif move == RIGHT:
            oppositeMove = LEFT
        elif move == LEFT:
            oppositeMove = RIGHT
        slideAnimation(board, oppositeMove, '', int(TILESIZE / 2))
        makeMove(board, oppositeMove)


if __name__ == '__main__':
    main()
```

Second Verse, Same as the First

Much of the code in Wormy is similar to the previous games we've looked at, especially the constants being set at the start of the code.

```
# Slide Puzzle
# By Al Sweigart al@inventwithpython.com
# http://inventwithpython.com/pygame
# Creative Commons BY-NC-SA 3.0 US

import pygame, sys, random
from pygame.locals import *

# Create the constants (go ahead and experiment with different values)
BOARDWIDTH = 4  # number of columns in the board
BOARDHEIGHT = 4 # number of rows in the board
TILESIZE = 80
WINDOWWIDTH = 640
```

```
WINDOWHEIGHT = 480
FPS = 30
BLANK = None
#                 R    G    B
BLACK =         (  0,   0,   0)
WHITE =         (255, 255, 255)
BRIGHTBLUE =    (  0,  50, 255)
DARKTURQUOISE = (  3,  54,  73)
GREEN =         (  0, 204,   0)
BGCOLOR = DARKTURQUOISE
TILECOLOR = GREEN
TEXTCOLOR = WHITE
BORDERCOLOR = BRIGHTBLUE
BASICFONTSIZE = 20
BUTTONCOLOR = WHITE
BUTTONTEXTCOLOR = BLACK
MESSAGECOLOR = WHITE
XMARGIN = int((WINDOWWIDTH - (TILESIZE * BOARDWIDTH + (BOARDWIDTH - 1))) / 2)
YMARGIN = int((WINDOWHEIGHT - (TILESIZE * BOARDHEIGHT + (BOARDHEIGHT - 1))) / 2)
UP = 'up'
DOWN = 'down'
LEFT = 'left'
RIGHT = 'right'
```

This code at the top of the program just handles all the basic importing of modules and creating constants. This is just like the beginning of the Memory Puzzle game from the last chapter.

SETTING UP THE BUTTONS

```
def main():
    global FPSCLOCK, DISPLAYSURF, BASICFONT, RESET_SURF, RESET_RECT, NEW_SURF, NEW_RECT, SOLVE_SURF, SOLVE_RECT
    pygame.init()
    FPSCLOCK = pygame.time.Clock()
    DISPLAYSURF = pygame.display.set_mode((WINDOWWIDTH, WINDOWHEIGHT))
    pygame.display.set_caption('Slide Puzzle')
    BASICFONT = pygame.font.Font('freesansbold.ttf', BASICFONTSIZE)
```

```
    # Store the option buttons and their rectangles in OPTIONS.
    RESET_SURF, RESET_RECT = makeText('Reset',    TEXTCOLOR, TILECOLOR, WINDOWWIDTH - 120, WINDOWHEIGHT - 90)
    NEW_SURF,   NEW_RECT   = makeText('New Game', TEXTCOLOR, TILECOLOR, WINDOWWIDTH - 120, WINDOWHEIGHT - 60)
    SOLVE_SURF, SOLVE_RECT = makeText('Solve',    TEXTCOLOR, TILECOLOR, WINDOWWIDTH - 120, WINDOWHEIGHT - 30)

    mainBoard, solutionSeq = generateNewPuzzle(80)
    SOLVEDBOARD = getStartingBoard() # a solved board is the same as the board in a start state.
```

Just like in the last chapter, the functions called from the main() function calls will be explained later in the chapter. For now, you just need to know what they do and what values they return. You don't need to know how they work.

The first part of the main() function will handle creating the window, Clock object, and Font object. The makeText() function is defined later in the program, but for now you just need to know that it returns a pygame.Surface object and pygame.Rect object which can be used to make clickable buttons. The Slide Puzzle game will have three buttons: a "Reset" button that will undo any moves the player has made, a "New" button that will create a new slide puzzle, and a "Solve" button that will solve the puzzle for the player.

We will need to have two board data structures for this program. One board will represent the current game state. The other board will have its tiles in the "solved" state, meaning that all the tiles are lined up in order. When the current game state's board is exactly the same as the solved board, then we know the player has won. (We won't ever change this second one. It'll just be there to compare the current game state board to.)

The generateNewPuzzle() will create a board data structure that started off in the ordered, solved state and then had 80 random slide moves performed on it (because we passed the integer 80 to it. If we want the board to be even more jumbled, then we can pass a larger integer to it). This will make the board into a randomly jumbled state that the player will have to solve (which will be stored in a variable named mainBoard). The generateNewBoard() also returns a list of all the random moves that were performed on it (which will be stored in a variable named solutionSeq).

BEING SMART BY USING STUPID CODE

```
    allMoves = [] # list of moves made from the solved configuration
```

Solving a slide puzzle can be really tricky. We could program the computer to do it, but that would require us to figure out an algorithm that can solve the slide puzzle. That would be very difficult and involve a lot of cleverness and effort to put into this program.

Fortunately, there's an easier way. We could just have the computer memorize all the random slides it made when it created the board data structure, and then the board can be solved just by performing the opposite slide. Since the board originally started in the solved state, undoing all the slides would return it to the solved state.

For example, below we perform a "right" slide on the board on the left side of the page, which leaves the board in the state that is on the right side of the page:

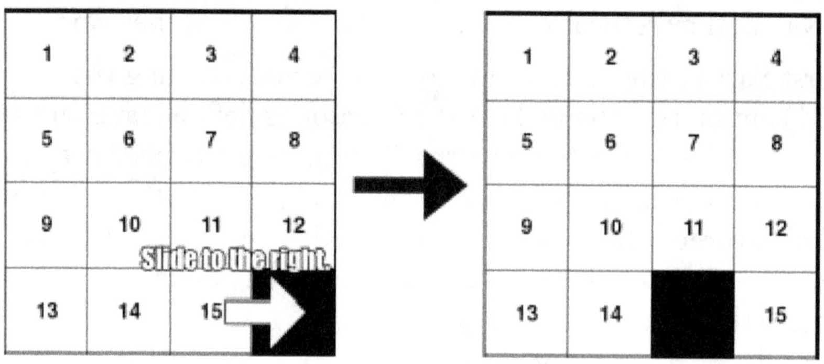

After the right slide, if we do the opposite slide (a left slide) then the board will be back in the original state. So to get back to the original state after several slides, we just have to do the opposite slides in reverse order. If we did a right slide, then another right slide, then a down slide, we would have to do an up slide, left slide, and left slide to undo those first three slides. This is much easier than writing a function that can solve these puzzles simply by looking at the current state of them.

THE MAIN GAME LOOP

```
    while True: # main game loop
        slideTo = None # the direction, if any, a tile should slide
        msg = '' # contains the message to show in the upper left corner.
        if mainBoard == SOLVEDBOARD:
            msg = 'Solved!'

        drawBoard(mainBoard, msg)
```

In the main game loop, the slideTo variable will track which direction the player wants to slide a tile (it starts off at the beginning of the game loop as None and is set later) and the msg variable tracks what string to display at the top of the window.

The program does a quick check on line 64 to see if the board data structure has the same value as the solved board data structure stored in SOLVEDBOARD. If so, then the msg variable is changed to the string 'Solved!'. This won't appear on the screen until drawBoard() has been called to draw it to the DISPLAYSURF Surface object (which is done on line 67) and pygame.display.update() is called to draw the display Surface object on the actual computer screen (which is done on line 291 at the end of the game loop).

CLICKING ON THE BUTTONS

```
69.         checkForQuit()
70.         for event in pygame.event.get(): # event handling loop
71.             if event.type == MOUSEBUTTONUP:
72.                 spotx, spoty = getSpotClicked(mainBoard, event.pos[0],
event.pos[1])
73.
74.                 if (spotx, spoty) == (None, None):
75.                     # check if the user clicked on an option button
76.                     if RESET_RECT.collidepoint(event.pos):
77.                         resetAnimation(mainBoard, allMoves) # clicked on
Reset button
78.                         allMoves = []
79.                     elif NEW_RECT.collidepoint(event.pos):
80.                         mainBoard, solutionSeq = generateNewPuzzle(80) #
clicked on New Game button
81.                         allMoves = []
82.                     elif SOLVE_RECT.collidepoint(event.pos):
83.                         resetAnimation(mainBoard, solutionSeq + allMoves)
# clicked on Solve button
84.                         allMoves = []
```

Before going into the event loop, the program calls checkForQuit() on line 69 to see if any QUIT events have been created (and terminates the program if there have). Why we have a separate function (the checkForQuit() function) for handling the QUIT events will be explained later. The for loop on line 70 executes the event handling code for any other event created since the last time pygame.event.get() was called (or since the program started, if pygame.event.get() has never been called before).

If the type of event was a MOUSEBUTTONUP event (that is, the player had released a mouse button somewhere over the window), then we pass the mouse coordinates to our getSpotClicked() function which will return the board coordinates of the spot on the board the mouse release happened. The event.pos[0] is the X coordinate and event.pos[1] is the Y coordinate.

If the mouse button release did not happen over one of the spaces on the board (but obviously still happened somewhere on the window, since a MOUSEBUTTONUP event was created), then getSpotClicked() will return None. If this is the case, we want to do an additional check to see if the player might have clicked on the Reset, New, or Solve buttons (which are not located on the board).

The coordinates of where these buttons are on the window are stored in the pygame.Rect objects that are stored in the RESET_RECT, NEW_RECT, and SOLVE_RECT variables. We can pass the mouse coordinates from the Event object to the collidepoint() method. This method will return True if the mouse coordinates are within the Rect object's area and False otherwise.

SLIDING TILES WITH THE MOUSE

```
85.                     else:
86.                         # check if the clicked tile was next to the blank spot
87.
88.                         blankx, blanky = getBlankPosition(mainBoard)
89.                         if spotx == blankx + 1 and spoty == blanky:
90.                             slideTo = LEFT
91.                         elif spotx == blankx - 1 and spoty == blanky:
92.                             slideTo = RIGHT
93.                         elif spotx == blankx and spoty == blanky + 1:
94.                             slideTo = UP
95.                         elif spotx == blankx and spoty == blanky - 1:
96.                             slideTo = DOWN
```

If getSpotClicked() did not return (None, None), then it will have returned a tuple of two integer values that represent the X and Y coordinate of the spot on the board that was clicked. Then the if and elif statements on lines 89 to 96 check if the spot that was clicked is a tile that is next to the blank spot (otherwise the tile will have no place to slide).

Our getBlankPosition() function will take the board data structure and return the X and Y board coordinates of the blank spot, which we store in the variables blankx and blanky. If the spot the user clicked on was next to the blank space, we set the slideTo variable with the value that the tile should slide.

SLIDING TILES WITH THE KEYBOARD

```
            elif event.type == KEYUP:
                # check if the user pressed a key to slide a tile
                if event.key in (K_LEFT, K_a) and isValidMove(mainBoard,
LEFT):
                    slideTo = LEFT
                elif event.key in (K_RIGHT, K_d) and
isValidMove(mainBoard, RIGHT):
                    slideTo = RIGHT
```

We can also let the user slide tiles by pressing keyboard keys. The if and elif statements on lines 100 to 107 let the user set the slideTo variable by either pressing the arrow keys or the WASD keys (explained later). Each if and elif statement also has a call to isValidMove() to make sure that the tile can slide in that direction. (We didn't have to make this call with the mouse clicks because the checks for the neighboring blank space did the same thing.)

"EQUAL TO ONE OF" TRICK WITH THE IN OPERATOR

The expression event.key in (K_LEFT, K_a) is just a Python trick to make the code simpler. It is a way of saying "evaluate to True if event.key is equal to one of K_LEFT or K_a". The following two expressions will evaluate the exact same way:

```
event.key in (K_LEFT, K_a)

event.key == K_LEFT or event.key == K_a
```

You can really save on some space by using this trick when you have to check if a value is equal to one of multiple values. The following two expressions will evaluate the exact same way:

```
spam == 'dog' or spam == 'cat' or spam == 'mouse' or spam == 'horse' or spam ==
42 or spam == 'dingo'

spam in ('dog', 'cat', 'mouse', 'horse', 42, 'dingo')
```

WASD AND ARROW KEYS

The W, A, S, and D keys (together called the WASD keys, pronounced "waz-dee") are commonly used in computer games to do the same thing as the arrow keys, except the player can use their left hand instead (since the WASD keys are on the left side of the keyboard). W is for up, A is for left, S is for down, and D is for right. You can easily remember this because the WASD keys have the same layout as the arrow keys:

ACTUALLY PERFORMING THE TILE SLIDE

```
        if slideTo:
            slideAnimation(mainBoard, slideTo, 'Click tile or press arrow keys to slide.', 8) # show slide on screen
            makeMove(mainBoard, slideTo)
            allMoves.append(slideTo) # record the slide
        pygame.display.update()
        FPSCLOCK.tick(FPS)
```

Now that the events have all been handled, we should update the variables of the game state and display the new state on the screen. If slideTo has been set (either by the mouse event or keyboard event handling code) then we can call slideAnimation() to perform the sliding animation. The parameters are the board data structure, the direction of the slide, a message to display while sliding the tile, and the speed of the sliding.

After it returns, we need to update the actual board data structure (which is done by the makeMove() function) and then add the slide to the allMoves list of all the slides made so far. This is done so that if the player clicks on the "Reset" button, we know how to undo all the player's slides.

IDLE AND TERMINATING PYGAME PROGRAMS

```
def terminate():
    pygame.quit()
    sys.exit()
```

This is a function that we can call that calls both the pygame.quit() and sys. exit() functions. This is a bit of syntactic sugar, so that instead of remembering to make both of these calls, there is just a single function we can call instead.

CHECKING FOR A SPECIFIC EVENT, AND POSTING EVENTS TO PYGAME'S EVENT QUEUE

```
def checkForQuit():
    for event in pygame.event.get(QUIT): # get all the QUIT events
        terminate() # terminate if any QUIT events are present
```

```
    for event in pygame.event.get(KEYUP): # get all the KEYUP events
        if event.key == K_ESCAPE:
            terminate() # terminate if the KEYUP event was for the Esc key
        pygame.event.post(event) # put the other KEYUP event objects back
```

The checkForQuit() function will check for QUIT events (or if the user has pressed the Esc key) and then call the terminate() function. But this is a bit tricky and requires some explanation.

Pygame internally has its own list data structure that it creates and appends Event objects to as they are made. This data structure is called the **event queue**. When the pygame.event.get() function is called with no parameters, the entire list is returned. However, you can pass a constant like QUIT to pygame.event.get() so that it will only return the QUIT events (if any) that are in the internal event queue. The rest of the events will stay in the event queue for the next time pygame.event.get() is called.

You should note that Pygame's event queue only stores up to 127 Event objects. If your program does not call pygame.event.get() frequently enough and the queue fills up, then any new events that happen won't be added to the event queue.

Line 123 pulls out a list of QUIT events from Pygame's event queue and returns them. If there are any QUIT events in the event queue, the program terminates.

Line 125 pulls out all the KEYUP events from the event queue and checks if any of them are for the Esc key. If one of the events is, then the program terminates. However, there could be KEYUP events for keys other than the Esc key. In this case, we need to put the KEYUP event back into Pygame's event queue. We can do this with the pygame.event.post() function, which adds the Event object passed to it to the end of the Pygame event queue. This way, when line 70 calls pygame.event.get() the non-Esc key KEYUP events will still be there. Otherwise calls to checkForQuit() would "consume" all of the KEYUP events and those events would never be handled.

The pygame.event.post() function is also handy if you ever want your program to add Event objects to the Pygame event queue.

CREATING THE BOARD DATA STRUCTURE

```
def getStartingBoard():
    # Return a board data structure with tiles in the solved state.
    # For example, if BOARDWIDTH and BOARDHEIGHT are both 3, this function
    # returns [[1, 4, 7], [2, 5, 8], [3, 6, None]]
    counter = 1
```

```
    board = []
    for x in range(BOARDWIDTH):
        column = []
        for y in range(BOARDHEIGHT):
            column.append(counter)
            counter += BOARDWIDTH
        board.append(column)
        counter -= BOARDWIDTH * (BOARDHEIGHT - 1) + BOARDWIDTH - 1

    board[BOARDWIDTH-1][BOARDHEIGHT-1] = None
    return board
```

The getStartingBoard() data structure will create and return a data structure that represents a "solved" board, where all the numbered tiles are in order and the blank tile is in the lower right corner. This is done with nested for loops, just like the board data structure in the Memory Puzzle game was made.

However, notice that the first column isn't going to be [1, 2, 3] but instead [1, 4, 7]. This is because the numbers on the tiles increase by 1 going across the row, not down the column. Going down the column, the numbers increase by the size of the board's width (which is stored in the BOARDWIDTH constant). We will use the counter variable to keep track of the number that should go on the next tile. When the numbering of the tiles in the column is finished, then we need to set counter to the number at the start of the next column.

NOT TRACKING THE BLANK POSITION

```
def getBlankPosition(board):
    # Return the x and y of board coordinates of the blank space.
    for x in range(BOARDWIDTH)):
        for y in range(BOARDHEIGHT):
            if board[x][y] == None:
                return (x, y)
```

Whenever our code needs to find the XY coordinates of the blank space, instead of keeping track of where the blank space is after each slide, we can just create a function that goes through the entire board and finds the blank space coordinates. The None value is used in the board data structure to represent the blank space. The code in getBlankPosition() simply uses nested for loops to find which space on the board is the blank space.

MAKING A MOVE BY UPDATING THE BOARD DATA STRUCTURE

```
def makeMove(board, move):
    # This function does not check if the move is valid.
```

```
    blankx, blanky = getBlankPosition(board)

    if move == UP:
        board[blankx][blanky], board[blankx][blanky + 1] = 
board[blankx][blanky + 1], board[blankx][blanky]
    elif move == DOWN:
        board[blankx][blanky], board[blankx][blanky - 1] = 
board[blankx][blanky - 1], board[blankx][blanky]
    elif move == LEFT:
        board[blankx][blanky], board[blankx + 1][blanky] = board[blankx + 
1][blanky], board[blankx][blanky]
    elif move == RIGHT:
        board[blankx][blanky], board[blankx - 1][blanky] = board[blankx - 
1][blanky], board[blankx][blanky]
```

The data structure in the board parameter is a 2D list that represents where all the tiles are. Whenever the player makes a move, the program needs to update this data structure. What happens is that the value for the tile is swapped with the value for the blank space.

The makeMove() function doesn't have to return any values, because the board parameter has a list reference passed for its argument. This means that any changes we make to board in this function will be made to the list value that was passed to makeMove().

WHEN NOT TO USE AN ASSERTION

```
171. def isValidMove(board, move):
172.     blankx, blanky = getBlankPosition(board)
173.     return (move == UP and blanky != len(board[0]) - 1) or \
174.            (move == DOWN and blanky != 0) or \
175.            (move == LEFT and blankx != len(board) - 1) or \
176.            (move == RIGHT and blankx != 0)
```

The isValidMove() function is passed a board data structure and a move the player would want to make. The return value is True if this move is possible and False if it is not. For example, you cannot slide a tile to the left one hundred times in a row, because eventually the blank space will be at the edge and there are no more tiles to slide to the left.

Whether a move is valid or not depends on where the blank space is. This function makes a call to getBlankPosition() to find the X and Y coordinates of the blank spot. Lines 173 to 176 are a return statement with a single expression. The \ slashes at the end of the first three lines tells the Python interpreter that that is not the end of the line of code (even though it is at the end of the line). This will let us split up a "line of code" across multiple lines to look pretty, rather than just have one very long unreadable line.

Because the parts of this expression in parentheses are joined by or operators, only one of them needs to be True for the entire expression to be True. Each of these parts checks what the intended move is and then sees if the coordinate of the blank space allows that move.

GETTING A NOT-SO-RANDOM MOVE

```
179. def getRandomMove(board, lastMove=None):
180.     # start with a full list of all four moves
181.     validMoves = [UP, DOWN, LEFT, RIGHT]
182.
183.     # remove moves from the list as they are disqualified
184.     if lastMove == UP or not isValidMove(board, DOWN):
185.         validMoves.remove(DOWN)
186.     if lastMove == DOWN or not isValidMove(board, UP):
187.         validMoves.remove(UP)
188.     if lastMove == LEFT or not isValidMove(board, RIGHT):
189.         validMoves.remove(RIGHT)
190.     if lastMove == RIGHT or not isValidMove(board, LEFT):
191.         validMoves.remove(LEFT)
192.
193.     # return a random move from the list of remaining moves
194.     return random.choice(validMoves)
```

At the beginning of the game, we start with the board data structure in the solved, ordered state and create the puzzle by randomly sliding around tiles. To decide which of the four directions we should slide, we'll call our getRandomMove() function. Normally we could just use the random.choice() function and pass it a tuple (UP, DOWN, LEFT, RIGHT) to have Python simply randomly choose a direction value for us. But the Sliding Puzzle game has a small restriction that prevents us from choosing a purely random number.

If you had a slide puzzle and slid a tile to left, and then slid a tile to the right, you would end up with the exact same board you had at the start. It's pointless to make a slide followed by the opposite slide. Also, if the blank space is in the lower right corner than it is impossible to slide a tile up or to the left.

The code in getRandomMove() will take these factors into account. To prevent the function from selecting the last move that was made, the caller of the function can pass a directional value for the lastMove parameter. Line 181 starts with a list of all four directional values stored in the validMoves variable. The lastMove value (if not set to None) is removed from validMoves. Depending on if the blank space is at the edge of the board, lines 184 to 191 will remove other directional values from the lastMove list.

Of the values that are left in lastMove, one of them is randomly selected with a call to random.choice() and returned.

CONVERTING TILE COORDINATES TO PIXEL COORDINATES

```
def getLeftTopOfTile(tileX, tileY):
    left = XMARGIN + (tileX * TILESIZE) + (tileX - 1)
    top = YMARGIN + (tileY * TILESIZE) + (tileY - 1)
    return (left, top)
```

The getLeftTopOfTile() function converts board coordinates to pixel coordinates. For the board XY coordinates that are passed in, the function calculates and returns the pixel XY coordinates of the pixel at the top left of that board space.

CONVERTING FROM PIXEL COORDINATES TO BOARD COORDINATES

```
203. def getSpotClicked(board, x, y):
204.     # from the x & y pixel coordinates, get the x & y board coordinates
205.     for tileX in range(len(board)):
206.         for tileY in range(len(board[0])):
207.             left, top = getLeftTopOfTile(tileX, tileY)
208.             tileRect = pygame.Rect(left, top, TILESIZE, TILESIZE)
209.             if tileRect.collidepoint(x, y):
210.                 return (tileX, tileY)
211.     return (None, None)
```

The getSpotClicked() function does the opposite of getLeftTopOfTile() and converts from pixel coordinates to board coordinates. The nested loops on lines 205 and 206 go through every possible XY board coordinate, and if the pixel coordinates that were passed in are within that space on the board, it returns those board coordinates. Since all of the tiles have a width and height that is set in the TILESIZE constant, we can create a Rect object that represents the space on the board by getting the pixel coordinates of the top left corner of the board space, and then use the collidepoint() Rect method to see if the pixel coordinates are inside that Rect object's area.

If the pixel coordinates that were passed in were not over any board space, then the value (None, None) is returned.

DRAWING A TILE

```
def drawTile(tilex, tiley, number, adjx=0, adjy=0):
```

```
    # draw a tile at board coordinates tilex and tiley, optionally a few
    # pixels over (determined by adjx and adjy)
    left, top = getLeftTopOfTile(tilex, tiley)
    pygame.draw.rect(DISPLAYSURF, TILECOLOR, (left + adjx, top + adjy, TILESIZE, TILESIZE))
    textSurf = BASICFONT.render(str(number), True, TEXTCOLOR)
    textRect = textSurf.get_rect()
    textRect.center = left + int(TILESIZE / 2) + adjx, top + int(TILESIZE / 2) + adjy
    DISPLAYSURF.blit(textSurf, textRect)
```

The drawTile() function will draw a single numbered tile on the board. The tilex and tiley parameters are the board coordinates of the tile. The number parameter is a string of the tile's number (like '3' or '12'). The adjx and adjy keyword parameters are for making minor adjustments to the position of the tile. For example, passing 5 for adjx would make the tile appear 5 pixels to the right of the tilex and tiley space on the board. Passing -10 for adjx would make the tile appear 10 pixels to the left of the space.

These adjustment values will be handy when we need to draw the tile in the middle of sliding. If no values are passed for these arguments when drawTile() is called, then by default they are set to 0. This means they will be exactly on the board space given by tilex and tiley.

The Pygame drawing functions only use pixel coordinates, so first line 217 converts the board coordinates in tilex and tiley to pixel coordinates, which we will store in variables left and top (since getLeftTopOfTile() returns the top left corner's coordinates). We draw the background square of the tile with a call to pygame.draw.rect() while adding the adjx and adjy values to left and top in case the code needs to adjust the position of the tile.

Lines 219 to 222 then create the Surface object that has the number text drawn on it. A Rect object for the Surface object is positioned, and then used to blit the Surface object to the display Surface. The drawTile() function doesn't call pygame.display.update() function, since the caller of drawTile() probably will want to draw more tiles for the rest of the board before making them appear on the screen.

THE MAKING TEXT APPEAR ON THE SCREEN

```
def makeText(text, color, bgcolor, top, left):
    # create the Surface and Rect objects for some text.
    textSurf = BASICFONT.render(text, True, color, bgcolor)
    textRect = textSurf.get_rect()
    textRect.topleft = (top, left)
    return (textSurf, textRect)
```

The makeText() function handles creating the Surface and Rect objects for positioning text on the screen. Instead of doing all these calls each time we want to make text on the screen, we can just call makeText() instead. This saves us on the amount of typing we have to do for our program. (Though drawTile() makes the calls to render() and get_rect() itself because it positions the text Surface object by the center point rather than the topleft point and uses a transparent background color.)

DRAWING THE BOARD

```
233. def drawBoard(board, message):
234.     DISPLAYSURF.fill(BGCOLOR)
235.     if message:
236.         textSurf, textRect = makeText(message, MESSAGECOLOR, BGCOLOR, 5,
5)
237.         DISPLAYSURF.blit(textSurf, textRect)
238.
239.     for tilex in range(len(board)):
240.         for tiley in range(len(board[0])):
241.             if board[tilex][tiley]:
242.                 drawTile(tilex, tiley, board[tilex][tiley])
```

This function handles drawing the entire board and all of its tiles to the DISPLAYSURF display Surface object. The fill() method on line 234 completely paints over anything that used to be drawn on the display Surface object before so that we start from scratch.

Line 235 to 237 handles drawing the message at the top of the window. We use this for the "Generating new puzzle..." and other text we want to display at the top of the window. Remember that if statement conditions consider the blank string to be a False value, so if message is set to '' then the condition is False and lines 236 and 237 are skipped.

Next, nested for loops are used to draw each tile to the display Surface object by calling the drawTile() function.

DRAWING THE BORDER OF THE BOARD

```
244.     left, top = getLeftTopOfTile(0, 0)
245.     width = BOARDWIDTH * TILESIZE
246.     height = BOARDHEIGHT * TILESIZE
247.     pygame.draw.rect(DISPLAYSURF, BORDERCOLOR, (left - 5, top - 5, width +
11, height + 11), 4)
```

Lines 244 to 247 draw a border around the tiles. The top left corner of the boarder will be 5 pixels to the left and 5 pixels above the top left corner of the tile at board coordinates (0, 0). The width and height of the border are calculated from the number of tiles wide and high the board is (stored in the BOARDWIDTH and BOARDHEIGHT constants) multiplied by the size of the tiles (stored in the TILESIZE constant).

The rectangle we draw on line 247 will have a thickness of 4 pixels, so we will move the boarder 5 pixels to the left and above where the top and left variables point so the thickness of the line won't overlap the tiles. We will also add 11 to the width and length (5 of those 11 pixels are to compensate for moving the rectangle to the left and up).

DRAWING THE BUTTONS

```
    DISPLAYSURF.blit(RESET_SURF, RESET_RECT)
    DISPLAYSURF.blit(NEW_SURF, NEW_RECT)
    DISPLAYSURF.blit(SOLVE_SURF, SOLVE_RECT)
```

Finally, we draw the buttons off to the slide of the screen. The text and position of these buttons never changes, which is why they were stored in constant variables at the beginning of the main() function.

ANIMATING THE TILE SLIDES

```
254. def slideAnimation(board, direction, message, animationSpeed):
255.     # Note: This function does not check if the move is valid.
256.
257.     blankx, blanky = getBlankPosition(board)
258.     if direction == UP:
259.         movex = blankx
260.         movey = blanky + 1
261.     elif direction == DOWN:
262.         movex = blankx
263.         movey = blanky - 1
264.     elif direction == LEFT:
265.         movex = blankx + 1
266.         movey = blanky
267.     elif direction == RIGHT:
268.         movex = blankx - 1
269.         movey = blanky
```

The first thing our tile sliding animation code needs to calculate is where the blank space is and where the moving tile is. The comment on line 255 reminds us that the code that calls slideAnimation() should make sure that the slide it passes for the direction parameter is a valid move to make.

The blank space's coordinates come from a call to getBlankPosition(). From these coordinates and the direction of the slide, we can figure out the XY board coordinates of the tile that will slide. These coordinates will be stored in the movex and movey variables.

THE COPY() SURFACE METHOD

```
    # prepare the base surface
    drawBoard(board, message)
    baseSurf = DISPLAYSURF.copy()
    # draw a blank space over the moving tile on the baseSurf Surface.
    moveLeft, moveTop = getLeftTopOfTile(movex, movey)
    pygame.draw.rect(baseSurf, BGCOLOR, (moveLeft, moveTop, TILESIZE, TILESIZE))
```

The copy() method of Surface objects will return a new Surface object that has the same image drawn to it. But they are two separate Surface objects. After calling the copy() method, if we draw on one Surface object using blit() or the Pygame drawing functions, it will not change the image on the other Surface object. We store this copy in the baseSurf variable on line 273.

Next, we paint another blank space over the tile that will slide. This is because when we draw each frame of the sliding animation, we will draw the sliding tile over different parts of the baseSurf Surface object. If we didn't blank out the moving tile on the baseSurf Surface, then it would still be there as we draw the sliding tile. In that case, here is what the baseSurf Surface would look like:

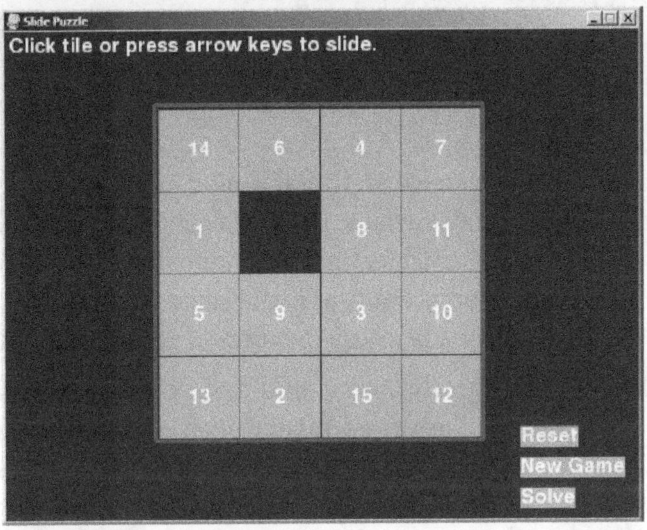

And then what it would look like when we draw the "9" tile sliding upwards on top of it:

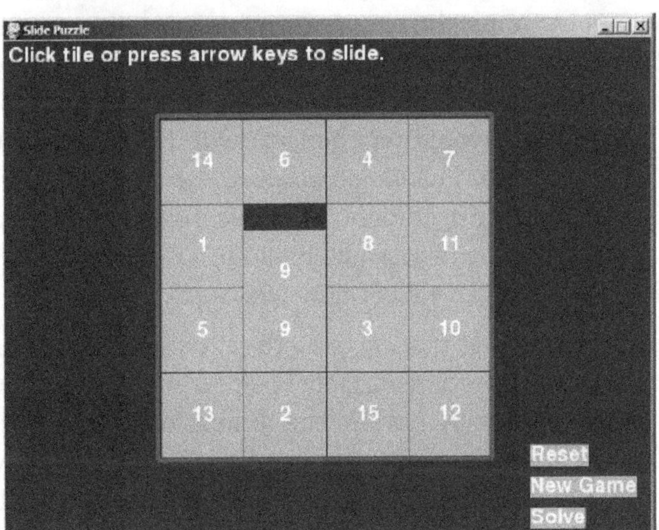

You can see this for yourself by commenting out line 276 and running the program.

```
278.     for i in range(0, TILESIZE, animationSpeed):
279.         # animate the tile sliding over
280.         checkForQuit()
281.         DISPLAYSURF.blit(baseSurf, (0, 0))
282.         if direction == UP:
283.             drawTile(movex, movey, board[movex][movey], 0, -i)
284.         if direction == DOWN:
285.             drawTile(movex, movey, board[movex][movey], 0, i)
286.         if direction == LEFT:
287.             drawTile(movex, movey, board[movex][movey], -i, 0)
288.         if direction == RIGHT:
289.             drawTile(movex, movey, board[movex][movey], i, 0)
290.
291.         pygame.display.update()
292.         FPSCLOCK.tick(FPS)
```

In order to draw the frames of the sliding animation, we must draw the baseSurf surface on the display Surface, then on each frame of the animation draw the sliding tile closer and closer to its final position where the original blank space was. The space between two adjacent tiles is the same size as a single tile, which we have stored in TILESIZE. The code uses a for loop to go from 0 to TILESIZE.

Normally this would mean that we would draw the tile 0 pixels over, then on the next frame draw the tile 1 pixel over, then 2 pixels, then 3, and so on. Each of these frames would take 1/30th of a second. If you have TILESIZE set to 80 (as the program in this book does on line 12) then sliding a tile would take over two and a half seconds, which is actually kind of slow.

So instead we will have the for loop iterate from 0 to TILESIZE by several pixels each frame. The number of pixels it jumps over is stored in animationSpeed, which is passed in when slideAnimation() is called. For example, if animationSpeed was set to 8 and the constant TILESIZE was set to 80, then the for loop and range(0, TILESIZE, animationSpeed) would set the i variable to the values 0, 8, 16, 24, 32, 40, 48, 56, 64, 72. (It does not include 80 because the range() function goes up to, but not including, the second argument.) This means the entire sliding animation would be done in 10 frames, which would mean it is done in 10/30th of a second (a third of a second) since the game runs at 30 FPS.

Lines 282 to 289 makes sure that we draw the tile sliding in the correct direction (based on what value the direction variable has). After the animation is done, then the function returns. Notice that while the animation is happening, any events being created by the user are not being handled. Those events will be handled the next time execution reaches line 70 in the main() function or the code in the checkForQuit() function.

CREATING A NEW PUZZLE

```
295. def generateNewPuzzle(numSlides):
296.     # From a starting configuration, make numSlides number of moves (and
297.     # animate these moves).
298.     sequence = []
299.     board = getStartingBoard()
300.     drawBoard(board, '')
301.     pygame.display.update()
302.     pygame.time.wait(500) # pause 500 milliseconds for effect
```

The generateNewPuzzle() function will be called at the start of each new game. It will create a new board data structure by calling getStartingBoard() and then randomly scramble it. The first few lines of generateNewPuzzle() get the board and then draw it to the screen (freezing for half a second to let the player see the fresh board for a moment).

```
303.     lastMove = None
304.     for i in range(numSlides):
305.         move = getRandomMove(board, lastMove)
306.         slideAnimation(board, move, 'Generating new puzzle...',
int(TILESIZE / 3))
307.         makeMove(board, move)
308.         sequence.append(move)
309.         lastMove = move
310.     return (board, sequence)
```

The numSlides parameter will show tell the function how many of these random moves to make. The code for doing a random move is the getRandomMove() call on line 305 to get the move itself, then call slideAnimation() to perform the animation on the screen. Because doing the slide animation does not actually update the board data structure, we update the board by calling makeMove() on line 307.

We need to keep track of each of the random moves that was made so that the player can click the "Solve" button later and have the program undo all these random moves. (The "Being Smart By Using Stupid Code" section talks about why and how we do this.) So the move is appended to the list of moves in sequence on line 308.

Then we store the random move in a variable called lastMove which will be passed to getRandomMove() on the next iteration. This prevents the next random move from undoing the random move we just performed.

All of this needs to happen numSlides number of times, so we put lines 305 to 309 inside a for loop. When the board is done being scrambled, then we return the board data structure and also the list of the random moves made on it.

ANIMATING THE BOARD RESET

```
313. def resetAnimation(board, allMoves):
314.     # make all of the moves in allMoves in reverse.
315.     revAllMoves = allMoves[:] # gets a copy of the list
316.     revAllMoves.reverse()
317.
318.     for move in revAllMoves:
319.         if move == UP:
320.             oppositeMove = DOWN
321.         elif move == DOWN:
322.             oppositeMove = UP
323.         elif move == RIGHT:
324.             oppositeMove = LEFT
325.         elif move == LEFT:
326.             oppositeMove = RIGHT
327.         slideAnimation(board, oppositeMove, '', int(TILESIZE / 2))
328.         makeMove(board, oppositeMove)
```

When the player clicks on "Reset" or "Solve", the Slide Puzzle game program needs to undo all of the moves that were made to the board. The list of directional values for the slides will be passed as the argument for the allMoves parameter.

Line 315 uses list slicing to create a duplicate of the allMoves list. Remember that if you don't specify a number before the :, then Python assumes the slice should start from the very beginning of the list. And if you don't specify a number after the :, then Python assumes the slice should keep going to the very end of the list. So allMoves[:] creates a list slice of the entire allMoves list. This makes a copy of the actual list to store in revAllMoves, rather than just a copy of the list reference.

To undo all the moves in allMoves, we need to perform the opposite move of the moves in allMoves, and in reverse order. There is a list method called reverse() which will reverse the order of the items in a list. We call this on the revAllMoves list on line 316.

The for loop on line 318 iterates over the list of directional values. Remember, we want the opposite move, so the if and elif statements from line 319 to 326 set the correct directional value in the oppositeMove variable. Then we call slideAnimation() to perform the animation, and makeMove() to update the board data structure.

```
if __name__ == '__main__':
    main()
```

Just like in the Memory Puzzle game, after all the def statements have been executed to create all the functions, we call the main() function to begin the meat of the program.

That's all there is to the Slide Puzzle program! But let's talk about some general programming concepts that came up in this game.

TIME VS. MEMORY TRADEOFFS

Of course, there are a few different ways to write the Slide Puzzle game so that it looks and acts the exact same way even though the code is different. There are many different ways the a program that does a task could be written. The most common differences are making tradeoffs between execution time and memory usage.

Usually, the faster a program can run, the better it is. This is especially true with programs that need to do a lot of calculations, whether they are scientific weather simulators or games with a large amount of detailed 3D graphics to draw. It's also good to use the least amount of memory possible. The more variables and the larger the lists your program uses, the more memory it takes up.

Right now, the programs in this book aren't big and complicated enough where you have to worry about conserving memory or optimizing the execution time. But it can be something to consider as you become a more skilled programmer.

For example, consider the getBlankPosition() function. This function takes time to run, since it goes through all the possible board coordinates to find where the blank space is. Instead, we could just have a blankspacex and blankspacey variable which would have these XY coordinates so we would not have to look through the entire board each time we want to know where it was. (We would also need code that updates the blankspacex and blankspacey variables whenever a move is done. This code could go in makeMove().) Using these variables would take up more memory, but they would save you on execution time so your program would run faster.

Another example is that we keep a board data structure in the solved state in the SOLVEDBOARD variable, so that we can compare the current board to SOLVEDBOARD to see if the player has solved the puzzle. Each time we wanted to do this check, we could just call the getStartingBoard() function and compare the returned value to the current board. Then we would not need the SOLVEDBOARD variable. This would save us a little bit of memory, but then our program would take longer to run because it is re-creating the solved-state board data structure each time we do this check.

There is one thing you must remember though. Writing code that is readable is a very important skill. Code that is "readable" is code that is easy to understand, especially by programmers who did not write the code. If another programmer can look at your program's source code and figure out what it does without much trouble, then that program is very readable. Readability is important because when you want to fix bugs or add new features to your program (and bugs and ideas for new features **always** come up), then having a readable program makes those tasks much easier.

NOBODY CARES ABOUT A FEW BYTES

Also, there is one thing that might seem kind of silly to say in this book because it seem obvious, but many people wonder about it. You should know that using short variable names like x or num instead of longer, more descriptive variable names like blankx or numSlides does not save you any memory when your program actually runs. Using these longer variable names is better because they'll make your program more readable.

You might also come up with some clever tricks that do save a few bytes of memory here and there. One trick is that when you no longer need a variable, you can reuse that variable name for a different purpose instead of just using two differently named variables.

Try to avoid the temptation to do this. Usually, these tricks reduce code readability and make it harder to debug your programs. Modern computers have billions of bytes of memory, and saving a few bytes here and there really isn't worth making the code more confusing for human programmers.

NOBODY CARES ABOUT A FEW MILLION NANOSECONDS

Similarly, there are times when you can rearrange your code in some way to make it slightly faster by a few nanoseconds. These tricks also usually make the code harder to read. When you consider that several billion nanoseconds have passed in the time it takes you to read this sentence, saving a few nanoseconds of execution time in your program won't be noticed by the player.

SUMMARY

This chapter hasn't introduced any new Pygame programming concepts that the Memory Puzzle game didn't use, aside from using the copy() method of Surface objects. Just knowing a few different concepts will let you create completely different games.

5 Chapter SIMULATE

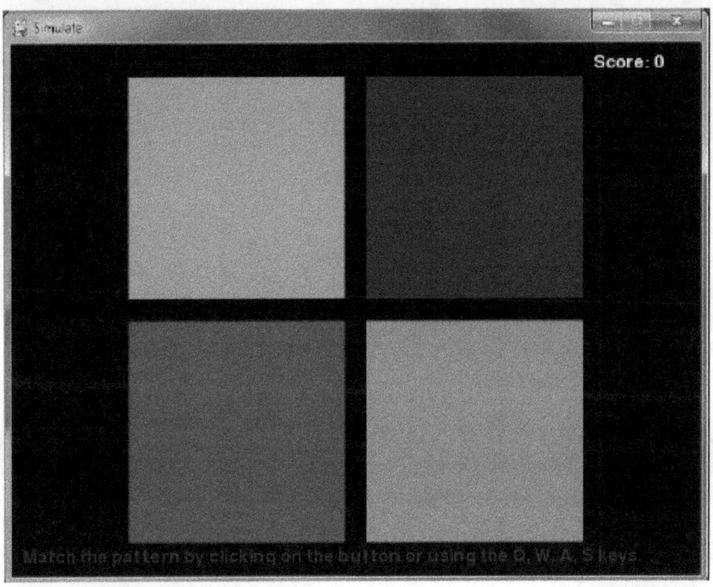

HOW TO PLAY SIMULATE

Simulate is a clone of the game Simon. There are four colored buttons on the screen. The buttons light up in a certain random pattern, and then the player must repeat this pattern by pressing the buttons in the correct order. Each time the player successfully simulates the pattern, the pattern gets longer. The player tries to match the pattern for as long as possible.

SOURCE CODE TO SIMULATE

```
# Simulate (a Simon clone)
# By Al Sweigart al@inventwithpython.com
# http://inventwithpython.com/pygame
```

```
# Creative Commons BY-NC-SA 3.0 US

import random, sys, time, pygame
from pygame.locals import *

FPS = 30
WINDOWWIDTH = 640
WINDOWHEIGHT = 480
FLASHSPEED = 500 # in milliseconds
FLASHDELAY = 200 # in milliseconds
BUTTONSIZE = 200
BUTTONGAPSIZE = 20
TIMEOUT = 4 # seconds before game over if no button is pushed.

#                R    G    B
WHITE        = (255, 255, 255)
BLACK        = (  0,   0,   0)
BRIGHTRED    = (255,   0,   0)
RED          = (155,   0,   0)
BRIGHTGREEN  = (  0, 255,   0)
GREEN        = (  0, 155,   0)
BRIGHTBLUE   = (  0,   0, 255)
BLUE         = (  0,   0, 155)
BRIGHTYELLOW = (255, 255,   0)
YELLOW       = (155, 155,   0)
DARKGRAY     = ( 40,  40,  40)
bgColor = BLACK

XMARGIN = int((WINDOWWIDTH - (2 * BUTTONSIZE) - BUTTONGAPSIZE) / 2)
YMARGIN = int((WINDOWHEIGHT - (2 * BUTTONSIZE) - BUTTONGAPSIZE) / 2)

# Rect objects for each of the four buttons
YELLOWRECT = pygame.Rect(XMARGIN, YMARGIN, BUTTONSIZE, BUTTONSIZE)
BLUERECT   = pygame.Rect(XMARGIN + BUTTONSIZE + BUTTONGAPSIZE, YMARGIN, BUTTONSIZE, BUTTONSIZE)
REDRECT    = pygame.Rect(XMARGIN, YMARGIN + BUTTONSIZE + BUTTONGAPSIZE, BUTTONSIZE, BUTTONSIZE)
GREENRECT  = pygame.Rect(XMARGIN + BUTTONSIZE + BUTTONGAPSIZE, YMARGIN + BUTTONSIZE + BUTTONGAPSIZE, BUTTONSIZE, BUTTONSIZE)

def main():
    global FPSCLOCK, DISPLAYSURF, BASICFONT, BEEP1, BEEP2, BEEP3, BEEP4

    pygame.init()
    FPSCLOCK = pygame.time.Clock()
    DISPLAYSURF = pygame.display.set_mode((WINDOWWIDTH, WINDOWHEIGHT))
```

```
    pygame.display.set_caption('Simulate')

    BASICFONT = pygame.font.Font('freesansbold.ttf', 16)

    infoSurf = BASICFONT.render('Match the pattern by clicking on the button or using the Q, W, A, S keys.', 1, DARKGRAY)
    infoRect = infoSurf.get_rect()
    infoRect.topleft = (10, WINDOWHEIGHT - 25)
    # load the sound files
    BEEP1 = pygame.mixer.Sound('beep1.ogg')
    BEEP2 = pygame.mixer.Sound('beep2.ogg')
    BEEP3 = pygame.mixer.Sound('beep3.ogg')
    BEEP4 = pygame.mixer.Sound('beep4.ogg')

    # Initialize some variables for a new game
    pattern = [] # stores the pattern of colors
    currentStep = 0 # the color the player must push next
    lastClickTime = 0 # timestamp of the player's last button push
    score = 0
    # when False, the pattern is playing. when True, waiting for the player to click a colored button:
    waitingForInput = False

    while True: # main game loop
        clickedButton = None # button that was clicked (set to YELLOW, RED, GREEN, or BLUE)
        DISPLAYSURF.fill(bgColor)
        drawButtons()

        scoreSurf = BASICFONT.render('Score: ' + str(score), 1, WHITE)
        scoreRect = scoreSurf.get_rect()
        scoreRect.topleft = (WINDOWWIDTH - 100, 10)
        DISPLAYSURF.blit(scoreSurf, scoreRect)

        DISPLAYSURF.blit(infoSurf, infoRect)

        checkForQuit()
        for event in pygame.event.get(): # event handling loop
            if event.type == MOUSEBUTTONUP:
                mousex, mousey = event.pos
                clickedButton = getButtonClicked(mousex, mousey)
            elif event.type == KEYDOWN:
                if event.key == K_q:
                    clickedButton = YELLOW
                elif event.key == K_w:
                    clickedButton = BLUE
```

```
                elif event.key == K_a:
                    clickedButton = RED
                elif event.key == K_s:
                    clickedButton = GREEN



        if not waitingForInput:
            # play the pattern
            pygame.display.update()
            pygame.time.wait(1000)
            pattern.append(random.choice((YELLOW, BLUE, RED, GREEN)))
            for button in pattern:
                flashButtonAnimation(button)
                pygame.time.wait(FLASHDELAY)
            waitingForInput = True
        else:
            # wait for the player to enter buttons
            if clickedButton and clickedButton == pattern[currentStep]:
                # pushed the correct button
                flashButtonAnimation(clickedButton)
                currentStep += 1
                lastClickTime = time.time()

                if currentStep == len(pattern):
                    # pushed the last button in the pattern
                    changeBackgroundAnimation()
                    score += 1
                    waitingForInput = False
                    currentStep = 0 # reset back to first step

            elif (clickedButton and clickedButton != pattern[currentStep]) or (currentStep != 0 and time.time() - TIMEOUT > lastClickTime):
                # pushed the incorrect button, or has timed out
                gameOverAnimation()
                # reset the variables for a new game:
                pattern = []
                currentStep = 0
                waitingForInput = False
                score = 0
                pygame.time.wait(1000)
                changeBackgroundAnimation()

        pygame.display.update()
        FPSCLOCK.tick(FPS)

```

```

def terminate():
    pygame.quit()
    sys.exit()


def checkForQuit():
    for event in pygame.event.get(QUIT): # get all the QUIT events
        terminate() # terminate if any QUIT events are present
    for event in pygame.event.get(KEYUP): # get all the KEYUP events
        if event.key == K_ESCAPE:
            terminate() # terminate if the KEYUP event was for the Esc key
        pygame.event.post(event) # put the other KEYUP event objects back


def flashButtonAnimation(color, animationSpeed=50):
    if color == YELLOW:
        sound = BEEP1
        flashColor = BRIGHTYELLOW
        rectangle = YELLOWRECT
    elif color == BLUE:
        sound = BEEP2
        flashColor = BRIGHTBLUE
        rectangle = BLUERECT
    elif color == RED:
        sound = BEEP3
        flashColor = BRIGHTRED
        rectangle = REDRECT
    elif color == GREEN:
        sound = BEEP4
        flashColor = BRIGHTGREEN
        rectangle = GREENRECT

    origSurf = DISPLAYSURF.copy()
    flashSurf = pygame.Surface((BUTTONSIZE, BUTTONSIZE))
    flashSurf = flashSurf.convert_alpha()
    r, g, b = flashColor
    sound.play()
    for start, end, step in ((0, 255, 1), (255, 0, -1)): # animation loop
        for alpha in range(start, end, animationSpeed * step):
            checkForQuit()
            DISPLAYSURF.blit(origSurf, (0, 0))
            flashSurf.fill((r, g, b, alpha))
            DISPLAYSURF.blit(flashSurf, rectangle.topleft)
            pygame.display.update()
            FPSCLOCK.tick(FPS)
```

```
    DISPLAYSURF.blit(origSurf, (0, 0))


def drawButtons():
    pygame.draw.rect(DISPLAYSURF, YELLOW, YELLOWRECT)
    pygame.draw.rect(DISPLAYSURF, BLUE,   BLUERECT)
    pygame.draw.rect(DISPLAYSURF, RED,    REDRECT)
    pygame.draw.rect(DISPLAYSURF, GREEN,  GREENRECT)


def changeBackgroundAnimation(animationSpeed=40):
    global bgColor
    newBgColor = (random.randint(0, 255), random.randint(0, 255), random.randint(0, 255))

    newBgSurf = pygame.Surface((WINDOWWIDTH, WINDOWHEIGHT))
    newBgSurf = newBgSurf.convert_alpha()
    r, g, b = newBgColor
    for alpha in range(0, 255, animationSpeed): # animation loop
        checkForQuit()
        DISPLAYSURF.fill(bgColor)

        newBgSurf.fill((r, g, b, alpha))
        DISPLAYSURF.blit(newBgSurf, (0, 0))

        drawButtons() # redraw the buttons on top of the tint

        pygame.display.update()
        FPSCLOCK.tick(FPS)
    bgColor = newBgColor


def gameOverAnimation(color=WHITE, animationSpeed=50):
    # play all beeps at once, then flash the background
    origSurf = DISPLAYSURF.copy()
    flashSurf = pygame.Surface(DISPLAYSURF.get_size())
    flashSurf = flashSurf.convert_alpha()
    BEEP1.play() # play all four beeps at the same time, roughly.
    BEEP2.play()
    BEEP3.play()
    BEEP4.play()
    r, g, b = color
    for i in range(3): # do the flash 3 times
        for start, end, step in ((0, 255, 1), (255, 0, -1)):
            # The first iteration in this loop sets the following for loop
            # to go from 0 to 255, the second from 255 to 0.
```

```
            for alpha in range(start, end, animationSpeed * step): # animation loop
                # alpha means transparency. 255 is opaque, 0 is invisible
                checkForQuit()
                flashSurf.fill((r, g, b, alpha))
                DISPLAYSURF.blit(origSurf, (0, 0))
                DISPLAYSURF.blit(flashSurf, (0, 0))
                drawButtons()
                pygame.display.update()
                FPSCLOCK.tick(FPS)



def getButtonClicked(x, y):
    if YELLOWRECT.collidepoint( (x, y) ):
        return YELLOW
    elif BLUERECT.collidepoint( (x, y) ):
        return BLUE
    elif REDRECT.collidepoint( (x, y) ):
        return RED
    elif GREENRECT.collidepoint( (x, y) ):
        return GREEN
    return None


if __name__ == '__main__':
    main()
```

THE USUAL STARTING STUFF

```
# Simulate (a Simon clone)
# By Al Sweigart al@inventwithpython.com
# http://inventwithpython.com/pygame
# Creative Commons BY-NC-SA 3.0 US

import random, sys, time, pygame
from pygame.locals import *

FPS = 30
WINDOWWIDTH = 640
WINDOWHEIGHT = 480
FLASHSPEED = 500 # in milliseconds
FLASHDELAY = 200 # in milliseconds
BUTTONSIZE = 200
BUTTONGAPSIZE = 20
TIMEOUT = 4 # seconds before game over if no button is pushed.
```

```
#              R    G    B
WHITE        = (255, 255, 255)
BLACK        = (  0,   0,   0)
BRIGHTRED    = (255,   0,   0)
RED          = (155,   0,   0)
BRIGHTGREEN  = (  0, 255,   0)
GREEN        = (  0, 155,   0)
BRIGHTBLUE   = (  0,   0, 255)
BLUE         = (  0,   0, 155)
BRIGHTYELLOW = (255, 255,   0)
YELLOW       = (155, 155,   0)
DARKGRAY     = ( 40,  40,  40)
bgColor = BLACK

XMARGIN = int((WINDOWWIDTH - (2 * BUTTONSIZE) - BUTTONGAPSIZE) / 2)
YMARGIN = int((WINDOWHEIGHT - (2 * BUTTONSIZE) - BUTTONGAPSIZE) / 2)
```

Here we set up the usual constants for things that we might want to modify later such as the size of the four buttons, the shades of color used for the buttons (the bright colors are used when the buttons light up) and the amount of time the player has to push the next button in the sequence before the game times out.

SETTING UP THE BUTTONS

```
35. # Rect objects for each of the four buttons
36. YELLOWRECT = pygame.Rect(XMARGIN, YMARGIN, BUTTONSIZE, BUTTONSIZE)
37. BLUERECT   = pygame.Rect(XMARGIN + BUTTONSIZE + BUTTONGAPSIZE, YMARGIN, BUTTONSIZE, BUTTONSIZE)
38. REDRECT    = pygame.Rect(XMARGIN, YMARGIN + BUTTONSIZE + BUTTONGAPSIZE, BUTTONSIZE, BUTTONSIZE)
39. GREENRECT  = pygame.Rect(XMARGIN + BUTTONSIZE + BUTTONGAPSIZE, YMARGIN + BUTTONSIZE + BUTTONGAPSIZE, BUTTONSIZE, BUTTONSIZE)
```

Just like the buttons in the Sliding Puzzle games for "Reset", "Solve" and "New Game", the Simulate game has four rectangular areas and code to handle when the player clicks inside of those areas. The program will need Rect objects for the areas of the four buttons so it can call the collidepoint() method on them. Lines 36 to 39 set up these Rect objects with the appropriate coordinates and sizes.

THE MAIN() FUNCTION

```
def main():
    global FPSCLOCK, DISPLAYSURF, BASICFONT, BEEP1, BEEP2, BEEP3, BEEP4
```

```
43.
44.      pygame.init()
45.      FPSCLOCK = pygame.time.Clock()
46.      DISPLAYSURF = pygame.display.set_mode((WINDOWWIDTH, WINDOWHEIGHT))
47.      pygame.display.set_caption('Simulate')
48.
49.      BASICFONT = pygame.font.Font('freesansbold.ttf', 16)
50.
51.      infoSurf = BASICFONT.render('Match the pattern by clicking on the
button or using the Q, W, A, S keys.', 1, DARKGRAY)
52.      infoRect = infoSurf.get_rect()
53.      infoRect.topleft = (10, WINDOWHEIGHT - 25)
54.      # load the sound files
55.      BEEP1 = pygame.mixer.Sound('beep1.ogg')
56.      BEEP2 = pygame.mixer.Sound('beep2.ogg')
57.      BEEP3 = pygame.mixer.Sound('beep3.ogg')
58.      BEEP4 = pygame.mixer.Sound('beep4.ogg')
```

The main() function will implement the bulk of the program and call the other functions as they are needed. The usual Pygame setup functions are called to initialize the library, create a Clock object, create a window, set the caption, and create a Font object that will be used to display the score and the instructions on the window. The objects that are created by these function calls will be stored in global variables so that they can be used in other functions. But they are basically constants since the value in them is never changed.

Lines 55 to 58 will load sound files so that Simulate can play sound effects as the player clicks on each button. The pygame.mixer.Sound() constructor function will return a Sound object, which we store in the variables BEEP1 to BEEP4 which were made into global variables on line 42.

SOME LOCAL VARIABLES USED IN THIS PROGRAM

```
    # Initialize some variables for a new game
    pattern = [] # stores the pattern of colors
    currentStep = 0 # the color the player must push next
    lastClickTime = 0 # timestamp of the player's last button push
    score = 0
    # when False, the pattern is playing. when True, waiting for the
player to click a colored button:
    waitingForInput = False
```

The pattern variable will be a list of color values (either YELLOW, RED, BLUE, or GREEN) to keep track of the pattern that the player must memorize. For example, if the value of pattern was [RED, RED, YELLOW, RED, BLUE, BLUE, RED, GREEN] then the player would have to first click the red button twice, then the yellow button, then the red button, and so on until the final green button. As the player finishes each round, a new random color is added to the end of the list.

The currentStep variable will keep track of which color in the pattern list the player has to click next. If currentStep was 0 and pattern was [GREEN, RED, RED, YELLOW], then the player would have to click the green button. If they clicked on any other button, the code will cause a game over.

There is a TIMEOUT constant that makes the player click on next button in the pattern within a number of seconds, otherwise the code causes a game over. In order to check if enough time has passed since the last button click, the lastClickTime variable needs to keep track of the last time the player clicked on a button. (Python has a module named time and a time.time() function to return the current time. This will be explained later.)

It may be hard to believe, but the score variable keeps track of the score. Inconceivable!

There are also two modes that our program will be in. Either the program is playing the pattern of buttons for the player (in which case, waitingForInput is set to False), or the program has finished playing the pattern and is waiting for the user to click the buttons in the correct order (in which case, waitingForInput is set to True).

DRAWING THE BOARD AND HANDLING INPUT

```
68.     while True: # main game loop
69.         clickedButton = None # button that was clicked (set to YELLOW, 
RED, GREEN, or BLUE)
70.         DISPLAYSURF.fill(bgColor)
71.         drawButtons()
72.
73.         scoreSurf = BASICFONT.render('Score: ' + str(score), 1, WHITE)
74.         scoreRect = scoreSurf.get_rect()
75.         scoreRect.topleft = (WINDOWWIDTH - 100, 10)
76.         DISPLAYSURF.blit(scoreSurf, scoreRect)
77.
78.         DISPLAYSURF.blit(infoSurf, infoRect)
```

Line 68 is the start of the main game loop. The clickedButton will be reset to None at the beginning of each iteration. If a button is clicked during this iteration, then clickedButton will be set to one of the color values to match the button (YELLOW, RED, GREEN, or BLUE).

The fill() method is called on line 70 to repaint the entire display Surface so that we can start drawing from scratch. The four colored buttons are drawn with a call to the drawButtons() (explained later). Then the text for the score is created on lines 73 to 76.

There will also be text that tells the player what their current score is. Unlike the call to the render() method on line 51 for the instruction text, the text for the score changes. It starts off as 'Score: 0' and then becomes 'Score: 1' and then 'Score: 2' and so on. This is why we create new Surface objects by calling the render() method on line 73 inside the game loop. Since the instruction text ("Match the pattern by...") never changes, we only need one call to render() outside the game loop on line 50.

CHECKING FOR MOUSE CLICKS

```
80.         checkForQuit()
81.         for event in pygame.event.get(): # event handling loop
82.             if event.type == MOUSEBUTTONUP:
83.                 mousex, mousey = event.pos
84.                 clickedButton = getButtonClicked(mousex, mousey)
```

Line 80 does a quick check for any QUIT events, and then line 81 is the start of the event handling loop. The XY coordinates of any mouse clicks will be stored in the mousex and mousey variables. If the mouse click was over one of the four buttons, then our getButtonClicked() function will return a Color object of the button clicked (otherwise it returns None).

CHECKING FOR KEYBOARD PRESSES

```
85.             elif event.type == KEYDOWN:
86.                 if event.key == K_q:
87.                     clickedButton = YELLOW
88.                 elif event.key == K_w:
89.                     clickedButton = BLUE
90.                 elif event.key == K_a:
91.                     clickedButton = RED
92.                 elif event.key == K_s:
93.                     clickedButton = GREEN
```

Lines 85 to 93 check for any KEYDOWN events (created when the user presses a key on the keyboard). The Q, W, A, and S keys correspond to the buttons because they are arranged in a square shape on the keyboard.

The Q key is in the upper left of the four keyboard keys, just like the yellow button on the screen is in the upper left, so we will make pressing the Q key the same as clicking on the yellow button. We can do this by setting the clickedButton variable to the value in the constant variable YELLOW. We can do the same for the three other keys. This way, the user can play Simulate with either the mouse or keyboard.

THE TWO STATES OF THE GAME LOOP

```
97.         if not waitingForInput:
98.             # play the pattern
99.             pygame.display.update()
100.            pygame.time.wait(1000)
101.            pattern.append(random.choice((YELLOW, BLUE, RED, GREEN)))
102.            for button in pattern:
103.                flashButtonAnimation(button)
104.                pygame.time.wait(FLASHDELAY)
105.            waitingForInput = True
```

There are two different "modes" or "states" that the program can be in. When waitingForInput is False, the program will be displaying the animation for the pattern. When waitingForInput is True, the program will be waiting for the user to select buttons.

Lines 97 to 105 will cover the case where the program displays the pattern animation. Since this is done at the start of the game or when the player finishes a pattern, line 101 will add a random color to the pattern list to make the pattern one step longer. Then lines 102 to 104 loops through each of the values in the pattern list and calls flashButtonAnimation() which makes that button light up. After it is done lighting up all the buttons in the pattern list, the program sets the waitingForInput variable to True.

FIGURING OUT IF THE PLAYER PRESSED THE RIGHT BUTTONS

```
106.        else:
107.            # wait for the player to enter buttons
108.            if clickedButton and clickedButton == pattern[currentStep]:
109.                # pushed the correct button
110.                flashButtonAnimation(clickedButton)
111.                currentStep += 1
112.                lastClickTime = time.time()
```

If waitingForInput is True, then the code in line 106's else statement will execute. Line 108 checks if the player has clicked on a button during this iteration of the game loop and if that button was the correct one. The currentStep variable keeps track of the index in the pattern list for the button that the player should click on next.

For example, if pattern was set to [YELLOW, RED, RED] and the currentStep variable was set to 0 (like it would be when the player first starts the game), then the correct button for the player to click would be pattern[0] (the yellow button).

If the player has clicked on the correct button, we want to flash the button the player clicked by calling flashButtonAnimation() then, increase the currentStep to the next step, and then update the lastClickTime variable to the current time. (The time.time() function returns a float value of the number of seconds since January 1st, 1970, so we can use it to keep track of time.)

```
114.                if currentStep == len(pattern):
115.                    # pushed the last button in the pattern
116.                    changeBackgroundAnimation()
117.                    score += 1
118.                    waitingForInput = False
119.                    currentStep = 0 # reset back to first step
```

Lines 114 to 119 are inside the else statement that started on line 106. If the execution is inside that else statement, we know the player clicked on a button and also it was the correct button. Line 114 checks if this was the last correct button in the pattern list by checking if the integer stored in currentStep is equal to the number of values inside the pattern list.

If this is True, then we want to change the background color by calling our changeBackgroundAnimation(). This is a simple way to let the player know they have entered the entire pattern correctly. The score is incremented, currentStep is set back to 0, and the waitingForInput variable is set to False so that on the next iteration of the game loop the code will add a new Color value to the pattern list and then flash the buttons.

```
121.            elif (clickedButton and clickedButton != pattern[currentStep])
or (currentStep != 0 and time.time() - TIMEOUT > lastClickTime):
```

If the player did not click on the correct button, the elif statement on line 121 handles the case where either the player clicked on the wrong button or the player has waited too long to click on a button. Either way, we need to show the "game over" animation and start a new game.

The (clickedButton and clickedButton != pattern[currentStep]) part of the elif statement's condition checks if a button was clicked and was the wrong button to click. You can compare this to line 108's if statement's condition clickedButton and clickedButton == pattern[currentStep] which evaluates to True if the player clicked a button and it was the correct button to click.

The other part of line 121's elif condition is (currentStep != 0 and time.time() - TIMEOUT > lastClickTime). This handles making sure the player did not "time out". Notice that this part of the condition has two expressions connected by an and keyword. That means both sides of the and keyword need to evaluate to True.

In order to "time out", it must not be the player's first button click. But once they've started to click buttons, they must keep clicking the buttons quickly enough until they've entered the entire pattern (or have clicked on the wrong pattern and gotten a "game over"). If currentStep != 0 is True, then we know the player has begun clicking the buttons.

EPOCH TIME

Also in order to "time out", the current time (returned by time.time()) minus four seconds (because 4 is stored in TIMEOUT) must be greater than the last time clicked a button (stored in lastClickTime). The reason why time.time() - TIMEOUT > lastClickTime works has to do with how epoch time works. Epoch time (also called Unix epoch time) is the number of seconds it has been since January 1st, 1970. This date is called the Unix epoch.

For example, when I run time.time() from the interactive shell (don't forget to import the time module first), it looks like this:

```
>>> import time
>>> time.time()
1320460242.118
```

What this number means is that the moment the time.time() function was called was a little over 1,320,460,242 seconds since midnight of January 1st, 1970.

If I call time.time() from the interactive shell a few seconds later, it might look like this:

```
>>> time.time()
1320460261.315
```

1320460261.315 seconds after midnight of the Unix epoch is November 4th, 2011 at 7:31:01pm. (Actually, it's 7:31 and 0.315 seconds if you want to be precise.)

Dealing with time would be difficult if we had to deal with strings. It's hard to tell that 19 seconds have passed if we only had the string values '7:30:42 PM' and '7:31:01 PM' to compare. But with epoch time, it's just a matter of subtracting the integers 1320460261.315 - 1320460242.118, which evaluates to 19.197000026702881. This value is the number of seconds between those two times. (The extra 0.000026702881 comes from very small rounding errors that happen when you do math with floating point numbers. They only happen sometimes and are usually too tiny to matter.

Going back to line 121, if time.time() - TIMEOUT > lastClickTime evaluates to True, then it has been longer than 4 seconds since time.time() was called and stored in lastClickTime. If it evaluates to False, then it has been less than 4 seconds.

```
            # pushed the incorrect button, or has timed out
            gameOverAnimation()
            # reset the variables for a new game:
            pattern = []
            currentStep = 0
            waitingForInput = False
            score = 0
            pygame.time.wait(1000)
            changeBackgroundAnimation()
```

If either the player clicked on the wrong button or has timed out, the program should play the "game over" animation and then reset the variables for a new game. This involves setting the pattern list to a blank list, currentStep to 0, waitingForInput to False, and then score to 0. A small pause and a new background color will be set to indicate to the player the start of a new game, which will begin on the next iteration of the game loop.

DRAWING THE BOARD TO THE SCREEN

```
        pygame.display.update()
        FPSCLOCK.tick(FPS)
```

Just like the other game programs, the last thing done in the game loop is drawing the display Surface object to the screen and calling the tick() method.

SAME OLD TERMINATE() FUNCTION

```
def terminate():
    pygame.quit()
    sys.exit()


def checkForQuit():
    for event in pygame.event.get(QUIT): # get all the QUIT events
        terminate() # terminate if any QUIT events are present
    for event in pygame.event.get(KEYUP): # get all the KEYUP events
```

```
        if event.key == K_ESCAPE:
            terminate() # terminate if the KEYUP event was for the Esc key
        pygame.event.post(event) # put the other KEYUP event objects back
```

REUSING THE CONSTANT VARIABLES

```
150. def flashButtonAnimation(color, animationSpeed=50):
151.     if color == YELLOW:
152.         sound = BEEP1
153.         flashColor = BRIGHTYELLOW
154.         rectangle = YELLOWRECT
155.     elif color == BLUE:
156.         sound = BEEP2
157.         flashColor = BRIGHTBLUE
158.         rectangle = BLUERECT
159.     elif color == RED:
160.         sound = BEEP3
161.         flashColor = BRIGHTRED
162.         rectangle = REDRECT
163.     elif color == GREEN:
164.         sound = BEEP4
165.         flashColor = BRIGHTGREEN
166.         rectangle = GREENRECT
```

Depending on which Color value is passed as an argument for the color parameter, the sound, color of the bright flash, and rectangular area of the flash will be different. Line 151 to 166 sets three local variables differently depending on the value in the color parameter: sound, flashColor, and rectangle.

ANIMATING THE BUTTON FLASH

```
    origSurf = DISPLAYSURF.copy()
    flashSurf = pygame.Surface((BUTTONSIZE, BUTTONSIZE))
    flashSurf = flashSurf.convert_alpha()
    r, g, b = flashColor
    sound.play()
```

The process of animating the button flash is simple: On each frame of the animation, the normal board is drawn and then on top of that, the bright color version of the button that is flashing is drawn over the button. The alpha value of the bright color starts off at 0 for the first frame of animation, but then on each frame after the alpha value is slowly increased until it is fully opaque and the bright color version completely paints over the normal button color. This will make it look like the button is slowly brightening up.

The brightening up is the first half of the animation. The second half is the button dimming. This is done with the same code, except that instead of the alpha value increasing for each frame, it will be decreasing. As the alpha value gets lower and lower, the bright color painted on top will become more and more invisible, until only the original board with the dull colors is visible.

To do this in code, line 168 creates a copy of the display Surface object and stores it in origSurf. Line 169 creates a new Surface object the size of a single button and stores it in flashSurf. The convert_alpha() method is called on flashSurf so that the Surface object can have transparent colors drawn on it (otherwise, the alpha value in the Color objects we use will be ignored and automatically assumed to be 255). In your own game programs, if you are having trouble getting color transparency to work, make sure that you have called the convert_alpha() method on any Surface objects that have transparent colors painted on them.

Line 171 creates individual local variables named r, g, and b to store the individual RGB values of the tuple stored in flashColor. This is just some syntactic sugar that makes the rest of the code in this function easier to read. Before we begin animating the button flash, line 172 will play the sound effect for that button. The program execution keeps going after the sound effect has started to play, so the sound will be playing during the button flash animation.

```
173.     for start, end, step in ((0, 255, 1), (255, 0, -1)): # animation loop
174.         for alpha in range(start, end, animationSpeed * step):
175.             checkForQuit()
176.             DISPLAYSURF.blit(origSurf, (0, 0))
177.             flashSurf.fill((r, g, b, alpha))
178.             DISPLAYSURF.blit(flashSurf, rectangle.topleft)
179.             pygame.display.update()
180.             FPSCLOCK.tick(FPS)
181.     DISPLAYSURF.blit(origSurf, (0, 0))
```

Remember that to do the animation, we want to first draw the flashSurf with color that has increasing alpha values from 0 to 255 to do the brightening part of the animation. Then to do the dimming, we want the alpha value to go from 255 to 0. We *could* do that with code like this:

```
    for alpha in range(0, 255, animationSpeed): # brightening
        checkForQuit()
        DISPLAYSURF.blit(origSurf, (0, 0))
        flashSurf.fill((r, g, b, alpha))
        DISPLAYSURF.blit(flashSurf, rectangle.topleft)
        pygame.display.update()
        FPSCLOCK.tick(FPS)
    for alpha in range(255, 0, -animationSpeed): # dimming
        checkForQuit()
        DISPLAYSURF.blit(origSurf, (0, 0))
        flashSurf.fill((r, g, b, alpha))
        DISPLAYSURF.blit(flashSurf, rectangle.topleft)
        pygame.display.update()
        FPSCLOCK.tick(FPS)
```

But notice that the code inside the for loops handles drawing the frame and are identical to each other. If we wrote the code like the above, then the first for loop would handle the brightening part of the animation (where the alpha value goes from 0 to 255) and the second for loop would handle the dimming part of the animation (where the alpha values goes from 255 to 0). Note that for the second for loop, the third argument to the range() call is a negative number.

Whenever we have identical code like this, we can probably shorten our code so we don't have to repeat it. This is what we do with the for loop on line 173, which supplies different values for the range() call on line 174:

```
173.     for start, end, step in ((0, 255, 1), (255, 0, -1)): # animation loop
174.         for alpha in range(start, end, animationSpeed * step):
```

On the first iteration of line 173's for loop, start is set to 0, end is set to 255, and step is set to 1. This way, when the for loop on line 174 is executed, it is calling range(0, 255, animationSpeed). (Note that animationSpeed * 1 is the same as animationSpeed. Multiplying a number by 1 gives us the same number.)

Line 174's for loop then executes and performs the brightening animation.

On the second iteration of line 173's for loop (there are always two and only two iterations of this inner for loop), start is set to 255, end is set to 0, and step is set to -1. When the line 174's for loop is executed, it is calling range(255, 0, -animationSpeed). (Note that animationSpeed * -1 evaluates to -animationSpeed, since multiplying any number by -1 returns the negative form of that same number.)

This way, we don't have to have two separate for loops and repeat all the code that is inside of them. Here's the code again that is inside line 174's for loop:

```
175.             checkForQuit()
176.             DISPLAYSURF.blit(origSurf, (0, 0))
177.             flashSurf.fill((r, g, b, alpha))
```

```
178.             DISPLAYSURF.blit(flashSurf, rectangle.topleft)
179.             pygame.display.update()
180.             FPSCLOCK.tick(FPS)
181.     DISPLAYSURF.blit(origSurf, (0, 0))
```

We check for any QUIT events (in case the user tried to close the program during the animation), then blit the origSurf Surface to the display Surface. Then we paint the flashSurf Surface by calling fill() (supplying the r, g, b values of the color we got on line 171 and the alpha value that the for loop sets in the alpha variable). Then the flashSurf Surface is blitted to the display Surface.

Then, to make the display Surface appear on the screen, pygame.display.update() is called on line 179. To make sure the animation doesn't play as fast as the computer can draw it, we add short pauses with a call to the tick() method. (If you want to see the flashing animation play very slowly, put a low number like 1 or 2 as the argument to tick() instead of FPS.)

DRAWING THE BUTTONS

```
def drawButtons():
    pygame.draw.rect(DISPLAYSURF, YELLOW, YELLOWRECT)
    pygame.draw.rect(DISPLAYSURF, BLUE,   BLUERECT)
    pygame.draw.rect(DISPLAYSURF, RED,    REDRECT)
    pygame.draw.rect(DISPLAYSURF, GREEN,  GREENRECT)
```

Since each of the buttons is just a rectangle of a certain color in a certain place, we just make four calls to pygame.draw.rect() to draw the buttons on the display Surface. The Color object and the Rect object we use to position them never change, which is why we stored them in constant variables like YELLOW and YELLOWRECT.

ANIMATING THE BACKGROUND CHANGE

```
191. def changeBackgroundAnimation(animationSpeed=40):
192.     global bgColor
193.     newBgColor = (random.randint(0, 255), random.randint(0, 255),
random.randint(0, 255))
194.
195.     newBgSurf = pygame.Surface((WINDOWWIDTH, WINDOWHEIGHT))
196.     newBgSurf = newBgSurf.convert_alpha()
197.     r, g, b = newBgColor
198.     for alpha in range(0, 255, animationSpeed): # animation loop
199.         checkForQuit()
200.         DISPLAYSURF.fill(bgColor)
201.
202.         newBgSurf.fill((r, g, b, alpha))
```

The background color change animation happens whenever the player finishes entering the entire pattern correctly. On each iteration through the loop which starts on line 198 the entire display Surface has to be redrawn (blended with a less and less transparent new background color, until the background is completely covered by the new color). The steps done on each iteration of the loop are:

- Line 200 fills in the entire display Surface (stored in DISPLAYSURF) with the old background color (which is stored in bgColor).
- Line 202 fills in a different Surface object (stored in newBgSurf) with the new background color's RGB values (and the alpha transparency value changes on each iteration since that is what the for loop on line 198 does).
- Line 203 then draws the newBgSurf Surface to the display Surface in DISPLAYSURF. The reason we didn't just paint our semitransparent new

background color on DISPLAYSURF to begin with is because the fill() method will just replace the color on the Surface, whereas the blit() method will blend the colors.

- Now that we have the background the way we want it, we'll draw the buttons over it with a call to drawButtons() on line 205.
- Line 207 and 208 then just draws the display Surface to the screen and adds a pause.

The reason there is a global statement at the beginning of the changeBackgroundAnimation() function is for the bgColor variable is because this function modifies the content of the variable with an assignment statement on line 209. Any function can read the value of a global variable without specifying the global statement.

If that function assigns a value to a global variable without a global statement, then Python considers that variable to be a local variable that just happens to have the same name as a global variable. The main() function uses the bgColor variable but doesn't need a global statement for it because it only reads the contents of the bgColor the main() function never assigns bgColor a new value.

THE GAME OVER ANIMATION

```
212. def gameOverAnimation(color=WHITE, animationSpeed=50):
```

```
213.     # play all beeps at once, then flash the background
214.     origSurf = DISPLAYSURF.copy()
215.     flashSurf = pygame.Surface(DISPLAYSURF.get_size())
216.     flashSurf = flashSurf.convert_alpha()
217.     BEEP1.play() # play all four beeps at the same time, roughly.
218.     BEEP2.play()
219.     BEEP3.play()
220.     BEEP4.play()
221.     r, g, b = color
222.     for i in range(3): # do the flash 3 times
```

Each of the iterations of the for loop on the next line (line 223 below) will perform a flash. To have three flashes done, we put all of that code in a for loop that has three iterations. If you want more or fewer flashes, then change the integer that is passed to range() on line 222.

```
223.         for start, end, step in ((0, 255, 1), (255, 0, -1)):
```

The for loop on line 223 is exactly the same as the one line 173. The start, end, and step variables will be used on the next for loop (on line 224) to control how the alpha variable changes. Reread the "Animating the Button Flash" section if you need to refresh yourself on how these loops work.

```
224.         # The first iteration in this loop sets the following for loop
225.         # to go from 0 to 255, the second from 255 to 0.
226.         for alpha in range(start, end, animationSpeed * step): # animation loop
227.             # alpha means transparency. 255 is opaque, 0 is invisible
228.             checkForQuit()
229.             flashSurf.fill((r, g, b, alpha))
230.             DISPLAYSURF.blit(origSurf, (0, 0))
231.             DISPLAYSURF.blit(flashSurf, (0, 0))
232.             drawButtons()
233.             pygame.display.update()
234.             FPSCLOCK.tick(FPS)
```

This animation loop works the same as the previous flashing animation code in the "Animating the Background Change" section. The copy of the original Surface object stored in origSurf is drawn on the display Surface, then flashSurf (which has the new flashing color painted on it) is blitted on top of the display Surface. After the background color is set up, the buttons are drawn on top on line 232. Finally the display Surface is drawn to the screen with the call to pygame.display.update().

The for loop on line 226 adjusts the alpha value for the color used for each frame of animation (increasing at first, and then decreasing).

CONVERTING FROM PIXEL COORDINATES TO BUTTONS

```
def getButtonClicked(x, y):
    if YELLOWRECT.collidepoint( (x, y) ):
        return YELLOW
    elif BLUERECT.collidepoint( (x, y) ):
        return BLUE
    elif REDRECT.collidepoint( (x, y) ):
        return RED
    elif GREENRECT.collidepoint( (x, y) ):
        return GREEN
    return None


if __name__ == '__main__':
    main()
```

The getButtonClicked() function simply takes XY pixel coordinates and returns either the values YELLOW, BLUE, RED, or GREEN if one of the buttons was clicked, or returns None if the XY pixel coordinates are not over any of the four buttons.

EXPLICIT IS BETTER THAN IMPLICIT

You may have noticed that the code for getButtonClicked() ends with a return None statement on line 247. This might seem like an odd thing to type out, since all functions return None if they don't have any return statement at all. We could have left line 47 out entirely and the program would have worked the exact same way. So why bother writing it in?

Normally when a function reaches the end and returns the None value implicitly (that is, there is no return statement outright saying that it is returning None) the code that calls it doesn't care about the return value. All function calls have to return a value (so that they can evaluate to something and be part of expressions), but our code doesn't always make use of the return value.

For example, think about the print() function. Technically, this function returns the None value, but we never care about it:

```
>>> spam = print('Hello')
Hello
>>> spam == None
True
>>>
```

However, when getButtonClicked() returns None, it means that the coordinates that were passed to it were not over any of the four buttons. To make it clear that in this case the value None is returned from getButtonClicked(), we have the return None line at the end of the function.

To make your code more readable, it is better to have your code be explicit (that is, clearly state something even if it might be obvious) rather than implicit (that is, leaving it up to the person reading code to know how it works without outright telling them). In fact, "explicit is better than implicit" is one of the Python Koans.

The koans are a group of little sayings about how to write good code. There's an Easter egg (that is, a little hidden surprise) in the Python interactive shell where if you try to import a module named this, then it will display "The Zen of Python" koans. Try it out in the interactive shell:

```
>>> import this
The Zen of Python, by Tim Peters

Beautiful is better than ugly.
Explicit is better than implicit.
Simple is better than complex.
Complex is better than complicated.
Flat is better than nested.
Sparse is better than dense.
Readability counts.
Special cases aren't special enough to break the rules.
Although practicality beats purity.
Errors should never pass silently.
Unless explicitly silenced.
In the face of ambiguity, refuse the temptation to guess.
There should be one-- and preferably only one --obvious way to do it.
Although that way may not be obvious at first unless you're Dutch.
Now is better than never.
Although never is often better than *right* now.
If the implementation is hard to explain, it's a bad idea.
If the implementation is easy to explain, it may be a good idea.
Namespaces are one honking great idea -- let's do more of those!
```

6 Chapter WORMY

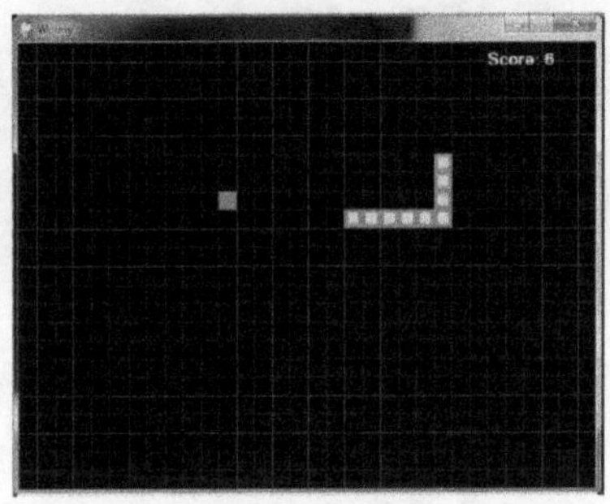

HOW TO PLAY WORMY

Wormy is a Nibbles clone. The player starts out controlling a short worm that is constantly moving around the screen. The player cannot stop or slow down the worm, but they can control which direction it turns. A red apple appears randomly on the screen, and the player must move the worm so that it eats the apple. Each time the worm eats an apple, the worm grows longer by one segment and a new apply randomly appears on the screen. The game is over if the worm crashes into itself or the edges of the screen.

SOURCE CODE TO WORMY

```
# Wormy (a Nibbles clone)
# By Al Sweigart al@inventwithpython.com
# http://inventwithpython.com/pygame
# Creative Commons BY-NC-SA 3.0 US

import random, pygame, sys
from pygame.locals import *

FPS = 15
WINDOWWIDTH = 640
WINDOWHEIGHT = 480
```

```
CELLSIZE = 20
assert WINDOWWIDTH % CELLSIZE == 0, "Window width must be a multiple of cell size."
assert WINDOWHEIGHT % CELLSIZE == 0, "Window height must be a multiple of cell size."
CELLWIDTH = int(WINDOWWIDTH / CELLSIZE)
CELLHEIGHT = int(WINDOWHEIGHT / CELLSIZE)

#             R    G    B
WHITE     = (255, 255, 255)
BLACK     = (  0,   0,   0)
RED       = (255,   0,   0)
GREEN     = (  0, 255,   0)
DARKGREEN = (  0, 155,   0)
DARKGRAY  = ( 40,  40,  40)
BGCOLOR = BLACK

UP = 'up'
DOWN = 'down'
LEFT = 'left'
RIGHT = 'right'

HEAD = 0 # syntactic sugar: index of the worm's head

def main():
    global FPSCLOCK, DISPLAYSURF, BASICFONT

    pygame.init()
    FPSCLOCK = pygame.time.Clock()
    DISPLAYSURF = pygame.display.set_mode((WINDOWWIDTH, WINDOWHEIGHT))
    BASICFONT = pygame.font.Font('freesansbold.ttf', 18)
    pygame.display.set_caption('Wormy')

    showStartScreen()
    while True:
        runGame()
        showGameOverScreen()


def runGame():
    # Set a random start point.
    startx = random.randint(5, CELLWIDTH - 6)
    starty = random.randint(5, CELLHEIGHT - 6)
    wormCoords = [{'x': startx,     'y': starty},
                  {'x': startx - 1, 'y': starty},
                  {'x': startx - 2, 'y': starty}]
```

```
    direction = RIGHT

    # Start the apple in a random place.
    apple = getRandomLocation()

    while True: # main game loop
        for event in pygame.event.get(): # event handling loop
            if event.type == QUIT:
                terminate()
            elif event.type == KEYDOWN:
                if (event.key == K_LEFT or event.key == K_a) and direction != RIGHT:
                    direction = LEFT
                elif (event.key == K_RIGHT or event.key == K_d) and direction != LEFT:
                    direction = RIGHT
                elif (event.key == K_UP or event.key == K_w) and direction != DOWN:
                    direction = UP
                elif (event.key == K_DOWN or event.key == K_s) and direction != UP:
                    direction = DOWN
                elif event.key == K_ESCAPE:
                    terminate()

        # check if the worm has hit itself or the edge
        if wormCoords[HEAD]['x'] == -1 or wormCoords[HEAD]['x'] == CELLWIDTH or wormCoords[HEAD]['y'] == -1 or wormCoords[HEAD]['y'] == CELLHEIGHT:
            return # game over
        for wormBody in wormCoords[1:]:
            if wormBody['x'] == wormCoords[HEAD]['x'] and wormBody['y'] == wormCoords[HEAD]['y']:
                return # game over

        # check if worm has eaten an apply
        if wormCoords[HEAD]['x'] == apple['x'] and wormCoords[HEAD]['y'] == apple['y']:
            # don't remove worm's tail segment
            apple = getRandomLocation() # set a new apple somewhere
        else:
            del wormCoords[-1] # remove worm's tail segment

        # move the worm by adding a segment in the direction it is moving
        if direction == UP:
```

```
            newHead = {'x': wormCoords[HEAD]['x'], 'y': wormCoords[HEAD]['y'] - 1}
        elif direction == DOWN:
            newHead = {'x': wormCoords[HEAD]['x'], 'y': wormCoords[HEAD]['y'] + 1}
        elif direction == LEFT:
            newHead = {'x': wormCoords[HEAD]['x'] - 1, 'y': wormCoords[HEAD]['y']}
        elif direction == RIGHT:
            newHead = {'x': wormCoords[HEAD]['x'] + 1, 'y': wormCoords[HEAD]['y']}
        wormCoords.insert(0, newHead)
        DISPLAYSURF.fill(BGCOLOR)
        drawGrid()
        drawWorm(wormCoords)
        drawApple(apple)
        drawScore(len(wormCoords) - 3)
        pygame.display.update()
        FPSCLOCK.tick(FPS)

def drawPressKeyMsg():
    pressKeySurf = BASICFONT.render('Press a key to play.', True, DARKGRAY)
    pressKeyRect = pressKeySurf.get_rect()
    pressKeyRect.topleft = (WINDOWWIDTH - 200, WINDOWHEIGHT - 30)
    DISPLAYSURF.blit(pressKeySurf, pressKeyRect)


def checkForKeyPress():
    if len(pygame.event.get(QUIT)) > 0:
        terminate()

    keyUpEvents = pygame.event.get(KEYUP)
    if len(keyUpEvents) == 0:
        return None
    if keyUpEvents[0].key == K_ESCAPE:
        terminate()
    return keyUpEvents[0].key


def showStartScreen():
    titleFont = pygame.font.Font('freesansbold.ttf', 100)
    titleSurf1 = titleFont.render('Wormy!', True, WHITE, DARKGREEN)
    titleSurf2 = titleFont.render('Wormy!', True, GREEN)

    degrees1 = 0
```

```
    degrees2 = 0
    while True:
        DISPLAYSURF.fill(BGCOLOR)
        rotatedSurf1 = pygame.transform.rotate(titleSurf1, degrees1)
        rotatedRect1 = rotatedSurf1.get_rect()
        rotatedRect1.center = (WINDOWWIDTH / 2, WINDOWHEIGHT / 2)
        DISPLAYSURF.blit(rotatedSurf1, rotatedRect1)

        rotatedSurf2 = pygame.transform.rotate(titleSurf2, degrees2)
        rotatedRect2 = rotatedSurf2.get_rect()
        rotatedRect2.center = (WINDOWWIDTH / 2, WINDOWHEIGHT / 2)
        DISPLAYSURF.blit(rotatedSurf2, rotatedRect2)

        drawPressKeyMsg()

        if checkForKeyPress():
            pygame.event.get() # clear event queue
            return
        pygame.display.update()
        FPSCLOCK.tick(FPS)
        degrees1 += 3 # rotate by 3 degrees each frame
        degrees2 += 7 # rotate by 7 degrees each frame


def terminate():
    pygame.quit()
    sys.exit()


def getRandomLocation():
    return {'x': random.randint(0, CELLWIDTH - 1), 'y': random.randint(0, CELLHEIGHT - 1)}


def showGameOverScreen():
    gameOverFont = pygame.font.Font('freesansbold.ttf', 150)
    gameSurf = gameOverFont.render('Game', True, WHITE)
    overSurf = gameOverFont.render('Over', True, WHITE)
    gameRect = gameSurf.get_rect()
    overRect = overSurf.get_rect()
    gameRect.midtop = (WINDOWWIDTH / 2, 10)
    overRect.midtop = (WINDOWWIDTH / 2, gameRect.height + 10 + 25)

    DISPLAYSURF.blit(gameSurf, gameRect)
    DISPLAYSURF.blit(overSurf, overRect)
    drawPressKeyMsg()
```

```
    pygame.display.update()
    pygame.time.wait(500)
    checkForKeyPress() # clear out any key presses in the event queue

    while True:
        if checkForKeyPress():
            pygame.event.get() # clear event queue
            return

def drawScore(score):
    scoreSurf = BASICFONT.render('Score: %s' % (score), True, WHITE)
    scoreRect = scoreSurf.get_rect()
    scoreRect.topleft = (WINDOWWIDTH - 120, 10)
    DISPLAYSURF.blit(scoreSurf, scoreRect)


def drawWorm(wormCoords):
    for coord in wormCoords:
        x = coord['x'] * CELLSIZE
        y = coord['y'] * CELLSIZE
        wormSegmentRect = pygame.Rect(x, y, CELLSIZE, CELLSIZE)
        pygame.draw.rect(DISPLAYSURF, DARKGREEN, wormSegmentRect)
        wormInnerSegmentRect = pygame.Rect(x + 4, y + 4, CELLSIZE - 8, CELLSIZE - 8)
        pygame.draw.rect(DISPLAYSURF, GREEN, wormInnerSegmentRect)


def drawApple(coord):
    x = coord['x'] * CELLSIZE
    y = coord['y'] * CELLSIZE
    appleRect = pygame.Rect(x, y, CELLSIZE, CELLSIZE)
    pygame.draw.rect(DISPLAYSURF, RED, appleRect)


def drawGrid():
    for x in range(0, WINDOWWIDTH, CELLSIZE): # draw vertical lines
        pygame.draw.line(DISPLAYSURF, DARKGRAY, (x, 0), (x, WINDOWHEIGHT))
    for y in range(0, WINDOWHEIGHT, CELLSIZE): # draw horizontal lines
        pygame.draw.line(DISPLAYSURF, DARKGRAY, (0, y), (WINDOWWIDTH, y))


if __name__ == '__main__':
    main()
```

THE GRID

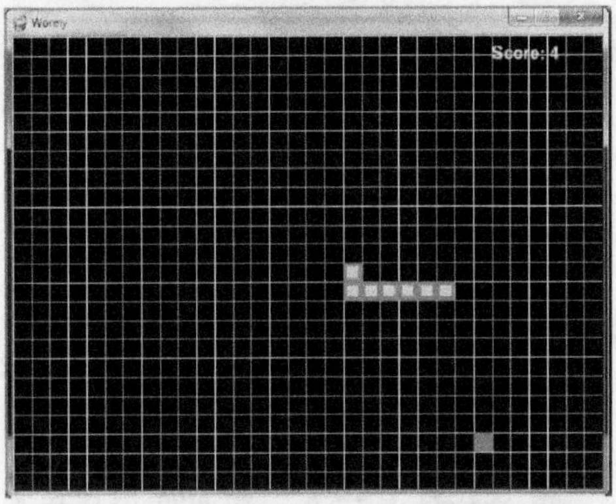

If you play the game a little, you'll notice that the apple and the segments of the worm's body always fit along a grid of lines. We will call each of the squares in this grid a cell (it's not always what a space in a grid is called, it's just a name I came up with). The cells have their own Cartesian coordinate system, with (0, 0) being the top left cell and (31, 23) being the bottom right cell.

THE SETUP CODE

```
1. # Wormy (a Nibbles clone)
2. # By Al Sweigart al@inventwithpython.com
3. # http://inventwithpython.com/pygame
4. # Creative Commons BY-NC-SA 3.0 US
5.
6. import random, pygame, sys
7. from pygame.locals import *
8.
9. FPS = 15
10. WINDOWWIDTH = 640
11. WINDOWHEIGHT = 480
12. CELLSIZE = 20
13. assert WINDOWWIDTH % CELLSIZE == 0, "Window width must be a multiple of cell size."
14. assert WINDOWHEIGHT % CELLSIZE == 0, "Window height must be a multiple of cell size."
15. CELLWIDTH = int(WINDOWWIDTH / CELLSIZE)
16. CELLHEIGHT = int(WINDOWHEIGHT / CELLSIZE)
```

The code at the start of the program just sets up some constant variables used in the game. The width and height of the cells are stored in CELLSIZE. The assert statements on lines 13 and 14 ensure that the cells fit perfectly in the window. For example, if the CELLSIZE was 10 and the WINDOWWIDTH or WINDOWHEIGHT constants were set to 15, then only 1.5 cells could fit. The assert statements make sure that only a whole integer number of cells fits in the window.

```
1. # Wormy (a Nibbles clone)
2. # By Al Sweigart al@inventwithpython.com
3. # http://inventwithpython.com/pygame
4. # Creative Commons BY-NC-SA 3.0 US
5.
6. import random, pygame, sys
7. from pygame.locals import *
8.
9. FPS = 15
10. WINDOWWIDTH = 640
11. WINDOWHEIGHT = 480
12. CELLSIZE = 20
13. assert WINDOWWIDTH % CELLSIZE == 0, "Window width must be a multiple of cell size."
14. assert WINDOWHEIGHT % CELLSIZE == 0, "Window height must be a multiple of cell size."
15. CELLWIDTH = int(WINDOWWIDTH / CELLSIZE)
16. CELLHEIGHT = int(WINDOWHEIGHT / CELLSIZE)
```

Some more constants are set on lines 19 to 32. The HEAD constant will be explained later in this chapter.

THE MAIN() FUNCTION

```
34. def main():
35.     global FPSCLOCK, DISPLAYSURF, BASICFONT
36.
37.     pygame.init()
38.     FPSCLOCK = pygame.time.Clock()
39.     DISPLAYSURF = pygame.display.set_mode((WINDOWWIDTH, WINDOWHEIGHT))
40.     BASICFONT = pygame.font.Font('freesansbold.ttf', 18)
41.     pygame.display.set_caption('Wormy')
42.
43.     showStartScreen()
44.     while True:
45.         runGame()
46.         showGameOverScreen()
```

In the Wormy game program, we've put the main part of the code in a function called runGame(). This is because we only want to show the "start screen" (the animation with the rotating "Wormy" text) once when the program starts (by calling the showStartScreen() function). Then we want to call runGame(), which will start a game of Wormy. This function will return when the player's worm collides into a wall or into itself and causes a game over.

AtthatpointwewillshowthegameoverscreenbycallingshowGameOverScreen(). When that function call returns, the loop goes back to the start and calls runGame() again. The while loop on line 44 will loop forever until the program terminates.

A SEPARATE RUNGAME() FUNCTION

```
49. def runGame():
50.     # Set a random start point.
51.     startx = random.randint(5, CELLWIDTH - 6)
52.     starty = random.randint(5, CELLHEIGHT - 6)
53.     wormCoords = [{'x': startx,     'y': starty},
54.                   {'x': startx - 1, 'y': starty},
55.                   {'x': startx - 2, 'y': starty}]
56.     direction = RIGHT
57.
58.     # Start the apple in a random place.
59.     apple = getRandomLocation()
```

At the beginning of a game, we want the worm to start in a random position (but not too close to the edges of the board) so we store a random coordinate in startx and starty. (Remember that CELLWIDTH and CELLHEIGHT is the number of cells wide and high the window is, not the number of pixels wide and high).

The body of the worm will be stored in a list of dictionary values. There will be one dictionary value per body segment of the worm. The dictionary will have keys 'x' and 'y' for the XY coordinates of that body segment. The head of the body to be at startx and starty. The other two body segments will be one and two cells to the left of the head.

The head of the worm will always be the body part at wormCoords[0]. To make this code more readable, we've set the HEAD constant to 0 on line 32, so that we can use wormCoords[HEAD] instead of wormCoords[0].

THE EVENT HANDLING LOOP

```
61.     while True: # main game loop
62.         for event in pygame.event.get(): # event handling loop
63.             if event.type == QUIT:
64.                 terminate()
65.             elif event.type == KEYDOWN:
66.                 if (event.key == K_LEFT or event.key == K_a) and direction
!= RIGHT:
```

```
67.                     direction = LEFT
68.                 elif (event.key == K_RIGHT or event.key == K_d) and direction != LEFT:
69.                     direction = RIGHT
70.                 elif (event.key == K_UP or event.key == K_w) and direction != DOWN:
71.                     direction = UP
72.                 elif (event.key == K_DOWN or event.key == K_s) and direction != UP:
73.                     direction = DOWN
74.                 elif event.key == K_ESCAPE:
75.                     terminate()
```

Line 61 is the start of the main game loop and line 62 is the start of the event handling loop. If the event is a QUIT event, then we call terminate() (which we've defined the same as the terminate() function in the previous game programs).

Otherwise, if the event is a KEYDOWN event, then we check if the key that was pressed down is an arrow key or a WASD key. We want an additional check so that the worm does not turn in on itself. For example, if the worm is moving left, then if the player accidentally presses the right arrow key, the worm would immediate start going right and crash into itself.

That is why we have this check for the current value of the direction variable. That way, if the player accidentally presses an arrow key that would cause them to immediately crash the worm, we just ignore that key press.

COLLISION DETECTION

```
77.         # check if the worm has hit itself or the edge
78.         if wormCoords[HEAD]['x'] == -1 or wormCoords[HEAD]['x'] == CELLWIDTH or wormCoords[HEAD]['y'] == -1 or wormCoords[HEAD]['y'] == CELLHEIGHT:
79.             return # game over
80.         for wormBody in wormCoords[1:]:
81.             if wormBody['x'] == wormCoords[HEAD]['x'] and wormBody['y'] == wormCoords[HEAD]['y']:
82.                 return # game over
```

The worm has crashed when the head has moved off the edge of the grid or when the head moves onto a cell that is already occupied by another body segment.

We can check if the head has moved off the edge of the grid by seeing if either the X coordinate of the head (which is stored in wormCoords[HEAD]['x']) is -1 (which is past the left edge of the grid) or equal to CELLWIDTH (which is past the right edge, since the rightmost X cell coordinate is one less than CELLWIDTH).

The head has also moved off the grid if the Y coordinate of the head (which is stored in wormCoords[HEAD]['y']) is either -1 (which is past the top edge) or CELLHEIGHT (which is past the bottom edge).

All we have to do to end the current game is to return out of runGame(). When runGame() returns to the function call in main(), the next line after the runGame() call (line 46) is the call to showGameOverScreen() which makes the large "Game Over" text appear. This is why we have the return statement on line 79.

Line 80 loops through every body segment in wormCoords after the head (which is at index 0. This is why the for loop iterates over wormCoords[1:] instead of just wormCoords). If both the 'x' and 'y' values of the body segment are the same as the 'x' and 'y' of the head, then we also end the game by returning out of the runGame() function.

DETECTING COLLISIONS WITH THE APPLE

```
84.        # check if worm has eaten an apply
85.        if wormCoords[HEAD]['x'] == apple['x'] and wormCoords[HEAD]['y']
== apple['y']:
86.            # don't remove worm's tail segment
87.            apple = getRandomLocation() # set a new apple somewhere
88.        else:
89.            del wormCoords[-1] # remove worm's tail segment
```

We do a similar collision detection check between the head of the worm and the apple's XY coordinates. If they match, we set the coordinates of the apple to a random new location (which we get from the return value of getRandomLocation()).

If the head has not collided with an apple, then we delete the last body segment in the wormCoords list. Remember that negative integers for indexes count from the end of the list. So while 0 is the index of the first item in the list and 1 is for the second item, -1 is for the last item in the list and -2 is for the second to last item.

The code on lines 91 to 100 (described next in the "Moving the Worm" section) will add a new body segment (for the head) in the direction that the worm is going. This will make the worm one segment longer. By not deleting the last body segment when the worm eats an apple, the overall length of the worm increases by one. But when line 89 deletes the last body segment, the size remains the same because a new head segment is added right afterwards.

MOVING THE WORM

```
91.         # move the worm by adding a segment in the direction it is moving
92.         if direction == UP:
93.             newHead = {'x': wormCoords[HEAD]['x'], 'y':
wormCoords[HEAD]['y'] - 1}
94.         elif direction == DOWN:
95.             newHead = {'x': wormCoords[HEAD]['x'], 'y':
wormCoords[HEAD]['y'] + 1}
96.         elif direction == LEFT:
97.             newHead = {'x': wormCoords[HEAD]['x'] - 1, 'y':
wormCoords[HEAD]['y']}
98.         elif direction == RIGHT:
99.             newHead = {'x': wormCoords[HEAD]['x'] + 1, 'y':
wormCoords[HEAD]['y']}
100.        wormCoords.insert(0, newHead)
```

To move the worm, we add a new body segment to the beginning of the wormCoords list. Because the body segment is being added to the beginning of the list, it will become the new head. The coordinates of the new head will be right next to the old head's coordinates. Whether 1 is added or subtracted from either the X or Y coordinate depends on the direction the worm was going.

This new head segment is added to wormCoords with the insert() list method on line 100.

THE INSERT() LIST METHOD

Unlike the append() list method that can only add items to the end of a list, the insert() list method can add items anywhere inside the list. The first parameter for insert() is the index where the item should go (all the items originally at this index and after have their indexes increase by one). If the argument passed for the first parameter is larger than the length of the list, the item is simply added to the end of the list (just like what append() does). The second parameter for insert() is the item value to be added. Type the following into the interactive shell to see how insert() works:

```
>>> spam = ['cat', 'dog', 'bat']
>>> spam.insert(0, 'frog')
>>> spam
['frog', 'cat', 'dog', 'bat']
>>> spam.insert(10, 42)
>>> spam
['frog', 'cat', 'dog', 'bat', 42]
>>> spam.insert(2, 'horse')
>>> spam
['frog', 'cat', 'horse', 'dog', 'bat', 42]
```

DRAWING THE SCREEN

```
101.         DISPLAYSURF.fill(BGCOLOR)
102.         drawGrid()
103.         drawWorm(wormCoords)
104.         drawApple(apple)
105.         drawScore(len(wormCoords) - 3)
106.         pygame.display.update()
107.         FPSCLOCK.tick(FPS)
```

The code for drawing the screen in the runGame() function is fairly simple. Line 101 fills in the entire display Surface with the background color. Lines 102 to 105 draw the grid, worm, apple, and score to the display Surface. Then the call to pygame.display.update() draws the display Surface to the actual computer screen.

DRAWING "PRESS A KEY" TEXT TO THE SCREEN

```
109. def drawPressKeyMsg():
110.     pressKeySurf = BASICFONT.render('Press a key to play.', True,
DARKGRAY)
111.     pressKeyRect = pressKeySurf.get_rect()
112.     pressKeyRect.topleft = (WINDOWWIDTH - 200, WINDOWHEIGHT - 30)
113.     DISPLAYSURF.blit(pressKeySurf, pressKeyRect)
```

While the start screen animation is playing or the game over screen is being shown, there will be some small text in the bottom right corner that says "Press a key to play." Rather than have the code typed out in both the showStartScreen() and the showGameOverScreen(), we put it in a this separate function and simply call the function from showStartScreen() and showGameOverScreen().

THE CHECKFORKEYPRESS() FUNCTION

```
116. def checkForKeyPress():
117.     if len(pygame.event.get(QUIT)) > 0:
118.         terminate()
119.
120.     keyUpEvents = pygame.event.get(KEYUP)
121.     if len(keyUpEvents) == 0:
122.         return None
123.     if keyUpEvents[0].key == K_ESCAPE:
124.         terminate()
125.     return keyUpEvents[0].key
```

This function first checks if there are any QUIT events in the event queue. The call to pygame.event.get() on line 117 returns a list of all the QUIT events in the event queue (because we pass QUIT as an argument). If there are not QUIT events in the event queue, then the list that pygame.event.get() returns will be the empty list: []

The len() call on line 117 will return 0 if pygame.event.get() returned an empty list. If there are more than zero items in the list returned by pygame.event.get() (and remember, any items in this list will only be QUIT events because we passed QUIT as the argument to pygame.event.get()), then the terminate() function gets called on line 118 and the program terminates.

After that, the call to pygame.event.get() gets a list of any KEYUP events in the event queue. If the key event is for the Esc key, then the program terminates in that case as well. Otherwise, the first key event object in the list that was returned by pygame.event.get() is returned from this checkForKeyPress() function.

THE START SCREEN

```
128. def showStartScreen():
129.     titleFont = pygame.font.Font('freesansbold.ttf', 100)
130.     titleSurf1 = titleFont.render('Wormy!', True, WHITE, DARKGREEN)
131.     titleSurf2 = titleFont.render('Wormy!', True, GREEN)
132.
133.     degrees1 = 0
134.     degrees2 = 0
135.     while True:
136.         DISPLAYSURF.fill(BGCOLOR)
```

When the Wormy game program first begins running, the player doesn't automatically begin playing the game. Instead, a start screen appears which tells the player what program they are running. A start screen also gives the player a chance to prepare for the game to begin (otherwise the player might not be ready and crash on their first game).

The Wormy start screen requires two Surface objects with the "Wormy!" text drawn on them. These are what the render() method calls create on lines 130 and 131. The text will be large: the Font() constructor function call on line 129 creates a Font object that is 100 points in size. The first "Wormy!" text will have white text with a dark green background, and the other will have green text with a transparent background.

Line 135 begins the animation loop for the start screen. During this animation, the two pieces of text will be rotated and drawn to the display Surface object.

ROTATING THE START SCREEN TEXT

```
        rotatedSurf1 = pygame.transform.rotate(titleSurf1, degrees1)
        rotatedRect1 = rotatedSurf1.get_rect()
        rotatedRect1.center = (WINDOWWIDTH / 2, WINDOWHEIGHT / 2)
        DISPLAYSURF.blit(rotatedSurf1, rotatedRect1)

        rotatedSurf2 = pygame.transform.rotate(titleSurf2, degrees2)
        rotatedRect2 = rotatedSurf2.get_rect()
        rotatedRect2.center = (WINDOWWIDTH / 2, WINDOWHEIGHT / 2)
        DISPLAYSURF.blit(rotatedSurf2, rotatedRect2)

        drawPressKeyMsg()

        if checkForKeyPress():
            pygame.event.get() # clear event queue
            return
        pygame.display.update()
        FPSCLOCK.tick(FPS)
```

The showStartScreen() function will rotate the images on the Surface objects that the "Wormy!" text is written on. The first parameter is the Surface object to make a rotated copy of. The second parameter is the number of degrees to rotate the Surface. The pygame.transform.rotate() function doesn't change the Surface object you pass it, but rather returns a new Surface object with the rotated image drawn on it.

Note that this new Surface object will probably be larger than the original one, since all Surface objects represent rectangular areas and the corners of the rotated Surface will stick out past the width and height of original Surface. The picture below has a black rectangle along with a slightly rotated version of itself. In order to make a Surface object that can fit the rotated rectangle (which is colored gray in the picture below), it must be larger than the original black rectangle's Surface object:

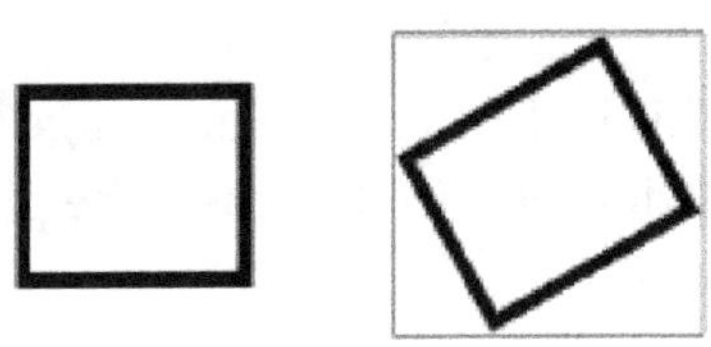

The amount you rotate it is given in degrees, which is a measure of rotation. There are 360 degrees in a circle. Not rotated at all is 0 degrees. Rotating to one quarter counter-clockwise is 90 degrees. To rotate clockwise, pass a negative integer. Rotating 360 degrees is rotating the image all the way around, which means you end up with the same image as if you rotated it 0 degrees. In fact, if the rotation argument you pass to pygame.transform.rotate() is 360 or larger, then Pygame automatically keeps subtracting 360 from it until it gets a number less than 360. This image shows several examples of different rotation amounts:

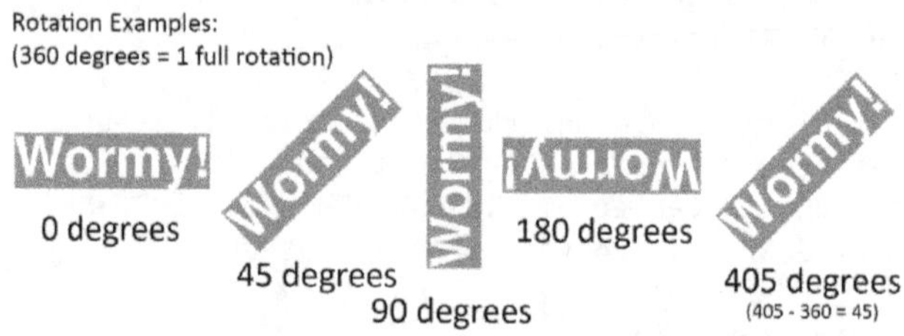

The two rotated "Wormy!" Surface objects are blitted to the display Surface on each frame of the animation loop on lines 140 and 145.

On line 147 the drawPressKeyMsg() function call draws the "Press a key to play." text in the lower corner of the display Surface object. This animation loop will keep looping until checkForKeyPress() returns a value that is not None, which happens if the player presses a key. Before returning, pygame.event.get() is called simply to clear out any other events that have accumulated in the event queue which the start screen was displayed.

ROTATIONS ARE NOT PERFECT

You may wonder why we store the rotated Surface in a separate variable, rather than just overwrite the titleSurf1 and titleSurf2 variables. There are two reasons.

First, rotating a 2D image is never completely perfect. The rotated image is always approximate. If you rotate an image by 10 degrees counterclockwise, and then rotate it back 10 degrees clockwise, the image you have will not be the exact same image you started with. Think of it as making a photocopy, and then a photocopy of the first photocopy, and the another photocopy of that photocopy. If you keep doing this, the image gets worse and worse as the slight distortions add up.

(The only exception to this is if you rotate an image by a multiple of 90 degrees, such as 0, 90, 180, 270, or 360 degrees. In that case, the pixels can be rotated without any distortion.)

Second, if you rotate a 2D image then the rotated image will be slightly larger than the original image. If you rotate that rotated image, then the next rotated image will be slightly larger again. If you keep doing this, eventually the image will become too large for Pygame to handle, and your program will crash with the error message, pygame.error: Width or height is too large.

```
        degrees1 += 3 # rotate by 3 degrees each frame
        degrees2 += 7 # rotate by 7 degrees each frame
```

The amount that we rotate the two "Wormy!" text Surface objects is stored in degrees1 and degrees2. On each iteration through the animation loop, we increase the number stored in degrees1 by 3 and degrees2 by 7. This means on the next iteration of the animation loop the white text "Wormy!" Surface object will be rotated by another 3 degrees and the green text "Wormy!" Surface object will be rotated by another 7 degrees. This is why the one of the Surface objects rotates slower than the other.

```
def terminate():
    pygame.quit()
    sys.exit()
```

The terminate() function calls pygame.quit() and sys.exit() so that the game correctly shuts down. It is identical to the terminate() functions in the previous game programs.

DECIDING WHERE THE APPLE APPEARS

```
def getRandomLocation():
    return {'x': random.randint(0, CELLWIDTH - 1), 'y': random.randint(0, 
CELLHEIGHT - 1)}
```

The getRandomLocation() function is called whenever new coordinates for the apple are needed. This function returns a dictionary with keys 'x' and 'y', with the values set to random XY coordinates.

GAME OVER SCREENS

```
def showGameOverScreen():
    gameOverFont = pygame.font.Font('freesansbold.ttf', 150)
    gameSurf = gameOverFont.render('Game', True, WHITE)
    overSurf = gameOverFont.render('Over', True, WHITE)
    gameRect = gameSurf.get_rect()
    overRect = overSurf.get_rect()
    gameRect.midtop = (WINDOWWIDTH / 2, 10)
    overRect.midtop = (WINDOWWIDTH / 2, gameRect.height + 10 + 25)

    DISPLAYSURF.blit(gameSurf, gameRect)
```

```
    DISPLAYSURF.blit(overSurf, overRect)
    drawPressKeyMsg()
    pygame.display.update()
```

The game over screen is similar to the start screen, except it isn't animated. The words "Game" and "Over" are rendered to two Surface objects which are then drawn on the screen.

```
180.     pygame.time.wait(500)
181.     checkForKeyPress() # clear out any key presses in the event queue
182.
183.     while True:
184.         if checkForKeyPress():
185.             pygame.event.get() # clear event queue
186.             return
```

The Game Over text will stay on the screen until the player pushes a key. Just to make sure the player doesn't accidentally press a key too soon, we will put a half second pause with the call to pygame.time.wait() on line 180. (The 500 argument stands for a 500 millisecond pause, which is half of one second.)

Then, checkForKeyPress() is called so that any key events that were made since the showGameOverScreen() function started are ignored. This pause and dropping of the key events is to prevent the following situation: Say the player was trying to turn away from the edge of the screen at the last minute, but pressed the key too late and crashed into the edge of the board. If this happens, then the key press would have happened after the showGameOverScreen() was called, and that key press would cause the game over screen to disappear almost instantly. The next game would start immediately after that, and might take the player by surprise. Adding this pause helps the make the game more "user friendly".

DRAWING FUNCTIONS

The code to draw the score, worm, apple, and grid are all put into separate functions.

```
188. def drawScore(score):
189.     scoreSurf = BASICFONT.render('Score: %s' % (score), True, WHITE)
190.     scoreRect = scoreSurf.get_rect()
191.     scoreRect.topleft = (WINDOWWIDTH - 120, 10)
192.     DISPLAYSURF.blit(scoreSurf, scoreRect)
```

The drawScore() function simply renders and draws the text of the score that was passed in its score parameter on the display Surface object.

```
195. def drawWorm(wormCoords):
196.     for coord in wormCoords:
197.         x = coord['x'] * CELLSIZE
198.         y = coord['y'] * CELLSIZE
199.         wormSegmentRect = pygame.Rect(x, y, CELLSIZE, CELLSIZE)
200.         pygame.draw.rect(DISPLAYSURF, DARKGREEN, wormSegmentRect)
201.         wormInnerSegmentRect = pygame.Rect(x + 4, y + 4, CELLSIZE - 8,
CELLSIZE - 8)
202.         pygame.draw.rect(DISPLAYSURF, GREEN, wormInnerSegmentRect)
```

The drawWorm() function will draw a green box for each of the segments of the worm's body. The segments are passed in the wormCoords parameter, which is a list of dictionaries each with an 'x' key and a 'y' key. The for loop on line 196 loops through each of the dictionary values in wormCoords.

Because the grid coordinates take up the entire window and also begin a 0, 0 pixel, it is fairly easy to convert from grid coordinates to pixel coordinates. Line 197 and 198 simply multiply the coord['x'] and coord['y'] coordinate by the CELLSIZE.

Line 199 creates a Rect object for the worm segment that will be passed to the pygame.draw.rect() function on line 200. Remember that each cell in the grid is CELLSIZE in width and height, so that's what the size of the segment's Rect object should be. Line 200 draws a dark green rectangle for the segment. Then on top of this, a smaller bright green rectangle is drawn. This makes the worm look a little nicer.

The inner bright green rectangle starts 4 pixels to the right and 4 pixels below the topleft corner of the cell. The width and height of this rectangle are 8 pixels less than the cell size, so there will be a 4 pixel margin on the right and bottom sides as well.

```
205. def drawApple(coord):
206.     x = coord['x'] * CELLSIZE
207.     y = coord['y'] * CELLSIZE
208.     appleRect = pygame.Rect(x, y, CELLSIZE, CELLSIZE)
209.     pygame.draw.rect(DISPLAYSURF, RED, appleRect)
```

The drawApple() function is very similar to drawWorm(), except since the red apple is just a single rectangle that fills up the cell, all the function needs to do is convert to pixel coordinates (which is what lines 206 and 207 do), create the Rect object with the location and size of the apple (line 208), and then pass this Rect object to the pygame.draw.rect() function.

```
def drawGrid():
    for x in range(0, WINDOWWIDTH, CELLSIZE): # draw vertical lines
```

```
        pygame.draw.line(DISPLAYSURF, DARKGRAY, (x, 0), (x, WINDOWHEIGHT))
    for y in range(0, WINDOWHEIGHT, CELLSIZE): # draw horizontal lines
        pygame.draw.line(DISPLAYSURF, DARKGRAY, (0, y), (WINDOWWIDTH, y))
```

Just to make it easier to visualize the grid of cells, we call pygame.draw.line() to draw out each of the vertical and horizontal lines of the grid.

Normally, to draw the 32 vertical lines needed, we would need 32 calls to pygame.draw.line() with the following coordinates:

```
pygame.draw.line(DISPLAYSURF, DARKGRAY, (0, 0), (0, WINDOWHEIGHT))
pygame.draw.line(DISPLAYSURF, DARKGRAY, (20, 0), (20, WINDOWHEIGHT))
pygame.draw.line(DISPLAYSURF, DARKGRAY, (40, 0), (40, WINDOWHEIGHT))
pygame.draw.line(DISPLAYSURF, DARKGRAY, (60, 0), (60, WINDOWHEIGHT))
...skipped for brevity...
pygame.draw.line(DISPLAYSURF, DARKGRAY, (560, 0), (560, WINDOWHEIGHT))
pygame.draw.line(DISPLAYSURF, DARKGRAY, (580, 0), (580, WINDOWHEIGHT))
pygame.draw.line(DISPLAYSURF, DARKGRAY, (600, 0), (600, WINDOWHEIGHT))
pygame.draw.line(DISPLAYSURF, DARKGRAY, (620, 0), (620, WINDOWHEIGHT))
```

Instead of typing out all these lines of code, we can just have one line of code inside a for loop. Notice that the pattern for the vertical lines is that the X coordinate of the start and end point starts at 0 and goes up to 620, increasing by 20 each time. The Y coordinate is always 0 for the start point and WINDOWHEIGHT for the end point parameter. That means the for loop should iterate over range(0, 640, 20). This is why the for loop on line 213 iterates over range(0, WINDOWWIDTH, CELLSIZE).

For the horizontal lines, the coordinates would have to be:

```
pygame.draw.line(DISPLAYSURF, DARKGRAY, (0, 0), (WINDOWWIDTH, 0))
pygame.draw.line(DISPLAYSURF, DARKGRAY, (0, 20), (WINDOWWIDTH, 20))
pygame.draw.line(DISPLAYSURF, DARKGRAY, (0, 40), (WINDOWWIDTH, 40))
pygame.draw.line(DISPLAYSURF, DARKGRAY, (0, 60), (WINDOWWIDTH, 60))
...skipped for brevity...
pygame.draw.line(DISPLAYSURF, DARKGRAY, (0, 400), (WINDOWWIDTH, 400))
pygame.draw.line(DISPLAYSURF, DARKGRAY, (0, 420), (WINDOWWIDTH, 420))
pygame.draw.line(DISPLAYSURF, DARKGRAY, (0, 440), (WINDOWWIDTH, 440))
pygame.draw.line(DISPLAYSURF, DARKGRAY, (0, 460), (WINDOWWIDTH, 460))
```

The Y coordinate ranges from 0 to 460, increasing by 20 each time. The X coordinate is always 0 for the start point and WINDOWWIDTH for the end point parameter. We can also use a for loop here so we don't have to type out all those pygame.draw.line() calls.

Noticing regular patterns needed by the calls and using loops is a clever programmer trick to save us from a lot of typing. We could have typed out all 56 pygame.draw.line() calls and the program would have worked the exact same. But by being a little bit clever, we can save ourselves a lot of work.

```
219. if __name__ == '__main__':
220.     main()
```

After all the functions and constants and global variables have been defined and created, the main() function is called to start the game.

DON'T REUSE VARIABLE NAMES

Take a look at a few lines of code from the drawWorm() function again:

```
199.         wormSegmentRect = pygame.Rect(x, y, CELLSIZE, CELLSIZE)
200.         pygame.draw.rect(DISPLAYSURF, DARKGREEN, wormSegmentRect)
201.         wormInnerSegmentRect = pygame.Rect(x + 4, y + 4, CELLSIZE - 8, CELLSIZE - 8)
202.         pygame.draw.rect(DISPLAYSURF, GREEN, wormInnerSegmentRect)
```

Notice that two different Rect objects are created on lines 199 and 201. The Rect object created on line 199 is stored in the wormSegmentRect local variable and is passed to the pygame.draw.rect() function on line 200. The Rect object created on line 201 is stored in the wormInnerSegmentRect local variable and is passed to the pygame.draw.rect() function on line 202.

Every time you create a variable, it takes up a small amount of the computer's memory. You might think it would be clever to reuse the wormSegmentRect variable for both Rect objects, like this:

```
199.         wormSegmentRect = pygame.Rect(x, y, CELLSIZE, CELLSIZE)
200.         pygame.draw.rect(DISPLAYSURF, DARKGREEN, wormSegmentRect)
201.         wormSegmentRect = pygame.Rect(x + 4, y + 4, CELLSIZE - 8, CELLSIZE - 8)
202.         pygame.draw.rect(DISPLAYSURF, GREEN, wormInnerSegmentRect)
```

Because the Rect object returned by pygame.Rect() on line 199 won't be needed after 200, we can overwrite this value and reuse the variable to store the Rect object returned by pygame.Rect() on line 201. Since we are now using fewer variables we are saving memory, right?

While this is technically true, you really are only saving a few bytes. Modern computers have memory of several billion bytes. So the savings aren't that great. Meanwhile, reusing variables reduces the code readability. If a programmer was reading through this code after it was written, they would see that wormSegmentRect is passed to the pygame.draw.rect() calls on line 200 and 202. If they tried to find the first time the wormSegmentRect variable was assigned a value, they would see the pygame.Rect() call on line 199. They might not realize that the Rect object returned by line 199's pygame.Rect() call isn't the same as the one that is passed to the pygame.draw.rect() call on line 202.

Little things like this make it harder to understand how exactly your program works. It won't just be other programmers looking at your code who will be confused. When you look at your own code a couple weeks after writing it, you may have a hard time remembering how exactly it works. Code readability is much more important than saving a few bytes of memory here and there.

7 Chapter

TETROMINO

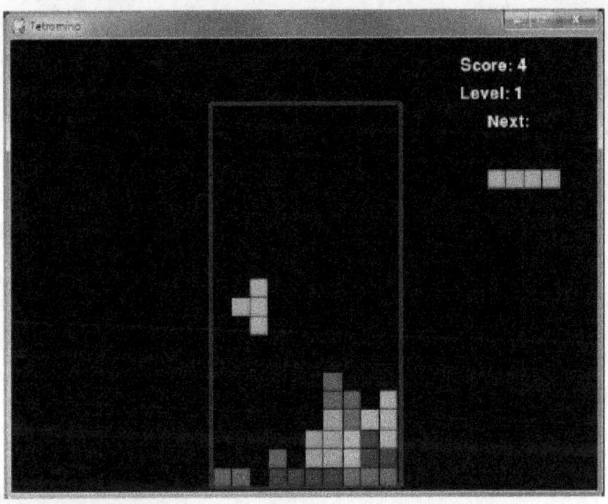

HOW TO PLAY TETROMINO

Tetromino is a Tetris clone. Differently shaped blocks (each made up of four boxes) fall from the top of the screen, and the player must guide them down to form complete rows that have no gaps in them. When a complete row is formed, the row disappears and each row above it moves down one row. The player tries to keep forming complete lines until the screen fills up and a new falling block cannot fit on the screen.

SOME TETROMINO NOMENCLATURE

In this chapter, I have come up with a set of terms for the different things in the game program.

- **Board** – The board is made up of 10 x 20 spaces that the blocks fall and stack up in.
- **Box** – A box is a single filled-in square space on the board.

- **Piece** – The things that fall from the top of the board that the player can rotate and position. Each piece has a shape and is made up of 4 boxes.
- **Shape** – The shapes are the different types of pieces in the game. The names of the shapes are T, S, Z, J, L, I, and O.

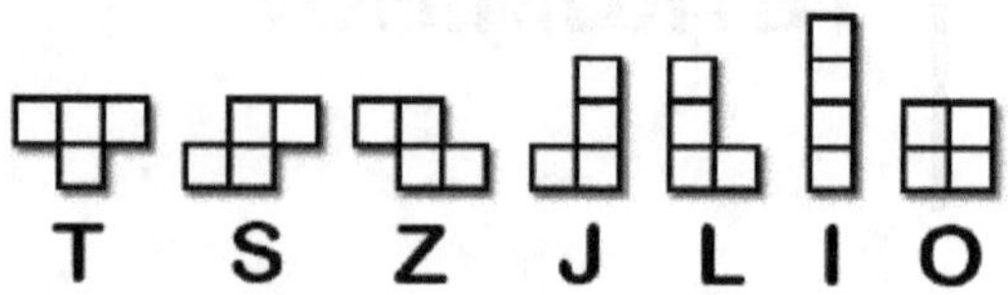

- **Template** – A list of shape data structures that represents all the possible rotations of a shape. These are store in variables with names like S_SHAPE_TEMPLATE or J_SHAPE_TEMPLATE.
- **Landed** – When a piece has either reached the bottom of the board or is touching a box on the board, we say that the piece has landed. At that point, the next piece should start falling.

SOURCE CODE TO TETROMINO

```
# Tetromino (a Tetris clone)
# By Al Sweigart al@inventwithpython.com
# http://inventwithpython.com/pygame
# Creative Commons BY-NC-SA 3.0 US

import random, time, pygame, sys
from pygame.locals import *

FPS = 25
WINDOWWIDTH = 640
WINDOWHEIGHT = 480
BOXSIZE = 20
BOARDWIDTH = 10
BOARDHEIGHT = 20
BLANK = '.'

MOVESIDEWAYSFREQ = 0.15
MOVEDOWNFREQ = 0.1

XMARGIN = int((WINDOWWIDTH - BOARDWIDTH * BOXSIZE) / 2)
TOPMARGIN = WINDOWHEIGHT - (BOARDHEIGHT * BOXSIZE) - 5

#               R    G    B
```

```
WHITE       = (255, 255, 255)
GRAY        = (185, 185, 185)
BLACK       = (  0,   0,   0)
RED         = (155,   0,   0)
LIGHTRED    = (175,  20,  20)
GREEN       = (  0, 155,   0)
LIGHTGREEN  = ( 20, 175,  20)
BLUE        = (  0,   0, 155)
LIGHTBLUE   = ( 20,  20, 175)
YELLOW      = (155, 155,   0)
LIGHTYELLOW = (175, 175,  20)

BORDERCOLOR = BLUE
BGCOLOR = BLACK
TEXTCOLOR = WHITE
TEXTSHADOWCOLOR = GRAY
COLORS      = (     BLUE,      GREEN,      RED,      YELLOW)
LIGHTCOLORS = (LIGHTBLUE, LIGHTGREEN, LIGHTRED, LIGHTYELLOW)
assert len(COLORS) == len(LIGHTCOLORS) # each color must have light color

TEMPLATEWIDTH = 5
TEMPLATEHEIGHT = 5

S_SHAPE_TEMPLATE = [['.....',
                     '.....',
                     '..OO.',
                     '.OO..',
                     '.....'],
                    ['.....',
                     '..O..',
                     '..OO.',
                     '...O.',
                     '.....']]

Z_SHAPE_TEMPLATE = [['.....',
                     '.....',
                     '.OO..',
                     '..OO.',
                     '.....'],
                    ['.....',
                     '..O..',
                     '.OO..',
                     '.O...',
                     '.....']]

I_SHAPE_TEMPLATE = [['..O..',
```

```
                     '..O..',
                     '..O..',
                     '..O..',
                     '.....'],
                    ['.....',
                     '.....',
                     'OOOO.',
                     '.....',
                     '.....']]

O_SHAPE_TEMPLATE = [['.....',
                     '.....',
                     '.OO..',
                     '.OO..',
                     '.....']]

J_SHAPE_TEMPLATE = [['.....',
                     '.O...',
                     '.OOO.',
                     '.....',
                     '.....'],
                    ['.....',
                     '..OO.',
                     '..O..',
                     '..O..',
                     '.....'],
                    ['.....',
                     '.....',
                     '.OOO.',
                     '...O.',
                     '.....'],
                    ['.....',
                     '..O..',
                     '..O..',
                     '.OO..',
                     '.....']]

L_SHAPE_TEMPLATE = [['.....',
                     '...O.',
                     '.OOO.',
                     '.....',
                     '.....'],
                    ['.....',
                     '..O..',
                     '..O..',
                     '..OO.',
```

```
                     '.....'],
                    ['.....',
                     '.....',
                     '.OOO.',
                     '.O...',
                     '.....'],
                    ['.....',
                     '.OO..',
                     '..O..',
                     '..O..',
                     '.....']]

T_SHAPE_TEMPLATE = [['.....',
                     '..O..',
                     '.OOO.',
                     '.....',
                     '.....'],
                    ['.....',
                     '..O..',
                     '..OO.',
                     '..O..',
                     '.....'],
                    ['.....',
                     '.....',
                     '.OOO.',
                     '..O..',
                     '.....'],
                    ['.....',
                     '..O..',
                     '.OO..',
                     '..O..',
                     '.....']]

SHAPES = {'S': S_SHAPE_TEMPLATE,
          'Z': Z_SHAPE_TEMPLATE,
          'J': J_SHAPE_TEMPLATE,
          'L': L_SHAPE_TEMPLATE,
          'I': I_SHAPE_TEMPLATE,
          'O': O_SHAPE_TEMPLATE,
          'T': T_SHAPE_TEMPLATE}


def main():
    global FPSCLOCK, DISPLAYSURF, BASICFONT, BIGFONT
    pygame.init()
    FPSCLOCK = pygame.time.Clock()
```

```
    DISPLAYSURF = pygame.display.set_mode((WINDOWWIDTH, WINDOWHEIGHT))
    BASICFONT = pygame.font.Font('freesansbold.ttf', 18)
    BIGFONT = pygame.font.Font('freesansbold.ttf', 100)
    pygame.display.set_caption('Tetromino')

    showTextScreen('Tetromino')
    while True: # game loop
        if random.randint(0, 1) == 0:
            pygame.mixer.music.load('tetrisb.mid')
        else:
            pygame.mixer.music.load('tetrisc.mid')
        pygame.mixer.music.play(-1, 0.0)
        runGame()
        pygame.mixer.music.stop()
        showTextScreen('Game Over')


def runGame():
    # setup variables for the start of the game
    board = getBlankBoard()
    lastMoveDownTime = time.time()
    lastMoveSidewaysTime = time.time()
    lastFallTime = time.time()
    movingDown = False # note: there is no movingUp variable
    movingLeft = False
    movingRight = False
    score = 0
    level, fallFreq = calculateLevelAndFallFreq(score)

    fallingPiece = getNewPiece()
    nextPiece = getNewPiece()

    while True: # main game loop
        if fallingPiece == None:
            # No falling piece in play, so start a new piece at the top
            fallingPiece = nextPiece
            nextPiece = getNewPiece()
            lastFallTime = time.time() # reset lastFallTime

            if not isValidPosition(board, fallingPiece):
                return # can't fit a new piece on the board, so game over

        checkForQuit()
        for event in pygame.event.get(): # event handling loop
            if event.type == KEYUP:
                if (event.key == K_p):
```

```
                    # Pausing the game
                    DISPLAYSURF.fill(BGCOLOR)
                    pygame.mixer.music.stop()
                    showTextScreen('Paused') # pause until a key press
                    pygame.mixer.music.play(-1, 0.0)
                    lastFallTime = time.time()
                    lastMoveDownTime = time.time()
                    lastMoveSidewaysTime = time.time()
                elif (event.key == K_LEFT or event.key == K_a):
                    movingLeft = False
                elif (event.key == K_RIGHT or event.key == K_d):
                    movingRight = False
                elif (event.key == K_DOWN or event.key == K_s):
                    movingDown = False

            elif event.type == KEYDOWN:
                # moving the block sideways
                if (event.key == K_LEFT or event.key == K_a) and isValidPosition(board, fallingPiece, adjX=-1):
                    fallingPiece['x'] -= 1
                    movingLeft = True
                    movingRight = False
                    lastMoveSidewaysTime = time.time()

                elif (event.key == K_RIGHT or event.key == K_d) and isValidPosition(board, fallingPiece, adjX=1):
                    fallingPiece['x'] += 1
                    movingRight = True
                    movingLeft = False
                    lastMoveSidewaysTime = time.time()

                # rotating the block (if there is room to rotate)
                elif (event.key == K_UP or event.key == K_w):
                    fallingPiece['rotation'] = (fallingPiece['rotation'] + 1) % len(SHAPES[fallingPiece['shape']])
                    if not isValidPosition(board, fallingPiece):
                        fallingPiece['rotation'] = (fallingPiece['rotation'] - 1) % len(SHAPES[fallingPiece['shape']])
                elif (event.key == K_q): # rotate the other direction
                    fallingPiece['rotation'] = (fallingPiece['rotation'] - 1) % len(SHAPES[fallingPiece['shape']])
                    if not isValidPosition(board, fallingPiece):
                        fallingPiece['rotation'] = (fallingPiece['rotation'] + 1) % len(SHAPES[fallingPiece['shape']])

                # making the block fall faster with the down key
```

```
                elif (event.key == K_DOWN or event.key == K_s):
                    movingDown = True
                    if isValidPosition(board, fallingPiece, adjY=1):
                        fallingPiece['y'] += 1
                    lastMoveDownTime = time.time()

                # move the current block all the way down
                elif event.key == K_SPACE:
                    movingDown = False
                    movingLeft = False
                    movingRight = False
                    for i in range(1, BOARDHEIGHT):
                        if not isValidPosition(board, fallingPiece, adjY=i):
                            break
                    fallingPiece['y'] += i - 1

        # handle moving the block because of user input
        if (movingLeft or movingRight) and time.time() - lastMoveSidewaysTime > MOVESIDEWAYSFREQ:
            if movingLeft and isValidPosition(board, fallingPiece, adjX=-1):
                fallingPiece['x'] -= 1
            elif movingRight and isValidPosition(board, fallingPiece, adjX=1):
                fallingPiece['x'] += 1
            lastMoveSidewaysTime = time.time()

        if movingDown and time.time() - lastMoveDownTime > MOVEDOWNFREQ and isValidPosition(board, fallingPiece, adjY=1):
            fallingPiece['y'] += 1
            lastMoveDownTime = time.time()

        # let the piece fall if it is time to fall
        if time.time() - lastFallTime > fallFreq:
            # see if the piece has landed
            if not isValidPosition(board, fallingPiece, adjY=1):
                # falling piece has landed, set it on the board
                addToBoard(board, fallingPiece)
                score += removeCompleteLines(board)
                level, fallFreq = calculateLevelAndFallFreq(score)
                fallingPiece = None
            else:
                # piece did not land, just move the block down
                fallingPiece['y'] += 1
                lastFallTime = time.time()
```

```
        # drawing everything on the screen
        DISPLAYSURF.fill(BGCOLOR)
        drawBoard(board)
        drawStatus(score, level)
        drawNextPiece(nextPiece)
        if fallingPiece != None:
            drawPiece(fallingPiece)

        pygame.display.update()
        FPSCLOCK.tick(FPS)


def makeTextObjs(text, font, color):
    surf = font.render(text, True, color)
    return surf, surf.get_rect()


def terminate():
    pygame.quit()
    sys.exit()


def checkForKeyPress():
    # Go through event queue looking for a KEYUP event.
    # Grab KEYDOWN events to remove them from the event queue.
    checkForQuit()

    for event in pygame.event.get([KEYDOWN, KEYUP]):
        if event.type == KEYDOWN:
            continue
        return event.key
    return None


def showTextScreen(text):
    # This function displays large text in the
    # center of the screen until a key is pressed.
    # Draw the text drop shadow
    titleSurf, titleRect = makeTextObjs(text, BIGFONT, TEXTSHADOWCOLOR)
    titleRect.center = (int(WINDOWWIDTH / 2), int(WINDOWHEIGHT / 2))
    DISPLAYSURF.blit(titleSurf, titleRect)

    # Draw the text
    titleSurf, titleRect = makeTextObjs(text, BIGFONT, TEXTCOLOR)
```

```
    titleRect.center = (int(WINDOWWIDTH / 2) - 3, int(WINDOWHEIGHT / 2) - 3)
    DISPLAYSURF.blit(titleSurf, titleRect)

    # Draw the additional "Press a key to play." text.
    pressKeySurf, pressKeyRect = makeTextObjs('Press a key to play.', BASICFONT, TEXTCOLOR)
    pressKeyRect.center = (int(WINDOWWIDTH / 2), int(WINDOWHEIGHT / 2) + 100)
    DISPLAYSURF.blit(pressKeySurf, pressKeyRect)

    while checkForKeyPress() == None:
        pygame.display.update()
        FPSCLOCK.tick()


def checkForQuit():
    for event in pygame.event.get(QUIT): # get all the QUIT events
        terminate() # terminate if any QUIT events are present
    for event in pygame.event.get(KEYUP): # get all the KEYUP events
        if event.key == K_ESCAPE:
            terminate() # terminate if the KEYUP event was for the Esc key
        pygame.event.post(event) # put the other KEYUP event objects back


def calculateLevelAndFallFreq(score):
    # Based on the score, return the level the player is on and
    # how many seconds pass until a falling piece falls one space.
    level = int(score / 10) + 1
    fallFreq = 0.27 - (level * 0.02)
    return level, fallFreq

def getNewPiece():
    # return a random new piece in a random rotation and color
    shape = random.choice(list(SHAPES.keys()))
    newPiece = {'shape': shape,
                'rotation': random.randint(0, len(SHAPES[shape]) - 1),
                'x': int(BOARDWIDTH / 2) - int(TEMPLATEWIDTH / 2),
                'y': -2, # start it above the board (i.e. less than 0)
                'color': random.randint(0, len(COLORS)-1)}
    return newPiece


def addToBoard(board, piece):
    # fill in the board based on piece's location, shape, and rotation
    for x in range(TEMPLATEWIDTH):
```

```
        for y in range(TEMPLATEHEIGHT):
            if SHAPES[piece['shape']][piece['rotation']][y][x] != BLANK:
                board[x + piece['x']][y + piece['y']] = piece['color']


def getBlankBoard():
    # create and return a new blank board data structure
    board = []
    for i in range(BOARDWIDTH):
        board.append([BLANK] * BOARDHEIGHT)
    return board


def isOnBoard(x, y):
    return x >= 0 and x < BOARDWIDTH and y < BOARDHEIGHT


def isValidPosition(board, piece, adjX=0, adjY=0):
    # Return True if the piece is within the board and not colliding
    for x in range(TEMPLATEWIDTH):
        for y in range(TEMPLATEHEIGHT):
            isAboveBoard = y + piece['y'] + adjY < 0
            if isAboveBoard or SHAPES[piece['shape']][piece['rotation']][y][x] == BLANK:
                continue
            if not isOnBoard(x + piece['x'] + adjX, y + piece['y'] + adjY):
                return False
            if board[x + piece['x'] + adjX][y + piece['y'] + adjY] != BLANK:
                return False
    return True

def isCompleteLine(board, y):
    # Return True if the line filled with boxes with no gaps.
    for x in range(BOARDWIDTH):
        if board[x][y] == BLANK:
            return False
    return True


def removeCompleteLines(board):
    # Remove any completed lines on the board, move everything above them down, and return the number of complete lines.
    numLinesRemoved = 0
    y = BOARDHEIGHT - 1 # start y at the bottom of the board
```

```
    while y >= 0:
        if isCompleteLine(board, y):
            # Remove the line and pull boxes down by one line.
            for pullDownY in range(y, 0, -1):
                for x in range(BOARDWIDTH):
                    board[x][pullDownY] = board[x][pullDownY-1]
            # Set very top line to blank.
            for x in range(BOARDWIDTH):
                board[x][0] = BLANK
            numLinesRemoved += 1
            # Note on the next iteration of the loop, y is the same.
            # This is so that if the line that was pulled down is also
            # complete, it will be removed.
        else:
            y -= 1 # move on to check next row up
    return numLinesRemoved


def convertToPixelCoords(boxx, boxy):
    # Convert the given xy coordinates of the board to xy
    # coordinates of the location on the screen.
    return (XMARGIN + (boxx * BOXSIZE)), (TOPMARGIN + (boxy * BOXSIZE))


def drawBox(boxx, boxy, color, pixelx=None, pixely=None):
    # draw a single box (each tetromino piece has four boxes)
    # at xy coordinates on the board. Or, if pixelx & pixely
    # are specified, draw to the pixel coordinates stored in
    # pixelx & pixely (this is used for the "Next" piece).
    if color == BLANK:
        return
    if pixelx == None and pixely == None:
        pixelx, pixely = convertToPixelCoords(boxx, boxy)
    pygame.draw.rect(DISPLAYSURF, COLORS[color], (pixelx + 1, pixely + 1, BOXSIZE - 1, BOXSIZE - 1))
    pygame.draw.rect(DISPLAYSURF, LIGHTCOLORS[color], (pixelx + 1, pixely + 1, BOXSIZE - 4, BOXSIZE - 4))


def drawBoard(board):
    # draw the border around the board
    pygame.draw.rect(DISPLAYSURF, BORDERCOLOR, (XMARGIN - 3, TOPMARGIN - 7, (BOARDWIDTH * BOXSIZE) + 8, (BOARDHEIGHT * BOXSIZE) + 8), 5)

    # fill the background of the board
```

```
    pygame.draw.rect(DISPLAYSURF, BGCOLOR, (XMARGIN, TOPMARGIN, BOXSIZE * BOARDWIDTH, BOXSIZE * BOARDHEIGHT))
    # draw the individual boxes on the board
    for x in range(BOARDWIDTH):
        for y in range(BOARDHEIGHT):
            drawBox(x, y, board[x][y])


def drawStatus(score, level):
    # draw the score text
    scoreSurf = BASICFONT.render('Score: %s' % score, True, TEXTCOLOR)
    scoreRect = scoreSurf.get_rect()
    scoreRect.topleft = (WINDOWWIDTH - 150, 20)
    DISPLAYSURF.blit(scoreSurf, scoreRect)

    # draw the level text
    levelSurf = BASICFONT.render('Level: %s' % level, True, TEXTCOLOR)
    levelRect = levelSurf.get_rect()
    levelRect.topleft = (WINDOWWIDTH - 150, 50)
    DISPLAYSURF.blit(levelSurf, levelRect)


def drawPiece(piece, pixelx=None, pixely=None):
    shapeToDraw = SHAPES[piece['shape']][piece['rotation']]
    if pixelx == None and pixely == None:
        # if pixelx & pixely hasn't been specified, use the location stored in the piece data structure
        pixelx, pixely = convertToPixelCoords(piece['x'], piece['y'])

    # draw each of the blocks that make up the piece
    for x in range(TEMPLATEWIDTH):
        for y in range(TEMPLATEHEIGHT):
            if shapeToDraw[y][x] != BLANK:
                drawBox(None, None, piece['color'], pixelx + (x * BOXSIZE), pixely + (y * BOXSIZE))


def drawNextPiece(piece):
    # draw the "next" text
    nextSurf = BASICFONT.render('Next:', True, TEXTCOLOR)
    nextRect = nextSurf.get_rect()
    nextRect.topleft = (WINDOWWIDTH - 120, 80)
    DISPLAYSURF.blit(nextSurf, nextRect)
    # draw the "next" piece
    drawPiece(piece, pixelx=WINDOWWIDTH-120, pixely=100)

```

```

if __name__ == '__main__':
    main()
```

THE USUAL SETUP CODE

```
# Tetromino (a Tetris clone)
# By Al Sweigart al@inventwithpython.com
# http://inventwithpython.com/pygame
# Creative Commons BY-NC-SA 3.0 US

import random, time, pygame, sys
from pygame.locals import *

FPS = 25
WINDOWWIDTH = 640
WINDOWHEIGHT = 480
BOXSIZE = 20
BOARDWIDTH = 10
BOARDHEIGHT = 20
BLANK = '.'
```

These are the constants used by our Tetromino game. Each box is a square that is 20 pixels wide and high. The board itself is 10 boxes wide and 20 boxes tall. The BLANK constant will be used as a value to represent blank spaces in the board's data structure.

SETTING UP TIMING CONSTANTS FOR HOLDING DOWN KEYS

```
MOVESIDEWAYSFREQ = 0.15
MOVEDOWNFREQ = 0.1
```

Every time the player pushes the left or right arrow key down, the falling piece should move one box over to the left or right, respectively. However, the player can also hold down the left or right arrow key to keep moving the falling piece. The MOVESIDEWAYSFREQ constant will set it so that every 0.15 seconds that passes with the left or right arrow key held down, the piece will move another space over.

The MOVEDOWNFREQ constant is the same thing except it tells how frequently the piece drops by one box while the player has the down arrow key held down.

MORE SETUP CODE

```
XMARGIN = int((WINDOWWIDTH - BOARDWIDTH * BOXSIZE) / 2)
```

```
TOPMARGIN = WINDOWHEIGHT - (BOARDHEIGHT * BOXSIZE) - 5
```

The program needs to calculate how many pixels are to the left and right side of the board to use later in the program. WINDOWWIDTH is the total number of pixels wide the entire window is. The board is BOARDWIDTH boxes wide and each box is BOXSIZE pixels wide. If we subtract BOXSIZE pixels from this for each of the boxes wide in the board (which is BOARDWIDTH * BOXSIZE), we'll have the size of the margin to the left and right of the board. If we divide this by 2, then we will have the size of just one margin. Since the margins are the same size, we can use XMARGIN for either the left-side or right-side margin.

We can calculate the size of the space between the top of the board and the top of the window in a similar manner. The board will be drawn 5 pixels above the bottom of the window, so 5 is subtracted from topmargin to account for this.

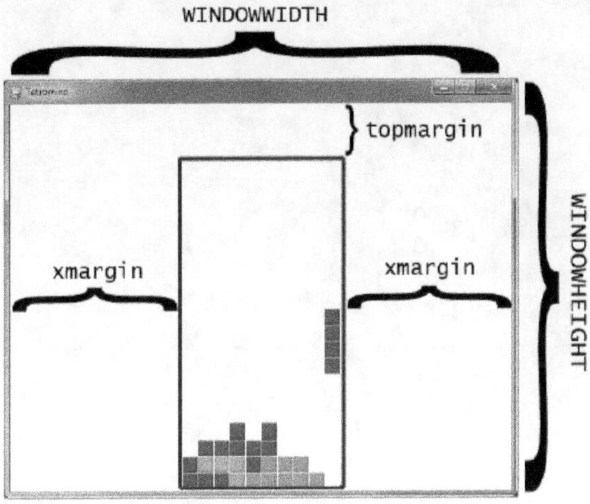


```
#                R    G    B
WHITE       = (255, 255, 255)
GRAY        = (185, 185, 185)
BLACK       = (  0,   0,   0)
RED         = (155,   0,   0)
LIGHTRED    = (175,  20,  20)
GREEN       = (  0, 155,   0)
LIGHTGREEN  = ( 20, 175,  20)
BLUE        = (  0,   0, 155)
LIGHTBLUE   = ( 20,  20, 175)
YELLOW      = (155, 155,   0)
LIGHTYELLOW = (175, 175,  20)
```

```

BORDERCOLOR = BLUE
BGCOLOR = BLACK
TEXTCOLOR = WHITE
TEXTSHADOWCOLOR = GRAY
COLORS      = (     BLUE,      GREEN,      RED,      YELLOW)
LIGHTCOLORS = (LIGHTBLUE, LIGHTGREEN, LIGHTRED, LIGHTYELLOW)
assert len(COLORS) == len(LIGHTCOLORS) # each color must have light color
```

The pieces will come in four colors: blue, green, red, and yellow. When we draw the boxes though, there will be a thin highlight on the box in a lighter color. So this means we need to create light blue, light green, light red, and light yellow colors as well.

Each of these four colors will be stored in tuples named COLORS (for the normal colors) and LIGHTCOLORS (for the lighter colors).

SETTING UP THE PIECE TEMPLATES

```
TEMPLATEWIDTH = 5
TEMPLATEHEIGHT = 5

S_SHAPE_TEMPLATE = [['.....',
                     '.....',
                     '..00.',
                     '.00..',
                     '.....'],
                    ['.....',
                     '..0..',
                     '..00.',
                     '...0.',
                     '.....']]

Z_SHAPE_TEMPLATE = [['.....',
                     '.....',
                     '.00..',
                     '..00.',
                     '.....'],
                    ['.....',
                     '..0..',
                     '.00..',
                     '.0...',
                     '.....']]

I_SHAPE_TEMPLATE = [['..0..',
                     '..0..',
                     '..0..',
                     '..0..',
                     '.....'],
                    ['.....',
                     '.....',
                     '0000.',
                     '.....',
                     '.....']]

O_SHAPE_TEMPLATE = [['.....',
                     '.....',
                     '.00..',
                     '.00..',
                     '.....']]

J_SHAPE_TEMPLATE = [['.....',
                     '.0...',
                     '.000.',
                     '.....',
```

```
                     '.....'],
                    ['.....',
                     '..OO.',
                     '..O..',
                     '..O..',
                     '.....'],
                    ['.....',
                     '.....',
                     '.OOO.',
                     '...O.',
                     '.....'],
                    ['.....',
                     '..O..',
                     '..O..',
                     '.OO..',
                     '.....']]

L_SHAPE_TEMPLATE = [['.....',
                     '...O.',
                     '.OOO.',
                     '.....',
                     '.....'],
                    ['.....',
                     '..O..',
                     '..O..',
                     '..OO.',
                     '.....'],
                    ['.....',
                     '.....',
                     '.OOO.',
                     '.O...',
                     '.....'],
                    ['.....',
                     '.OO..',
                     '..O..',
                     '..O..',
                     '.....']]

T_SHAPE_TEMPLATE = [['.....',
                     '..O..',
                     '.OOO.',
                     '.....',
                     '.....'],
                    ['.....',
                     '..O..',
                     '..OO.',
                     '..O..',
                     '.....'],
                    ['.....',
                     '.....',
                     '.OOO.',
                     '..O..',
```

```
                 '.....'],
                ['.....',
                 '..O..',
                 '.OO..',
                 '..O..',
                 '.....']]
```

Our game program needs to know how each of the shapes are shaped, including for all of their possible rotations. In order to do this, we will create lists of lists of strings. The inner list of strings will represent a single rotation of a shape, like this:

```
['.....',
 '.....',
 '..OO.',
 '.OO..',
 '.....']
```

We will write the rest of our code so that it interprets a list of strings like the one above to represent a shape where the periods are empty spaces and the O's are boxes, like this:

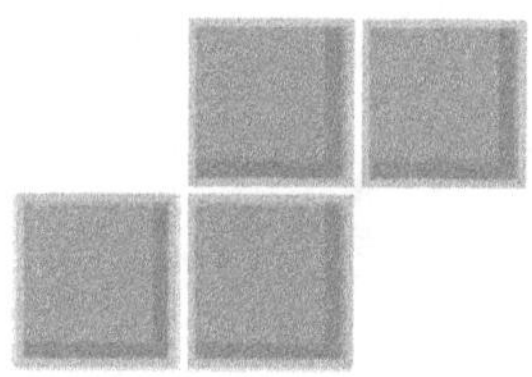

Splitting a "Line of Code" Across Multiple Lines

You can see that this list is spread across many lines in the file editor. This is perfectly valid Python, because the Python interpreter realizes that until it sees the] closing square bracket, the list isn't finished. The indentation doesn't matter because Python knows you won't have different indentation for a new block in the middle of a list. This code below works just fine:

```
spam = ['hello', 3.14, 'world', 42, 10, 'fuzz']
eggs = ['hello', 3.14,
    'world'
            , 42,
        10, 'fuzz']
```

Though, of course, the code for the eggs list would be much more readable if we lined up all the items in the list or put on a single line like spam.

Normally, splitting a line of code across multiple lines in the file editor would require putting a \ character at the end of the line. The \ tells Python, "This code continues onto the next line." (This slash was first used in the Sliding Puzzle game in the isValidMove() function.)

We will make "template" data structures of the shapes by creating a list of these list of strings, and store them in variables such as S_SHAPE_TEMPLATE. This way, len(S_SHAPE_TEMPLATE) will represent how many possible rotations there are for the S shape, and S_SHAPE_TEMPLATE[0] will represent the S shape's first possible rotation. Lines 47 to 147 will create "template" data structures for each of the shapes.

Imagine that each possible piece in a tiny 5 x 5 board of empty space, with some of the spaces on the board filled in with boxes. The following expressions that use S_SHAPE_TEMPLATE[0] are True:

```
S_SHAPE_TEMPLATE[0][2][2] == 'O'
S_SHAPE_TEMPLATE[0][2][3] == 'O'
S_SHAPE_TEMPLATE[0][3][1] == 'O'
S_SHAPE_TEMPLATE[0][3][2] == 'O'
```

If we represented this shape on paper, it would look something like this:

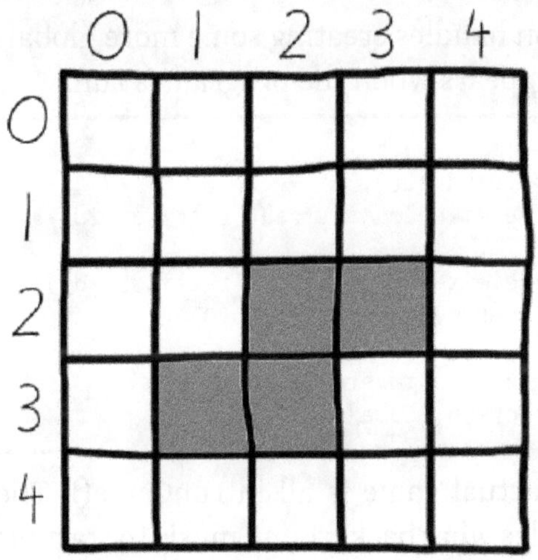

This is how we can represent things like Tetromino pieces as Python values such as strings and lists. The TEMPLATEWIDTH and TEMPLATEHEIGHT constants simply set how large each row and column for each shape's rotation should be. (The templates will always be 5x5.)

```
SHAPES = {'S': S_SHAPE_TEMPLATE,
          'Z': Z_SHAPE_TEMPLATE,
          'J': J_SHAPE_TEMPLATE,
          'L': L_SHAPE_TEMPLATE,
          'I': I_SHAPE_TEMPLATE,
          'O': O_SHAPE_TEMPLATE,
          'T': T_SHAPE_TEMPLATE}
```

The SHAPES variable will be a dictionary that stores all of the different templates. Because each template has all the possible rotations of a single shape, this means that the SHAPES variable contains all possible rotations of every possible shape. This will be the data structure that contains all of the shape data in our game.

THE MAIN() FUNCTION

```
158. def main():
159.     global FPSCLOCK, DISPLAYSURF, BASICFONT, BIGFONT
160.     pygame.init()
161.     FPSCLOCK = pygame.time.Clock()
162.     DISPLAYSURF = pygame.display.set_mode((WINDOWWIDTH, WINDOWHEIGHT))
163.     BASICFONT = pygame.font.Font('freesansbold.ttf', 18)
164.     BIGFONT = pygame.font.Font('freesansbold.ttf', 100)
165.     pygame.display.set_caption('Tetromino')
166.
167.     showTextScreen('Tetromino')
```

The main() function handles creating some more global constants and showing the start screen that appears when the program is run.

```
168.     while True: # game loop
169.         if random.randint(0, 1) == 0:
170.             pygame.mixer.music.load('tetrisb.mid')
171.         else:
172.             pygame.mixer.music.load('tetrisc.mid')
173.         pygame.mixer.music.play(-1, 0.0)
174.         runGame()
175.         pygame.mixer.music.stop()
176.         showTextScreen('Game Over')
```

The code for the actual game is all in runGame(). The main() function here simply randomly decides what background music to start playing (either the *tetrisb.mid* or *tetrisc.mid* MIDI music file), then calls runGame() to begin the game. When the player loses, runGame() will return to main(), which then stops the background music and displays the game over screen.

When the player presses a key, the showTextScreen() function that displays the game over screen will return. The game loop will loop back to the beginning at line 169 and start another game.

THE START OF A NEW GAME

```
179. def runGame():
180.     # setup variables for the start of the game
181.     board = getBlankBoard()
182.     lastMoveDownTime = time.time()
183.     lastMoveSidewaysTime = time.time()
184.     lastFallTime = time.time()
185.     movingDown = False # note: there is no movingUp variable
186.     movingLeft = False
187.     movingRight = False
188.     score = 0
189.     level, fallFreq = calculateLevelAndFallFreq(score)
190.
191.     fallingPiece = getNewPiece()
192.     nextPiece = getNewPiece()
```

Before the game begins and pieces start falling, we need to initialize some variables to their start-of-game values. On line 191 the fallingPiece variable will be set to the currently falling piece that can be rotated by the player. On line 192 the nextPiece variable will be set to the piece that shows up in the "Next" part of the screen so that player knows what piece is coming up after setting the falling piece.

THE GAME LOOP

```
194.     while True: # main game loop
195.         if fallingPiece == None:
196.             # No falling piece in play, so start a new piece at the top
197.             fallingPiece = nextPiece
198.             nextPiece = getNewPiece()
199.             lastFallTime = time.time() # reset lastFallTime
200.
201.             if not isValidPosition(board, fallingPiece):
202.                 return # can't fit a new piece on the board, so game over
203.
204.         checkForQuit()
```

The main game loop that starts on line 194 handles all of the code for the main part of the game when pieces are falling to the bottom. The fallingPiece variable is set to None after the falling piece has landed. This means that the piece in nextPiece should be copied to the fallingPiece variable, and a random new piece should be put into the nextPiece variable. A new piece can be generated from the getNewPiece() function. The lastFallTime variable is also reset to the current time so that the piece will fall in however many seconds is in fallFreq.

The pieces that getNewPiece() are positioned a little bit above the board, usually with part of the piece already on the board. But if this is an invalid position because the board is already filled up there (in which case the isValidPosition() call on line 201 will return False), then we know that the board is full and the player should lose the game. When this happens, the runGame() function returns.

THE EVENT HANDLING LOOP

```
        for event in pygame.event.get(): # event handling loop
            if event.type == KEYUP:
```

The event handling loop takes care of when the player rotates the falling piece, moves the falling piece, or pauses the game.

PAUSING THE GAME

```
207.                if (event.key == K_p):
208.                    # Pausing the game
209.                    DISPLAYSURF.fill(BGCOLOR)
210.                    pygame.mixer.music.stop()
211.                    showTextScreen('Paused') # pause until a key press
212.                    pygame.mixer.music.play(-1, 0.0)
```

```
213.                    lastFallTime = time.time()
214.                    lastMoveDownTime = time.time()
215.                    lastMoveSidewaysTime = time.time()
```

If the player has pressed the P key, then the game should pause. We need to hide the board from the player (otherwise the player could cheat by pausing the game and taking time to decide where to move the piece).

The code blanks out the display Surface with a call to DISPLAYSURF.fill(BGCOLOR) and stops the music. The showTextScreen() function is called to display the "Paused" text and wait for the player to press a key to continue.

Once the player has pressed a key, showTextScreen() will return. Line 212 will restart the background music. Also, since a large amount of time could have passed since the player paused the game, the lastFallTime, lastMoveDownTime, and lastMoveSidewaysTime variables should all be reset to the current time (which is done on lines 213 to 215).

USING MOVEMENT VARIABLES TO HANDLE USER INPUT

```
            elif (event.key == K_LEFT or event.key == K_a):
                movingLeft = False
            elif (event.key == K_RIGHT or event.key == K_d):
                movingRight = False
            elif (event.key == K_DOWN or event.key == K_s):
                movingDown = False
```

Letting up on one of the arrow keys (or the WASD keys) will set the movingLeft, movingRight, or movingDown variables back to False, indicating that the player no longer wants to move the piece in those directions. The code later will handle what to do based on the Boolean values inside these "moving" variables. Note that the up arrow and W keys are used for rotating the piece, not moving the piece up. This is why there is no movingUp variable.

CHECKING IF A SLIDE OR ROTATION IS VALID

```
        elif event.type == KEYDOWN:
            # moving the block sideways
            if (event.key == K_LEFT or event.key == K_a) and isValidPosition(board, fallingPiece, adjX=-1):
                fallingPiece['x'] -= 1
                movingLeft = True
                movingRight = False
                lastMoveSidewaysTime = time.time()
```

When the left arrow key is pressed down (and moving to the left is a valid move for the falling piece, as determined by the call to isValidPosition()), then we should change the position to one space to the left by subtracting the value of fallingPiece['x'] by 1. The isValidPosition() function has optional parameters called adjX and adjY. Normally the isValidPosition() function checks the position of the data provided by the piece object that is passed for the second parameter. However, sometimes we don't want to check where the piece is currently located, but rather a few spaces over from that position.

If we pass -1 for the adjX (a short name for "adjusted X"), then it doesn't check the validity of the position in the piece's data structure, but rather if the position of where the piece would be if it was one space to the left. Passing 1 for adjX would check one space to the right. There is also an adjY optional parameter. Passing -1 for adjY checks one space above where the piece is currently positioned, and passing a value like 3 for adjY would check three spaces down from where the piece is.

The movingLeft variable is set to True, and just to make sure the falling piece won't move both left *and* right, the movingRight variable is set to False on line 228. The lastMoveSidewaysTime variable will be updated to the current time on line 229.

These variables are set so that the player can just hold down the arrow key to keep moving the piece over. If the movingLeft variable is set to True, the program can know that the left arrow key (or A key) has been pressed and not yet let go. And if 0.15 seconds (the number stored in MOVESIDEWAYSFREQ) has passed since the time stored in lastMoveSidewaysTime, then it is time for the program to move the falling piece to the left again.

The lastMoveSidewaysTime works just like how the lastClickTime variable did in the Simulate chapter.

```
231.                elif (event.key == K_RIGHT or event.key == K_d) and
isValidPosition(board, fallingPiece, adjX=1):
232.                    fallingPiece['x'] += 1
233.                    movingRight = True
234.                    movingLeft = False
235.                    lastMoveSidewaysTime = time.time()
```

The code on lines 231 to 235 is almost identical to lines 225 to 229, except that it handles moving the falling piece to the right when the right arrow key (or D key) has been pressed.

```
237.                # rotating the block (if there is room to rotate)
238.                elif (event.key == K_UP or event.key == K_w):
```

```
239.                    fallingPiece['rotation'] = (fallingPiece['rotation'] +
1) % len(SHAPES[fallingPiece['shape']])
```

The up arrow key (or W key) will rotate the falling piece to its next rotation. All the code has to do is increment the 'rotation' key's value in the fallingPiece dictionary by 1. However, if incrementing the 'rotation' key's value makes it larger than the total number of rotations, then "modding" by the total number of possible rotations for that shape (which is what len(SHAPES[fallingPiece['shape']]) is) then it will "roll over" to 0.

Here's an example of this modding with the J shape, which has 4 possible rotations:

```
>>> 0 % 4
0
>>> 1 % 4
1
>>> 2 % 4
2
>>> 3 % 4
3
>>> 5 % 4
1
>>> 6 % 4
2
>>> 7 % 4
3
>>> 8 % 4
0
>>>
```

```
240.                     if not isValidPosition(board, fallingPiece):
241.                         fallingPiece['rotation'] =
(fallingPiece['rotation'] - 1) % len(SHAPES[fallingPiece['shape']])
```

If the new rotated position is not valid because it overlaps some boxes already on the board, then we want to switch it back to the original rotation by subtracting 1 from fallingPiece['rotation']. We can also mod it by len(SHAPES[fallingPiece['shape']]) so that if the new value is -1, the modding will change it back to the last rotation in the list. Here's an example of modding a negative number:

```
>>> -1 % 4
3
```

```
242.                 elif (event.key == K_q): # rotate the other direction
243.                     fallingPiece['rotation'] = (fallingPiece['rotation'] -
1) % len(SHAPES[fallingPiece['shape']])
244.                     if not isValidPosition(board, fallingPiece):
245.                         fallingPiece['rotation'] =
(fallingPiece['rotation'] + 1) % len(SHAPES[fallingPiece['shape']])
```

Lines 242 to 245 do the same thing 238 to 241, except they handle the case where the player has pressed the Q key which rotates the piece in the opposite direction. In this case, we *subtract* 1 from fallingPiece['rotation'] (which is done on line 243) instead of adding 1.

```
                # making the block fall faster with the down key
                elif (event.key == K_DOWN or event.key == K_s):
                    movingDown = True
                    if isValidPosition(board, fallingPiece, adjY=1):
                        fallingPiece['y'] += 1
                    lastMoveDownTime = time.time()
```

If the down arrow or S key is pressed down, then the player wants the piece to fall faster than normal. Line 251 moves the piece down one space on the board (but only if it is a valid space). The movingDown variable is set to True and lastMoveDownTime is reset to the current time. These variables will be checked later so that the piece keeps falling at the faster rate as long as the down arrow or S key is held down.

FINDING THE BOTTOM

```
254.                # move the current block all the way down
255.                elif event.key == K_SPACE:
256.                    movingDown = False
257.                    movingLeft = False
258.                    movingRight = False
259.                    for i in range(1, BOARDHEIGHT):
260.                        if not isValidPosition(board, fallingPiece, adjY=i):
261.                            break
262.                    fallingPiece['y'] += i - 1
```

When the player presses the space key the falling piece will immediately drop down as far as it can go on the board and land. The program first needs to find out how many spaces the piece can move until it lands.

Lines 256 to 258 will set all the moving variables to False (which makes the code in later parts of the programming think that the user has let up on any arrow keys that were held down). This is done because this code will move the piece to the absolute bottom and begin falling the next piece, and we don't want to surprise the player by having those pieces immediately start moving just because they were holding down an arrow key when they hit the space key.

To find the farthest that the piece can fall, we should first call isValidPosition() and pass the integer 1 for the adjY parameter. If isValidPosition() returns False, we know that the piece cannot fall any further and is already at the bottom. If isValidPosition() returns True, then we know that it can fall 1 space down.

In that case, we should call isValidPosition() with adjY set to 2. If it returns True again, we will call isValidPosition() with adjY set to 3, and so on. This is what the for loop on line 259 handles: calling isValidPosition() with increasing integer values to pass for adjY until the function call returns False. At that point, we know that the value in i is one space more past the bottom. This is why line 262 increases fallingPiece['y'] by i - 1 instead of i.

(Also note that the second parameter to range() on line 259's for statement is set to BOARDHEIGHT because this is the maximum amount that the piece could fall before it must hit the bottom of the board.)

MOVING BY HOLDING DOWN THE KEY

```
264.         # handle moving the block because of user input
265.         if (movingLeft or movingRight) and time.time() - lastMoveSidewaysTime > MOVESIDEWAYSFREQ:
266.             if movingLeft and isValidPosition(board, fallingPiece, adjX=-1):
267.                 fallingPiece['x'] -= 1
268.             elif movingRight and isValidPosition(board, fallingPiece, adjX=1):
269.                 fallingPiece['x'] += 1
270.             lastMoveSidewaysTime = time.time()
```

Remember that on line 227 the movingLeft variable was set to True if the player pressed down on the left arrow key? (The same for line 233 where movingRight was set to True if the player pressed down on the right arrow key.) The moving variables were set back to False if the user let up on these keys also (see line 217 and 219).

What also happened when the player pressed down on the left or right arrow key was that the lastMoveSidewaysTime variable was set to the current time (which was the return value of time.time()). If the player continued to hold down the arrow key without letting up on it, then the movingLeft or movingRight variable would still be set to True.

If the user held down on the key for longer than 0.15 seconds (the value stored in MOVESIDEWAYSFREQ is the float 0.15) then the expression time.time() - lastMoveSidewaysTime > MOVESIDEWAYSFREQ would evaluate to True. Line 265's condition is True if the user has both held down the arrow key and 0.15 seconds has passed, and in that case we should move the falling piece to the left or right even though the user hasn't pressed the arrow key again.

This is very useful because it would become tiresome for the player to repeatedly hit the arrow keys to get the falling piece to move over multiple spaces on the board. Instead, they can just hold down an arrow key and the piece will keep moving over until they let up on the key. When that happens, the code on lines 216 to 221 will set the moving variable to False and the condition on line 265 will be False. That is what stops the falling piece from sliding over more.

To demonstrate why the time.time() - lastMoveSidewaysTime > MOVESIDEWAYSFREQ returns True after the number of seconds in MOVESIDEWAYSFREQ has passed, run this short program:

```
import time

WAITTIME = 4
begin = time.time()

while True:
    now = time.time()
    message = '%s, %s, %s' % (begin, now, (now - begin))
    if now - begin > WAITTIME:
        print(message + ' PASSED WAIT TIME!')
    else:
        print(message + ' Not yet...')
    time.sleep(0.2)
```

This program has an infinite loop, so in order to terminate it, press Ctrl-C. The output of this program will look something like this:

```
1322106392.2, 1322106392.2, 0.0 Not yet...
1322106392.2, 1322106392.42, 0.219000101089 Not yet...
1322106392.2, 1322106392.65, 0.449000120163 Not yet...
1322106392.2, 1322106392.88, 0.680999994278 Not yet...
1322106392.2, 1322106393.11, 0.910000085831 Not yet...
1322106392.2, 1322106393.34, 1.1400001049 Not yet...
1322106392.2, 1322106393.57, 1.3710000515 Not yet...
1322106392.2, 1322106393.83, 1.6360001564 Not yet...
1322106392.2, 1322106394.05, 1.85199999809 Not yet...
```

```
1322106392.2, 1322106394.28, 2.08000016212 Not yet...
1322106392.2, 1322106394.51, 2.30900001526 Not yet...
1322106392.2, 1322106394.74, 2.54100012779 Not yet...
1322106392.2, 1322106394.97, 2.76999998093 Not yet...
1322106392.2, 1322106395.2, 2.99800014496 Not yet...
1322106392.2, 1322106395.42, 3.22699999809 Not yet...
1322106392.2, 1322106395.65, 3.45600008965 Not yet...
1322106392.2, 1322106395.89, 3.69200015068 Not yet...
1322106392.2, 1322106396.12, 3.92100000381 Not yet...
1322106392.2, 1322106396.35, 4.14899992943 PASSED WAIT TIME!
1322106392.2, 1322106396.58, 4.3789999485 PASSED WAIT TIME!
1322106392.2, 1322106396.81, 4.60700011253 PASSED WAIT TIME!
1322106392.2, 1322106397.04, 4.83700013161 PASSED WAIT TIME!
1322106392.2, 1322106397.26, 5.06500005722 PASSED WAIT TIME!
Traceback (most recent call last):
  File "C:\timetest.py", line 13, in <module>
    time.sleep(0.2)
KeyboardInterrupt
```

The first number on each line of output is the return value of time.time() when the program first started (and this value never changes). The second number is the latest return value from time.time() (this value keeps getting updated on each iteration of the loop). And the third number is the current time minus the start time. This third number is the number of seconds that have elapsed since the begin = time.time() line of code was executed.

If this number is greater than 4, the code will start printing "PASSED WAIT TIME!" instead of "Not yet...". This is how our game program can know if a certain amount of time has passed since a line of code was run.

In our Tetromino program, the time.time() – lastMoveSidewaysTime expression will evaluate to the number of seconds that has elapsed since the last time lastMoveSidewaysTime was set to the current time. If this value is greater than the value in MOVESIDEWAYSFREQ, we know it is time for the code to move the falling piece over one more space.

Don't forget to update lastMoveSidewaysTime to the current time again! This is what we do on line 270.

```
272.         if movingDown and time.time() - lastMoveDownTime > MOVEDOWNFREQ
and isValidPosition(board, fallingPiece, adjY=1):
273.             fallingPiece['y'] += 1
274.             lastMoveDownTime = time.time()
```

Lines 272 to 274 do almost the same thing as lines 265 to 270 do except for moving the falling piece down. This has a separate move variable (movingDown) and "last time" variable (lastMoveDownTime) as well as a different "move frequency" variable (MOVEDOWNFREQ).

LETTING THE PIECE "NATURALLY" FALL

```
276.         # let the piece fall if it is time to fall
277.         if time.time() - lastFallTime > fallFreq:
278.             # see if the piece has landed
279.             if not isValidPosition(board, fallingPiece, adjY=1):
280.                 # falling piece has landed, set it on the board
281.                 addToBoard(board, fallingPiece)
282.                 score += removeCompleteLines(board)
283.                 level, fallFreq = calculateLevelAndFallFreq(score)
284.                 fallingPiece = None
285.             else:
286.                 # piece did not land, just move the block down
287.                 fallingPiece['y'] += 1
288.                 lastFallTime = time.time()
```

The rate that the piece is naturally moving down (that is, falling) is tracked by the lastFallTime variable. If enough time has elapsed since the falling piece last fell down one space, lines 279 to 288 will handle dropping the piece by one space.

If the condition on line 279 is True, then the piece has landed. The call to addToBoard() will make the piece part of the board data structure (so that future pieces can land on it), and the removeCompleteLines() call will handle erasing any complete lines on the board and pulling the boxes down. The removeCompleteLines() function also returns an integer value of how many lines were removed, so we add this number to the score.

Because the score may have changed, we call the calculateLevelAndFallFreq() function to update the current level and frequency that the pieces fall. And finally, we set the fallingPiece variable to None to indicate that the next piece should become the new falling piece, and a random new piece should be generated for the new next piece. (That is done on lines 195 to 199 at the beginning of the game loop.)

If the piece has not landed, we simply set its Y position down one space (on line 287) and reset lastFallTime to the current time (on line 288).

DRAWING EVERYTHING ON THE SCREEN

```
290.         # drawing everything on the screen
291.         DISPLAYSURF.fill(BGCOLOR)
292.         drawBoard(board)
```

```
293.         drawStatus(score, level)
294.         drawNextPiece(nextPiece)
295.         if fallingPiece != None:
296.             drawPiece(fallingPiece)
297.
298.         pygame.display.update()
299.         FPSCLOCK.tick(FPS)
```

Now that the game loop has handled all events and updated the game state, the game loop just needs to draw the game state to the screen. Most of the drawing is handled by other functions, so the game loop code just needs to call those functions. Then the call to pygame.display.update() makes the display Surface appear on the actual computer screen, and the tick() method call adds a slight pause so the game doesn't run too fast.

MAKETEXTOBJS(), A SHORTCUT FUNCTION FOR MAKING TEXT

```
302. def makeTextObjs(text, font, color):
303.     surf = font.render(text, True, color)
304.     return surf, surf.get_rect()
```

The makeTextObjs() function just provides us with a shortcut. Given the text, Font object, and a Color object, it calls render() for us and returns the Surface and Rect object for this text. This just saves us from typing out the code to create the Surface and Rect object each time we need them.

THE SAME OLD TERMINATE() FUNCTION

```
307. def terminate():
308.     pygame.quit()
309.     sys.exit()
```

The terminate() function works the same as in the previous game programs.

WAITING FOR A KEY PRESS EVENT WITH THE CHECKFORKEYPRESS() FUNCTION

```
def checkForKeyPress():
    # Go through event queue looking for a KEYUP event.
    # Grab KEYDOWN events to remove them from the event queue.
    checkForQuit()

    for event in pygame.event.get([KEYDOWN, KEYUP]):
        if event.type == KEYDOWN:
```

```
            continue
        return event.key
    return None
```

The checkForKeyPress() function works almost the same as it did in the Wormy game. First it calls checkForQuit() to handle any QUIT events (or KEYUP events specifically for the Esc key) and terminates the program if there are any. Then it pulls out all the KEYUP and KEYDOWN events from the event queue. It ignores any KEYDOWN events (KEYDOWN was specified to pygame.event.get() only to clear those events out of the event queue).

If there were no KEYUP events in the event queue, then the function returns None.

SHOWTEXTSCREEN(), A GENERIC TEXT SCREEN FUNCTION

```
def showTextScreen(text):
    # This function displays large text in the
    # center of the screen until a key is pressed.
    # Draw the text drop shadow
    titleSurf, titleRect = makeTextObjs(text, BIGFONT, TEXTSHADOWCOLOR)
    titleRect.center = (int(WINDOWWIDTH / 2), int(WINDOWHEIGHT / 2))
    DISPLAYSURF.blit(titleSurf, titleRect)

    # Draw the text
    titleSurf, titleRect = makeTextObjs(text, BIGFONT, TEXTCOLOR)
    titleRect.center = (int(WINDOWWIDTH / 2) - 3, int(WINDOWHEIGHT / 2) -
3)
    DISPLAYSURF.blit(titleSurf, titleRect)

    # Draw the additional "Press a key to play." text.
    pressKeySurf, pressKeyRect = makeTextObjs('Press a key to play.',
BASICFONT, TEXTCOLOR)
    pressKeyRect.center = (int(WINDOWWIDTH / 2), int(WINDOWHEIGHT / 2) +
100)
    DISPLAYSURF.blit(pressKeySurf, pressKeyRect)
```

Instead of separate functions for the start screen and game over screens, we will create one generic function named showTextScreen(). The showTextScreen() function will draw whatever text we pass for the text parameter. Also, the text "Press a key to play." will be displayed in addition.

Notice that lines 328 to 330 draw the text in a darker shadow color first, and then lines 333 to 335 draw the same text again, except offset by 3 pixels to the left and 3 pixels upward. This creates a "drop shadow" effect that makes the text look a bit prettier. You can compare the difference by commenting out lines 328 to 330 to see the text without a drop shadow.

The showTextScreen() will be used for the start screen, the game over screen, and also for a pause screen. (The pause screen is explained later in this chapter.)

```
    while checkForKeyPress() == None:
        pygame.display.update()
        FPSCLOCK.tick()
```

We want the text to stay on the screen until the user presses a key. This small loop will constantly call pygame.display.update() and FPSCLOCK.tick() until checkForKeyPress() returns a value other than None. This happens when the user presses a key.

THE CHECKFORQUIT() FUNCTION

```
347. def checkForQuit():
348.     for event in pygame.event.get(QUIT): # get all the QUIT events
349.         terminate() # terminate if any QUIT events are present
350.     for event in pygame.event.get(KEYUP): # get all the KEYUP events
351.         if event.key == K_ESCAPE:
352.             terminate() # terminate if the KEYUP event was for the Esc key
353.         pygame.event.post(event) # put the other KEYUP event objects back
```

The checkForQuit() function can be called to handle any events that will cause the program to terminate. This happens if there are any QUIT events in the event queue (this is handle by lines 348 and 349), or if there is a KEYUP event of the Esc key. The player should be able to press the Esc key at any time to quit the program.

Because the pygame.event.get() call on line 350 pulls out all of the KEYUP events (including events for keys other than the Esc key), if the event is not for the Esc key, we want to put it back into the event queue by calling the pygame.event.post() function.

THE CALCULATELEVELANDFALLFREQ() FUNCTION

```
def calculateLevelAndFallFreq(score):
    # Based on the score, return the level the player is on and
    # how many seconds pass until a falling piece falls one space.
    level = int(score / 10) + 1
    fallFreq = 0.27 - (level * 0.02)
    return level, fallFreq
```

Every time the player completes a line, their score will increase by one point. Every ten points, the game goes up a level and the pieces start falling down faster. Both the level and the falling frequency can be calculated from the score that is passed to this function.

To calculate the level, we use the int() function to round down the score divided by 10. So if the score any number between 0 and 9, the int() call will round it down to 0. The + 1 part of the code is there because we want the first level to be level 1, not level 0. When the score reaches 10, then int(10 / 10) will evaluate to 1, and the + 1 will make the level 2. Here is a graph showing the values of level for the scores 1 to 34:

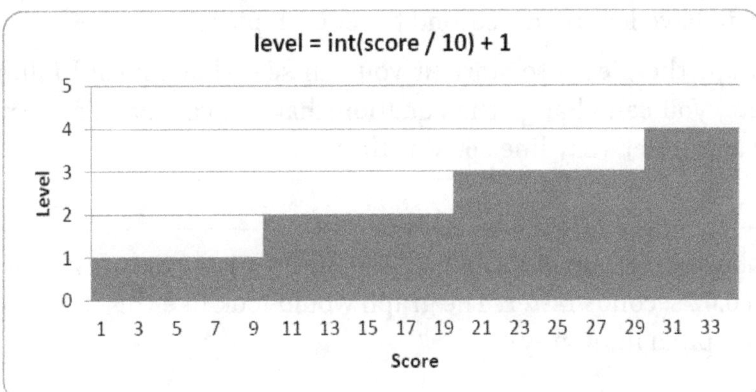

To calculate the falling frequency, we start with a base time of 0.27 (meaning that the piece will naturally fall once every 0.27 seconds). Then we multiply the level by 0.02, and subtract that from the 0.27 base time. So on level 1, we subtract 0.02 * 1 (that is, 0.02) from 0.27 to get 0.25. On level 2, we subtract 0.02 * 2 (that is, 0.04) to get 0.23. You can think of the level * 0.02 part of the equation as "for every level, the piece will fall 0.02 seconds faster than the previous level."

We can also make a graph showing how fast the pieces will fall at each level of the game:

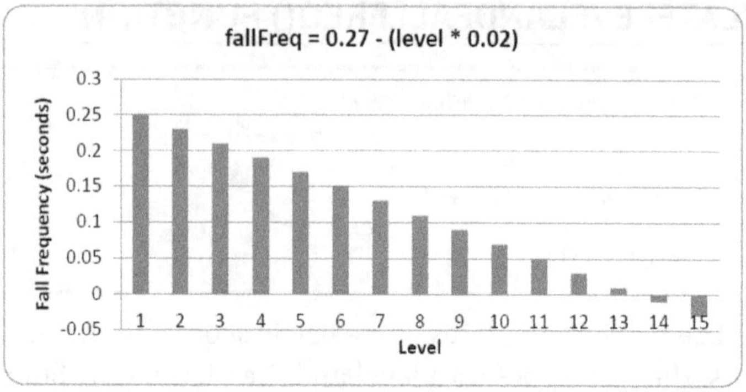

You can see that at level 14, the falling frequency will be less than 0. This won't cause any bugs with our code, because line 277 just checks that the elapsed time since the falling piece last fell one space is greater than the calculated falling frequency. So if the falling frequency is negative, then the condition on line 277 will always be True and the piece will fall on every iteration of the game loop. From level 14 and beyond, the piece cannot fall any faster.

If the FPS is set at 25, this means that at reaching level 14, the falling piece will fall 25 spaces a second. Considering that the board is only 20 spaces tall, that means the player will have less than a second to set each piece!

If you want the pieces to start (if you can see what I mean) falling faster at a slower rate, you can change the equation that the calculateLevelAndFallFreq() uses. For example, let's say line 360 was this:

```
360.        fallFreq = 0.27 - (level * 0.01)
```

In the above case, the pieces would only fall 0.01 seconds faster on each level rather than 0.02 seconds faster. The graph would look like this (the original line is also in the graph in light grey):

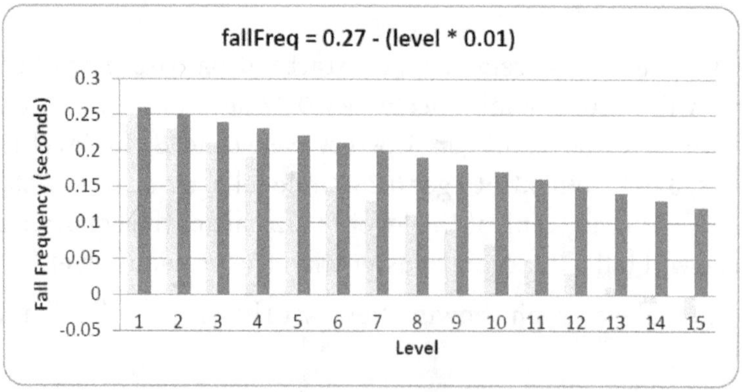

As you can see, with this new equation, level 14 would only be as hard as the original level 7. You can change the game to be as difficult or easy as you like by changing the equations in calculateLevelAndFallFreq().

GENERATING PIECES WITH THE GETNEWPIECE() FUNCTION

```
363. def getNewPiece():
364.     # return a random new piece in a random rotation and color
365.     shape = random.choice(list(SHAPES.keys()))
366.     newPiece = {'shape': shape,
367.                 'rotation': random.randint(0, len(SHAPES[shape]) - 1),
368.                 'x': int(BOARDWIDTH / 2) - int(TEMPLATEWIDTH / 2),
369.                 'y': -2, # start it above the board (i.e. less than 0)
370.                 'color': random.randint(0, len(COLORS)-1)}
371.     return newPiece
```

The getNewPiece() function generates a random piece that is positioned at the top of the board. First, to randomly choose the shape of the piece, we create a list of all the possible shapes by calling list(SHAPES.keys()) on line 365. The keys() dictionary method returns a value of the data type "dict_keys", which must be converted to a list value with the list() function before being passed to random.choice(). This is because the random.choice() function only accepts list values for its parameter. The random.choice() function then randomly returns the value of an item from the list.

The piece data structures are simply a dictionary value with the keys 'shape', 'rotation', 'x', 'y', and 'color'.

The value for the 'rotation' key is a random integer between 0 to one less than however many possible rotations there are for that shape. The number of rotations for a shape can be found from the expression len(SHAPES[shape]).

Notice that we don't store the list of string values (like the ones store in the constants like S_SHAPE_TEMPLATE) in each piece data structure to represent the boxes of each piece. Instead, we just store an index for the shape and rotation which refer to the PIECES constant.

The 'x' key's value is always set to the middle of the board (also accounting for the width of the pieces themselves, which is found from our TEMPLATEWIDTH constant). The 'y' key's value is always set to -2 to place it slightly above the board. (The top row of the board is row 0.)

Since the COLORS constant is a tuple of the different colors, selecting a random number from 0 to the length of COLORS (subtracting one) will give us a random index value for the piece's color.

Once all of the values in the newPiece dictionary are set, the getNewPiece() function returns newPiece.

ADDING PIECES TO THE BOARD DATA STRUCTURE

```
374. def addToBoard(board, piece):
375.     # fill in the board based on piece's location, shape, and rotation
376.     for x in range(TEMPLATEWIDTH):
377.         for y in range(TEMPLATEHEIGHT):
378.             if SHAPES[piece['shape']][piece['rotation']][y][x] != BLANK:
379.                 board[x + piece['x']][y + piece['y']] = piece['color']
```

The board data structure is a data representation for the rectangular space where pieces that have previously landed are tracked. The currently falling piece is not marked on the board data structure. What the addToBoard() function does is takes a piece data structure and adds its boxes to the board data structure. This happens after a piece has landed.

The nested for loops on lines 376 and 377 go through every space in the piece data structure, and if it finds a box in the space (line 378), it adds it to the board (line 379).

CREATING A NEW BOARD DATA STRUCTURE

```
382. def getBlankBoard():
383.     # create and return a new blank board data structure
384.     board = []
385.     for i in range(BOARDWIDTH):
386.         board.append([BLANK] * BOARDHEIGHT)
```

```
387.     return board
```

The data structure used for the board is fairly simple: it's a list of lists of values. If the value is the same as the value in BLANK, then it is an empty space. If the value is an integer, then it represents a box that is the color that the integer indexes in the COLORS constant list. That is, 0 is blue, 1 is green, 2 is red, and 3 is yellow.

In order to create a blank board, list replication is used to create the lists of BLANK values which represents a column. This is done on line 386. One of these lists is created for each of the columns in the board (this is what the for loop on line 385 does).

THE ISONBOARD() AND ISVALIDPOSITION() FUNCTIONS

```
def isOnBoard(x, y):
    return x >= 0 and x < BOARDWIDTH and y < BOARDHEIGHT
```

The isOnBoard() is a simple function which checks that the XY coordinates that are passed represent valid values that exist on the board. As long as both the

XY coordinates are not less 0 or greater than or equal to the BOARDWIDTH and BOARDHEIGHT constants, then the function returns True.

```
def isValidPosition(board, piece, adjX=0, adjY=0):
    # Return True if the piece is within the board and not colliding
    for x in range(TEMPLATEWIDTH):
        for y in range(TEMPLATEHEIGHT):
            isAboveBoard = y + piece['y'] + adjY < 0
            if isAboveBoard or
SHAPES[piece['shape']][piece['rotation']][y][x] == BLANK:
                continue
```

The isValidPosition() function is given a board data structure and a piece data structure, and returns True if all the boxes in the piece are both on the board and not overlapping any boxes on the board. This is done by taking the piece's XY coordinates (which is really the coordinate of the upper right box on the 5x5 boxes for the piece) and adding the coordinate inside the piece data structure. Here's a couple pictures to help illustrate this:

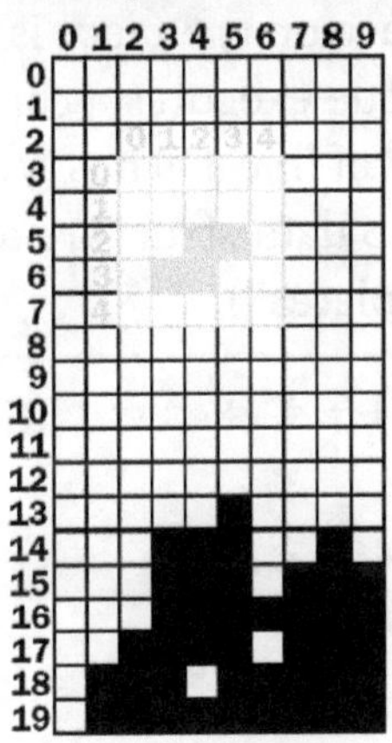

The board with a falling piece in a valid position.

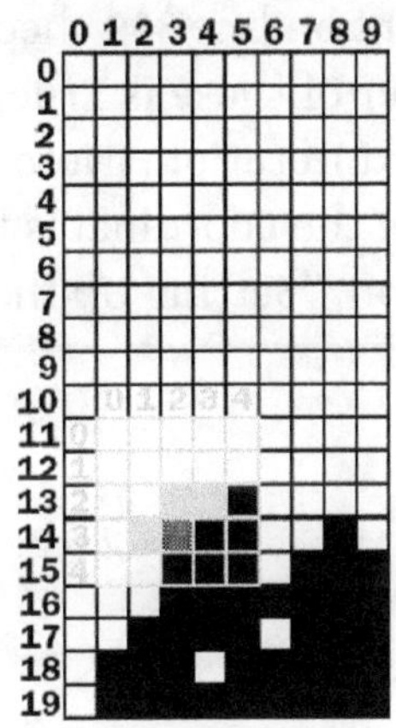

The board with the falling piece in an invalid position.

On the left board, the falling piece's (that is, the top left corner of the falling piece's) XY coordinates are (2, 3) on the board. But the boxes inside the falling piece's coordinate system have their own coordinates. To find the "board" coordinates of these pieces, we just have to add the "board" coordinates of the falling piece's top left box and the "piece" coordinates of the boxes.

On the left board, the falling piece's boxes are at the following "piece" coordinates:

(2, 2) (3, 2) (1, 3) (2, 3)

When we add the (2, 3) coordinate (the piece's coordinates on the board) to these coordinates, it looks like this:

(2 + 2, 2 + 3)   (3 + 2, 2 + 3)   (1 + 2, 3 + 3)   (2 + 2, 3 + 3)

After adding the (2, 3) coordinate the boxes are at the following "board" coordinates:

(4, 5)   (5, 5)   (3, 6)   (4, 6)

And now that we can figure out where the falling piece's boxes are as board coordinates, we can see if they overlap with the landed boxes that are already on the board. The nested for loops on lines 396 and 397 go through each of the possible coordinates on the falling piece.

We want to check if a box of the falling piece is either off of the board or overlapping a box on the board. (Although one exception is if the box is above the board, which is where it could be when the falling piece just begins falling.) Line 398 creates a variable named isAboveBoard that is set to True if the box on the falling piece at the coordinates pointed to be x and y is above the board. Otherwise it is set to False.

The if statement on line 399 checks if the space on the piece is above the board or is blank. If either of those is True, then the code executes a continue statement and goes to the next iteration. (Note that the end of line 399 has [y][x] instead of [x][y]. This is because the coordinates in the PIECES data structure are reversed. See the previous section, "Setting Up the Piece Templates").

```
401.             if not isOnBoard(x + piece['x'] + adjX, y + piece['y'] + adjY):
402.                 return False
403.             if board[x + piece['x'] + adjX][y + piece['y'] + adjY] != BLANK:
404.                 return False
405.     return True
```

The if statement on line 401 checks that the piece's box is not located on the board. The if statement on line 403 checks that the board space the piece's box is located is not blank. If either of these conditions are True, then the isValidPosition() function will return False. Notice that these if statements also adjust the coordinates for the adjX and adjY parameters that were passed in to the function.

If the code goes through the nested for loop and hasn't found a reason to return False, then the position of the piece must be valid and so the function returns True on line 405.

CHECKING FOR, AND REMOVING, COMPLETE LINES

```
407. def isCompleteLine(board, y):
408.     # Return True if the line filled with boxes with no gaps.
409.     for x in range(BOARDWIDTH):
410.         if board[x][y] == BLANK:
411.             return False
412.     return True
```

The isCompleteLine does a simple check at the row specified by the y parameter. A row on the board is considered to be "complete" when every space is filled by a box. The for loop on line 409 goes through each space in the row. If a space is blank (which is caused by it having the same value as the BLANK constant), then the function return False.

```
415. def removeCompleteLines(board):
416.     # Remove any completed lines on the board, move everything above them down, and return the number of complete lines.
417.     numLinesRemoved = 0
418.     y = BOARDHEIGHT - 1 # start y at the bottom of the board
419.     while y >= 0:
```

The removeCompleteLines() function will find any complete lines in the passed board data structure, remove the lines, and then shift all the boxes on the board above that line down one row. The function will return the number of lines that were removed (which is tracked by the numLinesRemoved variable) so that this can be added to the score.

The way this function works is by running in a loop starting on line 419 with the y variable starting at the lowest row (which is BOARDHEIGHT - 1). Whenever the row specified by y is not complete, y will be decremented to the next highest row. The loop finally stops once y reaches -1.

```
420.         if isCompleteLine(board, y):
421.             # Remove the line and pull boxes down by one line.
422.             for pullDownY in range(y, 0, -1):
423.                 for x in range(BOARDWIDTH):
424.                     board[x][pullDownY] = board[x][pullDownY-1]
425.             # Set very top line to blank.
426.             for x in range(BOARDWIDTH):
427.                 board[x][0] = BLANK
428.             numLinesRemoved += 1
429.             # Note on the next iteration of the loop, y is the same.
430.             # This is so that if the line that was pulled down is also
431.             # complete, it will be removed.
432.         else:
433.             y -= 1 # move on to check next row up
434.     return numLinesRemoved
```

The isCompleteLine() function will return True if the line that y is referring to is complete. In that case, the program needs to copy the values of each row above the removed line to the next lowest line. This is what the for loop on line 422 does (which is why its call to the range() function begins at y, rather than 0. Also note that it uses the three argument form of range(), so that the list it returns starts at y, ends at 0, and after each iteration "increases" by -1.)

Let's look at the following example. To save space, only the top five rows of the board are shown. Row 3 is a complete line, which means that all the rows above it (row 2, 1, and 0) must be "pulled down". First, row 2 is copied down to row 3. The board on the right shows what the board will look like after this is done:

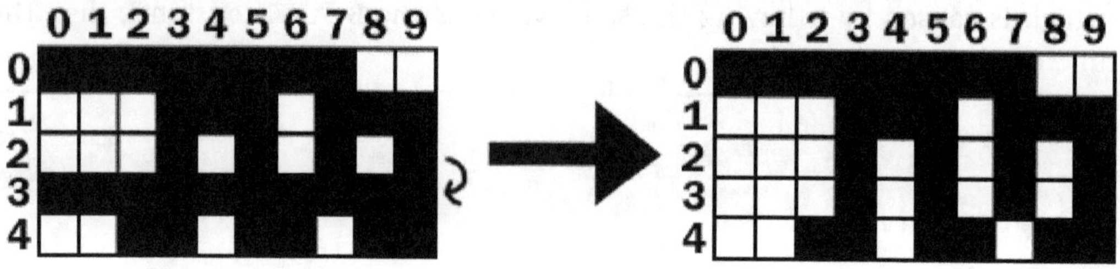

This "pulling down" is really just copying the higher row's values to the row below it on line 424. After row 2 is copied to row 3, then row 1 is copied to row 2 followed by row 0 copied to row 1:

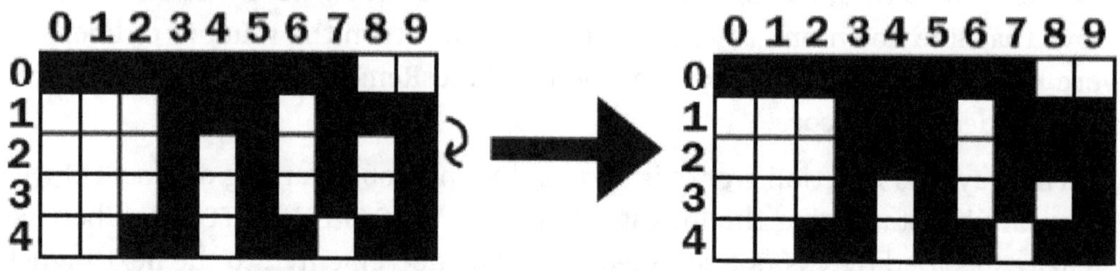

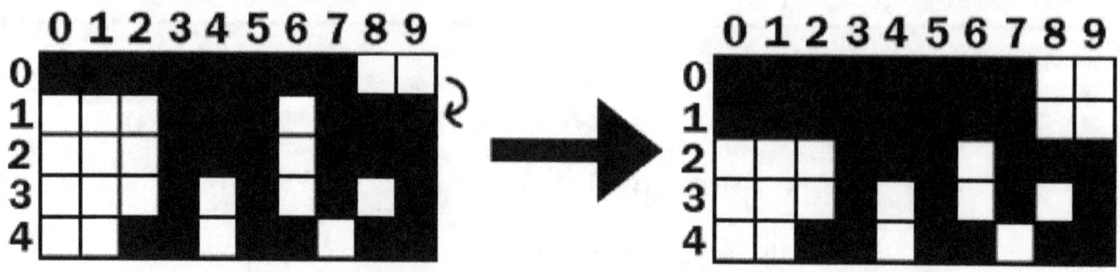

Row 0 (the row at the very top) doesn't have a row above it to copy values down. But row 0 doesn't need a row copied to it, it just needs all the spaces set to BLANK. This is what lines 426 and 427 do. After that, the board will have changed from the board shown below on the left to the board shown below on the right:

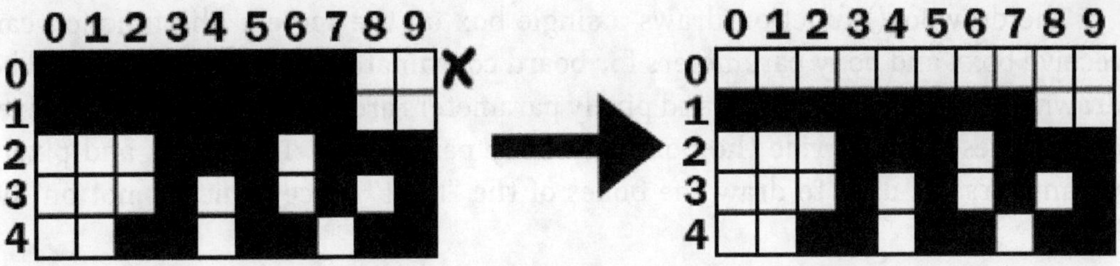

After the complete line is removed, the execution reaches the end of the while loop that started on line 419, so the execution jumps back to the beginning of the loop. Note that at no point when the line was being removed and the rows being pulled down that the y variable changed at all. So on the next iteration, the y variable is pointing to the same row as before.

This is needed because if there were two complete lines, then the second complete line would have been pulled down and would also have to be removed. The code will then remove this complete line, and then go to the next iteration. It is only when there is not a completed line that the y variable is decremented on line 433. Once the y variable has been decremented all the way to 0, the execution will exit the while loop.

CONVERT FROM BOARD COORDINATES TO PIXEL COORDINATES

```
def convertToPixelCoords(boxx, boxy):
    # Convert the given xy coordinates of the board to xy
    # coordinates of the location on the screen.
    return (XMARGIN + (boxx * BOXSIZE)), (TOPMARGIN + (boxy * BOXSIZE))
```

This helper function converts the board's box coordinates to pixel coordinates. This function works the same way to the other "convert coordinates" functions used in the previous game programs.

DRAWING A BOX ON THE BOARD OR ELSEWHERE ON THE SCREEN

```
def drawBox(boxx, boxy, color, pixelx=None, pixely=None):
    # draw a single box (each tetromino piece has four boxes)
    # at xy coordinates on the board. Or, if pixelx & pixely
    # are specified, draw to the pixel coordinates stored in
    # pixelx & pixely (this is used for the "Next" piece).
    if color == BLANK:
        return
    if pixelx == None and pixely == None:
        pixelx, pixely = convertToPixelCoords(boxx, boxy)
    pygame.draw.rect(DISPLAYSURF, COLORS[color], (pixelx + 1, pixely + 1,
BOXSIZE - 1, BOXSIZE - 1))
    pygame.draw.rect(DISPLAYSURF, LIGHTCOLORS[color], (pixelx + 1, pixely
+ 1, BOXSIZE - 4, BOXSIZE - 4))
```

The drawBox() function draws a single box on the screen. The function can receive boxx and boxy parameters for board coordinates where the box should be drawn. However, if the pixelx and pixely parameters are specified, then these pixel coordinates will override the boxx and boxy parameters. The pixelx and pixely parameters are used to draw the boxes of the "Next" piece, which is not on the board.

If the pixelx and pixely parameters are not set, then they will be set to None by default when the function first begins. Then the if statement on line 450 will overwrite the None values with the return values from convertToPixelCoords(). This call gets the pixel coordinates of the board coordinates specified by boxx and boxy.

The code won't fill the entire box's space with color. To have a black outline in between the boxes of a piece, the left and top parameters in the pygame.draw.rect() call have + 1 added to them and a - 1 is added to the width and height parameters. In order to draw the highlighted box, first the box is drawn with the darker color on line 452. Then, a slightly smaller box is drawn on top of the darker box on line 453.

DRAWING EVERYTHING TO THE SCREEN

```
def drawBoard(board):
    # draw the border around the board
    pygame.draw.rect(DISPLAYSURF, BORDERCOLOR, (XMARGIN - 3, TOPMARGIN - 7, (BOARDWIDTH * BOXSIZE) + 8, (BOARDHEIGHT * BOXSIZE) + 8), 5)

    # fill the background of the board
    pygame.draw.rect(DISPLAYSURF, BGCOLOR, (XMARGIN, TOPMARGIN, BOXSIZE * BOARDWIDTH, BOXSIZE * BOARDHEIGHT))
    # draw the individual boxes on the board
    for x in range(BOARDWIDTH):
        for y in range(BOARDHEIGHT):
            drawBox(x, y, board[x][y])
```

The drawBoard() function is responsible for calling the drawing functions for the board's border and all the boxes on the board. First the board's border is drawn on DISPLAYSURF, followed by the background color of the board. Then a call to drawBox() is made for each space on the board. The drawBox() function is smart enough to leave out the box if board[x][y] is set to BLANK.

DRAWING THE SCORE AND LEVEL TEXT

```
def drawStatus(score, level):
    # draw the score text
    scoreSurf = BASICFONT.render('Score: %s' % score, True, TEXTCOLOR)
    scoreRect = scoreSurf.get_rect()
    scoreRect.topleft = (WINDOWWIDTH - 150, 20)
    DISPLAYSURF.blit(scoreSurf, scoreRect)

    # draw the level text
    levelSurf = BASICFONT.render('Level: %s' % level, True, TEXTCOLOR)
    levelRect = levelSurf.get_rect()
    levelRect.topleft = (WINDOWWIDTH - 150, 50)
    DISPLAYSURF.blit(levelSurf, levelRect)
```

The drawStatus() function is responsible for rendering the text for the "Score:" and "Level:" information that appears in the upper right of the corner of the screen.

DRAWING A PIECE ON THE BOARD OR ELSEWHERE ON THE SCREEN

```
482. def drawPiece(piece, pixelx=None, pixely=None):
483.     shapeToDraw = SHAPES[piece['shape']][piece['rotation']]
484.     if pixelx == None and pixely == None:
485.         # if pixelx & pixely hasn't been specified, use the location stored in the piece data structure
486.         pixelx, pixely = convertToPixelCoords(piece['x'], piece['y'])
487.
488.     # draw each of the blocks that make up the piece
489.     for x in range(TEMPLATEWIDTH):
490.         for y in range(TEMPLATEHEIGHT):
491.             if shapeToDraw[y][x] != BLANK:
492.                 drawBox(None, None, piece['color'], pixelx + (x * BOXSIZE), pixely + (y * BOXSIZE))
```

The drawPiece() function will draw the boxes of a piece according to the piece data structure that is passed to it. This function will be used to draw the falling piece and the "Next" piece. Since the piece data structure will contain all of the shape, position, rotation, and color information, nothing else besides the piece data structure needs to be passed to the function.

However, the "Next" piece is not drawn on the board. In this case, we ignore the position information stored inside the piece data structure and instead let the caller of the drawPiece() function pass in arguments for the optional pixelx and pixely parameters to specify where exactly on the window the piece should be drawn.

If no pixelx and pixely arguments are passed in, then lines 484 and 486 will overwrite those variables with the return values of convertToPixelCoords() call.

The nested for loops on line 489 and 490 will then call drawBox() for each box of the piece that needs to be drawn.

Drawing the "Next" Piece

```
495. def drawNextPiece(piece):
496.     # draw the "next" text
497.     nextSurf = BASICFONT.render('Next:', True, TEXTCOLOR)
498.     nextRect = nextSurf.get_rect()
499.     nextRect.topleft = (WINDOWWIDTH - 120, 80)
500.     DISPLAYSURF.blit(nextSurf, nextRect)
501.     # draw the "next" piece
502.     drawPiece(piece, pixelx=WINDOWWIDTH-120, pixely=100)
```

```
503.
504.
505. if __name__ == '__main__':
506.     main()
```

The drawNextPiece() draws the "Next" piece in the upper right corner of the screen. It does this by calling the drawPiece() function and passing in arguments for drawPiece()'s pixelx and pixely parameters.

That's the last function. Line 505 and 506 are run after all the function definitions have been executed, and then the main() function is called to begin the main part of the program.

SUMMARY

The Tetromino game (which is a clone of the more popular game, "Tetris") is pretty easy to explain to someone in English: "Blocks fall from the top of a board, and the player moves and rotates them so that they form complete lines. The complete lines disappear (giving the player points) and the lines above them move down. The game keeps going until the blocks fill up the entire board and the player loses."

Explaining it in plain English is one thing, but when we have to tell a computer exactly what to do there are many details we have to fill in. The original Tetris game was designed and programmed one person, Alex Pajitnov, in the Soviet Union in 1984. The game is simple, fun, and addictive. It is one of the most popular video games ever made, and has sold 100 million copies with many people creating their own clones and variations of it.

And it was all created by one person who knew how to program.

With the right idea and some programming knowledge you can create incredibly fun games. And with some practice, you will be able to turn your game ideas into real programs that might become as popular as Tetris!

8 Chapter

SQUIRREL EAT SQUIRREL

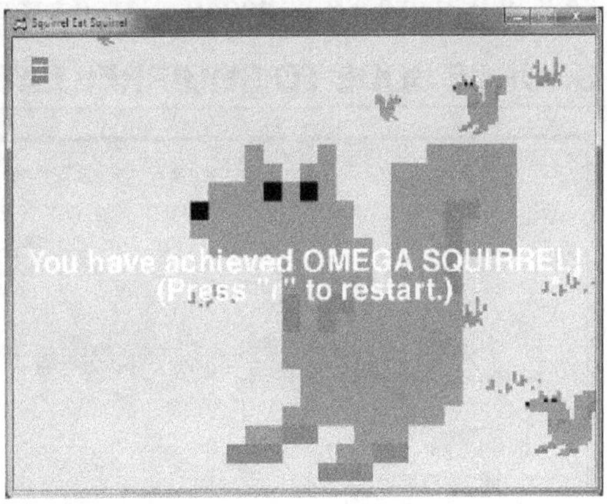

HOW TO PLAY SQUIRREL EAT SQUIRREL

Squirrel Eat Squirrel is loosely based on the game "Katamari Damacy". The player controls a small squirrel that must hop around the screen eating smaller squirrels and avoiding larger squirrels. Each time the player's squirrel eats a squirrel that is smaller than it, it grows larger. If the player's squirrel gets hit by a larger squirrel larger than it, it loses a life point. The player wins when the squirrel becomes a monstrously large squirrel called the Omega Squirrel. The player loses if their squirrel gets hit three times.

I'm not really sure where I got the idea for a video game where squirrels eat each other. I'm a little strange sometimes.

THE DESIGN OF SQUIRREL EAT SQUIRREL

There are three types of data structures in this game, which are represented as dictionary values. The types are player squirrels, enemy squirrels, and grass objects. There is only one player squirrel object at a time in the game.

Note: Technically, "object" means something specific in Object-Oriented Programming. Python does have OOP features, but they aren't covered in this book. Technically the Pygame objects such as "Rect object" or "Surface object" are objects. But I'm going to use the term "object" in this book to refer to "things that exist in the game world". But really, the player squirrel, enemy squirrels, and grass "objects" are just dictionary values.

All the objects have the following keys in their dictionary value: 'x', 'y', and 'rect'. The 'x' and 'y' key's value give the coordinates of the top left of the object in *game world coordinates*. These are different from pixel coordinates (which is what the 'rect' key's value tracks). The difference between game world and pixel coordinates will be explained when you learn about the concept of cameras.

In addition, the player squirrel, enemy squirrel, and grass objects have other keys which are explained in a large comment at the start of the source code.

SOURCE CODE TO SQUIRREL EAT SQUIRREL

```
# Squirrel Eat Squirrel (a 2D Katamari Damacy clone)
# By Al Sweigart al@inventwithpython.com
# http://inventwithpython.com/pygame
# Creative Commons BY-NC-SA 3.0 US

import random, sys, time, math, pygame
from pygame.locals import *

FPS = 30 # frames per second to update the screen
WINWIDTH = 640 # width of the program's window, in pixels
WINHEIGHT = 480 # height in pixels
HALF_WINWIDTH = int(WINWIDTH / 2)
HALF_WINHEIGHT = int(WINHEIGHT / 2)

GRASSCOLOR = (24, 255, 0)
WHITE = (255, 255, 255)
RED = (255, 0, 0)

```

```
CAMERASLACK = 90     # how far from the center the squirrel moves before moving the camera
MOVERATE = 9         # how fast the player moves
BOUNCERATE = 6       # how fast the player bounces (large is slower)
BOUNCEHEIGHT = 30    # how high the player bounces
STARTSIZE = 25       # how big the player starts off
WINSIZE = 300        # how big the player needs to be to win
INVULNTIME = 2       # how long the player is invulnerable after being hit in seconds
GAMEOVERTIME = 4     # how long the "game over" text stays on the screen in seconds
MAXHEALTH = 3        # how much health the player starts with

NUMGRASS = 80        # number of grass objects in the active area
NUMSQUIRRELS = 30    # number of squirrels in the active area
SQUIRRELMINSPEED = 3 # slowest squirrel speed
SQUIRRELMAXSPEED = 7 # fastest squirrel speed
DIRCHANGEFREQ = 2    # % chance of direction change per frame
LEFT = 'left'
RIGHT = 'right'

"""
This program has three data structures to represent the player, enemy squirrels, and grass background objects. The data structures are dictionaries with the following keys:

Keys used by all three data structures:
    'x' - the left edge coordinate of the object in the game world (not a pixel coordinate on the screen)
    'y' - the top edge coordinate of the object in the game world (not a pixel coordinate on the screen)
    'rect' - the pygame.Rect object representing where on the screen the object is located.
Player data structure keys:
    'surface' - the pygame.Surface object that stores the image of the squirrel which will be drawn to the screen.
    'facing' - either set to LEFT or RIGHT, stores which direction the player is facing.
    'size' - the width and height of the player in pixels. (The width & height are always the same.)
    'bounce' - represents at what point in a bounce the player is in. 0 means standing (no bounce), up to BOUNCERATE (the completion of the bounce)
    'health' - an integer showing how many more times the player can be hit by a larger squirrel before dying.
Enemy Squirrel data structure keys:
```

```
    'surface' - the pygame.Surface object that stores the image of the squirrel which will be drawn to the screen.
    'movex' - how many pixels per frame the squirrel moves horizontally. A negative integer is moving to the left, a positive to the right.
    'movey' - how many pixels per frame the squirrel moves vertically. A negative integer is moving up, a positive moving down.
    'width' - the width of the squirrel's image, in pixels
    'height' - the height of the squirrel's image, in pixels
    'bounce' - represents at what point in a bounce the player is in. 0 means standing (no bounce), up to BOUNCERATE (the completion of the bounce)
    'bouncerate' - how quickly the squirrel bounces. A lower number means a quicker bounce.
    'bounceheight' - how high (in pixels) the squirrel bounces
Grass data structure keys:
    'grassImage' - an integer that refers to the index of the pygame.Surface object in GRASSIMAGES used for this grass object
"""

def main():
    global FPSCLOCK, DISPLAYSURF, BASICFONT, L_SQUIR_IMG, R_SQUIR_IMG, GRASSIMAGES

    pygame.init()
    FPSCLOCK = pygame.time.Clock()
    pygame.display.set_icon(pygame.image.load('gameicon.png'))
    DISPLAYSURF = pygame.display.set_mode((WINWIDTH, WINHEIGHT))
    pygame.display.set_caption('Squirrel Eat Squirrel')
    BASICFONT = pygame.font.Font('freesansbold.ttf', 32)

    # load the image files
    L_SQUIR_IMG = pygame.image.load('squirrel.png')
    R_SQUIR_IMG = pygame.transform.flip(L_SQUIR_IMG, True, False)
    GRASSIMAGES = []
    for i in range(1, 5):
        GRASSIMAGES.append(pygame.image.load('grass%s.png' % i))

    while True:
        runGame()


def runGame():
    # set up variables for the start of a new game
    invulnerableMode = False  # if the player is invulnerable
    invulnerableStartTime = 0 # time the player became invulnerable
    gameOverMode = False      # if the player has lost
    gameOverStartTime = 0     # time the player lost
```

```
    winMode = False           # if the player has won

    # create the surfaces to hold game text
    gameOverSurf = BASICFONT.render('Game Over', True, WHITE)
    gameOverRect = gameOverSurf.get_rect()
    gameOverRect.center = (HALF_WINWIDTH, HALF_WINHEIGHT)

    winSurf = BASICFONT.render('You have achieved OMEGA SQUIRREL!', True, WHITE)
    winRect = winSurf.get_rect()
    winRect.center = (HALF_WINWIDTH, HALF_WINHEIGHT)

    winSurf2 = BASICFONT.render('(Press "r" to restart.)', True, WHITE)
    winRect2 = winSurf2.get_rect()
    winRect2.center = (HALF_WINWIDTH, HALF_WINHEIGHT + 30)

    # camerax and cameray are where the middle of the camera view is
    camerax = 0
    cameray = 0

    grassObjs = []    # stores all the grass objects in the game
    squirrelObjs = [] # stores all the non-player squirrel objects
    # stores the player object:
    playerObj = {'surface': pygame.transform.scale(L_SQUIR_IMG, (STARTSIZE, STARTSIZE)),
                 'facing': LEFT,
                 'size': STARTSIZE,
                 'x': HALF_WINWIDTH,
                 'y': HALF_WINHEIGHT,
                 'bounce':0,
                 'health': MAXHEALTH}

    moveLeft  = False
    moveRight = False
    moveUp    = False
    moveDown  = False

    # start off with some random grass images on the screen
    for i in range(10):
        grassObjs.append(makeNewGrass(camerax, cameray))
        grassObjs[i]['x'] = random.randint(0, WINWIDTH)
        grassObjs[i]['y'] = random.randint(0, WINHEIGHT)

    while True: # main game loop
        # Check if we should turn off invulnerability
```

```
        if invulnerableMode and time.time() - invulnerableStartTime > INVULNTIME:
            invulnerableMode = False

        # move all the squirrels
        for sObj in squirrelObjs:
            # move the squirrel, and adjust for their bounce
            sObj['x'] += sObj['movex']
            sObj['y'] += sObj['movey']
            sObj['bounce'] += 1
            if sObj['bounce'] > sObj['bouncerate']:
                sObj['bounce'] = 0 # reset bounce amount

            # random chance they change direction
            if random.randint(0, 99) < DIRCHANGEFREQ:
                sObj['movex'] = getRandomVelocity()
                sObj['movey'] = getRandomVelocity()
                if sObj['movex'] > 0: # faces right
                    sObj['surface'] = pygame.transform.scale(R_SQUIR_IMG, (sObj['width'], sObj['height']))
                else: # faces left
                    sObj['surface'] = pygame.transform.scale(L_SQUIR_IMG, (sObj['width'], sObj['height']))


        # go through all the objects and see if any need to be deleted.
        for i in range(len(grassObjs) - 1, -1, -1):
            if isOutsideActiveArea(camerax, cameray, grassObjs[i]):
                del grassObjs[i]
        for i in range(len(squirrelObjs) - 1, -1, -1):
            if isOutsideActiveArea(camerax, cameray, squirrelObjs[i]):
                del squirrelObjs[i]

        # add more grass & squirrels if we don't have enough.
        while len(grassObjs) < NUMGRASS:
            grassObjs.append(makeNewGrass(camerax, cameray))
        while len(squirrelObjs) < NUMSQUIRRELS:
            squirrelObjs.append(makeNewSquirrel(camerax, cameray))

        # adjust camerax and cameray if beyond the "camera slack"
        playerCenterx = playerObj['x'] + int(playerObj['size'] / 2)
        playerCentery = playerObj['y'] + int(playerObj['size'] / 2)
        if (camerax + HALF_WINWIDTH) - playerCenterx > CAMERASLACK:
            camerax = playerCenterx + CAMERASLACK - HALF_WINWIDTH
        elif playerCenterx - (camerax + HALF_WINWIDTH) > CAMERASLACK:
            camerax = playerCenterx - CAMERASLACK - HALF_WINWIDTH
```

```
        if (cameray + HALF_WINHEIGHT) - playerCentery > CAMERASLACK:
            cameray = playerCentery + CAMERASLACK - HALF_WINHEIGHT
        elif playerCentery - (cameray + HALF_WINHEIGHT) > CAMERASLACK:
            cameray = playerCentery - CAMERASLACK - HALF_WINHEIGHT

        # draw the green background
        DISPLAYSURF.fill(GRASSCOLOR)

        # draw all the grass objects on the screen
        for gObj in grassObjs:
            gRect = pygame.Rect( (gObj['x'] - camerax,
                                  gObj['y'] - cameray,
                                  gObj['width'],
                                  gObj['height']) )
            DISPLAYSURF.blit(GRASSIMAGES[gObj['grassImage']], gRect)


        # draw the other squirrels
        for sObj in squirrelObjs:
            sObj['rect'] = pygame.Rect( (sObj['x'] - camerax,
                                         sObj['y'] - cameray - 
getBounceAmount(sObj['bounce'], sObj['bouncerate'], sObj['bounceheight']),
                                         sObj['width'],
                                         sObj['height']) )
            DISPLAYSURF.blit(sObj['surface'], sObj['rect'])


        # draw the player squirrel
        flashIsOn = round(time.time(), 1) * 10 % 2 == 1
        if not gameOverMode and not (invulnerableMode and flashIsOn):
            playerObj['rect'] = pygame.Rect( (playerObj['x'] - camerax,
                                              playerObj['y'] - cameray - 
getBounceAmount(playerObj['bounce'], BOUNCERATE, BOUNCEHEIGHT),
                                              playerObj['size'],
                                              playerObj['size']) )
            DISPLAYSURF.blit(playerObj['surface'], playerObj['rect'])


        # draw the health meter
        drawHealthMeter(playerObj['health'])

        for event in pygame.event.get(): # event handling loop
            if event.type == QUIT:
                terminate()

            elif event.type == KEYDOWN:
```

```
                if event.key in (K_UP, K_w):
                    moveDown = False
                    moveUp = True
                elif event.key in (K_DOWN, K_s):
                    moveUp = False
                    moveDown = True
                elif event.key in (K_LEFT, K_a):
                    moveRight = False
                    moveLeft = True
                    if playerObj['facing'] == RIGHT: # change player image
                        playerObj['surface'] = pygame.transform.scale(L_SQUIR_IMG, (playerObj['size'], playerObj['size']))
                    playerObj['facing'] = LEFT
                elif event.key in (K_RIGHT, K_d):
                    moveLeft = False
                    moveRight = True
                    if playerObj['facing'] == LEFT: # change player image
                        playerObj['surface'] = pygame.transform.scale(R_SQUIR_IMG, (playerObj['size'], playerObj['size']))
                    playerObj['facing'] = RIGHT
                elif winMode and event.key == K_r:
                    return

            elif event.type == KEYUP:
                # stop moving the player's squirrel
                if event.key in (K_LEFT, K_a):
                    moveLeft = False
                elif event.key in (K_RIGHT, K_d):
                    moveRight = False
                elif event.key in (K_UP, K_w):
                    moveUp = False
                elif event.key in (K_DOWN, K_s):
                    moveDown = False

                elif event.key == K_ESCAPE:
                    terminate()

        if not gameOverMode:
            # actually move the player
            if moveLeft:
                playerObj['x'] -= MOVERATE
            if moveRight:
                playerObj['x'] += MOVERATE
            if moveUp:
                playerObj['y'] -= MOVERATE
            if moveDown:
```

```
                playerObj['y'] += MOVERATE

            if (moveLeft or moveRight or moveUp or moveDown) or playerObj['bounce'] != 0:
                playerObj['bounce'] += 1

            if playerObj['bounce'] > BOUNCERATE:
                playerObj['bounce'] = 0 # reset bounce amount

            # check if the player has collided with any squirrels
            for i in range(len(squirrelObjs)-1, -1, -1):
                sqObj = squirrelObjs[i]
                if 'rect' in sqObj and playerObj['rect'].colliderect(sqObj['rect']):
                    # a player/squirrel collision has occurred

                    if sqObj['width'] * sqObj['height'] <= playerObj['size']**2:
                        # player is larger and eats the squirrel
                        playerObj['size'] += int( (sqObj['width'] * sqObj['height'])**0.2 ) + 1
                        del squirrelObjs[i]

                        if playerObj['facing'] == LEFT:
                            playerObj['surface'] = pygame.transform.scale(L_SQUIR_IMG, (playerObj['size'], playerObj['size']))
                        if playerObj['facing'] == RIGHT:
                            playerObj['surface'] = pygame.transform.scale(R_SQUIR_IMG, (playerObj['size'], playerObj['size']))

                        if playerObj['size'] > WINSIZE:
                            winMode = True # turn on "win mode"

                    elif not invulnerableMode:
                        # player is smaller and takes damage
                        invulnerableMode = True
                        invulnerableStartTime = time.time()
                        playerObj['health'] -= 1
                        if playerObj['health'] == 0:
                            gameOverMode = True # turn on "game over mode"
                            gameOverStartTime = time.time()
        else:
            # game is over, show "game over" text
            DISPLAYSURF.blit(gameOverSurf, gameOverRect)
            if time.time() - gameOverStartTime > GAMEOVERTIME:
                return # end the current game
```

```

        # check if the player has won.
        if winMode:
            DISPLAYSURF.blit(winSurf, winRect)
            DISPLAYSURF.blit(winSurf2, winRect2)

        pygame.display.update()
        FPSCLOCK.tick(FPS)




def drawHealthMeter(currentHealth):
    for i in range(currentHealth): # draw red health bars
        pygame.draw.rect(DISPLAYSURF, RED,   (15, 5 + (10 * MAXHEALTH) - i * 10, 20, 10))
    for i in range(MAXHEALTH): # draw the white outlines
        pygame.draw.rect(DISPLAYSURF, WHITE, (15, 5 + (10 * MAXHEALTH) - i * 10, 20, 10), 1)


def terminate():
    pygame.quit()
    sys.exit()


def getBounceAmount(currentBounce, bounceRate, bounceHeight):
    # Returns the number of pixels to offset based on the bounce.
    # Larger bounceRate means a slower bounce.
    # Larger bounceHeight means a higher bounce.
    # currentBounce will always be less than bounceRate
    return int(math.sin( (math.pi / float(bounceRate)) * currentBounce ) * bounceHeight)

def getRandomVelocity():
    speed = random.randint(SQUIRRELMINSPEED, SQUIRRELMAXSPEED)
    if random.randint(0, 1) == 0:
        return speed
    else:
        return -speed


def getRandomOffCameraPos(camerax, cameray, objWidth, objHeight):
    # create a Rect of the camera view
    cameraRect = pygame.Rect(camerax, cameray, WINWIDTH, WINHEIGHT)
    while True:
```

```
        x = random.randint(camerax - WINWIDTH, camerax + (2 * WINWIDTH))
        y = random.randint(cameray - WINHEIGHT, cameray + (2 * WINHEIGHT))
        # create a Rect object with the random coordinates and use colliderect()
        # to make sure the right edge isn't in the camera view.
        objRect = pygame.Rect(x, y, objWidth, objHeight)
        if not objRect.colliderect(cameraRect):
            return x, y


def makeNewSquirrel(camerax, cameray):
    sq = {}
    generalSize = random.randint(5, 25)
    multiplier = random.randint(1, 3)
    sq['width']  = (generalSize + random.randint(0, 10)) * multiplier
    sq['height'] = (generalSize + random.randint(0, 10)) * multiplier
    sq['x'], sq['y'] = getRandomOffCameraPos(camerax, cameray, sq['width'], sq['height'])
    sq['movex'] = getRandomVelocity()
    sq['movey'] = getRandomVelocity()
    if sq['movex'] < 0: # squirrel is facing left
        sq['surface'] = pygame.transform.scale(L_SQUIR_IMG, (sq['width'], sq['height']))
    else: # squirrel is facing right
        sq['surface'] = pygame.transform.scale(R_SQUIR_IMG, (sq['width'], sq['height']))
    sq['bounce'] = 0
    sq['bouncerate'] = random.randint(10, 18)
    sq['bounceheight'] = random.randint(10, 50)
    return sq


def makeNewGrass(camerax, cameray):
    gr = {}
    gr['grassImage'] = random.randint(0, len(GRASSIMAGES) - 1)
    gr['width']  = GRASSIMAGES[0].get_width()
    gr['height'] = GRASSIMAGES[0].get_height()
    gr['x'], gr['y'] = getRandomOffCameraPos(camerax, cameray, gr['width'], gr['height'])
    gr['rect'] = pygame.Rect( (gr['x'], gr['y'], gr['width'], gr['height']) )
    return gr


def isOutsideActiveArea(camerax, cameray, obj):
    # Return False if camerax and cameray are more than
```

```
    # a half-window length beyond the edge of the window.
    boundsLeftEdge = camerax - WINWIDTH
    boundsTopEdge = cameray - WINHEIGHT
    boundsRect = pygame.Rect(boundsLeftEdge, boundsTopEdge, WINWIDTH * 3, WINHEIGHT * 3)
    objRect = pygame.Rect(obj['x'], obj['y'], obj['width'], obj['height'])
    return not boundsRect.colliderect(objRect)


if __name__ == '__main__':
    main()
```

THE USUAL SETUP CODE

```
# Squirrel Eat Squirrel (a 2D Katamari Damacy clone)
# By Al Sweigart al@inventwithpython.com
# http://inventwithpython.com/pygame
# Creative Commons BY-NC-SA 3.0 US

import random, sys, time, math, pygame
from pygame.locals import *

FPS = 30 # frames per second to update the screen
WINWIDTH = 640 # width of the program's window, in pixels
WINHEIGHT = 480 # height in pixels
HALF_WINWIDTH = int(WINWIDTH / 2)
HALF_WINHEIGHT = int(WINHEIGHT / 2)

GRASSCOLOR = (24, 255, 0)
WHITE = (255, 255, 255)
RED = (255, 0, 0)
```

The start of the program assigns several constant variables. This program frequently makes use of the half length of the width and height of the window so much that the HALF_WINWIDTH and HALF_WINHEIGHT variables store these numbers.

```
CAMERASLACK = 90     # how far from the center the squirrel moves before moving the camera
```

The "camera slack" is described later. Basically, it means that the camera will begin following the player squirrel when it moves 90 pixels away from the center of the window.

```
MOVERATE = 9         # how fast the player moves
BOUNCERATE = 6       # how fast the player bounces (large is slower)
```

```
BOUNCEHEIGHT = 30    # how high the player bounces
STARTSIZE = 25       # how big the player starts off
WINSIZE = 300        # how big the player needs to be to win
INVULNTIME = 2       # how long the player is invulnerable after being hit in seconds
GAMEOVERTIME = 4     # how long the "game over" text stays on the screen in seconds
MAXHEALTH = 3        # how much health the player starts with
NUMGRASS = 80        # number of grass objects in the active area
NUMSQUIRRELS = 30    # number of squirrels in the active area
SQUIRRELMINSPEED = 3 # slowest squirrel speed
SQUIRRELMAXSPEED = 7 # fastest squirrel speed
DIRCHANGEFREQ = 2    # % chance of direction change per frame
LEFT = 'left'
RIGHT = 'right'
```

The comments next to these constants explains what the constant variable is used for.

DESCRIBING THE DATA STRUCTURES

```
"""
This program has three data structures to represent the player, enemy squirrels, and grass background objects. The data structures are dictionaries with the following keys:
Keys used by all three data structures:
    'x' - the left edge coordinate of the object in the game world (not a pixel coordinate on the screen)
    'y' - the top edge coordinate of the object in the game world (not a pixel coordinate on the screen)
    'rect' - the pygame.Rect object representing where on the screen the object is located.
Player data structure keys:
    'surface' - the pygame.Surface object that stores the image of the squirrel which will be drawn to the screen.
    'facing' - either set to LEFT or RIGHT, stores which direction the player is facing.
    'size' - the width and height of the player in pixels. (The width & height are always the same.)
    'bounce' - represents at what point in a bounce the player is in. 0 means standing (no bounce), up to BOUNCERATE (the completion of the bounce)
    'health' - an integer showing how many more times the player can be hit by a larger squirrel before dying.
Enemy Squirrel data structure keys:
```

```
51.     'surface' - the pygame.Surface object that stores the image of the squirrel which will be drawn to the screen.
52.     'movex' - how many pixels per frame the squirrel moves horizontally. A negative integer is moving to the left, a positive to the right.
53.     'movey' - how many pixels per frame the squirrel moves vertically. A negative integer is moving up, a positive moving down.
54.     'width' - the width of the squirrel's image, in pixels
55.     'height' - the height of the squirrel's image, in pixels
56.     'bounce' - represents at what point in a bounce the player is in. 0 means standing (no bounce), up to BOUNCERATE (the completion of the bounce)
57.     'bouncerate' - how quickly the squirrel bounces. A lower number means a quicker bounce.
58.     'bounceheight' - how high (in pixels) the squirrel bounces
59. Grass data structure keys:
60.     'grassImage' - an integer that refers to the index of the pygame.Surface object in GRASSIMAGES used for this grass object
61. """
```

The comments from lines 37 to 61 are in one large, multi-line string. They describe the keys in the player squirrel, enemy squirrel, and grass objects. In Python, a multi-line string value by itself works as a multi-line comment.

THE MAIN() FUNCTION

```
63. def main():
64.     global FPSCLOCK, DISPLAYSURF, BASICFONT, L_SQUIR_IMG, R_SQUIR_IMG, GRASSIMAGES
65.
66.     pygame.init()
67.     FPSCLOCK = pygame.time.Clock()
68.     pygame.display.set_icon(pygame.image.load('gameicon.png'))
69.     DISPLAYSURF = pygame.display.set_mode((WINWIDTH, WINHEIGHT))
70.     pygame.display.set_caption('Squirrel Eat Squirrel')
71.     BASICFONT = pygame.font.Font('freesansbold.ttf', 32)
```

The first several lines of the main() function are the same setup code that we've seen in our previous game programs. The pygame.display.set_icon() is a Pygame function that sets the icon in the window's title bar (just like pygame.display.set_caption() sets the caption text in the title bar). The single argument to pygame.display.set_icon() is a Surface object of a small image. The ideal image size is 32 x 32 pixels, although you can use other sized images. The image will just be compressed into a smaller size to be used as the window's icon.

THE PYGAME.TRANSFORM.FLIP() FUNCTION

```
73.     # load the image files
74.     L_SQUIR_IMG = pygame.image.load('squirrel.png')
75.     R_SQUIR_IMG = pygame.transform.flip(L_SQUIR_IMG, True, False)
76.     GRASSIMAGES = []
77.     for i in range(1, 5):
78.         GRASSIMAGES.append(pygame.image.load('grass%s.png' % i))
```

The image for the player and enemy squirrels is loaded from *squirrel.png* on line 74. Make sure that this PNG file is in the same folder as *squirrel.py*, otherwise you will get the error pygame.error: Couldn't open squirrel.png.

The image in *squirrel.png* is of a squirrel facing to the left. We also need a Surface object that contains a picture of the squirrel facing to the right. Instead of creating a second PNG image file, we can call the pygame.transform.flip() function. This function has three parameters: the Surface object with the image to flip, a Boolean value to do a horizontal flip, and a Boolean value to do a vertical flip. By passing True for the second parameter and False for the third parameter, the Surface object that returns has the image of the squirrel facing to the right. The original Surface object in L_SQUIR_IMG that we passed in is unchanged.

Here are examples of images being horizontally and vertically flipped:

Original | Horizontal Flip | Vertical Flip | Horizontal and Vertical Flip

```
    while True:
        runGame()
```

After the setup in main() is complete, the game begins with runGame() being called.

A MORE DETAILED GAME STATE THAN USUAL

```
def runGame():
    # set up variables for the start of a new game
```

```
    invulnerableMode = False  # if the player is invulnerable
    invulnerableStartTime = 0 # time the player became invulnerable
    gameOverMode = False      # if the player has lost
    gameOverStartTime = 0     # time the player lost
    winMode = False           # if the player has won
```

The Squirrel Eat Squirrel game has quite a few variables that track the game state. These variables will be explained in more detail later when they are used in the code.

THE USUAL TEXT CREATION CODE

```
    # create the surfaces to hold game text
    gameOverSurf = BASICFONT.render('Game Over', True, WHITE)
    gameOverRect = gameOverSurf.get_rect()
    gameOverRect.center = (HALF_WINWIDTH, HALF_WINHEIGHT)

    winSurf = BASICFONT.render('You have achieved OMEGA SQUIRREL!', True,
WHITE)
    winRect = winSurf.get_rect()
    winRect.center = (HALF_WINWIDTH, HALF_WINHEIGHT)

    winSurf2 = BASICFONT.render('(Press "r" to restart.)', True, WHITE)
    winRect2 = winSurf2.get_rect()
    winRect2.center = (HALF_WINWIDTH, HALF_WINHEIGHT + 30)
```

These variables contain Surface objects with the "Game Over", "You have achieved OMEGA SQUIRREL!", and "(Press "r" to restart.)" text that appears on the screen after the game ends (with either the player losing or winning).

CAMERAS

```
    # camerax and cameray are where the middle of the camera view is
    camerax = 0
    cameray = 0
```

The camerax and cameray variables track the game coordinates of the "camera". Imagine the game world as an infinite 2D space. This could, of course, never fit on any screen. We can only draw a portion of the infinite 2D space on the screen. We call the area of this portion a **camera**, because it is as though our screen is just the area of the game world in front what a camera would see. Here's a picture of the game world (an infinite green field) and the area that the camera can view:

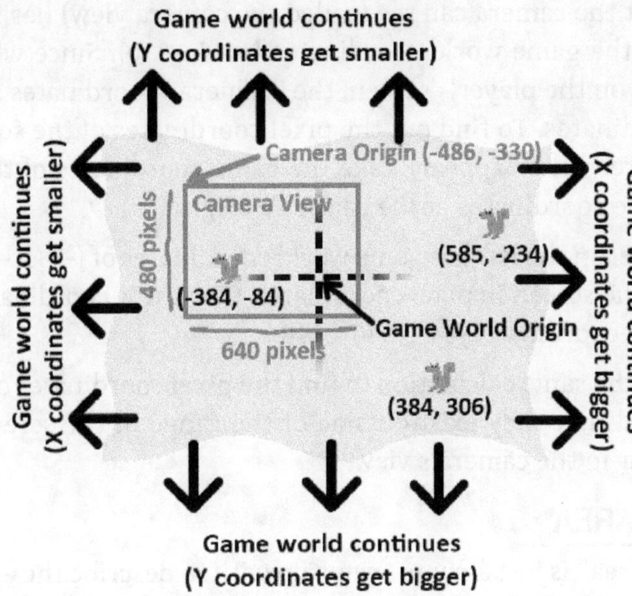

As you can see, the game world XY coordinates keep getting bigger and smaller forever. The game world origin is where the (0, 0) game world coordinates are. You can see that the three squirrels are located (in game world coordinates) at (-384, -84), (384, 306), and (585, -234).

But we can only display 640 x 480 pixel area on the screen (though this can change if we pass different numbers to the pygame.display.set_mode() function), so we need to track where the camera's origin is located in game world coordinates. In the picture above, the camera is placed at (-486, -330) in game world coordinates.

The picture below shows the same field and squirrels, except everything is given in camera coordinates:

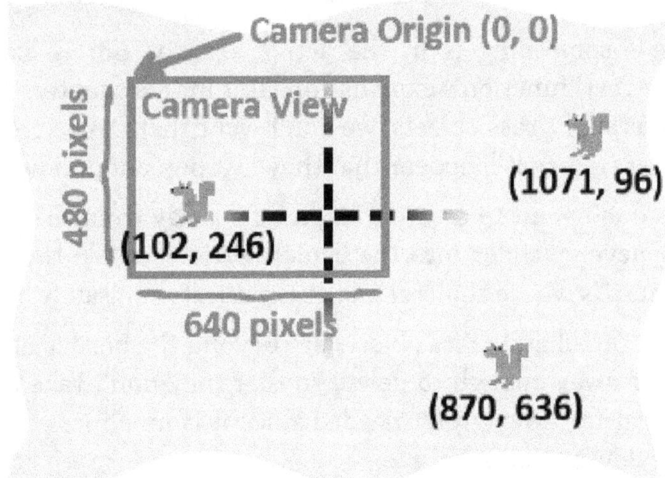

The area that the camera can see (called the camera view) has it's center (that is, its origin) at the game world coordinates (-486, -330). Since what the camera sees is displayed on the player's screen, the "camera" coordinates are the same as the "pixel" coordinates. To find out the pixel coordinates of the squirrels (that is, where on the screen they appear), take the game coordinates of the squirrel and subtract the game coordinates of the camera's origin.

So the squirrel on the left has game world coordinates of (-384, -84) but appears at (102, 246) on the screen in pixel coordinates. (For the X coordinate, -384 - -486 = 102 and for the Y coordinate, -84 - -330 = 246.)

When we do the same calculation to find the pixel coordinates of the other two squirrels, we find that they exist outside of the range of the screen. This is why they don't appear in the camera's view.

THE "ACTIVE AREA"

The "active area" is just a name I came up with to describe the area of the game world that the camera views plus an area around it the size of the camera area:

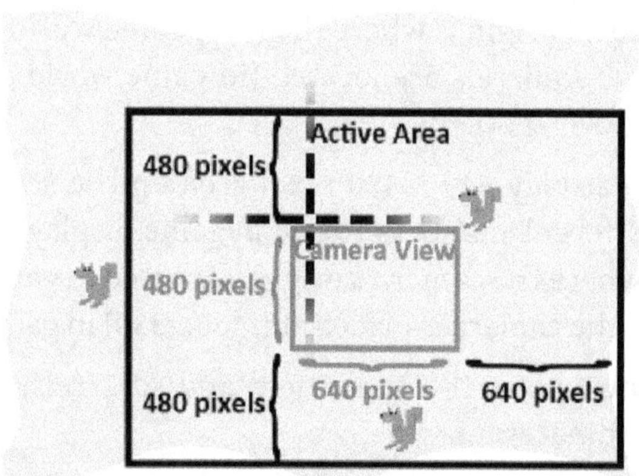

Calculating if something is in the active area or not is explained in the isOutsideActiveArea() function's explanation later in this chapter. When we create new enemy squirrel or grass objects, we don't want them to be created inside the view of the camera, since it'll appear that they just pop out of nowhere.

But we also don't want to create them too far away from the camera, because then they may never wander into the camera's view. Inside the active area but outside the camera is where squirrel and grass objects can safely be created.

Also, when squirrel and grass objects are beyond the border of the active area then they are far away enough to delete so that they don't take up memory any more. Objects that far away aren't needed since it is much less likely that they'll come back into view of the camera.

If you have ever played Super Mario World on the Super Nintendo, there is a good YouTube video explaining how Super Mario World's camera system works.

KEEPING TRACK OF THE LOCATION OF THINGS IN THE GAME WORLD

```
109.     grassObjs = []    # stores all the grass objects in the game
110.     squirrelObjs = [] # stores all the non-player squirrel objects
111.     # stores the player object:
112.     playerObj = {'surface': pygame.transform.scale(L_SQUIR_IMG,
(STARTSIZE, STARTSIZE)),
113.                  'facing': LEFT,
114.                  'size': STARTSIZE,
115.                  'x': HALF_WINWIDTH,
116.                  'y': HALF_WINHEIGHT,
117.                  'bounce':0,
118.                  'health': MAXHEALTH}
119.
120.     moveLeft  = False
121.     moveRight = False
122.     moveUp    = False
123.     moveDown  = False
```

The grassObjs variable holds a list of all the grass objects in the game. As new grass objects are created, they are added to this list. As grass objects are deleted, they are removed from this list. The same goes for the squirrelObjs variable and the enemy squirrel objects.

The playerObj variable is not a list, but just the dictionary value itself.

The move variables on lines 120 to 123 track which of arrow keys (or WASD keys) are being held down, just like in a few of the previous game programs.

STARTING OFF WITH SOME GRASS

```
    # start off with some random grass images on the screen
    for i in range(10):
        grassObjs.append(makeNewGrass(camerax, cameray))
        grassObjs[i]['x'] = random.randint(0, WINWIDTH)
        grassObjs[i]['y'] = random.randint(0, WINHEIGHT)
```

The active area should start off with a few grass objects visible on the screen. The makeNewGrass() function will create and return a grass object that is randomly located somewhere in the active area but outside the camera view. This is what we normally want when we call makeNewGrass(), but since we want to make sure the first few grass objects are on the screen, the X and Y coordinates are overwritten.

THE GAME LOOP

```
    while True: # main game loop
```

The game loop, like the game loops in the previous game programs, will do event handling, updating the game state, and drawing everything to the screen.

Checking to Disable Invulnerability

```
132.        # Check if we should turn off invulnerability
133.        if invulnerableMode and time.time() - invulnerableStartTime >
INVULNTIME:
134.            invulnerableMode = False
```

When the player gets hit by an enemy squirrel and does not die, we make the player invulnerable for a couple seconds (since the INVULNTIME constant is set to 2). During this time, the player's squirrel flashes and the won't take any damage from other squirrels. If the "invulnerability mode" time is over, line 134 will set invulnerableMode to False.

MOVING THE ENEMY SQUIRRELS

```
136.        # move all the squirrels
137.        for sObj in squirrelObjs:
138.            # move the squirrel, and adjust for their bounce
139.            sObj['x'] += sObj['movex']
140.            sObj['y'] += sObj['movey']
```

The enemy squirrels all move according to the values in their 'movex' and 'movey' keys. If these values are positive, the squirrels move right or down. If these values are negative, they move left or up. The larger the value, the farther they move on each iteration through the game loop (which means they move faster).

The for loop on line 137 will apply this moving code to each of the enemy squirrel objects in the squirrelObjs list. First, line 139 and 140 will adjust their 'x' and 'y' keys' values.

```
            sObj['bounce'] += 1
            if sObj['bounce'] > sObj['bouncerate']:
                sObj['bounce'] = 0 # reset bounce amount
```

The value in sObj['bounce'] is incremented on each iteration of the game loop for each squirrel. When this value is 0, the squirrel is at the very beginning of its bounce. When this value is equal to the value in sObj['bouncerate'] the value is at its end. (This is why a smaller sObj['bouncerate'] value makes for a faster bounce.

If sObj['bouncerate'] is 3, then it only takes three iterations through the game loop for the squirrel to do a full bounce. If sObj['bouncerate'] were 10, then it would take ten iterations.)

When sObj['bounce'] gets larger than sObj['bouncerate'], then it needs to be reset to 0. This is what lines 142 and 143 do.

```
145.         # random chance they change direction
146.         if random.randint(0, 99) < DIRCHANGEFREQ:
147.             sObj['movex'] = getRandomVelocity()
148.             sObj['movey'] = getRandomVelocity()
149.             if sObj['movex'] > 0: # faces right
150.                 sObj['surface'] = pygame.transform.scale(R_SQUIR_IMG,
(sObj['width'], sObj['height']))
151.             else: # faces left
152.                 sObj['surface'] = pygame.transform.scale(L_SQUIR_IMG,
(sObj['width'], sObj['height']))
```

There is a 2% chance on each iteration through the game loop that the squirrel will randomly change speed and direction. On line 146 the random.randint(0, 99) call randomly selects an integer out of 100 possible integers. If this number is less than DIRCHANGEFREQ (which we set to 2 on line 33) then a new value will be set for sObj['movex'] and sObj['movey'].

Because this means the squirrel might have changed direction, the Surface object in sObj['surface'] should be replaced by a new one that is properly facing left or right and scaled to the squirrel's size. This is what lines 149 to 152 determine. Note that line 150 gets a Surface object scaled from R_SQUIR_IMG and line 152 gets one scaled from L_SQUIR_IMG.

REMOVING THE FAR AWAY GRASS AND SQUIRREL OBJECTS

```
155.         # go through all the objects and see if any need to be deleted.
156.         for i in range(len(grassObjs) - 1, -1, -1):
157.             if isOutsideActiveArea(camerax, cameray, grassObjs[i]):
158.                 del grassObjs[i]
159.         for i in range(len(squirrelObjs) - 1, -1, -1):
160.             if isOutsideActiveArea(camerax, cameray, squirrelObjs[i]):
161.                 del squirrelObjs[i]
```

During each iteration of the game loop, the code will check all of the grass and enemy squirrel objects to see if they are outside the "active area". The isOutsideActiveArea() function takes the current coordinates of the camera (which are stored in camerax and cameray) and the grass/enemy squirrel object, and returns True if the object is not located in the active area.

If this is the case, this object is deleted on line 158 (for grass objects) or line 161 (for squirrel objects). This is how squirrel and grass objects get deleted when the player moves far enough away from them (or when the enemy squirrels move away far enough from the player). This ensures that there is always a number of squirrels and grass objects near the player.

WHEN DELETING ITEMS IN A LIST, ITERATE OVER THE LIST IN REVERSE

Deleting squirrel and grass objects is done with the del operator. However, notice that the for loop on line 156 and 159 pass arguments to the range() function so that the numbering starts at the index of the last item and then decrements by -1 (unlike incrementing by 1 as it normally does) until it reaches the number -1. We are iterating backwards over the list's indexes compared to how it is normally done. This is done because we are iterating over the list that we are also deleting items from.

To see why this reverse order is needed, say we had the following list value:

```
animals = ['cat', 'mouse', 'dog', 'horse']
```

So we wanted to write code to delete any instances of the string 'dog' from this list. We might think to write out code like this:

```
for i in range(len(animals)):
    if animals[i] == 'dog':
        del animals[i]
```

But if we ran this code, we would get an IndexError error that looks like this:

```
Traceback (most recent call last):
```

```
  File "<stdin>", line 2, in <module>
IndexError: list index out of range
```

To see why this error happens, let's walk through the code. First, the animals list would be set to ['cat', 'mouse', 'dog', 'horse'] and len(animals) would return 4. This means that the call to range(4) would cause the for loop to iterate with the values 0, 1, 2, and 3.

When the for loop iterates with i set to 2, the if statement's condition will be True and the del animals[i] statement will delete animals[2]. This means that afterwards the animals list will be ['cat', 'mouse', 'horse']. The indexes of all the items after 'dog' are all shifted down by one because the 'dog' value was removed.

But on the next iteration through the for loop, i is set to 3. But animals[3] is out of bounds because the valid indexes of the animals list is no longer 0 to 3 but 0 to

2. The original call to range() was for a list with 4 items in it. The list changed in length, but the for loop is set up for the original length.

However, if we iterate from the last index of the list to 0, we don't run into this problem. The following program deletes the 'dog' string from the animals list without causing an IndexError error:

```
animals = ['cat', 'mouse', 'dog', 'horse']
for i in range(len(animals) - 1, -1, -1):
    if animals[i] == 'dog':
        del animals[i]
```

The reason this code doesn't cause an error is because the for loop iterates over 3, 2, 1, and 0. On the first iteration, the code checks if animals[3] is equal to 'dog'. It isn't (animals[3] is 'horse') so the code moves on to the next iteration. Then animals[2] is checked if it equals 'dog'. It does, so animals[2] is deleted.

After animals[2] is deleted, the animals list is set to ['cat', 'mouse', 'horse']. On the next iteration, i is set to 1. There is a value at animals[1] (the 'mouse' value), so no error is caused. It doesn't matter that all the items in the list after 'dog' have shifted down by one, because since we started at the end of the list and are going towards the front, all of those items have already been checked.

Similarly, we can delete grass and squirrel objects from the grassObjs and squirrelObjs lists without error because the for loop on lines 156 and 159 iterate in reverse order.

ADDING NEW GRASS AND SQUIRREL OBJECTS

```
        # add more grass & squirrels if we don't have enough.
        while len(grassObjs) < NUMGRASS:
            grassObjs.append(makeNewGrass(camerax, cameray))
        while len(squirrelObjs) < NUMSQUIRRELS:
            squirrelObjs.append(makeNewSquirrel(camerax, cameray))
```

Remember that the NUMGRASS constant was set to 80 and the NUMSQUIRRELS constant was set to 30 at the beginning of the program? These variables are set so that we can be sure there are always plenty of grass and squirrel objects in the active area at all times. If the length of the grassObjs or squirrelObjs drops below NUMGRASS or NUMSQUIRRELS respectively, then new grass and squirrel objects are created. The makeNewGrass() and makeNewSquirrel() functions that create these objects are explained later in this chapter.

CAMERA SLACK, AND MOVING THE CAMERA VIEW

```
169.         # adjust camerax and cameray if beyond the "camera slack"
170.         playerCenterx = playerObj['x'] + int(playerObj['size'] / 2)
171.         playerCentery = playerObj['y'] + int(playerObj['size'] / 2)
172.         if (camerax + HALF_WINWIDTH) - playerCenterx > CAMERASLACK:
173.             camerax = playerCenterx + CAMERASLACK - HALF_WINWIDTH
174.         elif playerCenterx - (camerax + HALF_WINWIDTH) > CAMERASLACK:
175.             camerax = playerCenterx - CAMERASLACK - HALF_WINWIDTH
176.         if (cameray + HALF_WINHEIGHT) - playerCentery > CAMERASLACK:
177.             cameray = playerCentery + CAMERASLACK - HALF_WINHEIGHT
178.         elif playerCentery - (cameray + HALF_WINHEIGHT) > CAMERASLACK:
179.             cameray = playerCentery - CAMERASLACK - HALF_WINHEIGHT
```

The camera's position (which is stored as integers in the camerax and cameray variables) needs to be updated when the player moves over. I've called the number of pixels the player can move before the camera gets updated the "camera slack". Line 19 set the CAMERASLACK constant to 90, which our program will take to mean that the player squirrel can move 90 pixels from the center before the camera position gets updated to follow the squirrel.

In order to understand the equations used in the if statements on lines 172, 174, 176, and 178, you should note that (camerax + HALF_WINWIDTH) and (cameray + HALF_WINHEIGHT) are the XY game world coordinates currently at the center of the screen. The playerCenterx and playerCentery is set to the middle of the player's squirrel's position, also in game world coordinates.

For line 172, if the center X coordinate minus the player's center X coordinate is greater than the CAMERASLACK value, that means the player is more pixels to the right of the center of the camera than the camera slack should allow. The camerax value needs to be updated so that the player squirrel is just at the edge of the camera slack. This is why line 173 sets camerax to playerCenterx + CAMERASLACK – HALF_WINWIDTH. Note that the camerax variable is changed, not the playerObj['x'] value. We want to move the camera, not the player.

The other three if statements follow similar logic for the left, up and down sides.

DRAWING THE BACKGROUND, GRASS, SQUIRRELS, AND HEALTH METER

```
181.         # draw the green background
182.         DISPLAYSURF.fill(GRASSCOLOR)
```

Line 182 begins the code that starts drawing the contents of the display Surface object. First, line 182 draws a green color for the background. This will paint over all of the previous contents of the Surface so that we can start drawing the frame from scratch.

```
184.        # draw all the grass objects on the screen
185.        for gObj in grassObjs:
186.            gRect = pygame.Rect( (gObj['x'] - camerax,
187.                                  gObj['y'] - cameray,
188.                                  gObj['width'],
189.                                  gObj['height']) )
190.            DISPLAYSURF.blit(GRASSIMAGES[gObj['grassImage']], gRect)
```

The for loop on line 185 goes through all the grass objects in the grassObjs list and creates a Rect object from the x, y, width, and height information stored in it. This Rect object is stored in a variable named gRect. On line 190, gRect is used in the blit() method call to draw the grass image on the display Surface. Note that gObj['grassImage'] only contains an integer that is an index to GRASSIMAGES. GRASSIMAGES is a list of Surface objects that contain all the grass images. Surface objects take up much more memory than just a single integer, and all the grass objects with similar gObj['grassImage'] values look identical. So it makes sense to only have each grass image stored once in GRASSIMAGES and simply store integers in the grass objects themselves.

```
        # draw the other squirrels
        for sObj in squirrelObjs:
            sObj['rect'] = pygame.Rect( (sObj['x'] - camerax,
                                         sObj['y'] - cameray -
getBounceAmount(sObj['bounce'], sObj['bouncerate'], sObj['bounceheight']),
                                         sObj['width'],
                                         sObj['height']) )
```

```
            DISPLAYSURF.blit(sObj['surface'], sObj['rect'])
```

The for loop that draws all the enemy squirrel game objects is similar to the previous for loop, except that the Rect object it creates is saved in the 'rect' key's value of the squirrel dictionary. The reason the code does this is because we will use this Rect object later to check if the enemy squirrels have collided with the player squirrel.

Note that the top parameter for the Rect constructor is not just sObj['y'] - cameray but sObj['y'] - cameray - getBounceAmount(sObj['bounce'], sObj['bouncerate'], sObj['bounceheight']). The getBounceAmount() function will return the number of pixels that the top value should be raised.

Also, there is no common list of Surface objects of the squirrel images, like there was with grass game objects and GRASSIMAGES. Each enemy squirrel game object has its own Surface object stored in the 'surface' key. This is because the squirrel images can be scaled to different sizes.

```
202.        # draw the player squirrel
203.        flashIsOn = round(time.time(), 1) * 10 % 2 == 1
```

After drawing the grass and enemy squirrels, the code will draw the player's squirrel. However, there is one case where we would skip drawing the player's squirrel. When the player collides with a larger enemy squirrel, the player takes damage and flashes for a little bit to indicate that the player is temporarily invulnerable. This flashing effect is done by drawing the player squirrel on some iterations through the game loop but not on others.

The player squirrel will be drawn on game loop iterations for a tenth of a second, and then not drawn on the game loop iterations for a tenth of second. This repeats over and over again as long as the player is invulnerable (which, in the code, means that the invulnerableMode variable is set to True). Our code will make the flashing last for two seconds, since 2 was stored in the INVULNTIME constant variable on line 25.

To determine if the flash is on or not, line 202 grabs the current time from time.time(). Let's use the example where this function call returns 1323926893.622. This value is passed to round(), which rounds it to one digit past the decimal point (since 1 is passed as round()'s second parameter). This means round() will return the value 1323926893.6.

This value is then multiplied by 10, to become 13239268936. Once we have it as an integer, we can do the "mod two" trick first discussed in the Memory Puzzle chapter to see if it is even or odd. 13239268936 % 2 evaluates to 0, which means that flashIsOn will be set to False, since 0 == 1 is False.

In fact, time.time() will keep returning values that will end up putting False into flashIsOn until 1323926893.700, which is the next tenth second. This is why the flashIsOn variable will constantly have False for one tenth of a second, and then True for the next one tenth of a second (no matter how many iterations happen in that tenth of a second).

```
204.        if not gameOverMode and not (invulnerableMode and flashIsOn):
205.            playerObj['rect'] = pygame.Rect( (playerObj['x'] - camerax,
206.                                              playerObj['y'] - cameray -
getBounceAmount(playerObj['bounce'], BOUNCERATE, BOUNCEHEIGHT),
207.                                              playerObj['size'],
208.                                              playerObj['size']) )
209.            DISPLAYSURF.blit(playerObj['surface'], playerObj['rect'])
```

There are three things that must be True before we draw the player's squirrel. The game must currently be going on (which happens while gameOverMode is False) and the player is not invulnerable and not flashing (which happens while invulnerableMode and flashIsOn are False).

The code for drawing the player's squirrel is almost identical to the code for drawing the enemy squirrels.

```
        # draw the health meter
        drawHealthMeter(playerObj['health'])
```

The drawHealthMeter() function draws the indicator at the top left corner of the screen that tells the player how many times the player squirrel can be hit before dying. This function will be explained later in this chapter.

THE EVENT HANDLING LOOP

```
        for event in pygame.event.get(): # event handling loop
            if event.type == QUIT:
                terminate()
```

The first thing that is checked in the event handling loop is if the QUIT event has been generated. If so, then the program should be terminated.

```
            elif event.type == KEYDOWN:
                if event.key in (K_UP, K_w):
                    moveDown = False
                    moveUp = True
                elif event.key in (K_DOWN, K_s):
```

```
                    moveUp = False
                    moveDown = True
```

If the up or down arrow keys have been pressed (or their WASD equivalents), then the move variable (moveRight, moveDown, etc.) for that direction should be set to True and the move variable for the opposite direction should be set to False.

```
                elif event.key in (K_LEFT, K_a):
                    moveRight = False
                    moveLeft = True
                    if playerObj['facing'] == RIGHT: # change player image
                        playerObj['surface'] = pygame.transform.scale(L_SQUIR_IMG, (playerObj['size'], playerObj['size']))
                    playerObj['facing'] = LEFT
                elif event.key in (K_RIGHT, K_d):
                    moveLeft = False
                    moveRight = True
                    if playerObj['facing'] == LEFT: # change player image
                        playerObj['surface'] = pygame.transform.scale(R_SQUIR_IMG, (playerObj['size'], playerObj['size']))
                    playerObj['facing'] = RIGHT
```

The moveLeft and moveRight variables should also be set when the left or right arrow keys are pressed. Also, the value in playerObj['facing'] should be updated to either LEFT or RIGHT. If the player squirrel is now facing a new direction, the playerObj['surface'] value should be replaced with a correctly scaled image of the squirrel facing the new direction.

Line 229 is run if the left arrow key was pressed and checks if the player squirrel was facing right. If that was so, then a new scaled Surface object of the player squirrel image is stored in playerObj['surface']. The code in line 232's elif statement handles the opposite case.

```
238.                elif winMode and event.key == K_r:
239.                    return
```

If the player has won the game by growing large enough (in which case, winMode will be set to True) and the R key has been pressed, then runGame() should return. This will end the current game, and a new game will start the next time that runGame() gets called.

```
241.            elif event.type == KEYUP:
242.                # stop moving the player's squirrel
243.                if event.key in (K_LEFT, K_a):
244.                    moveLeft = False
```

```
245.                elif event.key in (K_RIGHT, K_d):
246.                    moveRight = False
247.                elif event.key in (K_UP, K_w):
248.                    moveUp = False
249.                elif event.key in (K_DOWN, K_s):
250.                    moveDown = False
```

If the player lets up on any of the arrow or WASD keys, then the code should set the move variable for that direction to False. This will stop the squirrel from moving in that direction any more.

```
252.                elif event.key == K_ESCAPE:
253.                    terminate()
```

If the key that was pressed was the Esc key, then terminate the program.

MOVING THE PLAYER, AND ACCOUNTING FOR BOUNCE

```
255.         if not gameOverMode:
256.             # actually move the player
257.             if moveLeft:
258.                 playerObj['x'] -= MOVERATE
259.             if moveRight:
260.                 playerObj['x'] += MOVERATE
261.             if moveUp:
262.                 playerObj['y'] -= MOVERATE
263.             if moveDown:
264.                 playerObj['y'] += MOVERATE
```

The code inside the if statement on line 255 will move the player's squirrel around only if the game is not over. (This is why pressing on the arrow keys after the player's squirrel dies will have no effect.) Depending on which of the move variables is set to True, the playerObj dictionary should have its playerObj['x'] and playerObj['y'] values changed by MOVERATE. (This is why a larger value in MOVERATE makes the squirrel move faster.)

```
266.             if (moveLeft or moveRight or moveUp or moveDown) or
playerObj['bounce'] != 0:
267.                 playerObj['bounce'] += 1
268.
269.             if playerObj['bounce'] > BOUNCERATE:
270.                 playerObj['bounce'] = 0 # reset bounce amount
```

The value in playerObj['bounce'] keeps track of at what point in bouncing the player is at. This variable stores an integer value from 0 to BOUNCERATE. Just like the bounce value for the enemy squirrels, a playerObj['bounce'] value of 0 means the player squirrel is at the start of a bounce and a value of BOUNCERATE means the player squirrel is at the end of the bounce.

The player squirrel will bounce whenever the player is moving, or if the player has stopped moving but the squirrel hasn't finished its current bounce. This condition is captured in the if statement on line 266. If any of the move variables is set to True or the current playerObj['bounce'] is not 0 (which means the player is currently in a bounce), then the variable should be incremented on line 267.

Because the playerObj['bounce'] variable should only be in the range of 0 to BOUNCERATE, if incrementing it makes it larger than BOUNCERATE, it should be reset back to 0.

COLLISION DETECTION: EAT OR BE EATEN

```
272.         # check if the player has collided with any squirrels
273.         for i in range(len(squirrelObjs)-1, -1, -1):
274.             sqObj = squirrelObjs[i]
```

The for loop on 273 will go run code on each of the enemy squirrel game objects in squirrelObjs. Notice that the parameters to range() on line 273 start at the last index of squirrelObjs and decrement. This is because the code inside this for loop may end up deleting some of these enemy squirrel game objects (if the player's squirrel ends up eating them), so it is important to iterate from the end down to the front. The reason why was explained previously in the "When Deleting Items in a List, Iterate Over the List in Reverse" section.

```
275.             if 'rect' in sqObj and
playerObj['rect'].colliderect(sqObj['rect']):
276.                 # a player/squirrel collision has occurred
277.
278.                 if sqObj['width'] * sqObj['height'] <=
playerObj['size']**2:
279.                     # player is larger and eats the squirrel
280.                     playerObj['size'] += int( (sqObj['width'] *
sqObj['height'])**0.2 ) + 1
281.                     del squirrelObjs[i]
```

If the player's squirrel is equal or larger than the size of the enemy squirrel it has collided with, then the player's squirrel will eat that squirrel and grow. The number that is added to the 'size' key in the player object (that is, the growth) is calculated based on the enemy squirrel's size on line 280. Here's a graph showing the growth from different sized squirrels. Notice that larger squirrels cause more growth:

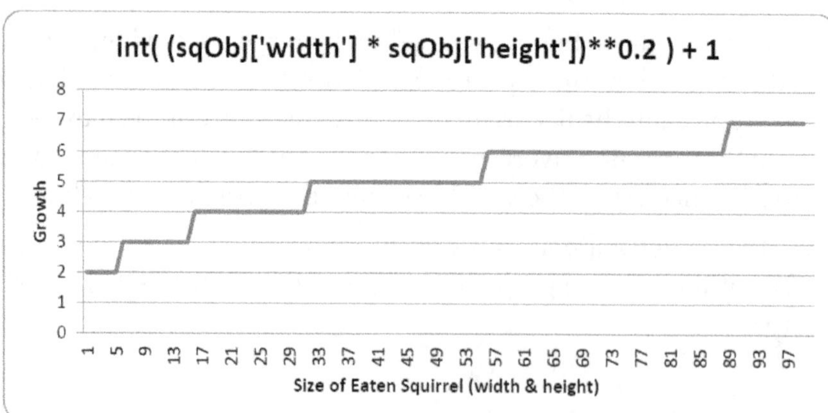

So, according to the chart, eating a squirrel that has a width and height of 45 (that is, an area of 1600 pixels) would cause the player to grow 5 pixels wider and taller.

Line 281 deletes the eaten squirrel object from the squirrelObjs list so that it will no longer appear on the screen or have its position updated.

```
283.                     if playerObj['facing'] == LEFT:
284.                         playerObj['surface'] =
pygame.transform.scale(L_SQUIR_IMG, (playerObj['size'], playerObj['size']))
285.                     if playerObj['facing'] == RIGHT:
286.                         playerObj['surface'] =
pygame.transform.scale(R_SQUIR_IMG, (playerObj['size'], playerObj['size']))
```

The player's squirrel image needs to be updated now that the squirrel is larger. This can be done by passing the original squirrel image in L_SQUIR_IMG or R_SQUIR_IMG to the pygame.transform.scale() function, which will return an enlarged version of the image. Depending on whether playerObj['facing'] is equal to LEFT or RIGHT determines which original squirrel image we pass to the function.

```
288.                     if playerObj['size'] > WINSIZE:
289.                         winMode = True # turn on "win mode"
```

The way the player wins the game is by getting the squirrel to have a size larger than the integer stored in the WINSIZE constant variable. If this is true, then the winMode variable is set to True. Code in the other parts of this function will handle displaying the congratulations text and checking for the player to press the R key to restart the game.

```
291.                 elif not invulnerableMode:
292.                     # player is smaller and takes damage
293.                     invulnerableMode = True
294.                     invulnerableStartTime = time.time()
295.                     playerObj['health'] -= 1
296.                     if playerObj['health'] == 0:
297.                         gameOverMode = True # turn on "game over mode"
298.                         gameOverStartTime = time.time()
```

If the player's area was not equal to or larger than the area of the enemy squirrel, and invulnerableMode was not set to True, then the player will take damage from colliding with this larger squirrel.

To prevent the player from being damaged several times by the same squirrel immediately, we will briefly make the player invulnerable to further squirrel attacks by setting invulnerableMode to True on line 293. Line 294 will set invulnerableStartTime to the current time (which is returned by time.time()) so that lines 133 and 134 can know when to set invulnerableMode to False.

Line 295 decrements the player's health by 1. Because there is a chance that the player's health is now at 0, line 296 checks for this and, if so, sets gameOverMode to True and gameOverStartTime to the current time.

THE GAME OVER SCREEN

```
299.         else:
300.             # game is over, show "game over" text
301.             DISPLAYSURF.blit(gameOverSurf, gameOverRect)
302.             if time.time() - gameOverStartTime > GAMEOVERTIME:
303.                 return # end the current game
```

When the player has died, the "Game Over" text (which is on the Surface object in the gameOverSurf variable) will be shown on the screen for the number of seconds that is in the GAMEOVERTIME constant. Once this amount of time has elapsed, then the runGame() function will return.

This lets the enemy squirrels continue to be animated and moving around for a few seconds after the player dies and before the next game starts. The "game over screen" in Squirrel Eat Squirrel does not wait until the player presses a key before a new game starts.

WINNING

```
305.         # check if the player has won.
306.         if winMode:
307.             DISPLAYSURF.blit(winSurf, winRect)
308.             DISPLAYSURF.blit(winSurf2, winRect2)
309.
310.         pygame.display.update()
311.         FPSCLOCK.tick(FPS)
```

The winMode variable is set to True on line 289 if the player has reached a certain size (which is dictated by the WINSIZE constant). All that happens when the player has won is that the "You have achieved OMEGA SQUIRREL!" text (which is on the Surface object stored in the winSurf variable) and the "(Press "r" to restart.)" text (which is on the Surface object stored in the winSurf2 variable) appears on the screen. The game continues until the user presses the R key, at which point the program execution will return from runGame(). The event handling code for the R key is done on lines 238 and 239.

DRAWING A GRAPHICAL HEALTH METER

```
316. def drawHealthMeter(currentHealth):
317.     for i in range(currentHealth): # draw red health bars
318.         pygame.draw.rect(DISPLAYSURF, RED,   (15, 5 + (10 * MAXHEALTH) - i * 10, 20, 10))
319.     for i in range(MAXHEALTH): # draw the white outlines
320.         pygame.draw.rect(DISPLAYSURF, WHITE, (15, 5 + (10 * MAXHEALTH) - i * 10, 20, 10), 1)
```

To draw the health meter, first the for loop on line 317 draws the filled-in red rectangle for the amount of health the player has. Then the for loop on line 319 draws an unfilled white rectangle for all of the possible health the player could have (which is the integer value stored in the MAXHEALTH constant). Note that the pygame.display.update() function is not called in drawHealthMeter().

THE SAME OLD TERMINATE() FUNCTION

```
323. def terminate():
324.     pygame.quit()
325.     sys.exit()
```

The terminate() function works the same as in the previous game programs.

THE MATHEMATICS OF THE SINE FUNCTION

```
328. def getBounceAmount(currentBounce, bounceRate, bounceHeight):
329.     # Returns the number of pixels to offset based on the bounce.
330.     # Larger bounceRate means a slower bounce.
331.     # Larger bounceHeight means a higher bounce.
332.     # currentBounce will always be less than bounceRate
333.     return int(math.sin( (math.pi / float(bounceRate)) * currentBounce ) * bounceHeight)
334.
```

There is a mathematical function (which is similar to functions in programming in that they both "return" or "evaluate" to a number based on their parameters) called **sine** (pronounced like "sign" and often abbreviated as "sin"). You may have learned about it in math class, but if you haven't it will be explained here. Python has this mathematic function as a Python function in the math module. You can pass an int or float value to math.sin(), and it will return a float value that is called the "sine value"

In the interactive shell, let's see what math.sin() returns for some values:

```
>>> import math
>>> math.sin(1)
0.8414709848078965
>>> math.sin(2)
0.9092974268256817
>>> math.sin(3)
0.1411200080598672
>>> math.sin(4)
-0.7568024953079282
>>> math.sin(5)
-0.9589242746631385
```

It seems really hard to predict what value math.sin() is going to return based on what value we pass it (which might make you wonder what math.sin() is useful for). But if we graph the sine values of the integers 1 through 10 on a graph, we would get this:

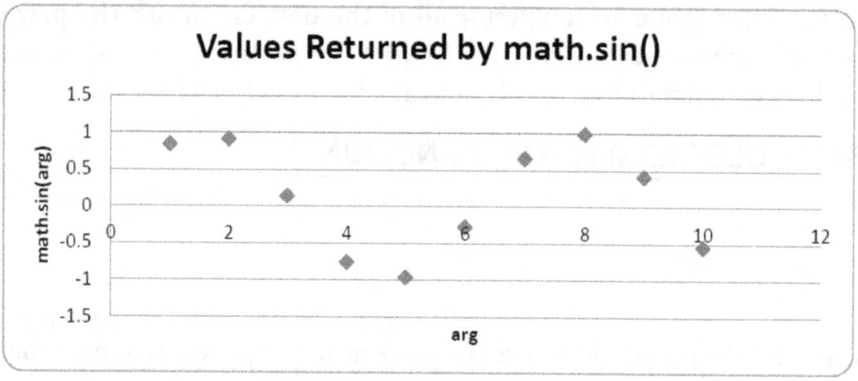

You can kind of see a wavy pattern in the values returned by math.sin(). If you figure out the sine values for more numbers besides integers (for example, 1.5 and 2.5 and so on) and then connect the dots with lines, you can see this wavy pattern more easily:

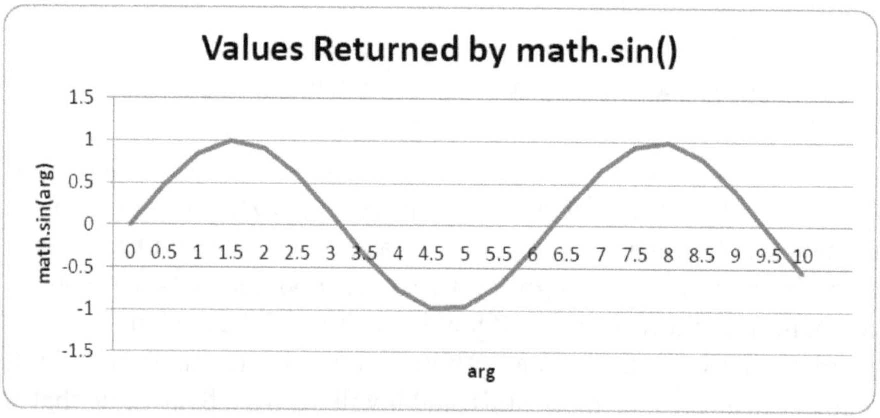

In fact, if you kept adding more and more data points to this graph, you would see that the sine wave looks like this:

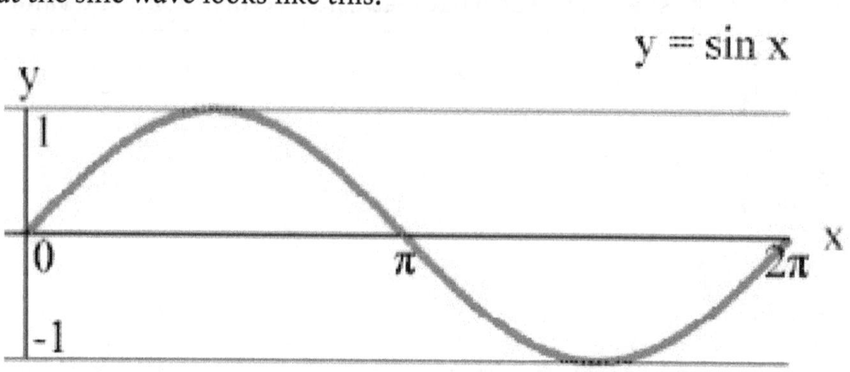

Notice that math.sin(0) returns 0, then gradually increases until math.sin(3.14 / 2) returns 1, then it begins to decrease until math.sin(3.14) returns 0. The number 3.14 is a special number in mathematics called **pi** (pronounced the same as delicious "pie"). This value is also stored in the constant variable pi in the math module (which is why line 333 uses the variable, math.pi), which is technically the float value 3.1415926535897931. Since we want a wavy-looking bounce for our squirrel, we'll only pay attention to the return values of math.sin() for the arguments 0 to 3.14:

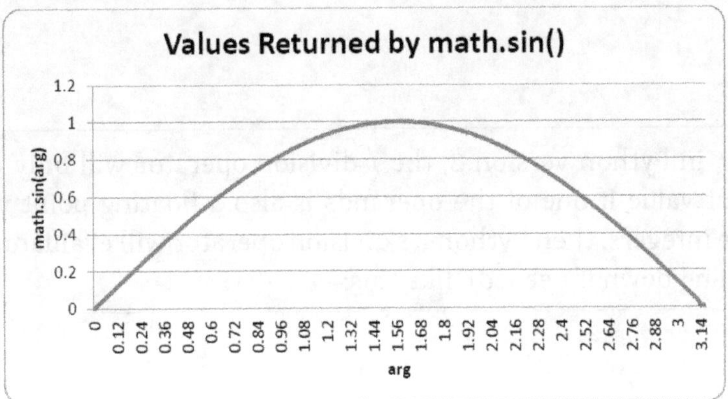

Let's take a look at the return value of getBounceAmount() and figure out what it does exactly.

```
333.      return int(math.sin( (math.pi / float(bounceRate)) * currentBounce ) *
bounceHeight)
```

Remember that on line 21 we set the BOUNCERATE constant to 6. This means that our code will only increment playerObj['bounce'] from 0 to 6 and that we want to split up the range of floating-point values from 0 to 3.14 into 6 parts, which we can do with simple division: 3.14 / 6 = 0.5235. Each of the 6 equal parts of the 3.14 length on the graph for the "sine wave bounce" is 0.5235.

You can see that when playerObj['bounce'] is at 3 (halfway between 0 and 6), the value passed to the math.sin() call is math.pi / 6 * 3, which is 1.5707 (halfway between 0 and 3.1415). Then math.sin(1.5707) will return 1.0, which is the highest part of the sine wave (and the highest part of the sine wave happens half way through the wave).

As playerObj['bounce'] gets its value incremented, the getBounceAmount() function will return values that have the same bounce shape that the sine wave has from 0 to 3.14. If you want to make the bounce higher, than increase the BOUNCEHEIGHT constant. If you want to make the bounce slower, than increase the BOUNCERATE constant.

The sine function is a concept from trigonometry mathematics.

BACKWARDS COMPATIBILITY WITH PYTHON VERSION 2

The reason we call float() to convert bounceRate to a floating point number is simply so that this program will work in Python version 2. In Python version 3, the division operator will evaluate to a floating point value even if both of the operands are integers, like this:

```
>>> # Python version 3
...
>>> 10 / 5
2.0
>>> 10 / 4
2.5
>>>
```

However, in Python version 2, the / division operator will only evaluate to a floating point value if one of the operands is also a floating point value. If both operands are integers, then Python 2's division operator will evaluate to an integer value (rounding down if needed), like this:

```
>>> # Python version 2
...
>>> 10 / 5
2
>>> 10 / 4
2
>>> 10 / 4.0
2.5
>>> 10.0 / 4
2.5
>>> 10.0 / 4.0
2.5
```

But if we always convert one of the values to a floating point value with the float() function, then the division operator will evaluate to a float value no matter which version of Python runs this source code. Making these changes so that our code works with older versions of software is called **backwards compatibility.** It is important to maintain backwards compatibility, because not everyone will always be running the latest version of software and you want to ensure that the code you write works with as many computers as possible.

You can't always make your Python 3 code backwards compatible with Python 2, but if it's possible then you should do it. Otherwise, when people with Python 2 try to run your games will get error messages and think that your program is buggy.

THE GETRANDOMVELOCITY() FUNCTION

```
def getRandomVelocity():
    speed = random.randint(SQUIRRELMINSPEED, SQUIRRELMAXSPEED)
    if random.randint(0, 1) == 0:
        return speed
    else:
        return -speed
```

The getRandomVelocity() function is used to randomly determine how fast an enemy squirrel will move. The range of this velocity is set in the SQUIRRELMINSPEED and SQUIRRELMAXSPEED constants, but on top of that, the speed is either negative (indicating the squirrel goes to the left or up) or positive (indicating the squirrel goes to the right or down). There is a fifty-fifty chance for the random speed to be positive or negative.

FINDING A PLACE TO ADD NEW SQUIRRELS AND GRASS

```
def getRandomOffCameraPos(camerax, cameray, objWidth, objHeight):
    # create a Rect of the camera view
    cameraRect = pygame.Rect(camerax, cameray, WINWIDTH, WINHEIGHT)
    while True:
        x = random.randint(camerax - WINWIDTH, camerax + (2 * WINWIDTH))
        y = random.randint(cameray - WINHEIGHT, cameray + (2 * WINHEIGHT))
        # create a Rect object with the random coordinates and use
colliderect()
        # to make sure the right edge isn't in the camera view.
        objRect = pygame.Rect(x, y, objWidth, objHeight)
        if not objRect.colliderect(cameraRect):
            return x, y
```

When a new squirrel or grass object is created in the game world, we want it to be within the active area (so that it is near the player's squirrel) but not within the view of the camera (so that it doesn't just suddenly pop into existence on the screen). To do this, we create a Rect object that represents the area of the camera (using camerax, cameray, WINWIDTH, and WINHEIGHT constants).

Next, we randomly generate numbers for the XY coordinates that would be within the active area. The active area's left and top edge are WINWIDTH and WINHEIGHT pixels to the left and up of camerax and cameray. So the active area's left and top edge are at camerax - WINWIDTH and cameray - WINHEIGHT. The active area's width and height are also three times the size of the WINWIDTH and WINHEIGHT, as you can see in this image (where WINWIDTH is set to 640 pixels and WINHEIGHT set to 480 pixels):

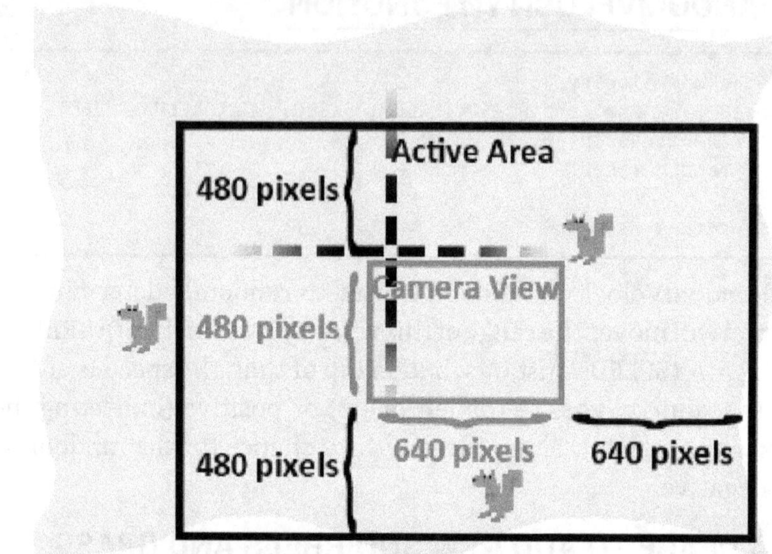

This means the right and bottom edges will be at camerax + (2 * WINWIDTH) and cameray + (2 * WINHEIGHT). Line 352 will check if the random XY coordinates would collide with the camera view's Rect object. If not, then those coordinates are returned. If so, then the while loop on line 346 will keep generating new coordinates until it finds acceptable ones.

CREATING ENEMY SQUIRREL DATA STRUCTURES

```
356. def makeNewSquirrel(camerax, cameray):
357.     sq = {}
358.     generalSize = random.randint(5, 25)
359.     multiplier = random.randint(1, 3)
360.     sq['width']  = (generalSize + random.randint(0, 10)) * multiplier
361.     sq['height'] = (generalSize + random.randint(0, 10)) * multiplier
362.     sq['x'], sq['y'] = getRandomOffCameraPos(camerax, cameray,
sq['width'], sq['height'])
363.     sq['movex'] = getRandomVelocity()
364.     sq['movey'] = getRandomVelocity()
```

Creating enemy squirrel game objects is similar to making the grass game objects. The data for each enemy squirrel is also stored in a dictionary. The width and height are set to random sizes on line 360 and 361. The generalSize variable is used so that the width and height of each squirrel aren't too different from each other. Otherwise, using completely random numbers for width and height could give us very tall and skinny squirrels or very short and wide squirrels. The width and height of the squirrel are this general size with a random number from 0 to 10 added to it (for slight variation), and then multiplied by the multiplier variable.

The original XY coordinate position of the squirrel will be a random location that the camera cannot see, to prevent the squirrels from just "popping" into existence on the screen.

The speed and direction are also randomly selected by the getRandomVelocity() function.

FLIPPING THE SQUIRREL IMAGE

```
365.     if sq['movex'] < 0: # squirrel is facing left
366.         sq['surface'] = pygame.transform.scale(L_SQUIR_IMG, (sq['width'], sq['height']))
367.     else: # squirrel is facing right
368.         sq['surface'] = pygame.transform.scale(R_SQUIR_IMG, (sq['width'], sq['height']))
369.     sq['bounce'] = 0
370.     sq['bouncerate'] = random.randint(10, 18)
371.     sq['bounceheight'] = random.randint(10, 50)
372.     return sq
```

The L_SQUIR_IMG and R_SQUIR_IMG constants contain Surface objects with left-facing and right-facing squirrel images on them. New Surface objects will be made using the pygame.transform.scale() function to match the squirrel's width and height (stored in sq['width'] and sq['height'] respectively).

After that, the three bounce-related values are randomly generated (except for sq['bounce'] which is 0 because the squirrel always starts at the beginning of the bounce) and the dictionary is returned on line 372.

CREATING GRASS DATA STRUCTURES

```
def makeNewGrass(camerax, cameray):
    gr = {}
    gr['grassImage'] = random.randint(0, len(GRASSIMAGES) - 1)
    gr['width']  = GRASSIMAGES[0].get_width()
    gr['height'] = GRASSIMAGES[0].get_height()
    gr['x'], gr['y'] = getRandomOffCameraPos(camerax, cameray, gr['width'], gr['height'])
    gr['rect'] = pygame.Rect( (gr['x'], gr['y'], gr['width'], gr['height']) )
    return gr
```

The grass game objects are dictionaries with the usual 'x', 'y', 'width', 'height', and 'rect' keys but also a 'grassImage' key which is a number from 0 to one less than the length of the GRASSIMAGES list. This number will determine what image the grass game object has. For example, if the value of the grass object's 'grassImage' key is 3, then it will use the Surface object stored at GRASSIMAGES[3] for its image.

CHECKING IF OUTSIDE THE ACTIVE AREA

```
def isOutsideActiveArea(camerax, cameray, obj):
    # Return False if camerax and cameray are more than
    # a half-window length beyond the edge of the window.
    boundsLeftEdge = camerax - WINWIDTH
    boundsTopEdge = cameray - WINHEIGHT
    boundsRect = pygame.Rect(boundsLeftEdge, boundsTopEdge, WINWIDTH * 3,
WINHEIGHT * 3)
    objRect = pygame.Rect(obj['x'], obj['y'], obj['width'], obj['height'])
    return not boundsRect.colliderect(objRect)
```

The isOutsideActiveArea() will return True if the object you pass it is outside of the "active area" that is dictated by the camerax and cameray parameters. Remember that the active area is an area around the camera view the size of the camera view (which has a width and height set by WINWIDTH and WINHEIGHT), like this:

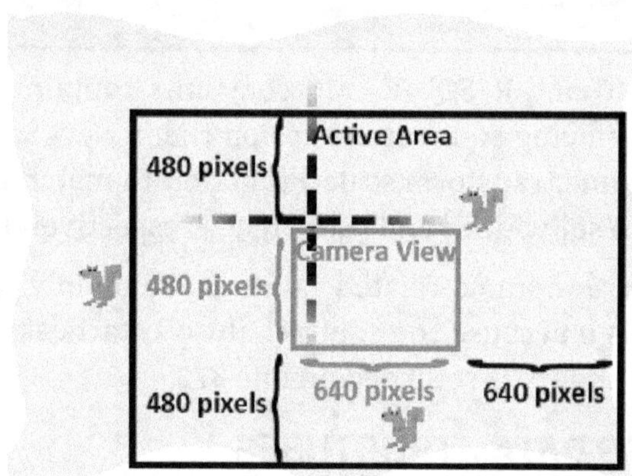

We can create a Rect object that represents the active area by passing camerax - WINWIDTH for the left edge value and cameray - WINHEIGHT for the top edge value, and then WINWIDTH * 3 and WINHEIGHT * 3 for the width and height. Once we have the active area represented as a Rect object, we can use the colliderect() method to determine if the object in the obj parameter is collides with (that is, is inside of) the active area Rect object.

Since the player squirrel, enemy squirrel and grass objects all have 'x', 'y', 'width' and 'height' keys, the isOutsideActiveArea() code can work with any type of those game objects.

```
if __name__ == '__main__':
    main()
```

Finally, after all the functions have been defined, the program will run the main() function and start the game.

SUMMARY

Squirrel Eat Squirrel was our first game to have multiple enemies moving around the board at once. The key to having several enemies was using a dictionary value with identical keys for each enemy squirrel, so that the same code could be run on each of them during an iteration through the game loop.

The concept of the camera was also introduced. Cameras weren't needed for our previous games because the entire game world fit onto one screen. However, when you make your own games that involve a player moving around a large game world, you will need code to handle converting between the game world's coordinate system and the screen's pixel coordinate system.

Finally, the mathematical sine function was introduced to give realistic squirrel hops (no matter how tall or long each hop was). You don't need to know a lot of math to do programming. In most cases, just knowing addition, multiplication, and negative numbers is fine. However, if you study mathematics, you'll often find several uses for math to make your games cooler.

9 Chapter | STAR PUSHER

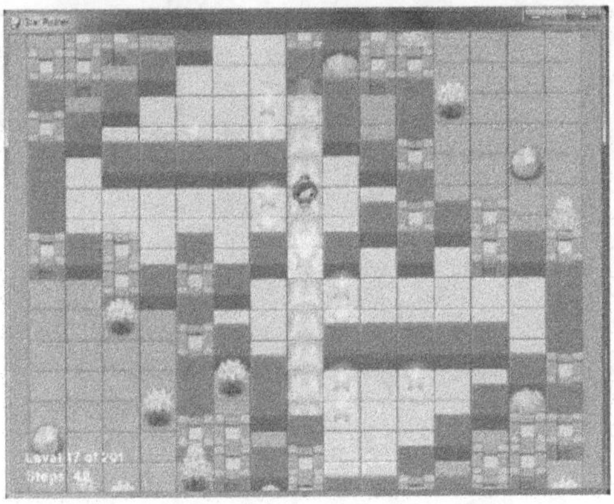

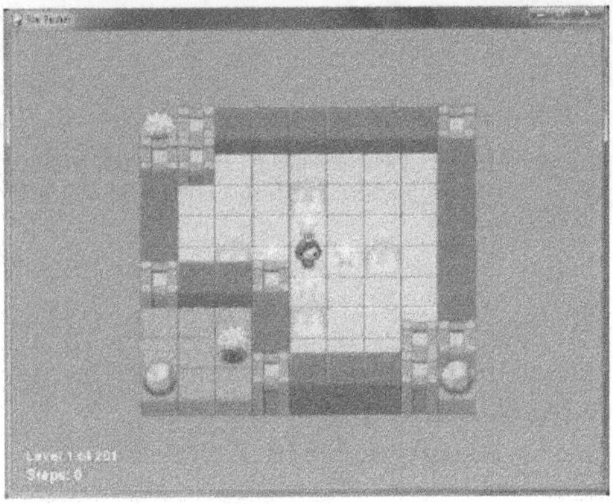

HOW TO PLAY STAR PUSHER

Star Pusher is a Sokoban or “Box Pusher” clone. The player is in a room with several stars. There are star marks on the grounds of some of the tile sprites in the room. The player must figure out how to push the stars on top of the tiles with star marks. The player cannot push a star if there is a wall or another star behind it. The player cannot pull stars, so if a star gets pushed into a corner, the player will have to restart the level. When all of the stars have been pushed onto star-marked floor tiles, the level is complete and the next level starts.

Each level is made up of a 2D grid of tile images. **Tile sprites** are images of the same size that can be placed next to each other to form more complex images. With a few floor and wall tiles, we can create levels of many interesting shapes and sizes.

The level files are not included in the source code. Instead, you can create the level files yourself. When you run the Star Pusher program, make sure that this level file is in the same folder as the *starpusher.py* file. Otherwise you will get this error message: AssertionError: Cannot find the level file: starPusherLevels.txt

SOURCE CODE TO STAR PUSHER

Just like the squirrel, grass, and enemy "objects" in the Squirrel Eat Squirrel game, when I say "map objects", "game state objects", or "level objects" in this chapter, I do not mean objects in the Object-Oriented Programming sense. These "objects" are really just dictionary values, but it is easier to refer to them as objects since they represent things in the game world.

```
# Star Pusher (a Sokoban clone)
# By Al Sweigart al@inventwithpython.com
# http://inventwithpython.com/pygame
# Creative Commons BY-NC-SA 3.0 US

import random, sys, copy, os, pygame
from pygame.locals import *

FPS = 30 # frames per second to update the screen
WINWIDTH = 800 # width of the program's window, in pixels
WINHEIGHT = 600 # height in pixels
HALF_WINWIDTH = int(WINWIDTH / 2)
HALF_WINHEIGHT = int(WINHEIGHT / 2)

# The total width and height of each tile in pixels.
TILEWIDTH = 50
TILEHEIGHT = 85
TILEFLOORHEIGHT = 45

CAM_MOVE_SPEED = 5 # how many pixels per frame the camera moves

# The percentage of outdoor tiles that have additional
# decoration on them, such as a tree or rock.
OUTSIDE_DECORATION_PCT = 20

BRIGHTBLUE = (  0, 170, 255)
WHITE      = (255, 255, 255)
BGCOLOR = BRIGHTBLUE
TEXTCOLOR = WHITE

UP = 'up'
DOWN = 'down'
LEFT = 'left'
RIGHT = 'right'
```

```


def main():
    global FPSCLOCK, DISPLAYSURF, IMAGESDICT, TILEMAPPING,
OUTSIDEDECOMAPPING, BASICFONT, PLAYERIMAGES, currentImage

    # Pygame initialization and basic set up of the global variables.
    pygame.init()
    FPSCLOCK = pygame.time.Clock()

    # Because the Surface object stored in DISPLAYSURF was returned
    # from the pygame.display.set_mode() function, this is the
    # Surface object that is drawn to the actual computer screen
    # when pygame.display.update() is called.
    DISPLAYSURF = pygame.display.set_mode((WINWIDTH, WINHEIGHT))

    pygame.display.set_caption('Star Pusher')
    BASICFONT = pygame.font.Font('freesansbold.ttf', 18)

    # A global dict value that will contain all the Pygame
    # Surface objects returned by pygame.image.load().
    IMAGESDICT = {'uncovered goal': pygame.image.load('RedSelector.png'),
                  'covered goal': pygame.image.load('Selector.png'),
                  'star': pygame.image.load('Star.png'),
                  'corner': pygame.image.load('Wall Block Tall.png'),
                  'wall': pygame.image.load('Wood Block Tall.png'),
                  'inside floor': pygame.image.load('Plain Block.png'),
                  'outside floor': pygame.image.load('Grass Block.png'),
                  'title': pygame.image.load('star_title.png'),
                  'solved': pygame.image.load('star_solved.png'),
                  'princess': pygame.image.load('princess.png'),
                  'boy': pygame.image.load('boy.png'),
                  'catgirl': pygame.image.load('catgirl.png'),
                  'horngirl': pygame.image.load('horngirl.png'),
                  'pinkgirl': pygame.image.load('pinkgirl.png'),
                  'rock': pygame.image.load('Rock.png'),
                  'short tree': pygame.image.load('Tree_Short.png'),
                  'tall tree': pygame.image.load('Tree_Tall.png'),
                  'ugly tree': pygame.image.load('Tree_Ugly.png')}

    # These dict values are global, and map the character that appears
    # in the level file to the Surface object it represents.
    TILEMAPPING = {'x': IMAGESDICT['corner'],
                   '#': IMAGESDICT['wall'],
                   'o': IMAGESDICT['inside floor'],
                   ' ': IMAGESDICT['outside floor']}
```

```
    OUTSIDEDECOMAPPING = {'1': IMAGESDICT['rock'],
                          '2': IMAGESDICT['short tree'],
                          '3': IMAGESDICT['tall tree'],
                          '4': IMAGESDICT['ugly tree']}

    # PLAYERIMAGES is a list of all possible characters the player can be.
    # currentImage is the index of the player's current player image.
    currentImage = 0
    PLAYERIMAGES = [IMAGESDICT['princess'],
                    IMAGESDICT['boy'],
                    IMAGESDICT['catgirl'],
                    IMAGESDICT['horngirl'],
                    IMAGESDICT['pinkgirl']]

    startScreen() # show the title screen until the user presses a key

    # Read in the levels from the text file. See the readLevelsFile() for
    # details on the format of this file and how to make your own levels.
    levels = readLevelsFile('starPusherLevels.txt')
    currentLevelIndex = 0

    # The main game loop. This loop runs a single level, when the user
    # finishes that level, the next/previous level is loaded.
    while True: # main game loop
        # Run the level to actually start playing the game:
        result = runLevel(levels, currentLevelIndex)

        if result in ('solved', 'next'):
            # Go to the next level.
            currentLevelIndex += 1
            if currentLevelIndex >= len(levels):
                # If there are no more levels, go back to the first one.
                currentLevelIndex = 0
        elif result == 'back':
            # Go to the previous level.
            currentLevelIndex -= 1
            if currentLevelIndex < 0:
                # If there are no previous levels, go to the last one.
                currentLevelIndex = len(levels)-1
        elif result == 'reset':
            pass # Do nothing. Loop re-calls runLevel() to reset the level


def runLevel(levels, levelNum):
    global currentImage
    levelObj = levels[levelnum]
```

```
    mapObj = decorateMap(levelObj['mapObj'], levelObj['startState']['player'])
    gameStateObj = copy.deepcopy(levelObj['startState'])
    mapNeedsRedraw = True # set to True to call drawMap()
    levelSurf = BASICFONT.render('Level %s of %s' % (levelObj['levelNum'] + 1, totalNumOfLevels), 1, TEXTCOLOR)
    levelRect = levelSurf.get_rect()
    levelRect.bottomleft = (20, WINHEIGHT - 35)
    mapWidth = len(mapObj) * TILEWIDTH
    mapHeight = (len(mapObj[0]) - 1) * (TILEHEIGHT - TILEFLOORHEIGHT) + TILEHEIGHT
    MAX_CAM_X_PAN = abs(HALF_WINHEIGHT - int(mapHeight / 2)) + TILEWIDTH
    MAX_CAM_Y_PAN = abs(HALF_WINWIDTH - int(mapWidth / 2)) + TILEHEIGHT

    levelIsComplete = False
    # Track how much the camera has moved:
    cameraOffsetX = 0
    cameraOffsetY = 0
    # Track if the keys to move the camera are being held down:
    cameraUp = False
    cameraDown = False
    cameraLeft = False
    cameraRight = False

    while True: # main game loop
        # Reset these variables:
        playerMoveTo = None
        keyPressed = False

        for event in pygame.event.get(): # event handling loop
            if event.type == QUIT:
                # Player clicked the "X" at the corner of the window.
                terminate()

            elif event.type == KEYDOWN:
                # Handle key presses
                keyPressed = True
                if event.key == K_LEFT:
                    playerMoveTo = LEFT
                elif event.key == K_RIGHT:
                    playerMoveTo = RIGHT
                elif event.key == K_UP:
                    playerMoveTo = UP
                elif event.key == K_DOWN:
                    playerMoveTo = DOWN

```

```
                # Set the camera move mode.
                elif event.key == K_a:
                    cameraLeft = True
                elif event.key == K_d:
                    cameraRight = True
                elif event.key == K_w:
                    cameraUp = True
                elif event.key == K_s:
                    cameraDown = True

                elif event.key == K_n:
                    return 'next'
                elif event.key == K_b:
                    return 'back'

                elif event.key == K_ESCAPE:
                    terminate() # Esc key quits.
                elif event.key == K_BACKSPACE:
                    return 'reset' # Reset the level.
                elif event.key == K_p:
                    # Change the player image to the next one.
                    currentImage += 1
                    if currentImage >= len(PLAYERIMAGES):
                        # After the last player image, use the first one.
                        currentImage = 0
                    mapNeedsRedraw = True

            elif event.type == KEYUP:
                # Unset the camera move mode.
                if event.key == K_a:
                    cameraLeft = False
                elif event.key == K_d:
                    cameraRight = False
                elif event.key == K_w:
                    cameraUp = False
                elif event.key == K_s:
                    cameraDown = False

        if playerMoveTo != None and not levelIsComplete:
            # If the player pushed a key to move, make the move
            # (if possible) and push any stars that are pushable.
            moved = makeMove(mapObj, gameStateObj, playerMoveTo)

            if moved:
                # increment the step counter.
                gameStateObj['stepCounter'] += 1
```

```
                mapNeedsRedraw = True

            if isLevelFinished(levelObj, gameStateObj):
                # level is solved, we should show the "Solved!" image.
                levelIsComplete = True
                keyPressed = False

        DISPLAYSURF.fill(BGCOLOR)

        if mapNeedsRedraw:
            mapSurf = drawMap(mapObj, gameStateObj, levelObj['goals'])
            mapNeedsRedraw = False

        if cameraUp and cameraOffsetY < MAX_CAM_X_PAN:
            cameraOffsetY += CAM_MOVE_SPEED
        elif cameraDown and cameraOffsetY > -MAX_CAM_X_PAN:
            cameraOffsetY -= CAM_MOVE_SPEED
        if cameraLeft and cameraOffsetX < MAX_CAM_Y_PAN:
            cameraOffsetX += CAM_MOVE_SPEED
        elif cameraRight and cameraOffsetX > -MAX_CAM_Y_PAN:
            cameraOffsetX -= CAM_MOVE_SPEED

        # Adjust mapSurf's Rect object based on the camera offset.
        mapSurfRect = mapSurf.get_rect()
        mapSurfRect.center = (HALF_WINWIDTH + cameraOffsetX, HALF_WINHEIGHT + cameraOffsetY)

        # Draw mapSurf to the DISPLAYSURF Surface object.
        DISPLAYSURF.blit(mapSurf, mapSurfRect)

        DISPLAYSURF.blit(levelSurf, levelRect)
        stepSurf = BASICFONT.render('Steps: %s' % (gameStateObj['stepCounter']), 1, TEXTCOLOR)
        stepRect = stepSurf.get_rect()
        stepRect.bottomleft = (20, WINHEIGHT - 10)
        DISPLAYSURF.blit(stepSurf, stepRect)

        if levelIsComplete:
            # is solved, show the "Solved!" image until the player
            # has pressed a key.
            solvedRect = IMAGESDICT['solved'].get_rect()
            solvedRect.center = (HALF_WINWIDTH, HALF_WINHEIGHT)
            DISPLAYSURF.blit(IMAGESDICT['solved'], solvedRect)

            if keyPressed:
                return 'solved'
```

```

        pygame.display.update() # draw DISPLAYSURF to the screen.
        FPSCLOCK.tick()


def decorateMap(mapObj, startxy):
    """Makes a copy of the given map object and modifies it.
    Here is what is done to it:
        * Walls that are corners are turned into corner pieces.
        * The outside/inside floor tile distinction is made.
        * Tree/rock decorations are randomly added to the outside tiles.

    Returns the decorated map object."""

    startx, starty = startxy # Syntactic sugar

    # Copy the map object so we don't modify the original passed
    mapObjCopy = copy.deepcopy(mapObj)

    # Remove the non-wall characters from the map data
    for x in range(len(mapObjCopy)):
        for y in range(len(mapObjCopy[0])):
            if mapObjCopy[x][y] in ('$', '.', '@', '+', '*'):
                mapObjCopy[x][y] = ' '

    # Flood fill to determine inside/outside floor tiles.
    floodFill(mapObjCopy, startx, starty, ' ', 'o')

    # Convert the adjoined walls into corner tiles.
    for x in range(len(mapObjCopy)):
        for y in range(len(mapObjCopy[0])):

            if mapObjCopy[x][y] == '#':
                if (isWall(mapObjCopy, x, y-1) and isWall(mapObjCopy, x+1, y)) or \
                   (isWall(mapObjCopy, x+1, y) and isWall(mapObjCopy, x, y+1)) or \
                   (isWall(mapObjCopy, x, y+1) and isWall(mapObjCopy, x-1, y)) or \
                   (isWall(mapObjCopy, x-1, y) and isWall(mapObjCopy, x, y-1)):
                    mapObjCopy[x][y] = 'x'

            elif mapObjCopy[x][y] == ' ' and random.randint(0, 99) < OUTSIDE_DECORATION_PCT:
```

```
                mapObjCopy[x][y] =
random.choice(list(OUTSIDEDECOMAPPING.keys()))

    return mapObjCopy


def isBlocked(mapObj, gameStateObj, x, y):
    """Returns True if the (x, y) position on the map is
    blocked by a wall or star, otherwise return False."""

    if isWall(mapObj, x, y):
        return True

    elif x < 0 or x >= len(mapObj) or y < 0 or y >= len(mapObj[x]):
        return True # x and y aren't actually on the map.

    elif (x, y) in gameStateObj['stars']:
        return True # a star is blocking

    return False


def makeMove(mapObj, gameStateObj, playerMoveTo):
    """Given a map and game state object, see if it is possible for the
    player to make the given move. If it is, then change the player's
    position (and the position of any pushed star). If not, do nothing.

    Returns True if the player moved, otherwise False."""

    # Make sure the player can move in the direction they want.
    playerx, playery = gameStateObj['player']

    # This variable is "syntactic sugar". Typing "stars" is more
    # readable than typing "gameStateObj['stars']" in our code.
    stars = gameStateObj['stars']

    # The code for handling each of the directions is so similar aside
    # from adding or subtracting 1 to the x/y coordinates. We can
    # simplify it by using the xOffset and yOffset variables.
    if playerMoveTo == UP:
        xOffset = 0
        yOffset = -1
    elif playerMoveTo == RIGHT:
        xOffset = 1
        yOffset = 0
    elif playerMoveTo == DOWN:
```

```
        xOffset = 0
        yOffset = 1
    elif playerMoveTo == LEFT:
        xOffset = -1
        yOffset = 0

    # See if the player can move in that direction.
    if isWall(mapObj, playerx + xOffset, playery + yOffset):
        return False
    else:
        if (playerx + xOffset, playery + yOffset) in stars:
            # There is a star in the way, see if the player can push it.
            if not isBlocked(mapObj, gameStateObj, playerx + (xOffset*2), playery + (yOffset*2)):
                # Move the star.
                ind = stars.index((playerx + xOffset, playery + yOffset))
                stars[ind] = (stars[ind][0] + xOffset, stars[ind][1] + yOffset)
            else:
                return False
        # Move the player upwards.
        gameStateObj['player'] = (playerx + xOffset, playery + yOffset)
        return True


def startScreen():
    """Display the start screen (which has the title and instructions)
    until the player presses a key. Returns None."""

    # Position the title image.
    titleRect = IMAGESDICT['title'].get_rect()
    topCoord = 50 # topCoord tracks where to position the top of the text
    titleRect.top = topCoord
    titleRect.centerx = HALF_WINWIDTH
    topCoord += titleRect.height

    # Unfortunately, Pygame's font & text system only shows one line at
    # a time, so we can't use strings with \n newline characters in them.
    # So we will use a list with each line in it.
    instructionText = ['Push the stars over the marks.',
                       'Arrow keys to move, WASD for camera control, P to change character.',
                       'Backspace to reset level, Esc to quit.',
                       'N for next level, B to go back a level.']

    # Start with drawing a blank color to the entire window:
```

```
    DISPLAYSURF.fill(BGCOLOR)

    # Draw the title image to the window:
    DISPLAYSURF.blit(IMAGESDICT['title'], titleRect)

    # Position and draw the text.
    for i in range(len(instructionText)):
        instSurf = BASICFONT.render(instructionText[i], 1, TEXTCOLOR)
        instRect = instSurf.get_rect()
        topCoord += 10 # 10 pixels will go in between each line of text.
        instRect.top = topCoord
        instRect.centerx = HALF_WINWIDTH
        topCoord += instRect.height # Adjust for the height of the line.
        DISPLAYSURF.blit(instSurf, instRect)

    while True: # Main loop for the start screen.
        for event in pygame.event.get():
            if event.type == QUIT:
                terminate()
            elif event.type == KEYDOWN:
                if event.key == K_ESCAPE:
                    terminate()
                return # user has pressed a key, so return.

        # Display the DISPLAYSURF contents to the actual screen.
        pygame.display.update()
        FPSCLOCK.tick()


def readLevelsFile(filename):
    assert os.path.exists(filename), 'Cannot find the level file: %s' %
(filename)
    mapFile = open(filename, 'r')
    # Each level must end with a blank line
    content = mapFile.readlines() + ['\r\n']
    mapFile.close()

    levels = [] # Will contain a list of level objects.
    levelNum = 0
    mapTextLines = [] # contains the lines for a single level's map.
    mapObj = [] # the map object made from the data in mapTextLines
    for lineNum in range(len(content)):
        # Process each line that was in the level file.
        line = content[lineNum].rstrip('\r\n')

        if ';' in line:
```

```
            # Ignore the ; lines, they're comments in the level file.
            line = line[:line.find(';')]

        if line != '':
            # This line is part of the map.
            mapTextLines.append(line)
        elif line == '' and len(mapTextLines) > 0:
            # A blank line indicates the end of a level's map in the file.
            # Convert the text in mapTextLines into a level object.

            # Find the longest row in the map.
            maxWidth = -1
            for i in range(len(mapTextLines)):
                if len(mapTextLines[i]) > maxWidth:
                    maxWidth = len(mapTextLines[i])
            # Add spaces to the ends of the shorter rows. This
            # ensures the map will be rectangular.
            for i in range(len(mapTextLines)):
                mapTextLines[i] += ' ' * (maxWidth - len(mapTextLines[i]))

            # Convert mapTextLines to a map object.
            for x in range(len(mapTextLines[0])):
                mapObj.append([])
            for y in range(len(mapTextLines)):
                for x in range(maxWidth):
                    mapObj[x].append(mapTextLines[y][x])

            # Loop through the spaces in the map and find the @, ., and $
            # characters for the starting game state.
            startx = None # The x and y for the player's starting position
            starty = None
            goals = [] # list of (x, y) tuples for each goal.
            stars = [] # list of (x, y) for each star's starting position.
            for x in range(maxWidth):
                for y in range(len(mapObj[x])):
                    if mapObj[x][y] in ('@', '+'):
                        # '@' is player, '+' is player & goal
                        startx = x
                        starty = y
                    if mapObj[x][y] in ('.', '+', '*'):
                        # '.' is goal, '*' is star & goal
                        goals.append((x, y))
                    if mapObj[x][y] in ('$', '*'):
                        # '$' is star
                        stars.append((x, y))

```

```
            # Basic level design sanity checks:
            assert startx != None and starty != None, 'Level %s (around line %s) in %s is missing a "@" or "+" to mark the start point.' % (levelNum+1, lineNum, filename)
            assert len(goals) > 0, 'Level %s (around line %s) in %s must have at least one goal.' % (levelNum+1, lineNum, filename)
            assert len(stars) >= len(goals), 'Level %s (around line %s) in %s is impossible to solve. It has %s goals but only %s stars.' % (levelNum+1, lineNum, filename, len(goals), len(stars))

            # Create level object and starting game state object.
            gameStateObj = {'player': (startx, starty),
                            'stepCounter': 0,
                            'stars': stars}
            levelObj = {'width': maxWidth,
                        'height': len(mapObj),
                        'mapObj': mapObj,
                        'goals': goals,
                        'startState': gameStateObj}

            levels.append(levelObj)

            # Reset the variables for reading the next map.
            mapTextLines = []
            mapObj = []
            gameStateObj = {}
            levelNum += 1
    return levels


def floodFill(mapObj, x, y, oldCharacter, newCharacter):
    """Changes any values matching oldCharacter on the map object to
    newCharacter at the (x, y) position, and does the same for the
    positions to the left, right, down, and up of (x, y), recursively."""

    # In this game, the flood fill algorithm creates the inside/outside
    # floor distinction. This is a "recursive" function.
    # For more info on the Flood Fill algorithm, see:
    #   http://en.wikipedia.org/wiki/Flood_fill
    if mapObj[x][y] == oldCharacter:
        mapObj[x][y] = newCharacter

    if x < len(mapObj) - 1 and mapObj[x+1][y] == oldCharacter:
        floodFill(mapObj, x+1, y, oldCharacter, newCharacter) # call right
    if x > 0 and mapObj[x-1][y] == oldCharacter:
```

```
            floodFill(mapObj, x-1, y, oldCharacter, newCharacter) # call left
    if y < len(mapObj[x]) - 1 and mapObj[x][y+1] == oldCharacter:
            floodFill(mapObj, x, y+1, oldCharacter, newCharacter) # call down
    if y > 0 and mapObj[x][y-1] == oldCharacter:
            floodFill(mapObj, x, y-1, oldCharacter, newCharacter) # call up


def drawMap(mapObj, gameStateObj, goals):
    """Draws the map to a Surface object, including the player and
    stars. This function does not call pygame.display.update(), nor
    does it draw the "Level" and "Steps" text in the corner."""

    # mapSurf will be the single Surface object that the tiles are drawn
    # on, so that it is easy to position the entire map on the DISPLAYSURF
    # Surface object. First, the width and height must be calculated.
    mapSurfWidth = len(mapObj) * TILEWIDTH
    mapSurfHeight = (len(mapObj[0]) - 1) * (TILEHEIGHT - TILEFLOORHEIGHT)
+ TILEHEIGHT
    mapSurf = pygame.Surface((mapSurfWidth, mapSurfHeight))
    mapSurf.fill(BGCOLOR) # start with a blank color on the surface.

    # Draw the tile sprites onto this surface.
    for x in range(len(mapObj)):
        for y in range(len(mapObj[x])):
            spaceRect = pygame.Rect((x * TILEWIDTH, y * (TILEHEIGHT -
TILEFLOORHEIGHT), TILEWIDTH, TILEHEIGHT))
            if mapObj[x][y] in TILEMAPPING:
                baseTile = TILEMAPPING[mapObj[x][y]]
            elif mapObj[x][y] in OUTSIDEDECOMAPPING:
                baseTile = TILEMAPPING[' ']

            # First draw the base ground/wall tile.
            mapSurf.blit(baseTile, spaceRect)

            if mapObj[x][y] in OUTSIDEDECOMAPPING:
                # Draw any tree/rock decorations that are on this tile.
                mapSurf.blit(OUTSIDEDECOMAPPING[mapObj[x][y]], spaceRect)
            elif (x, y) in gameStateObj['stars']:
                if (x, y) in goals:
                    # A goal AND star are on this space, draw goal first.
                    mapSurf.blit(IMAGESDICT['covered goal'], spaceRect)
                # Then draw the star sprite.
                mapSurf.blit(IMAGESDICT['star'], spaceRect)
            elif (x, y) in goals:
                # Draw a goal without a star on it.
                mapSurf.blit(IMAGESDICT['uncovered goal'], spaceRect)
```

```

            # Last draw the player on the board.
            if (x, y) == gameStateObj['player']:
                # Note: The value "currentImage" refers
                # to a key in "PLAYERIMAGES" which has the
                # specific player image we want to show.
                mapSurf.blit(PLAYERIMAGES[currentImage], spaceRect)

    return mapSurf


def isLevelFinished(levelObj, gameStateObj):
    """Returns True if all the goals have stars in them."""
    for goal in levelObj['goals']:
        if goal not in gameStateObj['stars']:
            # Found a space with a goal but no star on it.
            return False
    return True


def terminate():
    pygame.quit()
    sys.exit()


if __name__ == '__main__':
    main()
```

THE INITIAL SETUP

```
# Star Pusher (a Sokoban clone)
# By Al Sweigart al@inventwithpython.com
# http://inventwithpython.com/pygame
# Creative Commons BY-NC-SA 3.0 US

import random, sys, copy, os, pygame
from pygame.locals import *

FPS = 30 # frames per second to update the screen
WINWIDTH = 800 # width of the program's window, in pixels
WINHEIGHT = 600 # height in pixels
HALF_WINWIDTH = int(WINWIDTH / 2)
HALF_WINHEIGHT = int(WINHEIGHT / 2)

# The total width and height of each tile in pixels.
TILEWIDTH = 50
```

```
TILEHEIGHT = 85
TILEFLOORHEIGHT = 45

CAM_MOVE_SPEED = 5 # how many pixels per frame the camera moves

# The percentage of outdoor tiles that have additional
# decoration on them, such as a tree or rock.
OUTSIDE_DECORATION_PCT = 20

BRIGHTBLUE = (  0, 170, 255)
WHITE      = (255, 255, 255)
BGCOLOR = BRIGHTBLUE
TEXTCOLOR = WHITE

UP = 'up'
DOWN = 'down'
LEFT = 'left'
RIGHT = 'right'
```

These constants are used in various parts of the program. The TILEWIDTH and TILEHEIGHT variables show that each of the tile images are 50 pixels wide and 85 pixels tall. However, these tiles overlap with each other when drawn on the screen. (This is explained later.) The TILEFLOORHEIGHT refers to the fact that the part of the tile that represents the floor is 45 pixels tall. Here is a diagram of the plain floor image:

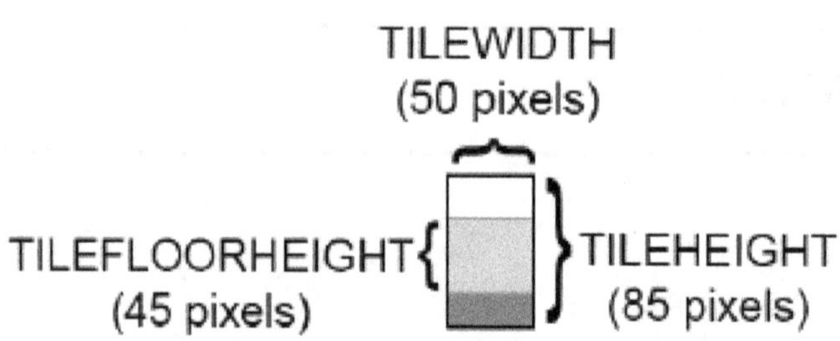

The grassy tiles outside of the level's room will sometimes have extra decorations added to them (such as trees or rocks). The OUTSIDE_DECORATION_PCT constant shows what percentage of these tiles will randomly have these decorations.

```
def main():
    global FPSCLOCK, DISPLAYSURF, IMAGESDICT, TILEMAPPING, OUTSIDEDECOMAPPING, BASICFONT, PLAYERIMAGES, currentImage

    # Pygame initialization and basic set up of the global variables.
    pygame.init()
    FPSCLOCK = pygame.time.Clock()

    # Because the Surface object stored in DISPLAYSURF was returned
```

```
    # from the pygame.display.set_mode() function, this is the
    # Surface object that is drawn to the actual computer screen
    # when pygame.display.update() is called.
    DISPLAYSURF = pygame.display.set_mode((WINWIDTH, WINHEIGHT))

    pygame.display.set_caption('Star Pusher')
    BASICFONT = pygame.font.Font('freesansbold.ttf', 18)
```

This is the usual Pygame setup that happens at the beginning of the program.

```
    # A global dict value that will contain all the Pygame
    # Surface objects returned by pygame.image.load().
    IMAGESDICT = {'uncovered goal': pygame.image.load('RedSelector.png'),
                  'covered goal': pygame.image.load('Selector.png'),
                  'star': pygame.image.load('Star.png'),
                  'corner': pygame.image.load('Wall Block Tall.png'),
                  'wall': pygame.image.load('Wood Block Tall.png'),
                  'inside floor': pygame.image.load('Plain Block.png'),
                  'outside floor': pygame.image.load('Grass Block.png'),
                  'title': pygame.image.load('star_title.png'),
                  'solved': pygame.image.load('star_solved.png'),
                  'princess': pygame.image.load('princess.png'),
                  'boy': pygame.image.load('boy.png'),
                  'catgirl': pygame.image.load('catgirl.png'),
                  'horngirl': pygame.image.load('horngirl.png'),
                  'pinkgirl': pygame.image.load('pinkgirl.png'),
                  'rock': pygame.image.load('Rock.png'),
                  'short tree': pygame.image.load('Tree_Short.png'),
                  'tall tree': pygame.image.load('Tree_Tall.png'),
                  'ugly tree': pygame.image.load('Tree_Ugly.png')}
```

The IMAGESDICT is a dictionary where all of the loaded images are stored. This makes it easier to use in other functions, since only the IMAGESDICT variable needs to be made global. If we stored each of these images in separate variables, then all 18 variables (for the 18 images used in this game) would need to be made global. A dictionary containing all of the Surface objects with the images is easier to handle.

```
    # These dict values are global, and map the character that appears
    # in the level file to the Surface object it represents.
    TILEMAPPING = {'x': IMAGESDICT['corner'],
                   '#': IMAGESDICT['wall'],
                   'o': IMAGESDICT['inside floor'],
                   ' ': IMAGESDICT['outside floor']}
```

The data structure for the map is just a 2D list of single character strings. The TILEMAPPING dictionary links the characters used in this map data structure to the images that they represent. (This will become more clear in the drawMap() function's explanation.)

```
    OUTSIDEDECOMAPPING = {'1': IMAGESDICT['rock'],
                          '2': IMAGESDICT['short tree'],
                          '3': IMAGESDICT['tall tree'],
                          '4': IMAGESDICT['ugly tree']}
```

The OUTSIDEDECOMAPPING is also a dictionary that links the characters used in the map data structure to images that were loaded. The "outside decoration" images are drawn on top of the outdoor grassy tile.

```
    # PLAYERIMAGES is a list of all possible characters the player can be.
    # currentImage is the index of the player's current player image.
    currentImage = 0
    PLAYERIMAGES = [IMAGESDICT['princess'],
                    IMAGESDICT['boy'],
                    IMAGESDICT['catgirl'],
                    IMAGESDICT['horngirl'],
                    IMAGESDICT['pinkgirl']]
```

The PLAYERIMAGES list stores the images used for the player. The currentImage variable tracks the index of the currently selected player image. For example, when currentImage is set to 0 then PLAYERIMAGES[0], which is the "princess" player image, is drawn to the screen.

```
    startScreen() # show the title screen until the user presses a key

    # Read in the levels from the text file. See the readLevelsFile() for
    # details on the format of this file and how to make your own levels.
    levels = readLevelsFile('starPusherLevels.txt')
    currentLevelIndex = 0
```

The startScreen() function will keep displaying the initial start screen (which also has the instructions for the game) until the player presses a key. When the player presses a key, the startScreen() function returns and then reads in the levels from the level file. The player starts off on the first level, which is the level object in the levels list at index 0.

```
    # The main game loop. This loop runs a single level, when the user
    # finishes that level, the next/previous level is loaded.
    while True: # main game loop
        # Run the level to actually start playing the game:
```

```
        result = runLevel(levels, currentLevelIndex)
```

The runLevel() function handles all the action for the game. It is passed a list of level objects, and the integer index of the level in that list to be played. When the player has finished playing the level, runLevel() will return one of the following strings: 'solved' (because the player has finished putting all the stars on the goals), 'next' (because the player wants to skip to the next level), 'back' (because the player wants to go back to the previous level), and 'reset' (because the player wants to start playing the current level over again, maybe because they pushed a star into a corner).

```
        if result in ('solved', 'next'):
            # Go to the next level.
            currentLevelIndex += 1
            if currentLevelIndex >= len(levels):
                # If there are no more levels, go back to the first one.
                currentLevelIndex = 0
        elif result == 'back':
            # Go to the previous level.
            currentLevelIndex -= 1
            if currentLevelIndex < 0:
                # If there are no previous levels, go to the last one.
                currentLevelIndex = len(levels)-1
```

If runLevel() has returned the strings 'solved' or 'next', then we need to increment levelNum by 1. If this increments levelNum beyond the number of levels there are, then levelNum is set back at 0.

The opposite is done if 'back' is returned, then levelNum is decremented by 1. If this makes it go below 0, then it is set to the last level (which is len(levels)-1).

```
119.        elif result == 'reset':
120.            pass # Do nothing. Loop re-calls runLevel() to reset the level
```

If the return value was 'reset', then the code does nothing. The pass statement does nothing (like a comment), but is needed because the Python interpreter expects an indented line of code after an elif statement.

We could remove lines 119 and 120 from the source code entirely, and the program will still work just the same. The reason we include it here is for program readability, so that if we make changes to the code later, we won't forget that runLevel() can also return the string 'reset'.

```
def runLevel(levels, levelNum):
    global currentImage
    levelObj = levels[levelnum]
    mapObj = decorateMap(levelObj['mapObj'], levelObj['startState']['player'])
    gameStateObj = copy.deepcopy(levelObj['startState'])
```

The levels list contains all the level objects that were loaded from the level file. The level object for the current level (which is what levelNum is set to) is stored in the levelObj variable. A map object (which makes a distinction between indoor and outdoor tiles, and decorates the outdoor tiles with trees and rocks) is returned from the decorateMap() function. And to track the state of the game while the player plays this level, a copy of the game state object that is stored in levelObj is made using the copy.deepcopy() function.

The game state object copy is made because the game state object stored in levelObj['startState'] represents the game state at the very beginning of the level, and we do not want to modify this. Otherwise, if the player restarts the level, the original game state for that level will be lost.

The copy.deepcopy() function is used because the game state object is a dictionary of that has tuples. But technically, the dictionary contains references to tuples. Using an assignment statement to make a copy of the dictionary will make a copy of the references but not the values they refer to, so that both the copy and the original dictionary still refer to the same tuples.

The copy.deepcopy() function solves this problem by making copies of the actual tuples in the dictionary. This way we can guarantee that changing one dictionary will not affect the other dictionary.

```
    mapNeedsRedraw = True # set to True to call drawMap()
    levelSurf = BASICFONT.render('Level %s of %s' % (levelObj['levelNum'] + 1, totalNumOfLevels), 1, TEXTCOLOR)
    levelRect = levelSurf.get_rect()
    levelRect.bottomleft = (20, WINHEIGHT - 35)
    mapWidth = len(mapObj) * TILEWIDTH
    mapHeight = (len(mapObj[0]) - 1) * (TILEHEIGHT - TILEFLOORHEIGHT) + TILEHEIGHT
    MAX_CAM_X_PAN = abs(HALF_WINHEIGHT - int(mapHeight / 2)) + TILEWIDTH
    MAX_CAM_Y_PAN = abs(HALF_WINWIDTH - int(mapWidth / 2)) + TILEHEIGHT

    levelIsComplete = False
    # Track how much the camera has moved:
    cameraOffsetX = 0
```

```
    cameraOffsetY = 0
    # Track if the keys to move the camera are being held down:
    cameraUp = False
    cameraDown = False
    cameraLeft = False
    cameraRight = False
```

More variables are set at the start of playing a level. The mapWidth and mapHeight variables are the size of the maps in pixels. The expression for calculating mapHeight is a bit complicated since the tiles overlap each other. Only the bottom row of tiles is the full height (which accounts for the + TILEHEIGHT part of the expression), all of the other rows of tiles (which number as (len(mapObj[0]) - 1)) are slightly overlapped. This means that they are effectively each only (TILEHEIGHT - TILEFLOORHEIGHT) pixels tall.

The camera in Star Pusher can be moved independently of the player moving around the map. This is why the camera needs its own set of "moving" variables: cameraUp, cameraDown, cameraLeft, and cameraRight. The cameraOffsetX and cameraOffsetY variables track the position of the camera.

```
    while True: # main game loop
        # Reset these variables:
        playerMoveTo = None
        keyPressed = False

        for event in pygame.event.get(): # event handling loop
            if event.type == QUIT:
                # Player clicked the "X" at the corner of the window.
                terminate()

```

The playerMoveTo variable will be set to the direction constant that the player intends to move the player character on the map. The keyPressed variable tracks if any key has been pressed during this iteration of the game loop. This variable is checked later when the player has solved the level.

```
            elif event.type == KEYDOWN:
                # Handle key presses
                keyPressed = True
                if event.key == K_LEFT:
                    playerMoveTo = LEFT
                elif event.key == K_RIGHT:
                    playerMoveTo = RIGHT
                elif event.key == K_UP:
```

```
                playerMoveTo = UP
            elif event.key == K_DOWN:
                playerMoveTo = DOWN

            # Set the camera move mode.
            elif event.key == K_a:
                cameraLeft = True
            elif event.key == K_d:
                cameraRight = True
            elif event.key == K_w:
                cameraUp = True
            elif event.key == K_s:
                cameraDown = True

            elif event.key == K_n:
                return 'next'
            elif event.key == K_b:
                return 'back'

            elif event.key == K_ESCAPE:
                terminate() # Esc key quits.
            elif event.key == K_BACKSPACE:
                return 'reset' # Reset the level.
            elif event.key == K_p:
                # Change the player image to the next one.
                currentImage += 1
                if currentImage >= len(PLAYERIMAGES):
                    # After the last player image, use the first one.
                    currentImage = 0
                mapNeedsRedraw = True

        elif event.type == KEYUP:
            # Unset the camera move mode.
            if event.key == K_a:
                cameraLeft = False
            elif event.key == K_d:
                cameraRight = False
            elif event.key == K_w:
                cameraUp = False
            elif event.key == K_s:
                cameraDown = False
```

This code handles what to do when the various keys are pressed.

```
    if playerMoveTo != None and not levelIsComplete:
        # If the player pushed a key to move, make the move
```

```
209.             # (if possible) and push any stars that are pushable.
210.             moved = makeMove(mapObj, gameStateObj, playerMoveTo)
211.
212.             if moved:
213.                 # increment the step counter.
214.                 gameStateObj['stepCounter'] += 1
215.                 mapNeedsRedraw = True
216.
217.             if isLevelFinished(levelObj, gameStateObj):
218.                 # level is solved, we should show the "Solved!" image.
219.                 levelIsComplete = True
220.                 keyPressed = False
```

If the playerMoveTo variable is no longer set to None, then we know the player intended to move. The call to makeMove() handles changing the XY coordinates of the player's position in the gameStateObj, as well as pushing any stars. The return value of makeMove() is stored in moved. If this value is True, then the player character was moved in that direction. If the value was False, then the player must have tried to move into a tile that was a wall, or push a star that had something behind it. In this case, the player can't move and nothing on the map changes.

```
222.         DISPLAYSURF.fill(BGCOLOR)
223.
224.         if mapNeedsRedraw:
225.             mapSurf = drawMap(mapObj, gameStateObj, levelObj['goals'])
226.             mapNeedsRedraw = False
```

The map does not need to be redrawn on each iteration through the game loop. In fact, this game program is complicated enough that doing so would cause a slight (but noticeable) slowdown in the game. And the map really only needs to be redrawn when something has changed (such as the player moving or a star being pushed). So the Surface object in the mapSurf variable is only updated with a call to the drawMap() function when the mapNeedsRedraw variable is set to True.

After the map has been drawn on line 225, the mapNeedsRedraw variable is set to False. If you want to see how the program slows down by drawing on each iteration through the game loop, comment out line 226 and rerun the program. You will notice that moving the camera is significantly slower.

```
228.         if cameraUp and cameraOffsetY < MAX_CAM_X_PAN:
229.             cameraOffsetY += CAM_MOVE_SPEED
230.         elif cameraDown and cameraOffsetY > -MAX_CAM_X_PAN:
```

```
231.            cameraOffsetY -= CAM_MOVE_SPEED
232.        if cameraLeft and cameraOffsetX < MAX_CAM_Y_PAN:
233.            cameraOffsetX += CAM_MOVE_SPEED
234.        elif cameraRight and cameraOffsetX > -MAX_CAM_Y_PAN:
235.            cameraOffsetX -= CAM_MOVE_SPEED
```

If the camera movement variables are set to True and the camera has not gone past (i.e. panned passed) the boundaries set by the MAX_CAM_X_PAN and MAX_CAM_Y_PAN, then the camera location (stored in cameraOffsetX and cameraOffsetY) should move over by CAM_MOVE_SPEED pixels.

Note that there is an if and elif statement on lines 228 and 230 for moving the camera up and down, and then a separate if and elif statement on lines 232 and 234. This way, the user can move the camera both vertically and horizontally at the same time. This wouldn't be possible if line 232 were an elif statement.

```
237.        # Adjust mapSurf's Rect object based on the camera offset.
238.        mapSurfRect = mapSurf.get_rect()
239.        mapSurfRect.center = (HALF_WINWIDTH + cameraOffsetX,
HALF_WINHEIGHT + cameraOffsetY)
240.
241.        # Draw mapSurf to the DISPLAYSURF Surface object.
242.        DISPLAYSURF.blit(mapSurf, mapSurfRect)
243.
244.        DISPLAYSURF.blit(levelSurf, levelRect)
245.        stepSurf = BASICFONT.render('Steps: %s' %
(gameStateObj['stepCounter']), 1, TEXTCOLOR)
246.        stepRect = stepSurf.get_rect()
247.        stepRect.bottomleft = (20, WINHEIGHT - 10)
248.        DISPLAYSURF.blit(stepSurf, stepRect)
249.
250.        if levelIsComplete:
251.            # is solved, show the "Solved!" image until the player
252.            # has pressed a key.
253.            solvedRect = IMAGESDICT['solved'].get_rect()
254.            solvedRect.center = (HALF_WINWIDTH, HALF_WINHEIGHT)
255.            DISPLAYSURF.blit(IMAGESDICT['solved'], solvedRect)
256.
257.            if keyPressed:
258.                return 'solved'
259.
260.        pygame.display.update() # draw DISPLAYSURF to the screen.
261.        FPSCLOCK.tick()
262.
```

```
263.
```

Lines 237 to 261 position the camera and draw the map and other graphics to the display Surface object in DISPLAYSURF. If the level is solved, then the victory graphic is also drawn on top of everything else. The keyPressed variable will be set to True if the user pressed a key during this iteration, at which point the runLevel() function returns.

```
def isWall(mapObj, x, y):
    """Returns True if the (x, y) position on
    the map is a wall, otherwise return False."""
    if x < 0 or x >= len(mapObj) or y < 0 or y >= len(mapObj[x]):
        return False # x and y aren't actually on the map.
    elif mapObj[x][y] in ('#', 'x'):
        return True # wall is blocking
    return False
```

The isWall() function returns True if there is a wall on the map object at the XY coordinates passed to the function. Wall objects are represented as either a 'x' or '#' string in the map object.

```
def decorateMap(mapObj, startxy):
    """Makes a copy of the given map object and modifies it.
    Here is what is done to it:
        * Walls that are corners are turned into corner pieces.
        * The outside/inside floor tile distinction is made.
        * Tree/rock decorations are randomly added to the outside tiles.

    Returns the decorated map object."""

    startx, starty = startxy # Syntactic sugar

    # Copy the map object so we don't modify the original passed
    mapObjCopy = copy.deepcopy(mapObj)
```

The decorateMap() function alters the data structure mapObj so that it isn't as plain as it appears in the map file. The three things that decorateMap() changes are explained in the comment at the top of the function.

```
    # Remove the non-wall characters from the map data
    for x in range(len(mapObjCopy)):
        for y in range(len(mapObjCopy[0])):
            if mapObjCopy[x][y] in ('$', '.', '@', '+', '*'):
```

```
                mapObjCopy[x][y] = ' '
```

The map object has characters that represent the position of the player, goals, and stars. These are necessary for the map object (they're stored in other data structures after the map file is read) so they are converted to blank spaces.

```
    # Flood fill to determine inside/outside floor tiles.
    floodFill(mapObjCopy, startx, starty, ' ', 'o')
```

The floodFill() function will change all of the tiles inside the walls from ' ' characters to 'o' characters. It does this using a programming concept called recursion, which is explained in "Recursive Functions" section later in this chapter.

```
297.     # Convert the adjoined walls into corner tiles.
298.     for x in range(len(mapObjCopy)):
299.         for y in range(len(mapObjCopy[0])):
300.
301.             if mapObjCopy[x][y] == '#':
302.                 if (isWall(mapObjCopy, x, y-1) and isWall(mapObjCopy, x+1, y)) or \
303.                    (isWall(mapObjCopy, x+1, y) and isWall(mapObjCopy, x, y+1)) or \
304.                    (isWall(mapObjCopy, x, y+1) and isWall(mapObjCopy, x-1, y)) or \
305.                    (isWall(mapObjCopy, x-1, y) and isWall(mapObjCopy, x, y-1)):
306.                     mapObjCopy[x][y] = 'x'
307.
308.             elif mapObjCopy[x][y] == ' ' and random.randint(0, 99) < OUTSIDE_DECORATION_PCT:
309.                 mapObjCopy[x][y] = random.choice(list(OUTSIDEDECOMAPPING.keys()))
310.
311.     return mapObjCopy
```

The large, multi-line if statement on line 301 checks if the wall tile at the current XY coordinates are a corner wall tile by checking if there are wall tiles adjacent to it that form a corner shape. If so, the '#' string in the map object that represents a normal wall is changed to a 'x' string which represents a corner wall tile.

```
314. def isBlocked(mapObj, gameStateObj, x, y):
315.     """Returns True if the (x, y) position on the map is
316.     blocked by a wall or star, otherwise return False."""
```

```
317.
318.     if isWall(mapObj, x, y):
319.         return True
320.
321.     elif x < 0 or x >= len(mapObj) or y < 0 or y >= len(mapObj[x]):
322.         return True # x and y aren't actually on the map.
323.
324.     elif (x, y) in gameStateObj['stars']:
325.         return True # a star is blocking
326.
327.     return False
```

There are three cases where a space on the map would be blocked: if there is a star, a wall, or the coordinates of the space are past the edges of the map. The isBlocked() function checks for these three cases and returns True if the XY coordinates are blocked and False if not.

```
def makeMove(mapObj, gameStateObj, playerMoveTo):
    """Given a map and game state object, see if it is possible for the
    player to make the given move. If it is, then change the player's
    position (and the position of any pushed star). If not, do nothing.

    Returns True if the player moved, otherwise False."""

    # Make sure the player can move in the direction they want.
    playerx, playery = gameStateObj['player']

    # This variable is "syntactic sugar". Typing "stars" is more
    # readable than typing "gameStateObj['stars']" in our code.
    stars = gameStateObj['stars']

    # The code for handling each of the directions is so similar aside
    # from adding or subtracting 1 to the x/y coordinates. We can
    # simplify it by using the xOffset and yOffset variables.
    if playerMoveTo == UP:
        xOffset = 0
        yOffset = -1
    elif playerMoveTo == RIGHT:
        xOffset = 1
        yOffset = 0
    elif playerMoveTo == DOWN:
        xOffset = 0
        yOffset = 1
    elif playerMoveTo == LEFT:
        xOffset = -1
        yOffset = 0

    # See if the player can move in that direction.
    if isWall(mapObj, playerx + xOffset, playery + yOffset):
        return False
    else:
        if (playerx + xOffset, playery + yOffset) in stars:
            # There is a star in the way, see if the player can push it.
            if not isBlocked(mapObj, gameStateObj, playerx + (xOffset*2), playery + (yOffset*2)):
                # Move the star.
                ind = stars.index((playerx + xOffset, playery + yOffset))
                stars[ind] = (stars[ind][0] + xOffset, stars[ind][1] + yOffset)
            else:
                return False
        # Move the player upwards.
        gameStateObj['player'] = (playerx + xOffset, playery + yOffset)
        return True
```

The makeMove() function checks to make sure if moving the player in a particular direction is a valid move. As long as there isn't a wall blocking the path, or a star that has a wall or star behind it, the player will be able to move in that direction. The gameStateObj variable will be updated to reflect this, and the True value will be returned to tell the function's caller that the player was moved.

If there was a star in the space that the player wanted to move, that star's position is also changed and this information is updated in the gameStateObj variable as well. This is how the "star pushing" is implemented.

If the player is blocked from moving in the desired direction, then the gameStateObj is not modified and the function returns False.

```
377. def startScreen():
378.     """Display the start screen (which has the title and instructions)
379.     until the player presses a key. Returns None."""
380.
381.     # Position the title image.
382.     titleRect = IMAGESDICT['title'].get_rect()
383.     topCoord = 50 # topCoord tracks where to position the top of the text
384.     titleRect.top = topCoord
385.     titleRect.centerx = HALF_WINWIDTH
386.     topCoord += titleRect.height
387.
388.     # Unfortunately, Pygame's font & text system only shows one line at
```

```
389.     # a time, so we can't use strings with \n newline characters in them.
390.     # So we will use a list with each line in it.
391.     instructionText = ['Push the stars over the marks.',
392.                        'Arrow keys to move, WASD for camera control, P to
change character.',
393.                        'Backspace to reset level, Esc to quit.',
394.                        'N for next level, B to go back a level.']
```

The startScreen() function needs to display a few different pieces of text down the center of the window. We will store each line as a string in the instructionText list. The title image (stored in IMAGESDICT['title'] as a Surface object (that was originally loaded from the *star_title.png* file)) will be positioned 50 pixels from the top of the window. This is because the integer 50 was stored in the topCoord variable on line 383. The topCoord variable will track the Y axis positioning of the title image and the instructional text. The X axis is always going to be set so that the images and text are centered, as it is on line 385 for the title image.

On line 386, the topCoord variable is increased by whatever the height of that image is. This way we can modify the image and the start screen code won't have to be changed.

```
396.     # Start with drawing a blank color to the entire window:
397.     DISPLAYSURF.fill(BGCOLOR)
398.
399.     # Draw the title image to the window:
400.     DISPLAYSURF.blit(IMAGESDICT['title'], titleRect)
401.
402.     # Position and draw the text.
403.     for i in range(len(instructionText)):
404.         instSurf = BASICFONT.render(instructionText[i], 1, TEXTCOLOR)
405.         instRect = instSurf.get_rect()
406.         topCoord += 10 # 10 pixels will go in between each line of text.
407.         instRect.top = topCoord
408.         instRect.centerx = HALF_WINWIDTH
409.         topCoord += instRect.height # Adjust for the height of the line.
410.         DISPLAYSURF.blit(instSurf, instRect)
```

Line 400 is where the title image is blitted to the display Surface object. The for loop starting on line 403 will render, position, and blit each instructional string in the instructionText loop. The topCoord variable will always be incremented by the size of the previously rendered text (line 409) and 10 additional pixels (on line 406, so that there will be a 10 pixel gap between the lines of text).

```
412.     while True: # Main loop for the start screen.
413.         for event in pygame.event.get():
```

```
414.             if event.type == QUIT:
415.                 terminate()
416.             elif event.type == KEYDOWN:
417.                 if event.key == K_ESCAPE:
418.                     terminate()
419.                 return # user has pressed a key, so return.
420.
421.         # Display the DISPLAYSURF contents to the actual screen.
422.         pygame.display.update()
423.         FPSCLOCK.tick()
```

There is a game loop in startScreen() that begins on line 412 and handles events that indicate if the program should terminate or return from the startScreen() function. Until the player does either, the loop will keep calling pygame.display.update() and FPSCLOCK.tick() to keep the start screen displayed on the screen.

DATA STRUCTURES IN STAR PUSHER

Star Pusher has a specific format for the levels, maps, and game state data structures.

THE "GAME STATE" DATA STRUCTURE

The game state object will be a dictionary with three keys: 'player', 'stepCounter', and 'stars'.

- The value at the 'player' key will be a tuple of two integers for the current XY position of the player.
- The value at the 'stepCounter' key will be an integer that tracks how many moves the player has made in this level (so the player can try to solve the puzzle in the future with fewer steps).
- The value at the 'stars' key is a list of two-integer tuples of XY values for each of the stars on the current level.

THE "MAP" DATA STRUCTURE

The map data structure is simply a 2D list of lists where the two indexes used represent the X and Y coordinates of the map. The value at each index in the list of lists is a single-character string that represents the title that is on that map at each space:

- '#' – A wooden wall.
- 'x' – A corner wall.
- '@' – The starting space for the player on this level.
- '.' – A goal space.
- '$' – A space where a star is at the start of the level.
- '+' – A space with a goal and the starting player's space.
- '*' – A space with a goal and a star at the start of the level.
- ' ' – A grassy outdoor space.
- 'o' – An inside floor space. (This is a lowercase letter O, not a zero.)
- '1' – A rock on grass.
- '2' – A short tree on grass.
- '3' – A tall tree on grass.
- '4' – An ugly tree on grass.

THE "LEVELS" DATA STRUCTURE

The level object contains a game state object (which will be the state used when the level first starts), a map object, and a few other values. The level object itself is a dictionary with the following keys:

- The value at the key 'width' is an integer of how many tiles wide the entire map is.

- The value at the key 'height' is an integer of how many tiles tall the entire map is.
- The value at the key 'mapObj' is the map object for this level.
- The value at the key 'goals' is a list of two-integer tuples with the XY coordinates of each goal space on the map.
- The value at the key 'startState' is a game state object used to show the starting position of the stars and player at the start of the level.

READING AND WRITING TEXT FILES

Python has functions for reading files off of the player's hard drive. This will be useful for having a separate file keep all of the data for each level. This is also a good idea because in order to get new levels, the player doesn't have to change the source code of the game but instead can just download new level files.

TEXT FILES AND BINARY FILES

Text files are files that contain simple text data. Text files are created in Windows by the Notepad application, Gedit on Ubuntu, and TextEdit on Mac OS X. There are many other programs called text editors that can create and modify text files. IDLE's own file editor is a text editor.

The difference between text editors and word processors (like Microsoft Word, or OpenOffice Writer, or iWork Pages) is that text editors have text only. You can't set the font, size, or color of the text. (IDLE automatically sets the color of the text based on what kind of Python code it is, but you can't change this yourself, so it is still a text editor.) The difference between text and binary files isn't important for this game program. All you need to know is the this chapter and the Star Pusher program only deal with text files.

WRITING TO FILES

To create a file, call the open() function pass it two arguments: a string for the name of the file, and the string 'w' to tell the open() function you want to open the file in "write" mode. The open() function returns a file object:

```
>>> textFile = open('hello.txt', 'w')
>>>
```

If you run this code from the interactive shell, the *hello.txt* file that this function creates will be created in the same folder that the python.exe program is in (on Windows, this will probably be C:\Python32). If the open() function is called from a .py program, the file is created in the same folder that the .py file is in.

The "write" mode tells open() to create the file if it does not exist. If it does exist, then open() will delete that file and create a new, blank file. This is just like how an assignment statement can create a new variable, or overwrite the current value in an already existing variable. **This can be somewhat dangerous.** If you accidentally send a filename of an important file to the open() function with 'w' as the second parameter, it will be deleted. This could result in having to reinstall the operating system on your computer and/or the launching of nuclear missiles.

The file object has a method called write() which can be used to write text to the file. Just pass it a string like you would pass a string to the print() function. The difference is that write() does not automatically add a newline character ('\n') to the end of the string. If you want to add a newline, you will have to include it in the string:

```
>>> textFile = open('hello.txt', 'w')
>>> textFile.write('This will be the content of the file.\nHello world!\n')
>>>
```

To tell Python that you are done writing content to this file, you should call the close() method of the file object. (Although Python will automatically close any opened file objects when the program ends.)

```
>>> textFile.close()
```

READING FROM FILES

To read the content of a file, pass the string 'r' instead of 'w' to the open() function. Then call the readlines() method on the file object to read in the contents of the file. Last, close the file by calling the close() method.

```
>>> textFile = open('hello.txt', 'r')
>>> content = textFile.readlines()
>>> textFile.close()
```

The readlines() method returns a list of strings: one string for each line of text in the file:

```
>>> content
['This will be the content of the file.\n', 'Hello world!\n']
>>>
```

If you want to re-read the contents of that file, you will have to call close() on the file object and re-open it.

As an alternative to readlines(), you can also call the read() method, which will return the entire contents of the file as a single string value:

```
>>> textFile = open('hello.txt', 'r')
>>> content = textFile.read()
>>> content
'This will be the content of the file.\nHello world!\n'
```

On a side note, if you leave out the second parameter to the open() function, Python will assume you mean to open the file in read mode. So open('foobar.txt', 'r') and open('foobar.txt') do the exact same thing.

ABOUT THE STAR PUSHER MAP FILE FORMAT

We need the level text file to be in a specific format. Which characters represent walls, or stars, or the player's starting position? If we have the maps for multiple levels, how can we tell when one level's map ends and the next one begins?

Fortunately, the map file format we will use is already defined for us. There are many Sokoban games out there, and they all use the same map file format. If you open it in a text editor, you'll see something like this:

```
; Star Pusher (Sokoban clone)
```

```
; http://inventwithpython.com/blog
; By Al Sweigart al@inventwithpython.com
;
; Everything after the ; is a comment and will be ignored by the game that
; reads in this file.
;
; The format is described at:
; http://sokobano.de/wiki/index.php?title=Level_format
;   @ - The starting position of the player.
;   $ - The starting position for a pushable star.
;   . - A goal where a star needs to be pushed.
;   + - Player & goal
;   * - Star & goal
;  (space) - an empty open space.
;   # - A wall.
;
; Level maps are separated by a blank line (I like to use a ; at the start
; of the line since it is more visible.)
;
; I tried to use the same format as other people use for their Sokoban games,
; so that loading new levels is easy. Just place the levels in a text file
; and name it "starPusherLevels.txt" (after renaming this file, of course).


; Starting demo level:
 ########
##      #
#   .   #
#   $   #
# .$@$. #
####$   #
   #.   #
   #   ##
   #####
```

The comments at the top of the file explain the file's format. When you load the first level, it looks like this:

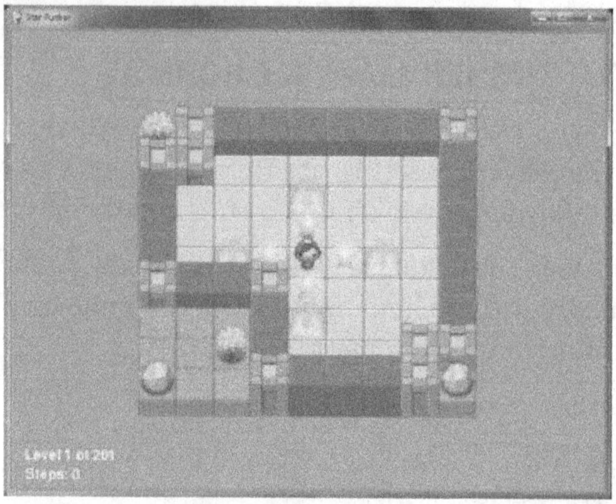


```
def readLevelsFile(filename):
    assert os.path.exists(filename), 'Cannot find the level file: %s' % (filename)
```

The os.path.exists() function will return True if the file specified by the string passed to the function exists. If it does not exist, os.path.exists() returns False.

```
    mapFile = open(filename, 'r')
    # Each level must end with a blank line
    content = mapFile.readlines() + ['\r\n']
    mapFile.close()

    levels = [] # Will contain a list of level objects.
    levelNum = 0
    mapTextLines = [] # contains the lines for a single level's map.
    mapObj = [] # the map object made from the data in mapTextLines
```

The file object for the level file that is opened for reading is stored in mapFile. All of the text from the level file is stored as a list of strings in the content variable, with a blank line added to the end. (The reason that this is done is explained later.)

After the level objects are created, they will be stored in the levels list. The levelNum variable will keep track of how many levels are found inside the level file. The mapTextLines list will be a list of strings from the content list for a single map (as opposed to how content stores the strings of all maps in the level file). The mapObj variable will be a 2D list.

```
    for lineNum in range(len(content)):
        # Process each line that was in the level file.
        line = content[lineNum].rstrip('\r\n')
```

The for loop on line 437 will go through each line that was read from the level file one line at a time. The line number will be stored in lineNum and the string of text for the line will be stored in line. Any newline characters at the end of the string will be stripped off.

```
441.         if ';' in line:
442.             # Ignore the ; lines, they're comments in the level file.
443.             line = line[:line.find(';')]
```

Any text that exists after a semicolon in the map file is treated like a comment and is ignored. This is just like the # sign for Python comments. To make sure that our code does not accidentally think the comment is part of the map, the line variable is modified so that it only consists of the text up to (but not including) the semicolon character. (Remember that this is only changing the string in the content list. It is not changing the level file on the hard drive.)

```
445.         if line != '':
446.             # This line is part of the map.
447.             mapTextLines.append(line)
```

There can be maps for multiple levels in the map file. The mapTextLines list will contain the lines of text from the map file for the current level being loaded. As long as the current line is not blank, the line will be appended to the end of mapTextLines.

```
448.         elif line == '' and len(mapTextLines) > 0:
449.             # A blank line indicates the end of a level's map in the file.
450.             # Convert the text in mapTextLines into a level object.
```

When there is a blank line in the map file, that indicates that the map for the current level has ended. And future lines of text will be for the later levels. Note however, that there must at least be one line in mapTextLines so that multiple blank lines together are not counted as the start and stop to multiple levels.

```
452.             # Find the longest row in the map.
453.             maxWidth = -1
454.             for i in range(len(mapTextLines)):
455.                 if len(mapTextLines[i]) > maxWidth:
456.                     maxWidth = len(mapTextLines[i])
```

All of the strings in mapTextLines need to be the same length (so that they form a rectangle), so they should be padded with extra blank spaces until they are all as long as the longest string. The for loop goes through each of the strings in mapTextLines and updates maxWidth when it finds a new longest string. After this loop finishes executing, the maxWidth variable will be set to the length of the longest string in mapTextLines.

```
457.         # Add spaces to the ends of the shorter rows. This
458.         # ensures the map will be rectangular.
459.         for i in range(len(mapTextLines)):
460.             mapTextLines[i] += ' ' * (maxWidth - len(mapTextLines[i]))
```

The for loop on line 459 goes through the strings in mapTextLines again, this time to add enough space characters to pad each to be as long as maxWidth.

```
462.         # Convert mapTextLines to a map object.
463.         for x in range(len(mapTextLines[0])):
464.             mapObj.append([])
465.         for y in range(len(mapTextLines)):
466.             for x in range(maxWidth):
467.                 mapObj[x].append(mapTextLines[y][x])
```

The mapTextLines variable just stores a list of strings. (Each string in the list represents a row, and each character in the string represents a character at a different column. This is why line 467 has the Y and X indexes reversed, just like the SHAPES data structure in the Tetromino game.) But the map object will have to be a list of list of single-character strings such that mapObj[x][y] refers to the tile at the XY coordinates. The for loop on line 463 adds an empty list to mapObj for each column in mapTextLines.

The nested for loops on line 465 and 466 will fill these lists with single-character strings to represent each tile on the map. This creates the map object that Star Pusher uses.

```
469.         # Loop through the spaces in the map and find the @, ., and $
470.         # characters for the starting game state.
471.         startx = None # The x and y for the player's starting position
472.         starty = None
473.         goals = [] # list of (x, y) tuples for each goal.
474.         stars = [] # list of (x, y) for each star's starting position.
475.         for x in range(maxWidth):
476.             for y in range(len(mapObj[x])):
477.                 if mapObj[x][y] in ('@', '+'):
478.                     # '@' is player, '+' is player & goal
479.                     startx = x
480.                     starty = y
481.                 if mapObj[x][y] in ('.', '+', '*'):
482.                     # '.' is goal, '*' is star & goal
483.                     goals.append((x, y))
```

```
484.                 if mapObj[x][y] in ('$', '*'):
485.                     # '$' is star
486.                     stars.append((x, y))
```

After creating the map object, the nested for loops on lines 475 and 476 will go through each space to find the XY coordinates three things:

The player's starting position. This will be stored in the startx and starty variables, which will then be stored in the game state object later on line 494.

The starting position of all the stars These will be stored in the stars list, which is later stored in the game state object on line 496.

The position of all the goals. These will be stored in the goals list, which is later stored in the level object on line 500.

Remember, the game state object contains all the things that can change. This is why the player's position is stored in it (because the player can move around) and why the stars are stored in it (because the stars can be pushed around by the player). But the goals are stored in the level object, since they will never move around.

```
488.             # Basic level design sanity checks:
489.             assert startx != None and starty != None, 'Level %s (around line %s) in %s is missing a "@" or "+" to mark the start point.' % (levelNum+1, lineNum, filename)
490.             assert len(goals) > 0, 'Level %s (around line %s) in %s must have at least one goal.' % (levelNum+1, lineNum, filename)
491.             assert len(stars) >= len(goals), 'Level %s (around line %s) in %s is impossible to solve. It has %s goals but only %s stars.' % (levelNum+1, lineNum, filename, len(goals), len(stars))
```

At this point, the level has been read in and processed. To be sure that this level will work properly, a few assertions must pass. If any of the conditions for these assertions are False, then Python will produce an error (using the string from the assert statement) saying what is wrong with the level file.

The first assertion on line 489 checks to make sure that there is a player starting point listed somewhere on the map. The second assertion on line 490 checks to make sure there is at least one goal (or more) somewhere on the map. And the third assertion on line 491 checks to make sure that there is at least one star for each goal (but having more stars than goals is allowed).

```
493.             # Create level object and starting game state object.
494.             gameStateObj = {'player': (startx, starty),
495.                             'stepCounter': 0,
```

```
496.                         'stars': stars}
497.             levelObj = {'width': maxWidth,
498.                         'height': len(mapObj),
499.                         'mapObj': mapObj,
500.                         'goals': goals,
501.                         'startState': gameStateObj}
502.
503.             levels.append(levelObj)
```

Finally, these objects are stored in the game state object, which itself is stored in the level object. The level object is added to a list of level objects on line 503. It is this levels list that will be returned by the readLevelsFile() function when all of the maps have been processed.

```
505.             # Reset the variables for reading the next map.
506.             mapTextLines = []
507.             mapObj = []
508.             gameStateObj = {}
509.             levelNum += 1
510.     return levels
```

Now that this level is done processing, the variables for mapTextLines, mapObj, and gameStateObj should be reset to blank values for the next level that will be read in from the level file. The levelNum variable is also incremented by 1 for the next level's level number.

RECURSIVE FUNCTIONS

Before you can learn how the floodFill() function works, you need to learn about recursion. Recursion is a simple concept: A **recursive function** is just a function that calls itself, like the one in the following program: (don't type the letters at the beginning of each line though)

```
A. def passFortyTwoWhenYouCallThisFunction(param):
B.     print('Start of function.')
C.     if param != 42:
D.         print('You did not pass 42 when you called this function.')
E.         print('Fine. I will do it myself.')
F.         passFortyTwoWhenYouCallThisFunction(42) # this is the recursive call
G.     if param == 42:
H.         print('Thank you for passing 42 when you called this function.')
I.     print('End of function.')
J.
K. passFortyTwoWhenYouCallThisFunction(41)
```

(In your own programs, don't make functions have names as long as passFortyTwoWhenYouCallThisFunction(). I'm just being stupid and silly. Stupilly.)

When you run this program, the function gets defined when the def statement on line A executes. The next line of code that is executed is line K, which calls passFortyTwoWhenYouCallThisFunction() and passes (gasp!) 41. As a result, the function calls itself on line F and passes 42. We call this call the **recursive call**.

This is what our program outputs:

```
Start of function.
You did not pass 42 when you called this function.
Fine. I will do it myself.
Start of function.
Thank you for passing 42 when you called this function.
End of function.
End of function.
```

Notice that the "Start of function." and "End of function." text appears twice. Let's figure out what exactly happens and what order it happens in.

On line K, the function is called and 41 is passed for the param parameter. Line B prints out "Start of function.". The condition on line C will be True (since 41 != 42) so Line C and D will print out their messages. Line F will then make a call, recursively, to the function and passes 42 for the param parameter. So execution starts on line B again and prints out "Start of function.". Line C's condition this time is False, so it skips to line G and finds that condition to be True. This causes line H to be called and displays "Thank you..." on the screen. Then the last line of the function, line I, will execute to print out "End of function." and the function returns to the line that called it.

But remember, the line of code that called the function was line F. And in this original call, param was set to 41. The code goes down to line G and checks the condition, which is False (since 41 == 42 is False) so it skips the print() call on line H. Instead, it runs the print() call on line I which makes "End of function." display for a second time.

Since it has reached the end of the function, it returns to the line of code that called this function call, which was line K. There are no more lines of code after line K, so the program terminates.

Note that local variables are not just local to the function, but to a specific call of the function.

STACK OVERFLOWS

Each time a function is called, the Python interpreter remembers which line of code made the call. That way when the function returns Python knows where to resume the execution. Remembering this takes up a tiny bit of memory. This isn't normally a big deal, but take a look at this code:

```
def funky():
    funky()

funky()
```

If you run this program, you'll get a large amount of output which looks like this:

```
...
  File "C:\test67.py", line 2, in funky
    funky()
  File "C:\test67.py", line 2, in funky
    funky()
  File "C:\test67.py", line 2, in funky
    funky()
  File "C:\test67.py", line 2, in funky
    funky()
  File "C:\test67.py", line 2, in funky
    funky()
RuntimeError: maximum recursion depth exceeded
```

The funky() function does nothing but call itself. And then in that call, the function calls itself again. Then it calls itself again, and again, and again. Each time it calls itself, Python has to remember what line of code made that call so that when the function returns it can resume the execution there. But the funky() function never returns, it just keeps making calls to itself.

This is just like the infinite loop bug, where the program keeps going and never stops. To prevent itself from running out of memory, Python will cause an error after you are a 1000 calls deep and crash the program. This type of bug is called a **stack overflow.**

This code also causes a stack overflow, even though there are no recursive functions:

```
def spam():
    eggs()

def eggs():
    spam()

spam()
```

When you run this program, it causes an error that looks like this:

```
...
  File "C:\test67.py", line 2, in spam
    eggs()
```

```
  File "C:\test67.py", line 5, in eggs
    spam()
  File "C:\test67.py", line 2, in spam
    eggs()
  File "C:\test67.py", line 5, in eggs
    spam()
  File "C:\test67.py", line 2, in spam
    eggs()
RuntimeError: maximum recursion depth exceeded
```

PREVENTING STACK OVERFLOWS WITH A BASE CASE

In order to prevent stack overflow bugs, you must have a **base case** where the function stops make new recursive calls. If there is no base case then the function calls will never stop and eventually a stack overflow will occur. Here is an example of a recursive function with a base case. The base case is when the param parameter equals 2.

```
def fizz(param):
    print(param)
    if param == 2:
        return
    fizz(param - 1)

fizz(5)
```

When you run this program, the output will look like this:

```
5
4
3
2
```

This program does not have a stack overflow error because once the param parameter is set to 2, the if statement's condition will be True and the function will return, and then the rest of the calls will also return in turn.

Though if your code never reaches the base case, then this will cause a stack overflow. If we changed the fizz(5) call to fizz(0), then the program's output would look like this:

```
  File "C:\rectest.py", line 5, in fizz
    fizz(param - 1)
  File "C:\rectest.py", line 5, in fizz
    fizz(param - 1)
  File "C:\rectest.py", line 5, in fizz
```

```
    fizz(param - 1)
  File "C:\rectest.py", line 2, in fizz
    print(param)
RuntimeError: maximum recursion depth exceeded
```

Recursive calls and base cases will be used to perform the flood fill algorithm, which is described next.

THE FLOOD FILL ALGORITHM

The flood fill algorithm is used in Star Pusher to change all of the floor tiles inside the walls of the level to use the "inside floor" tile image instead of the "outside floor" tile (which all the tiles on the map are by default). The original floodFill() call is on line 295. It will convert any tiles represented with the ' ' string (which represents an outdoor floor) to a 'o' string (which represents an indoor floor).

```
513. def floodFill(mapObj, x, y, oldCharacter, newCharacter):
514.     """Changes any values matching oldCharacter on the map object to
515.     newCharacter at the (x, y) position, and does the same for the
516.     positions to the left, right, down, and up of (x, y), recursively."""
517.
518.     # In this game, the flood fill algorithm creates the inside/outside
519.     # floor distinction. This is a "recursive" function.
520.     # For more info on the Flood Fill algorithm, see:
521.     #   http://en.wikipedia.org/wiki/Flood_fill
522.     if mapObj[x][y] == oldCharacter:
523.         mapObj[x][y] = newCharacter
```

Line 522 and 523 converts the tile at the XY coordinate passed to floodFill() to the newCharacter string if it originally was the same as the oldCharacter string.

```
525.     if x < len(mapObj) - 1 and mapObj[x+1][y] == oldCharacter:
526.         floodFill(mapObj, x+1, y, oldCharacter, newCharacter) # call right
527.     if x > 0 and mapObj[x-1][y] == oldCharacter:
528.         floodFill(mapObj, x-1, y, oldCharacter, newCharacter) # call left
529.     if y < len(mapObj[x]) - 1 and mapObj[x][y+1] == oldCharacter:
530.         floodFill(mapObj, x, y+1, oldCharacter, newCharacter) # call down
531.     if y > 0 and mapObj[x][y-1] == oldCharacter:
532.         floodFill(mapObj, x, y-1, oldCharacter, newCharacter) # call up
```

These four if statements check if the tile to the right, left, down, and up of the XY coordinate are the same as oldCharacter, and if so, a recursive call is made to floodFill() with those coordinates.

To better understand how the floodFill() function works, here is a version that does not use recursive calls, but instead uses a list of XY coordinates to keep track of which spaces on the map should be checked and possibly changed to newCharacter.

```
def floodFill(mapObj, x, y, oldCharacter, newCharacter):
    spacesToCheck = []
    if mapObj[x][y] == oldCharacter:
        spacesToCheck.append((x, y))
    while spacesToCheck != []:
        x, y = spacesToCheck.pop()
        mapObj[x][y] = newCharacter

        if x < len(mapObj) - 1 and mapObj[x+1][y] == oldCharacter:
            spacesToCheck.append((x+1, y)) # check right
        if x > 0 and mapObj[x-1][y] == oldCharacter:
            spacesToCheck.append((x-1, y)) # check left
        if y < len(mapObj[x]) - 1 and mapObj[x][y+1] == oldCharacter:
            spacesToCheck.append((x, y+1)) # check down
        if y > 0 and mapObj[x][y-1] == oldCharacter:
            spacesToCheck.append((x, y-1)) # check up
```

DRAWING THE MAP

```
535. def drawMap(mapObj, gameStateObj, goals):
536.     """Draws the map to a Surface object, including the player and
537.     stars. This function does not call pygame.display.update(), nor
538.     does it draw the "Level" and "Steps" text in the corner."""
539.
540.     # mapSurf will be the single Surface object that the tiles are drawn
541.     # on, so that it is easy to position the entire map on the DISPLAYSURF
542.     # Surface object. First, the width and height must be calculated.
543.     mapSurfWidth = len(mapObj) * TILEWIDTH
544.     mapSurfHeight = (len(mapObj[0]) - 1) * (TILEHEIGHT - TILEFLOORHEIGHT)
+ TILEHEIGHT
545.     mapSurf = pygame.Surface((mapSurfWidth, mapSurfHeight))
546.     mapSurf.fill(BGCOLOR) # start with a blank color on the surface.
```

The drawMap() function will return a Surface object with the entire map (and the player and stars) drawn on it. The width and height needed for this Surface have to be calculated from mapObj (which is done on line 543 and 544). The Surface object that everything will be drawn on is created on line 545. To begin with, the entire Surface object is painted to the background color on line 546.

```
548.     # Draw the tile sprites onto this surface.
549.     for x in range(len(mapObj)):
550.         for y in range(len(mapObj[x])):
551.             spaceRect = pygame.Rect((x * TILEWIDTH, y * (TILEHEIGHT -
TILEFLOORHEIGHT), TILEWIDTH, TILEHEIGHT))
```

The set of nested for loops on line 549 and 550 will go through every possible XY coordinate on the map and draw the appropriate tile image at that location.

```
552.            if mapObj[x][y] in TILEMAPPING:
553.                baseTile = TILEMAPPING[mapObj[x][y]]
554.            elif mapObj[x][y] in OUTSIDEDECOMAPPING:
555.                baseTile = TILEMAPPING[' ']
556.
557.            # First draw the base ground/wall tile.
558.            mapSurf.blit(baseTile, spaceRect)
559.
```

The baseTile variable is set to the Surface object of the tile image to be drawn at the iteration's current XY coordinate. If the single-character string is in the OUTSIDEDECOMAPPING dictionary, then TILEMAPPING[' '] (the single-character string for the basic outdoor floor tile) will be used.

```
560.            if mapObj[x][y] in OUTSIDEDECOMAPPING:
561.                # Draw any tree/rock decorations that are on this tile.
562.                mapSurf.blit(OUTSIDEDECOMAPPING[mapObj[x][y]], spaceRect)
```

Additionally, if the tile was listed in the OUTSIDEDECOMAPPING dictionary, the corresponding tree or rock image should be drawn on top of the tile that was just drawn at that XY coordinate.

```
563.            elif (x, y) in gameStateObj['stars']:
564.                if (x, y) in goals:
565.                    # A goal AND star are on this space, draw goal first.
566.                    mapSurf.blit(IMAGESDICT['covered goal'], spaceRect)
567.                # Then draw the star sprite.
568.                mapSurf.blit(IMAGESDICT['star'], spaceRect)
```

If there is a star located at this XY coordinate on the map (which can be found out by checking for (x, y) in the list at gameStateObj['stars']), then a star should be drawn at this XY coordinate (which is done on line 568). Before the star is drawn, the code should first check if there is also a goal at this location, in which case, the "covered goal" tile should be drawn first.

```
569.            elif (x, y) in goals:
570.                # Draw a goal without a star on it.
571.                mapSurf.blit(IMAGESDICT['uncovered goal'], spaceRect)
```

If there is a goal at this XY coordinate on the map, then the "uncovered goal" should be drawn on top of the tile. The uncovered goal is drawn because if execution has reached the elif statement on line 569, we know that the elif statement's condition on line 563 was False and there is no star that is also at this XY coordinate.

```
573.            # Last draw the player on the board.
574.            if (x, y) == gameStateObj['player']:
575.                # Note: The value "currentImage" refers
576.                # to a key in "PLAYERIMAGES" which has the
577.                # specific player image we want to show.
578.                mapSurf.blit(PLAYERIMAGES[currentImage], spaceRect)
579.
580.    return mapSurf
```

Finally, the drawMap() function checks if the player is located at this XY coordinate, and if so, the player's image is drawn over the tile. Line 580 is outside of the nested for loops that began on line 549 and 550, so by the time the Surface object is returned, the entire map has been drawn on it.

CHECKING IF THE LEVEL IS FINISHED

```
583. def isLevelFinished(levelObj, gameStateObj):
584.     """Returns True if all the goals have stars in them."""
585.     for goal in levelObj['goals']:
586.         if goal not in gameStateObj['stars']:
587.             # Found a space with a goal but no star on it.
588.             return False
589.     return True
```

The isLevelFinished() function returns True if all the goals are covered stars. Some levels could have more stars than goals, so it's important to check that all the goals are covered by stars, rather than checking if all the stars are over goals.

The for loop on line 585 goes through the goals in levelObj['goals'] (which is a list of tuples of XY coordinates for each goal) and checks if there is a star in the gameStateObj['stars'] list that has those same XY coordinates (the not in operators work here because gameStateObj['stars'] is a list of those same tuples of XY coordinates). The first time the code finds a goal with no star at the same position, the function returns False.

If it gets through all of the goals and finds a star on each of them, isLevelFinished() returns True.

```
def terminate():
    pygame.quit()
    sys.exit()
```

This terminate() function is the same as in all the previous programs.

```
if __name__ == '__main__':
    main()
```

After all the functions have been defined, the main() function is called on line 602 to begin the game.

SUMMARY

In the Squirrel Eat Squirrel game, the game world was pretty simple: just an infinite green plain with grass images randomly scattered around it. The Star Pusher game introduced something new: having uniquely designed levels with tile graphics. In order to store these levels in a format that the computer can read, they are typed out into a text file and code in the program reads those files and creates the data structures for the level.

Really, rather than just make a simple game with a single map, the Star Pusher program is more of a system for loading custom maps based on the level file. Just by modifying the level file, we can change where walls, stars, and goals appear in the game world. The Star Pusher program can handle any configuration that the level file is set to (as long as it passes the assert statements that ensure the map makes sense).

You won't even have to know how to program Python to make your own levels. A text editor program that modifies the *starPusherLevels.txt* file is all that anyone needs to have their own level editor for the Star Pusher game.

10 Chapter FOUR EXTRA GAMES

Included in this chapter is the source code for four extra games. Unfortunately, only the source code (including comments) is in this chapter without any detailed explanation of the code. By now, you can play these games and figure out how the code works by looking at the source code and comments.

The games are:

- **Flippy** – An "Othello" clone where the player tries to flip the computer AI player's tiles.
- **Ink Spill** – A "Flood It" clone that makes use of the flood fill algorithm.
- **Four in a Row** – A "Connect Four" clone against the computer AI player.
- **Gemgem** – A "Bejeweled" clone where the player swaps gems to try to get three identical gems in a row.

FLIPPY, AN "OTHELLO" CLONE

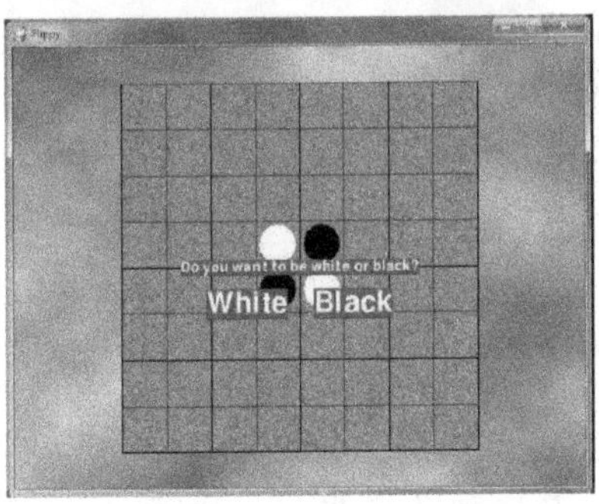

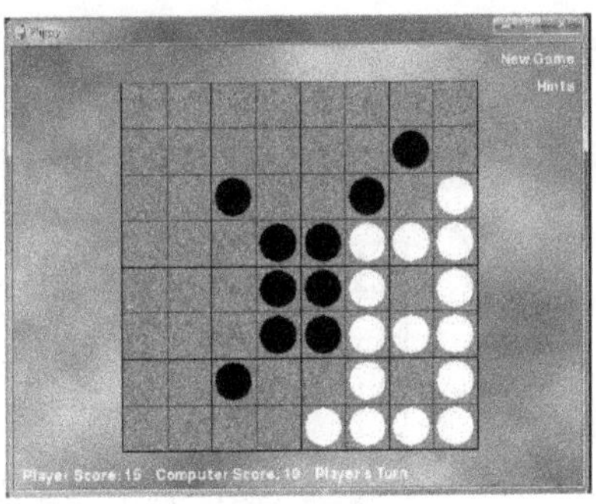

Othello, also known by the generic name Reversi, has an 8 x 8 board with tiles that are black on one side and white on the other. The starting board looks like Figure 10-1. Each player takes turn placing down a new tile of their color. Any of the opponent's tiles that are between the new tile and the other tiles of that color is flipped. The goal of the game is to have as many of the tiles with your color as possible. For example, Figure 10-2 is what it looks like if the white player places a new white tile on space 5, 6.

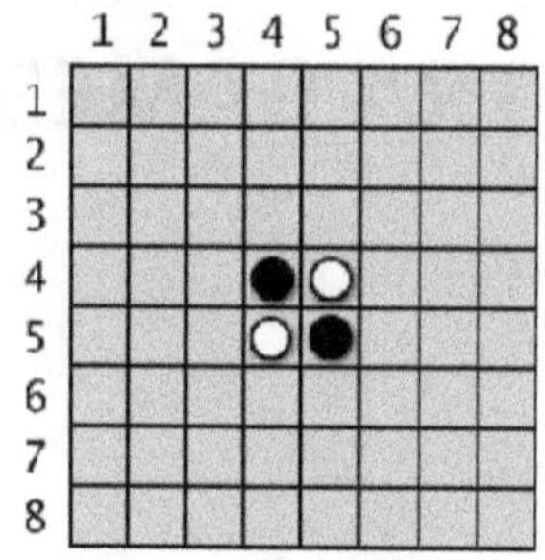

The starting Reversi board has two white tiles and two black tiles.

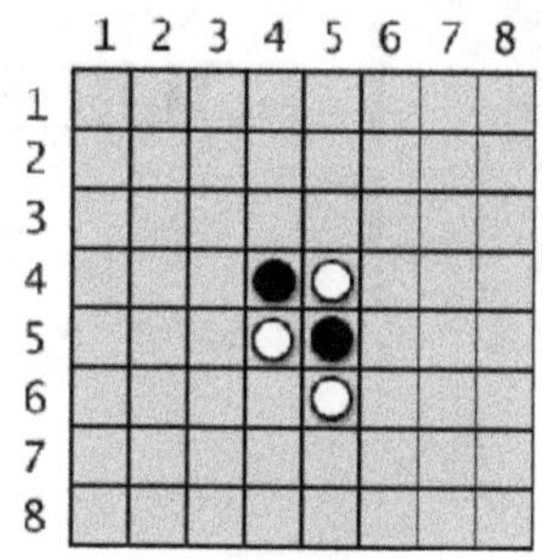

White places a new tile.

The black tile at 5, 5 is in between the new white tile and the existing white tile at 5, 4. That black tile is flipped over and becomes a new white tile, making the board look like Figure 10-3. Black makes a similar move next, placing a black tile on 4, 6 which flips the white tile at 4, 5. This results in a board that looks like Figure 10-4.

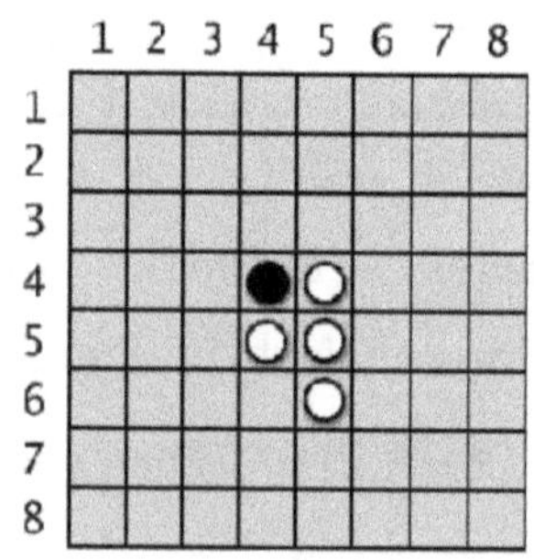

White's move will flip over one of black's tiles.

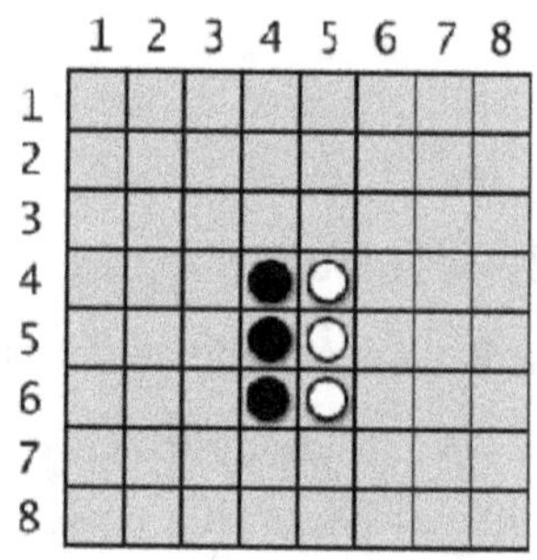

Black places a new tile, which flips over one of white's tiles.

Tiles in all directions are flipped as long as they are in between the player's new tile and existing tile. In Figure 10-5, the white player places a tile at 3, 6 and flips black tiles in both directions (marked by the lines). The result is in Figure 10-6.

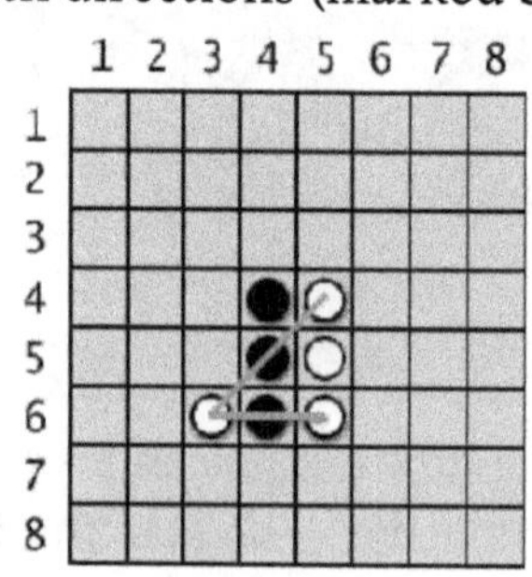

White's second move at 3, 6 will flip two of black's tiles.

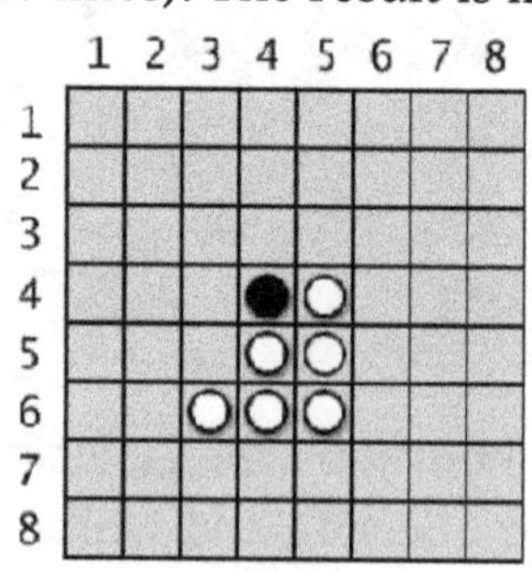

The board after white's second move.

As you can see, each player can quickly grab a majority of the tiles on the board in just one or two moves. Players must always make a move that captures at least one tile. The game ends when a player either cannot make a move, or the board is completely full. The player with the most tiles of their color wins.

A text version of this game that uses print() and input() instead of Pygame is featured in Chapter 15 of "Invent Your Own Computer Games with Python".

The computer AI for this game is pretty good, because it is easy for a computer to simulate every possible move and take the one that flips over the most tiles. It usually beats me whenever I play it.

SOURCE CODE FOR FLIPPY

```
# Flippy (an Othello or Reversi clone)
# By Al Sweigart al@inventwithpython.com
# http://inventwithpython.com/pygame
# Released under a "Simplified BSD" license

# Based on the "reversi.py" code that originally appeared in "Invent
# Your Own Computer Games with Python", chapter 15:
#   http://inventwithpython.com/chapter15.html

import random, sys, pygame, time, copy
from pygame.locals import *

FPS = 10 # frames per second to update the screen
WINDOWWIDTH = 640 # width of the program's window, in pixels
WINDOWHEIGHT = 480 # height in pixels
SPACESIZE = 50 # width & height of each space on the board, in pixels
BOARDWIDTH = 8 # how many columns of spaces on the game board
BOARDHEIGHT = 8 # how many rows of spaces on the game board
WHITE_TILE = 'WHITE_TILE' # an arbitrary but unique value
BLACK_TILE = 'BLACK_TILE' # an arbitrary but unique value
EMPTY_SPACE = 'EMPTY_SPACE' # an arbitrary but unique value
HINT_TILE = 'HINT_TILE' # an arbitrary but unique value
ANIMATIONSPEED = 25 # integer from 1 to 100, higher is faster animation

# Amount of space on the left & right side (XMARGIN) or above and below
# (YMARGIN) the game board, in pixels.
XMARGIN = int((WINDOWWIDTH - (BOARDWIDTH * SPACESIZE)) / 2)
YMARGIN = int((WINDOWHEIGHT - (BOARDHEIGHT * SPACESIZE)) / 2)

#              R    G    B
WHITE      = (255, 255, 255)
BLACK      = (  0,   0,   0)
GREEN      = (  0, 155,   0)
BRIGHTBLUE = (  0,  50, 255)
BROWN      = (174,  94,   0)

```

```
TEXTBGCOLOR1 = BRIGHTBLUE
TEXTBGCOLOR2 = GREEN
GRIDLINECOLOR = BLACK
TEXTCOLOR = WHITE
HINTCOLOR = BROWN


def main():
    global MAINCLOCK, DISPLAYSURF, FONT, BIGFONT, BGIMAGE

    pygame.init()
    MAINCLOCK = pygame.time.Clock()
    DISPLAYSURF = pygame.display.set_mode((WINDOWWIDTH, WINDOWHEIGHT))
    pygame.display.set_caption('Flippy')
    FONT = pygame.font.Font('freesansbold.ttf', 16)
    BIGFONT = pygame.font.Font('freesansbold.ttf', 32)

    # Set up the background image.
    boardImage = pygame.image.load('flippyboard.png')
    # Use smoothscale() to stretch the board image to fit the entire board:
    boardImage = pygame.transform.smoothscale(boardImage, (BOARDWIDTH * SPACESIZE, BOARDHEIGHT * SPACESIZE))
    boardImageRect = boardImage.get_rect()
    boardImageRect.topleft = (XMARGIN, YMARGIN)
    BGIMAGE = pygame.image.load('flippybackground.png')
    # Use smoothscale() to stretch the background image to fit the entire window:
    BGIMAGE = pygame.transform.smoothscale(BGIMAGE, (WINDOWWIDTH, WINDOWHEIGHT))
    BGIMAGE.blit(boardImage, boardImageRect)

    # Run the main game.
    while True:
        if runGame() == False:
            break


def runGame():
    # Plays a single game of reversi each time this function is called.

    # Reset the board and game.
    mainBoard = getNewBoard()
    resetBoard(mainBoard)
    showHints = False
    turn = random.choice(['computer', 'player'])

    # Draw the starting board and ask the player what color they want.
    drawBoard(mainBoard)
    playerTile, computerTile = enterPlayerTile()

    # Make the Surface and Rect objects for the "New Game" and "Hints" buttons
```

```
    newGameSurf = FONT.render('New Game', True, TEXTCOLOR, TEXTBGCOLOR2)
    newGameRect = newGameSurf.get_rect()
    newGameRect.topright = (WINDOWWIDTH - 8, 10)
    hintsSurf = FONT.render('Hints', True, TEXTCOLOR, TEXTBGCOLOR2)
    hintsRect = hintsSurf.get_rect()
    hintsRect.topright = (WINDOWWIDTH - 8, 40)

    while True: # main game loop
        # Keep looping for player and computer's turns.
        if turn == 'player':
            # Player's turn:
            if getValidMoves(mainBoard, playerTile) == []:
                # If it's the player's turn but they
                # can't move, then end the game.
                break
            movexy = None
            while movexy == None:
                # Keep looping until the player clicks on a valid space.

                # Determine which board data structure to use for display.
                if showHints:
                    boardToDraw = getBoardWithValidMoves(mainBoard, playerTile)
                else:
                    boardToDraw = mainBoard

                checkForQuit()
                for event in pygame.event.get(): # event handling loop
                    if event.type == MOUSEBUTTONUP:
                        # Handle mouse click events
                        mousex, mousey = event.pos
                        if newGameRect.collidepoint( (mousex, mousey) ):
                            # Start a new game
                            return True
                        elif hintsRect.collidepoint( (mousex, mousey) ):
                            # Toggle hints mode
                            showHints = not showHints
                        # movexy is set to a two-item tuple XY coordinate, or None value
                        movexy = getSpaceClicked(mousex, mousey)
                        if movexy != None and not isValidMove(mainBoard, playerTile, movexy[0], movexy[1]):
                            movexy = None

                # Draw the game board.
                drawBoard(boardToDraw)
                drawInfo(boardToDraw, playerTile, computerTile, turn)

                # Draw the "New Game" and "Hints" buttons.
                DISPLAYSURF.blit(newGameSurf, newGameRect)
```

```
                DISPLAYSURF.blit(hintsSurf, hintsRect)

                MAINCLOCK.tick(FPS)
                pygame.display.update()

            # Make the move and end the turn.
            makeMove(mainBoard, playerTile, movexy[0], movexy[1], True)
            if getValidMoves(mainBoard, computerTile) != []:
                # Only set for the computer's turn if it can make a move.
                turn = 'computer'

        else:
            # Computer's turn:
            if getValidMoves(mainBoard, computerTile) == []:
                # If it was set to be the computer's turn but
                # they can't move, then end the game.
                break

            # Draw the board.
            drawBoard(mainBoard)
            drawInfo(mainBoard, playerTile, computerTile, turn)

            # Draw the "New Game" and "Hints" buttons.
            DISPLAYSURF.blit(newGameSurf, newGameRect)
            DISPLAYSURF.blit(hintsSurf, hintsRect)

            # Make it look like the computer is thinking by pausing a bit.
            pauseUntil = time.time() + random.randint(5, 15) * 0.1
            while time.time() < pauseUntil:
                pygame.display.update()

            # Make the move and end the turn.
            x, y = getComputerMove(mainBoard, computerTile)
            makeMove(mainBoard, computerTile, x, y, True)
            if getValidMoves(mainBoard, playerTile) != []:
                # Only set for the player's turn if they can make a move.
                turn = 'player'

    # Display the final score.
    drawBoard(mainBoard)
    scores = getScoreOfBoard(mainBoard)

    # Determine the text of the message to display.
    if scores[playerTile] > scores[computerTile]:
        text = 'You beat the computer by %s points! Congratulations!' % \
               (scores[playerTile] - scores[computerTile])
```

```
    elif scores[playerTile] < scores[computerTile]:
        text = 'You lost. The computer beat you by %s points.' % \
            (scores[computerTile] - scores[playerTile])
    else:
        text = 'The game was a tie!'

    textSurf = FONT.render(text, True, TEXTCOLOR, TEXTBGCOLOR1)
    textRect = textSurf.get_rect()
    textRect.center = (int(WINDOWWIDTH / 2), int(WINDOWHEIGHT / 2))
    DISPLAYSURF.blit(textSurf, textRect)

    # Display the "Play again?" text with Yes and No buttons.
    text2Surf = BIGFONT.render('Play again?', True, TEXTCOLOR,
TEXTBGCOLOR1)
    text2Rect = text2Surf.get_rect()
    text2Rect.center = (int(WINDOWWIDTH / 2), int(WINDOWHEIGHT / 2) + 50)

    # Make "Yes" button.
    yesSurf = BIGFONT.render('Yes', True, TEXTCOLOR, TEXTBGCOLOR1)
    yesRect = yesSurf.get_rect()
    yesRect.center = (int(WINDOWWIDTH / 2) - 60, int(WINDOWHEIGHT / 2) +
90)

    # Make "No" button.
    noSurf = BIGFONT.render('No', True, TEXTCOLOR, TEXTBGCOLOR1)
    noRect = noSurf.get_rect()
    noRect.center = (int(WINDOWWIDTH / 2) + 60, int(WINDOWHEIGHT / 2) +
90)

    while True:
        # Process events until the user clicks on Yes or No.
        checkForQuit()
        for event in pygame.event.get(): # event handling loop
            if event.type == MOUSEBUTTONUP:
                mousex, mousey = event.pos
                if yesRect.collidepoint( (mousex, mousey) ):
                    return True
                elif noRect.collidepoint( (mousex, mousey) ):
                    return False
        DISPLAYSURF.blit(textSurf, textRect)
        DISPLAYSURF.blit(text2Surf, text2Rect)
        DISPLAYSURF.blit(yesSurf, yesRect)
        DISPLAYSURF.blit(noSurf, noRect)
        pygame.display.update()
        MAINCLOCK.tick(FPS)
```

```
def translateBoardToPixelCoord(x, y):
    return XMARGIN + x * SPACESIZE + int(SPACESIZE / 2), YMARGIN + y * SPACESIZE + int(SPACESIZE / 2)
def animateTileChange(tilesToFlip, tileColor, additionalTile):
    # Draw the additional tile that was just laid down. (Otherwise we'd
    # have to completely redraw the board & the board info.)
    if tileColor == WHITE_TILE:
        additionalTileColor = WHITE
    else:
        additionalTileColor = BLACK
    additionalTileX, additionalTileY = translateBoardToPixelCoord(additionalTile[0], additionalTile[1])
    pygame.draw.circle(DISPLAYSURF, additionalTileColor, (additionalTileX, additionalTileY), int(SPACESIZE / 2) - 4)
    pygame.display.update()
    for rgbValues in range(0, 255, int(ANIMATIONSPEED * 2.55)):
        if rgbValues > 255:
            rgbValues = 255
        elif rgbValues < 0:
            rgbValues = 0
        if tileColor == WHITE_TILE:
            color = tuple([rgbValues] * 3) # rgbValues goes from 0 to 255
        elif tileColor == BLACK_TILE:
            color = tuple([255 - rgbValues] * 3) # rgbValues goes from 255 to 0
        for x, y in tilesToFlip:
            centerx, centery = translateBoardToPixelCoord(x, y)
            pygame.draw.circle(DISPLAYSURF, color, (centerx, centery), int(SPACESIZE / 2) - 4)
        pygame.display.update()
        MAINCLOCK.tick(FPS)
        checkForQuit()
def drawBoard(board):
    # Draw background of board.
    DISPLAYSURF.blit(BGIMAGE, BGIMAGE.get_rect())
    # Draw grid lines of the board.
    for x in range(BOARDWIDTH + 1):
```

```
        # Draw the horizontal lines.
        startx = (x * SPACESIZE) + XMARGIN
        starty = YMARGIN
        endx = (x * SPACESIZE) + XMARGIN
        endy = YMARGIN + (BOARDHEIGHT * SPACESIZE)
        pygame.draw.line(DISPLAYSURF, GRIDLINECOLOR, (startx, starty), (endx, endy))
    for y in range(BOARDHEIGHT + 1):
        # Draw the vertical lines.
        startx = XMARGIN
        starty = (y * SPACESIZE) + YMARGIN
        endx = XMARGIN + (BOARDWIDTH * SPACESIZE)
        endy = (y * SPACESIZE) + YMARGIN
        pygame.draw.line(DISPLAYSURF, GRIDLINECOLOR, (startx, starty), (endx, endy))

    # Draw the black & white tiles or hint spots.
    for x in range(BOARDWIDTH):
        for y in range(BOARDHEIGHT):
            centerx, centery = translateBoardToPixelCoord(x, y)
            if board[x][y] == WHITE_TILE or board[x][y] == BLACK_TILE:
                if board[x][y] == WHITE_TILE:
                    tileColor = WHITE
                else:
                    tileColor = BLACK
                pygame.draw.circle(DISPLAYSURF, tileColor, (centerx, centery), int(SPACESIZE / 2) - 4)
            if board[x][y] == HINT_TILE:
                pygame.draw.rect(DISPLAYSURF, HINTCOLOR, (centerx - 4, centery - 4, 8, 8))


def getSpaceClicked(mousex, mousey):
    # Return a tuple of two integers of the board space coordinates where
    # the mouse was clicked. (Or returns None not in any space.)
    for x in range(BOARDWIDTH):
        for y in range(BOARDHEIGHT):
            if mousex > x * SPACESIZE + XMARGIN and \
               mousex < (x + 1) * SPACESIZE + XMARGIN and \
               mousey > y * SPACESIZE + YMARGIN and \
               mousey < (y + 1) * SPACESIZE + YMARGIN:
                return (x, y)
    return None


def drawInfo(board, playerTile, computerTile, turn):
```

```
    # Draws scores and whose turn it is at the bottom of the screen.
    scores = getScoreOfBoard(board)
    scoreSurf = FONT.render("Player Score: %s    Computer Score: %s    %s's Turn" % (str(scores[playerTile]), str(scores[computerTile]), turn.title()), True, TEXTCOLOR)
    scoreRect = scoreSurf.get_rect()
    scoreRect.bottomleft = (10, WINDOWHEIGHT - 5)
    DISPLAYSURF.blit(scoreSurf, scoreRect)


def resetBoard(board):
    # Blanks out the board it is passed, and sets up starting tiles.
    for x in range(BOARDWIDTH):
        for y in range(BOARDHEIGHT):
            board[x][y] = EMPTY_SPACE

    # Add starting pieces to the center
    board[3][3] = WHITE_TILE
    board[3][4] = BLACK_TILE
    board[4][3] = BLACK_TILE
    board[4][4] = WHITE_TILE


def getNewBoard():
    # Creates a brand new, empty board data structure.
    board = []
    for i in range(BOARDWIDTH):
        board.append([EMPTY_SPACE] * BOARDHEIGHT)

    return board


def isValidMove(board, tile, xstart, ystart):
    # Returns False if the player's move is invalid. If it is a valid
    # move, returns a list of spaces of the captured pieces.
    if board[xstart][ystart] != EMPTY_SPACE or not isOnBoard(xstart, ystart):
        return False

    board[xstart][ystart] = tile # temporarily set the tile on the board.

    if tile == WHITE_TILE:
        otherTile = BLACK_TILE
    else:
        otherTile = WHITE_TILE

```

```
    tilesToFlip = []
    # check each of the eight directions:
    for xdirection, ydirection in [[0, 1], [1, 1], [1, 0], [1, -1], [0, -1], [-1, -1], [-1, 0], [-1, 1]]:
        x, y = xstart, ystart
        x += xdirection
        y += ydirection
        if isOnBoard(x, y) and board[x][y] == otherTile:
            # The piece belongs to the other player next to our piece.
            x += xdirection
            y += ydirection
            if not isOnBoard(x, y):
                continue
            while board[x][y] == otherTile:
                x += xdirection
                y += ydirection
                if not isOnBoard(x, y):
                    break # break out of while loop, continue in for loop
            if not isOnBoard(x, y):
                continue
            if board[x][y] == tile:
                # There are pieces to flip over. Go in the reverse
                # direction until we reach the original space, noting all
                # the tiles along the way.
                while True:
                    x -= xdirection
                    y -= ydirection
                    if x == xstart and y == ystart:
                        break
                    tilesToFlip.append([x, y])

    board[xstart][ystart] = EMPTY_SPACE # make space empty
    if len(tilesToFlip) == 0: # If no tiles flipped, this move is invalid
        return False
    return tilesToFlip


def isOnBoard(x, y):
    # Returns True if the coordinates are located on the board.
    return x >= 0 and x < BOARDWIDTH and y >= 0 and y < BOARDHEIGHT


def getBoardWithValidMoves(board, tile):
    # Returns a new board with hint markings.
    dupeBoard = copy.deepcopy(board)

```

```
    for x, y in getValidMoves(dupeBoard, tile):
        dupeBoard[x][y] = HINT_TILE
    return dupeBoard


def getValidMoves(board, tile):
    # Returns a list of (x,y) tuples of all valid moves.
    validMoves = []

    for x in range(BOARDWIDTH):
        for y in range(BOARDHEIGHT):
            if isValidMove(board, tile, x, y) != False:
                validMoves.append((x, y))
    return validMoves


def getScoreOfBoard(board):
    # Determine the score by counting the tiles.
    xscore = 0
    oscore = 0
    for x in range(BOARDWIDTH):
        for y in range(BOARDHEIGHT):
            if board[x][y] == WHITE_TILE:
                xscore += 1
            if board[x][y] == BLACK_TILE:
                oscore += 1
    return {WHITE_TILE:xscore, BLACK_TILE:oscore}


def enterPlayerTile():
    # Draws the text and handles the mouse click events for letting
    # the player choose which color they want to be.  Returns
    # [WHITE_TILE, BLACK_TILE] if the player chooses to be White,
    # [BLACK_TILE, WHITE_TILE] if Black.

    # Create the text.
    textSurf = FONT.render('Do you want to be white or black?', True, TEXTCOLOR, TEXTBGCOLOR1)
    textRect = textSurf.get_rect()
    textRect.center = (int(WINDOWWIDTH / 2), int(WINDOWHEIGHT / 2))

    xSurf = BIGFONT.render('White', True, TEXTCOLOR, TEXTBGCOLOR1)
    xRect = xSurf.get_rect()
    xRect.center = (int(WINDOWWIDTH / 2) - 60, int(WINDOWHEIGHT / 2) + 40)

    oSurf = BIGFONT.render('Black', True, TEXTCOLOR, TEXTBGCOLOR1)
```

```
    oRect = oSurf.get_rect()
    oRect.center = (int(WINDOWWIDTH / 2) + 60, int(WINDOWHEIGHT / 2) + 40)

    while True:
        # Keep looping until the player has clicked on a color.
        checkForQuit()
        for event in pygame.event.get(): # event handling loop
            if event.type == MOUSEBUTTONUP:
                mousex, mousey = event.pos
                if xRect.collidepoint( (mousex, mousey) ):
                    return [WHITE_TILE, BLACK_TILE]
                elif oRect.collidepoint( (mousex, mousey) ):
                    return [BLACK_TILE, WHITE_TILE]

        # Draw the screen.
        DISPLAYSURF.blit(textSurf, textRect)
        DISPLAYSURF.blit(xSurf, xRect)
        DISPLAYSURF.blit(oSurf, oRect)
        pygame.display.update()
        MAINCLOCK.tick(FPS)


def makeMove(board, tile, xstart, ystart, realMove=False):
    # Place the tile on the board at xstart, ystart, and flip tiles
    # Returns False if this is an invalid move, True if it is valid.
    tilesToFlip = isValidMove(board, tile, xstart, ystart)

    if tilesToFlip == False:
        return False

    board[xstart][ystart] = tile

    if realMove:
        animateTileChange(tilesToFlip, tile, (xstart, ystart))

    for x, y in tilesToFlip:
        board[x][y] = tile
    return True


def isOnCorner(x, y):
    # Returns True if the position is in one of the four corners.
    return (x == 0 and y == 0) or \
           (x == BOARDWIDTH and y == 0) or \
           (x == 0 and y == BOARDHEIGHT) or \
           (x == BOARDWIDTH and y == BOARDHEIGHT)
```

```
def getComputerMove(board, computerTile):
    # Given a board and the computer's tile, determine where to
    # move and return that move as a [x, y] list.
    possibleMoves = getValidMoves(board, computerTile)
    # randomize the order of the possible moves
    random.shuffle(possibleMoves)
    # always go for a corner if available.
    for x, y in possibleMoves:
        if isOnCorner(x, y):
            return [x, y]
    # Go through all possible moves and remember the best scoring move
    bestScore = -1
    for x, y in possibleMoves:
        dupeBoard = copy.deepcopy(board)
        makeMove(dupeBoard, computerTile, x, y)
        score = getScoreOfBoard(dupeBoard)[computerTile]
        if score > bestScore:
            bestMove = [x, y]
            bestScore = score
    return bestMove
def checkForQuit():
    for event in pygame.event.get((QUIT, KEYUP)): # event handling loop
        if event.type == QUIT or (event.type == KEYUP and event.key == K_ESCAPE):
            pygame.quit()
            sys.exit()
if __name__ == '__main__':
    main()
```

INK SPILL, A "FLOOD IT" CLONE

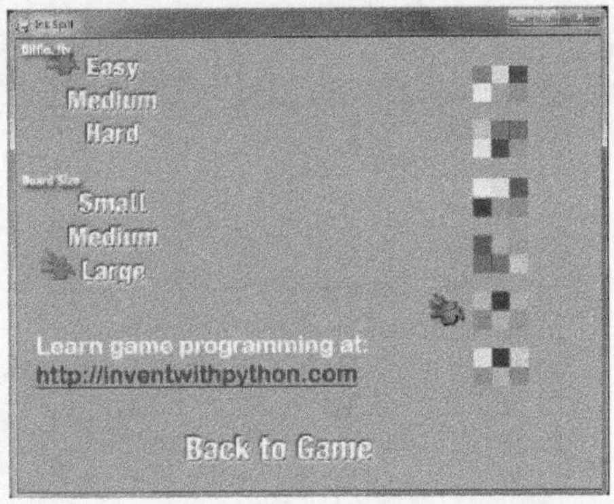

The game "Flood It" begins with a board filled with colored tiles. On each turn the player chooses a new color to paint the top left tile and any tiles adjacent to it of that same color. This game makes use of the flood fill algorithm (described in the Star Pusher chapter). The goal of the game is to turn the entire board into a single color before running out of turns.

This game also has a Settings screen where the player can change the size of the board and the difficulty of the game. If the player gets board of the colors, there are a few other color schemes they can switch to as well.

SOURCE CODE FOR INK SPILL

```
# Ink Spill (a Flood It clone)
# http://inventwithpython.com/pygame
# By Al Sweigart al@inventwithpython.com
# Released under a "Simplified BSD" license

import random, sys, webbrowser, copy, pygame
from pygame.locals import *

# There are different box sizes, number of boxes, and
# life depending on the "board size" setting selected.
SMALLBOXSIZE  = 60 # size is in pixels
MEDIUMBOXSIZE = 20
LARGEBOXSIZE  = 11

SMALLBOARDSIZE  = 6 # size is in boxes
```

```
MEDIUMBOARDSIZE = 17
LARGEBOARDSIZE  = 30

SMALLMAXLIFE  = 10 # number of turns
MEDIUMMAXLIFE = 30
LARGEMAXLIFE  = 64

FPS = 30
WINDOWWIDTH = 640
WINDOWHEIGHT = 480
boxSize = MEDIUMBOXSIZE
PALETTEGAPSIZE = 10
PALETTESIZE = 45
EASY = 0   # arbitrary but unique value
MEDIUM = 1 # arbitrary but unique value
HARD = 2   # arbitrary but unique value

difficulty = MEDIUM # game starts in "medium" mode
maxLife = MEDIUMMAXLIFE
boardWidth = MEDIUMBOARDSIZE
boardHeight = MEDIUMBOARDSIZE


#            R    G    B
WHITE    = (255, 255, 255)
DARKGRAY = ( 70,  70,  70)
BLACK    = (  0,   0,   0)
RED      = (255,   0,   0)
GREEN    = (  0, 255,   0)
BLUE     = (  0,   0, 255)
YELLOW   = (255, 255,   0)
ORANGE   = (255, 128,   0)
PURPLE   = (255,   0, 255)

# The first color in each scheme is the background color, the next six are the palette colors.
COLORSCHEMES = (((150, 200, 255), RED, GREEN, BLUE, YELLOW, ORANGE, PURPLE),
                ((0, 155, 104),  (97, 215, 164),  (228, 0, 69),  (0, 125, 50),  (204, 246, 0),  (148, 0, 45),   (241, 109, 149)),
                ((195, 179, 0),  (255, 239, 115), (255, 226, 0), (147, 3, 167), (24, 38, 176),  (166, 147, 0),  (197, 97, 211)),
                ((85, 0, 0),     (155, 39, 102),  (0, 201, 13),  (255, 118, 0), (206, 0, 113),  (0, 130, 9),    (255, 180, 115)),
                ((191, 159, 64), (183, 182, 208), (4, 31, 183),  (167, 184, 45), (122, 128, 212), (37, 204, 7),  (88, 155, 213)),
```

```
                  ((200, 33, 205), (116, 252, 185), (68, 56, 56), (52, 238, 83), (23, 149, 195), (222, 157, 227), (212, 86, 185)))
for i in range(len(COLORSCHEMES)):
    assert len(COLORSCHEMES[i]) == 7, 'Color scheme %s does not have exactly 7 colors.' % (i)
bgColor = COLORSCHEMES[0][0]
paletteColors =  COLORSCHEMES[0][1:]

def main():
    global FPSCLOCK, DISPLAYSURF, LOGOIMAGE, SPOTIMAGE, SETTINGSIMAGE, SETTINGSBUTTONIMAGE, RESETBUTTONIMAGE

    pygame.init()
    FPSCLOCK = pygame.time.Clock()
    DISPLAYSURF = pygame.display.set_mode((WINDOWWIDTH, WINDOWHEIGHT))

    # Load images
    LOGOIMAGE = pygame.image.load('inkspilllogo.png')
    SPOTIMAGE = pygame.image.load('inkspillspot.png')
    SETTINGSIMAGE = pygame.image.load('inkspillsettings.png')
    SETTINGSBUTTONIMAGE = pygame.image.load('inkspillsettingsbutton.png')
    RESETBUTTONIMAGE = pygame.image.load('inkspillresetbutton.png')

    pygame.display.set_caption('Ink Spill')
    mousex = 0
    mousey = 0
    mainBoard = generateRandomBoard(boardWidth, boardHeight, difficulty)
    life = maxLife
    lastPaletteClicked = None

    while True: # main game loop
        paletteClicked = None
        resetGame = False

        # Draw the screen.
        DISPLAYSURF.fill(bgColor)
        drawLogoAndButtons()
        drawBoard(mainBoard)
        drawLifeMeter(life)
        drawPalettes()

        checkForQuit()
        for event in pygame.event.get(): # event handling loop
            if event.type == MOUSEBUTTONUP:
                mousex, mousey = event.pos
```

```
                    if pygame.Rect(WINDOWWIDTH - SETTINGSBUTTONIMAGE.get_width(),
                                   WINDOWHEIGHT - SETTINGSBUTTONIMAGE.get_height(),
                                   SETTINGSBUTTONIMAGE.get_width(),
                                   SETTINGSBUTTONIMAGE.get_height()).collidepoint(mousex, mousey):
                        resetGame = showSettingsScreen() # clicked on Settings button
                    elif pygame.Rect(WINDOWWIDTH - RESETBUTTONIMAGE.get_width(),
                                     WINDOWHEIGHT - SETTINGSBUTTONIMAGE.get_height() - RESETBUTTONIMAGE.get_height(),
                                     RESETBUTTONIMAGE.get_width(),
                                     RESETBUTTONIMAGE.get_height()).collidepoint(mousex, mousey):
                        resetGame = True # clicked on Reset button
                    else:
                        # check if a palette button was clicked
                        paletteClicked = getColorOfPaletteAt(mousex, mousey)

            if paletteClicked != None and paletteClicked != lastPaletteClicked:
                # a palette button was clicked that is different from the
                # last palette button clicked (this check prevents the player
                # from accidentally clicking the same palette twice)
                lastPaletteClicked = paletteClicked
                floodAnimation(mainBoard, paletteClicked)
                life -= 1

                resetGame = False
                if hasWon(mainBoard):
                    for i in range(4): # flash border 4 times
                        flashBorderAnimation(WHITE, mainBoard)
                    resetGame = True
                    pygame.time.wait(2000) # pause so the player can bask in victory
                elif life == 0:
                    # life is zero, so player has lost
                    drawLifeMeter(0)
                    pygame.display.update()
                    pygame.time.wait(400)
                    for i in range(4):
                        flashBorderAnimation(BLACK, mainBoard)
                    resetGame = True
```

```
                pygame.time.wait(2000) # pause so the player can suffer in their defeat

        if resetGame:
            # start a new game
            mainBoard = generateRandomBoard(boardWidth, boardHeight, difficulty)
            life = maxLife
            lastPaletteClicked = None

        pygame.display.update()
        FPSCLOCK.tick(FPS)


def checkForQuit():
    # Terminates the program if there are any QUIT or escape key events.
    for event in pygame.event.get(QUIT): # get all the QUIT events
        pygame.quit() # terminate if any QUIT events are present
        sys.exit()
    for event in pygame.event.get(KEYUP): # get all the KEYUP events
        if event.key == K_ESCAPE:
            pygame.quit() # terminate if the KEYUP event was for the Esc key
            sys.exit()
        pygame.event.post(event) # put the other KEYUP event objects back


def hasWon(board):
    # if the entire board is the same color, player has won
    for x in range(boardWidth):
        for y in range(boardHeight):
            if board[x][y] != board[0][0]:
                return False # found a different color, player has not won
    return True


def showSettingsScreen():
    global difficulty, boxSize, boardWidth, boardHeight, maxLife, paletteColors, bgColor

    # The pixel coordinates in this function were obtained by loading
    # the inkspillsettings.png image into a graphics editor and reading
    # the pixel coordinates from there. Handy trick.

    origDifficulty = difficulty
    origBoxSize = boxSize
```

```
    screenNeedsRedraw = True

    while True:
        if screenNeedsRedraw:
            DISPLAYSURF.fill(bgColor)
            DISPLAYSURF.blit(SETTINGSIMAGE, (0,0))

            # place the ink spot marker next to the selected difficulty
            if difficulty == EASY:
                DISPLAYSURF.blit(SPOTIMAGE, (30, 4))
            if difficulty == MEDIUM:
                DISPLAYSURF.blit(SPOTIMAGE, (8, 41))
            if difficulty == HARD:
                DISPLAYSURF.blit(SPOTIMAGE, (30, 76))

            # place the ink spot marker next to the selected size
            if boxSize == SMALLBOXSIZE:
                DISPLAYSURF.blit(SPOTIMAGE, (22, 150))
            if boxSize == MEDIUMBOXSIZE:
                DISPLAYSURF.blit(SPOTIMAGE, (11, 185))
            if boxSize == LARGEBOXSIZE:
                DISPLAYSURF.blit(SPOTIMAGE, (24, 220))

            for i in range(len(COLORSCHEMES)):
                drawColorSchemeBoxes(500, i * 60 + 30, i)

            pygame.display.update()

        screenNeedsRedraw = False # by default, don't redraw the screen
        for event in pygame.event.get(): # event handling loop
            if event.type == QUIT:
                pygame.quit()
                sys.exit()
            elif event.type == KEYUP:
                if event.key == K_ESCAPE:
                    # Esc key on settings screen goes back to game
                    return not (origDifficulty == difficulty and origBoxSize == boxSize)
            elif event.type == MOUSEBUTTONUP:
                screenNeedsRedraw = True # screen should be redrawn
                mousex, mousey = event.pos # syntactic sugar

                # check for clicks on the difficulty buttons
                if pygame.Rect(74, 16, 111, 30).collidepoint(mousex, mousey):
                    difficulty = EASY
```

```
                elif pygame.Rect(53, 50, 104, 29).collidepoint(mousex, mousey):
                    difficulty = MEDIUM
                elif pygame.Rect(72, 85, 65, 31).collidepoint(mousex, mousey):
                    difficulty = HARD

                # check for clicks on the size buttons
                elif pygame.Rect(63, 156, 84, 31).collidepoint(mousex, mousey):
                    # small board size setting:
                    boxSize = SMALLBOXSIZE
                    boardWidth = SMALLBOARDSIZE
                    boardHeight = SMALLBOARDSIZE
                    maxLife = SMALLMAXLIFE
                elif pygame.Rect(52, 192, 106,32).collidepoint(mousex, mousey):
                    # medium board size setting:
                    boxSize = MEDIUMBOXSIZE
                    boardWidth = MEDIUMBOARDSIZE
                    boardHeight = MEDIUMBOARDSIZE
                    maxLife = MEDIUMMAXLIFE
                elif pygame.Rect(67, 228, 58, 37).collidepoint(mousex, mousey):
                    # large board size setting:
                    boxSize = LARGEBOXSIZE
                    boardWidth = LARGEBOARDSIZE
                    boardHeight = LARGEBOARDSIZE
                    maxLife = LARGEMAXLIFE
                elif pygame.Rect(14, 299, 371, 97).collidepoint(mousex, mousey):
                    # clicked on the "learn programming" ad
                    webbrowser.open('http://inventwithpython.com') # opens a web browser
                elif pygame.Rect(178, 418, 215, 34).collidepoint(mousex, mousey):
                    # clicked on the "back to game" button
                    return not (origDifficulty == difficulty and origBoxSize == boxSize)

                for i in range(len(COLORSCHEMES)):
                    # clicked on a color scheme button
                    if pygame.Rect(500, 30 + i * 60, MEDIUMBOXSIZE * 3, MEDIUMBOXSIZE * 2).collidepoint(mousex, mousey):
                        bgColor = COLORSCHEMES[i][0]
                        paletteColors  = COLORSCHEMES[i][1:]
```

```


def drawColorSchemeBoxes(x, y, schemeNum):
    # Draws the color scheme boxes that appear on the "Settings" screen.
    for boxy in range(2):
        for boxx in range(3):
            pygame.draw.rect(DISPLAYSURF, COLORSCHEMES[schemeNum][3 * boxy
+ boxx + 1], (x + MEDIUMBOXSIZE * boxx, y + MEDIUMBOXSIZE * boxy,
MEDIUMBOXSIZE, MEDIUMBOXSIZE))
            if paletteColors == COLORSCHEMES[schemeNum][1:]:
                # put the ink spot next to the selected color scheme
                DISPLAYSURF.blit(SPOTIMAGE, (x - 50, y))


def flashBorderAnimation(color, board, animationSpeed=30):
    origSurf = DISPLAYSURF.copy()
    flashSurf = pygame.Surface(DISPLAYSURF.get_size())
    flashSurf = flashSurf.convert_alpha()
    for start, end, step in ((0, 256, 1), (255, 0, -1)):
        # the first iteration on the outer loop will set the inner loop
        # to have transparency go from 0 to 255, the second iteration will
        # have it go from 255 to 0. This is the "flash".
        for transparency in range(start, end, animationSpeed * step):
            DISPLAYSURF.blit(origSurf, (0, 0))
            r, g, b = color
            flashSurf.fill((r, g, b, transparency))
            DISPLAYSURF.blit(flashSurf, (0, 0))
            drawBoard(board) # draw board ON TOP OF the transparency layer
            pygame.display.update()
            FPSCLOCK.tick(FPS)
    DISPLAYSURF.blit(origSurf, (0, 0)) # redraw the original surface


def floodAnimation(board, paletteClicked, animationSpeed=25):
    origBoard = copy.deepcopy(board)
    floodFill(board, board[0][0], paletteClicked, 0, 0)

    for transparency in range(0, 255, animationSpeed):
        # The "new" board slowly become opaque over the original board.
        drawBoard(origBoard)
        drawBoard(board, transparency)
        pygame.display.update()
        FPSCLOCK.tick(FPS)


def generateRandomBoard(width, height, difficulty=MEDIUM):
```

```
    # Creates a board data structure with random colors for each box.
    board = []
    for x in range(width):
        column = []
        for y in range(height):
            column.append(random.randint(0, len(paletteColors) - 1))
        board.append(column)

    # Make board easier by setting some boxes to same color as a neighbor.

    # Determine how many boxes to change.
    if difficulty == EASY:
        if boxSize == SMALLBOXSIZE:
            boxesToChange = 100
        else:
            boxesToChange = 1500
    elif difficulty == MEDIUM:
        if boxSize == SMALLBOXSIZE:
            boxesToChange = 5
        else:
            boxesToChange = 200
    else:
        boxesToChange = 0

    # Change neighbor's colors:
    for i in range(boxesToChange):
        # Randomly choose a box whose color to copy
        x = random.randint(1, width-2)
        y = random.randint(1, height-2)

        # Randomly choose neighbors to change.
        direction = random.randint(0, 3)
        if direction == 0: # change left and up neighbor
            board[x-1][y] == board[x][y]
            board[x][y-1] == board[x][y]
        elif direction == 1: # change right and down neighbor
            board[x+1][y] == board[x][y]
            board[x][y+1] == board[x][y]
        elif direction == 2: # change right and up neighbor
            board[x][y-1] == board[x][y]
            board[x+1][y] == board[x][y]
        else: # change left and down neighbor
            board[x][y+1] == board[x][y]
            board[x-1][y] == board[x][y]
    return board
```

```

def drawLogoAndButtons():
    # draw the Ink Spill logo and Settings and Reset buttons.
    DISPLAYSURF.blit(LOGOIMAGE, (WINDOWWIDTH - LOGOIMAGE.get_width(), 0))
    DISPLAYSURF.blit(SETTINGSBUTTONIMAGE, (WINDOWWIDTH - SETTINGSBUTTONIMAGE.get_width(), WINDOWHEIGHT - SETTINGSBUTTONIMAGE.get_height()))
    DISPLAYSURF.blit(RESETBUTTONIMAGE, (WINDOWWIDTH - RESETBUTTONIMAGE.get_width(), WINDOWHEIGHT - SETTINGSBUTTONIMAGE.get_height() - RESETBUTTONIMAGE.get_height()))


def drawBoard(board, transparency=255):
    # The colored squares are drawn to a temporary surface which is then
    # drawn to the DISPLAYSURF surface. This is done so we can draw the
    # squares with transparency on top of DISPLAYSURF as it currently is.
    tempSurf = pygame.Surface(DISPLAYSURF.get_size())
    tempSurf = tempSurf.convert_alpha()
    tempSurf.fill((0, 0, 0, 0))

    for x in range(boardWidth):
        for y in range(boardHeight):
            left, top = leftTopPixelCoordOfBox(x, y)
            r, g, b = paletteColors[board[x][y]]
            pygame.draw.rect(tempSurf, (r, g, b, transparency), (left, top, boxSize, boxSize))
    left, top = leftTopPixelCoordOfBox(0, 0)
    pygame.draw.rect(tempSurf, BLACK, (left-1, top-1, boxSize * boardWidth + 1, boxSize * boardHeight + 1), 1)
    DISPLAYSURF.blit(tempSurf, (0, 0))


def drawPalettes():
    # Draws the six color palettes at the bottom of the screen.
    numColors = len(paletteColors)
    xmargin = int((WINDOWWIDTH - ((PALETTESIZE * numColors) + (PALETTEGAPSIZE * (numColors - 1)))) / 2)
    for i in range(numColors):
        left = xmargin + (i * PALETTESIZE) + (i * PALETTEGAPSIZE)
        top = WINDOWHEIGHT - PALETTESIZE - 10
        pygame.draw.rect(DISPLAYSURF, paletteColors[i], (left, top, PALETTESIZE, PALETTESIZE))
        pygame.draw.rect(DISPLAYSURF, bgColor,   (left + 2, top + 2, PALETTESIZE - 4, PALETTESIZE - 4), 2)


```

```
def drawLifeMeter(currentLife):
    lifeBoxSize = int((WINDOWHEIGHT - 40) / maxLife)

    # Draw background color of life meter.
    pygame.draw.rect(DISPLAYSURF, bgColor, (20, 20, 20, 20 + (maxLife * lifeBoxSize)))

    for i in range(maxLife):
        if currentLife >= (maxLife - i): # draw a solid red box
            pygame.draw.rect(DISPLAYSURF, RED, (20, 20 + (i * lifeBoxSize), 20, lifeBoxSize))
        pygame.draw.rect(DISPLAYSURF, WHITE, (20, 20 + (i * lifeBoxSize), 20, lifeBoxSize), 1) # draw white outline


def getColorOfPaletteAt(x, y):
    # Returns the index of the color in paletteColors that the x and y parameters
    # are over. Returns None if x and y are not over any palette.
    numColors = len(paletteColors)
    xmargin = int((WINDOWWIDTH - ((PALETTESIZE * numColors) + (PALETTEGAPSIZE * (numColors - 1)))) / 2)
    top = WINDOWHEIGHT - PALETTESIZE - 10
    for i in range(numColors):
        # Find out if the mouse click is inside any of the palettes.
        left = xmargin + (i * PALETTESIZE) + (i * PALETTEGAPSIZE)
        r = pygame.Rect(left, top, PALETTESIZE, PALETTESIZE)
        if r.collidepoint(x, y):
            return i
    return None # no palette exists at these x, y coordinates


def floodFill(board, oldColor, newColor, x, y):
    # This is the flood fill algorithm.
    if oldColor == newColor or board[x][y] != oldColor:
        return

    board[x][y] = newColor # change the color of the current box

    # Make the recursive call for any neighboring boxes:
    if x > 0:
        floodFill(board, oldColor, newColor, x - 1, y) # on box to the left
    if x < boardWidth - 1:
        floodFill(board, oldColor, newColor, x + 1, y) # on box to the right
```

```
    if y > 0:
        floodFill(board, oldColor, newColor, x, y - 1) # on box to up
    if y < boardHeight - 1:
        floodFill(board, oldColor, newColor, x, y + 1) # on box to down


def leftTopPixelCoordOfBox(boxx, boxy):
    # Returns the x and y of the left-topmost pixel of the xth & yth box.
    xmargin = int((WINDOWWIDTH - (boardWidth * boxSize)) / 2)
    ymargin = int((WINDOWHEIGHT - (boardHeight * boxSize)) / 2)
    return (boxx * boxSize + xmargin, boxy * boxSize + ymargin)


if __name__ == '__main__':
    main()
```

FOUR-IN-A-ROW, A "CONNECT FOUR" CLONE

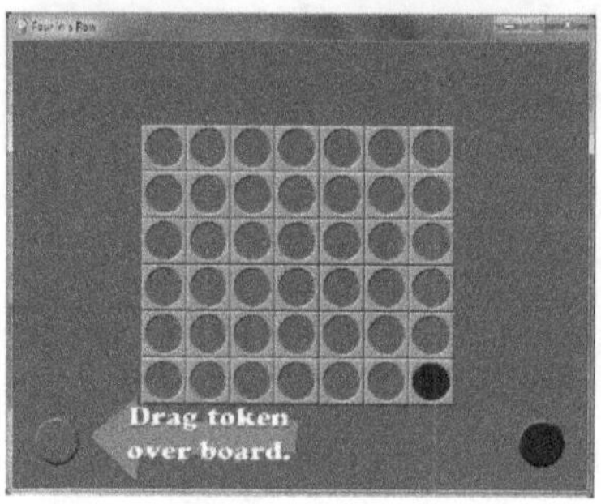

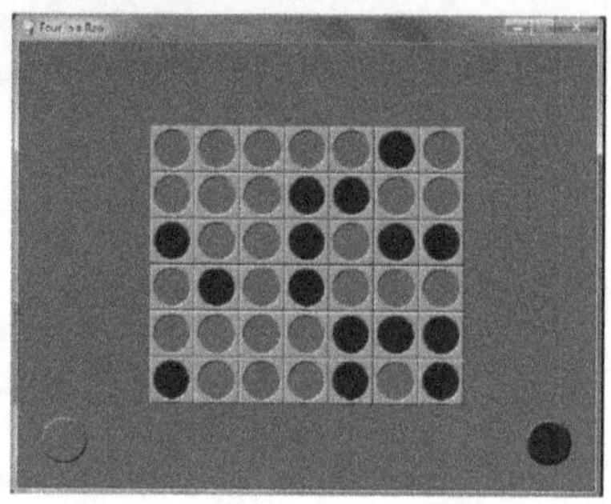

The game "Connect Four" has a 7 x 6 board where the players take turns dropping tokens from the top of the board. The tokens will fall from the top of each column and come to rest on the bottom of the board or on top of the topmost token in that column. A player wins when four of their tokens line up in a row either horizontally, vertically, or diagonally.

The AI for this game is pretty good. It simulates every possible move it can make, then simulates every possible move the human player can make in response to each of those moves, and then simulates every possible move it can make *in response to that*, and then simulates every possible move the human player could make *in response to each of those moves!* After all that thinking, the computer determines which move is most likely to lead to it winning.

So the computer is kind of tough to beat. I usually lose to it.

Since there are seven possible moves you can make on your turn (unless some columns are full), and seven possible moves the opponent could make, and seven moves in response to that, and seven moves in response to that, that means that on each turn the computer is considering 7 x 7 x 7 x 7 = 2,401 possible moves. You can make the computer consider the game even further by setting the DIFFICULTY constant to a higher number, but when I set to a value larger than 2, the computer takes a long time to calculate its turn.

You can also make the computer easier by setting DIFFICULTY to 1. Then the computer only considers each of its moves and the player's possible responses to those moves. If you set the DIFFICULTY to 0, then the computer loses all intelligence and simply makes random moves.

SOURCE CODE FOR FOUR-IN-A-ROW

```
# Four-In-A-Row (a Connect Four clone)
# By Al Sweigart al@inventwithpython.com
# http://inventwithpython.com/pygame
# Released under a "Simplified BSD" license

import random, copy, sys, pygame
from pygame.locals import *

BOARDWIDTH = 7  # how many spaces wide the board is
BOARDHEIGHT = 6 # how many spaces tall the board is
assert BOARDWIDTH >= 4 and BOARDHEIGHT >= 4, 'Board must be at least 4x4.'

DIFFICULTY = 2 # how many moves to look ahead. (>2 is usually too slow)

SPACESIZE = 50 # size of the tokens and individual board spaces in pixels

FPS = 30 # frames per second to update the screen
WINDOWWIDTH = 640 # width of the program's window, in pixels
WINDOWHEIGHT = 480 # height in pixels

XMARGIN = int((WINDOWWIDTH - BOARDWIDTH * SPACESIZE) / 2)
YMARGIN = int((WINDOWHEIGHT - BOARDHEIGHT * SPACESIZE) / 2)

BRIGHTBLUE = (0, 50, 255)
WHITE = (255, 255, 255)

BGCOLOR = BRIGHTBLUE
TEXTCOLOR = WHITE

RED = 'red'
BLACK = 'black'
EMPTY = None
HUMAN = 'human'
COMPUTER = 'computer'


def main():
    global FPSCLOCK, DISPLAYSURF, REDPILERECT, BLACKPILERECT, REDTOKENIMG
    global BLACKTOKENIMG, BOARDIMG, ARROWIMG, ARROWRECT, HUMANWINNERIMG
    global COMPUTERWINNERIMG, WINNERRECT, TIEWINNERIMG

    pygame.init()
    FPSCLOCK = pygame.time.Clock()
    DISPLAYSURF = pygame.display.set_mode((WINDOWWIDTH, WINDOWHEIGHT))
```

```
    pygame.display.set_caption('Four in a Row')

    REDPILERECT = pygame.Rect(int(SPACESIZE / 2), WINDOWHEIGHT - int(3 * SPACESIZE / 2), SPACESIZE, SPACESIZE)
    BLACKPILERECT = pygame.Rect(WINDOWWIDTH - int(3 * SPACESIZE / 2), WINDOWHEIGHT - int(3 * SPACESIZE / 2), SPACESIZE, SPACESIZE)
    REDTOKENIMG = pygame.image.load('4row_red.png')
    REDTOKENIMG = pygame.transform.smoothscale(REDTOKENIMG, (SPACESIZE, SPACESIZE))
    BLACKTOKENIMG = pygame.image.load('4row_black.png')
    BLACKTOKENIMG = pygame.transform.smoothscale(BLACKTOKENIMG, (SPACESIZE, SPACESIZE))
    BOARDIMG = pygame.image.load('4row_board.png')
    BOARDIMG = pygame.transform.smoothscale(BOARDIMG, (SPACESIZE, SPACESIZE))

    HUMANWINNERIMG = pygame.image.load('4row_humanwinner.png')
    COMPUTERWINNERIMG = pygame.image.load('4row_computerwinner.png')
    TIEWINNERIMG = pygame.image.load('4row_tie.png')
    WINNERRECT = HUMANWINNERIMG.get_rect()
    WINNERRECT.center = (int(WINDOWWIDTH / 2), int(WINDOWHEIGHT / 2))

    ARROWIMG = pygame.image.load('4row_arrow.png')
    ARROWRECT = ARROWIMG.get_rect()
    ARROWRECT.left = REDPILERECT.right + 10
    ARROWRECT.centery = REDPILERECT.centery

    isFirstGame = True

    while True:
        runGame(isFirstGame)
        isFirstGame = False


def runGame(isFirstGame):
    if isFirstGame:
        # Let the computer go first on the first game, so the player
        # can see how the tokens are dragged from the token piles.
        turn = COMPUTER
        showHelp = True
    else:
        # Randomly choose who goes first.
        if random.randint(0, 1) == 0:
            turn = COMPUTER
        else:
            turn = HUMAN
```

```
        showHelp = False

    # Set up a blank board data structure.
    mainBoard = getNewBoard()

    while True: # main game loop
        if turn == HUMAN:
            # Human player's turn.
            getHumanMove(mainBoard, showHelp)
            if showHelp:
                # turn off help arrow after the first move
                showHelp = False
            if isWinner(mainBoard, RED):
                winnerImg = HUMANWINNERIMG
                break
            turn = COMPUTER # switch to other player's turn
        else:
            # Computer player's turn.
            column = getComputerMove(mainBoard)
            animateComputerMoving(mainBoard, column)
            makeMove(mainBoard, BLACK, column)
            if isWinner(mainBoard, BLACK):
                winnerImg = COMPUTERWINNERIMG
                break
            turn = HUMAN # switch to other player's turn

        if isBoardFull(mainBoard):
            # A completely filled board means it's a tie.
            winnerImg = TIEWINNERIMG
            break

    while True:
        # Keep looping until player clicks the mouse or quits.
        drawBoard(mainBoard)
        DISPLAYSURF.blit(winnerImg, WINNERRECT)
        pygame.display.update()
        FPSCLOCK.tick()
        for event in pygame.event.get(): # event handling loop
            if event.type == QUIT or (event.type == KEYUP and event.key == K_ESCAPE):
                pygame.quit()
                sys.exit()
            elif event.type == MOUSEBUTTONUP:
                return
```

```
def makeMove(board, player, column):
    lowest = getLowestEmptySpace(board, column)
    if lowest != -1:
        board[column][lowest] = player


def drawBoard(board, extraToken=None):
    DISPLAYSURF.fill(BGCOLOR)

    # draw tokens
    spaceRect = pygame.Rect(0, 0, SPACESIZE, SPACESIZE)
    for x in range(BOARDWIDTH):
        for y in range(BOARDHEIGHT):
            spaceRect.topleft = (XMARGIN + (x * SPACESIZE), YMARGIN + (y * SPACESIZE))
            if board[x][y] == RED:
                DISPLAYSURF.blit(REDTOKENIMG, spaceRect)
            elif board[x][y] == BLACK:
                DISPLAYSURF.blit(BLACKTOKENIMG, spaceRect)

    # draw the extra token
    if extraToken != None:
        if extraToken['color'] == RED:
            DISPLAYSURF.blit(REDTOKENIMG, (extraToken['x'], extraToken['y'], SPACESIZE, SPACESIZE))
        elif extraToken['color'] == BLACK:
            DISPLAYSURF.blit(BLACKTOKENIMG, (extraToken['x'], extraToken['y'], SPACESIZE, SPACESIZE))

    # draw board over the tokens
    for x in range(BOARDWIDTH):
        for y in range(BOARDHEIGHT):
            spaceRect.topleft = (XMARGIN + (x * SPACESIZE), YMARGIN + (y * SPACESIZE))
            DISPLAYSURF.blit(BOARDIMG, spaceRect)

    # draw the red and black tokens off to the side
    DISPLAYSURF.blit(REDTOKENIMG, REDPILERECT) # red on the left
    DISPLAYSURF.blit(BLACKTOKENIMG, BLACKPILERECT) # black on the right


def getNewBoard():
    board = []
    for x in range(BOARDWIDTH):
        board.append([EMPTY] * BOARDHEIGHT)
    return board
```

```
def getHumanMove(board, isFirstMove):
    draggingToken = False
    tokenx, tokeny = None, None
    while True:
        for event in pygame.event.get(): # event handling loop
            if event.type == QUIT:
                pygame.quit()
                sys.exit()
            elif event.type == MOUSEBUTTONDOWN and not draggingToken and REDPILERECT.collidepoint(event.pos):
                # start of dragging on red token pile.
                draggingToken = True
                tokenx, tokeny = event.pos
            elif event.type == MOUSEMOTION and draggingToken:
                # update the position of the red token being dragged
                tokenx, tokeny = event.pos
            elif event.type == MOUSEBUTTONUP and draggingToken:
                # let go of the token being dragged
                if tokeny < YMARGIN and tokenx > XMARGIN and tokenx < WINDOWWIDTH - XMARGIN:
                    # let go at the top of the screen.
                    column = int((tokenx - XMARGIN) / SPACESIZE)
                    if isValidMove(board, column):
                        animateDroppingToken(board, column, RED)
                        board[column][getLowestEmptySpace(board, column)] = RED
                        drawBoard(board)
                        pygame.display.update()
                        return
                tokenx, tokeny = None, None
                draggingToken = False
        if tokenx != None and tokeny != None:
            drawBoard(board, {'x':tokenx - int(SPACESIZE / 2), 'y':tokeny - int(SPACESIZE / 2), 'color':RED})
        else:
            drawBoard(board)

        if isFirstMove:
            # Show the help arrow for the player's first move.
            DISPLAYSURF.blit(ARROWIMG, ARROWRECT)

        pygame.display.update()
        FPSCLOCK.tick()
```

```
def animateDroppingToken(board, column, color):
    x = XMARGIN + column * SPACESIZE
    y = YMARGIN - SPACESIZE
    dropSpeed = 1.0

    lowestEmptySpace = getLowestEmptySpace(board, column)

    while True:
        y += int(dropSpeed)
        dropSpeed += 0.5
        if int((y - YMARGIN) / SPACESIZE) >= lowestEmptySpace:
            return
        drawBoard(board, {'x':x, 'y':y, 'color':color})
        pygame.display.update()
        FPSCLOCK.tick()


def animateComputerMoving(board, column):
    x = BLACKPILERECT.left
    y = BLACKPILERECT.top
    speed = 1.0
    # moving the black tile up
    while y > (YMARGIN - SPACESIZE):
        y -= int(speed)
        speed += 0.5
        drawBoard(board, {'x':x, 'y':y, 'color':BLACK})
        pygame.display.update()
        FPSCLOCK.tick()
    # moving the black tile over
    y = YMARGIN - SPACESIZE
    speed = 1.0
    while x > (XMARGIN + column * SPACESIZE):
        x -= int(speed)
        speed += 0.5
        drawBoard(board, {'x':x, 'y':y, 'color':BLACK})
        pygame.display.update()
        FPSCLOCK.tick()
    # dropping the black tile
    animateDroppingToken(board, column, BLACK)


def getComputerMove(board):
    potentialMoves = getPotentialMoves(board, BLACK, DIFFICULTY)
    # get the best fitness from the potential moves
    bestMoveFitness = -1
```

```
    for i in range(BOARDWIDTH):
        if potentialMoves[i] > bestMoveFitness and isValidMove(board, i):
            bestMoveFitness = potentialMoves[i]
    # find all potential moves that have this best fitness
    bestMoves = []
    for i in range(len(potentialMoves)):
        if potentialMoves[i] == bestMoveFitness and isValidMove(board, i):
            bestMoves.append(i)
    return random.choice(bestMoves)


def getPotentialMoves(board, tile, lookAhead):
    if lookAhead == 0 or isBoardFull(board):
        return [0] * BOARDWIDTH

    if tile == RED:
        enemyTile = BLACK
    else:
        enemyTile = RED

    # Figure out the best move to make.
    potentialMoves = [0] * BOARDWIDTH
    for firstMove in range(BOARDWIDTH):
        dupeBoard = copy.deepcopy(board)
        if not isValidMove(dupeBoard, firstMove):
            continue
        makeMove(dupeBoard, tile, firstMove)
        if isWinner(dupeBoard, tile):
            # a winning move automatically gets a perfect fitness
            potentialMoves[firstMove] = 1
            break # don't bother calculating other moves
        else:
            # do other player's counter moves and determine best one
            if isBoardFull(dupeBoard):
                potentialMoves[firstMove] = 0
            else:
                for counterMove in range(BOARDWIDTH):
                    dupeBoard2 = copy.deepcopy(dupeBoard)
                    if not isValidMove(dupeBoard2, counterMove):
                        continue
                    makeMove(dupeBoard2, enemyTile, counterMove)
                    if isWinner(dupeBoard2, enemyTile):
                        # a losing move automatically gets the worst fitness
                        potentialMoves[firstMove] = -1
                        break
```

```
                    else:
                        # do the recursive call to getPotentialMoves()
                        results = getPotentialMoves(dupeBoard2, tile, lookAhead - 1)
                        potentialMoves[firstMove] += (sum(results) / BOARDWIDTH) / BOARDWIDTH
    return potentialMoves


def getLowestEmptySpace(board, column):
    # Return the row number of the lowest empty row in the given column.
    for y in range(BOARDHEIGHT-1, -1, -1):
        if board[column][y] == EMPTY:
            return y
    return -1


def isValidMove(board, column):
    # Returns True if there is an empty space in the given column.
    # Otherwise returns False.
    if column < 0 or column >= (BOARDWIDTH) or board[column][0] != EMPTY:
        return False
    return True


def isBoardFull(board):
    # Returns True if there are no empty spaces anywhere on the board.
    for x in range(BOARDWIDTH):
        for y in range(BOARDHEIGHT):
            if board[x][y] == EMPTY:
                return False
    return True


def isWinner(board, tile):
    # check horizontal spaces
    for x in range(BOARDWIDTH - 3):
        for y in range(BOARDHEIGHT):
            if board[x][y] == tile and board[x+1][y] == tile and board[x+2][y] == tile and board[x+3][y] == tile:
                return True
    # check vertical spaces
    for x in range(BOARDWIDTH):
        for y in range(BOARDHEIGHT - 3):
            if board[x][y] == tile and board[x][y+1] == tile and board[x][y+2] == tile and board[x][y+3] == tile:
```

```
                return True
    # check / diagonal spaces
    for x in range(BOARDWIDTH - 3):
        for y in range(3, BOARDHEIGHT):
            if board[x][y] == tile and board[x+1][y-1] == tile and board[x+2][y-2] == tile and board[x+3][y-3] == tile:
                return True
    # check \ diagonal spaces
    for x in range(BOARDWIDTH - 3):
        for y in range(BOARDHEIGHT - 3):
            if board[x][y] == tile and board[x+1][y+1] == tile and board[x+2][y+2] == tile and board[x+3][y+3] == tile:
                return True
    return False


if __name__ == '__main__':
    main()
```

GEMGEM, A "BEJEWELED" CLONE

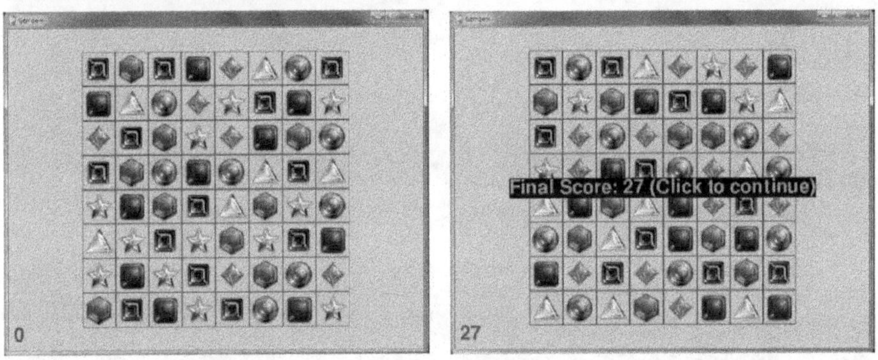

"Bejeweled" is a game where gems fall to fill up a board. The player can swap any two adjacent gems to try to match three gems in a row (vertically or horizontally, but not diagonally). The matched gems then disappear, making way for new gems to fall from the top. Matching more than three gems, or causing a chain reaction of gem matches will result in more points. The player's score slowly drops over time, so the player must constantly be making new matches. The game ends when no possible match can be made on the board.

SOURCE CODE FOR GEMGEM

```
# Gemgem (a Bejeweled clone)
# By Al Sweigart al@inventwithpython.com
# http://inventwithpython.com/pygame
# Released under a "Simplified BSD" license

"""
This program has "gem data structures", which are basically dictionaries
with the following keys:
  'x' and 'y' - The location of the gem on the board. 0,0 is the top left.
                There is also a ROWABOVEBOARD row that 'y' can be set to,
                to indicate that it is above the board.
  'direction' - one of the four constant variables UP, DOWN, LEFT, RIGHT.
                This is the direction the gem is moving.
  'imageNum'  - The integer index into GEMIMAGES to denote which image
                this gem uses.
"""

import random, time, pygame, sys, copy
from pygame.locals import *

FPS = 30 # frames per second to update the screen
WINDOWWIDTH = 600  # width of the program's window, in pixels
WINDOWHEIGHT = 600 # height in pixels

BOARDWIDTH = 8 # how many columns in the board
BOARDHEIGHT = 8 # how many rows in the board
GEMIMAGESIZE = 64 # width & height of each space in pixels

# NUMGEMIMAGES is the number of gem types. You will need .png image
# files named gem0.png, gem1.png, etc. up to gem(N-1).png.
NUMGEMIMAGES = 7
assert NUMGEMIMAGES >= 5 # game needs at least 5 types of gems to work

# NUMMATCHSOUNDS is the number of different sounds to choose from when
# a match is made. The .wav files are named match0.wav, match1.wav, etc.
NUMMATCHSOUNDS = 6

MOVERATE = 25 # 1 to 100, larger num means faster animations
DEDUCTSPEED = 0.8 # reduces score by 1 point every DEDUCTSPEED seconds.

#              R    G    B
PURPLE    = (255,   0, 255)
LIGHTBLUE = (170, 190, 255)
BLUE      = (  0,   0, 255)
RED       = (255, 100, 100)
BLACK     = (  0,   0,   0)
BROWN     = ( 85,  65,   0)
HIGHLIGHTCOLOR = PURPLE # color of the selected gem's border
BGCOLOR = LIGHTBLUE # background color on the screen
```

```
GRIDCOLOR = BLUE # color of the game board
GAMEOVERCOLOR = RED # color of the "Game over" text.
GAMEOVERBGCOLOR = BLACK # background color of the "Game over" text.
SCORECOLOR = BROWN # color of the text for the player's score

# The amount of space to the sides of the board to the edge of the window
# is used several times, so calculate it once here and store in variables.
XMARGIN = int((WINDOWWIDTH - GEMIMAGESIZE * BOARDWIDTH) / 2)
YMARGIN = int((WINDOWHEIGHT - GEMIMAGESIZE * BOARDHEIGHT) / 2)

# constants for direction values
UP = 'up'
DOWN = 'down'
LEFT = 'left'
RIGHT = 'right'

EMPTY_SPACE = -1 # an arbitrary, nonpositive value
ROWABOVEBOARD = 'row above board' # an arbitrary, noninteger value

def main():
    global FPSCLOCK, DISPLAYSURF, GEMIMAGES, GAMESOUNDS, BASICFONT, BOARDRECTS

    # Initial set up.
    pygame.init()
    FPSCLOCK = pygame.time.Clock()
    DISPLAYSURF = pygame.display.set_mode((WINDOWWIDTH, WINDOWHEIGHT))
    pygame.display.set_caption('Gemgem')
    BASICFONT = pygame.font.Font('freesansbold.ttf', 36)

    # Load the images
    GEMIMAGES = []
    for i in range(1, NUMGEMIMAGES+1):
        gemImage = pygame.image.load('gem%s.png' % i)
        if gemImage.get_size() != (GEMIMAGESIZE, GEMIMAGESIZE):
            gemImage = pygame.transform.smoothscale(gemImage, (GEMIMAGESIZE, GEMIMAGESIZE))
        GEMIMAGES.append(gemImage)

    # Load the sounds.
    GAMESOUNDS = {}
    GAMESOUNDS['bad swap'] = pygame.mixer.Sound('badswap.wav')
    GAMESOUNDS['match'] = []
    for i in range(NUMMATCHSOUNDS):
        GAMESOUNDS['match'].append(pygame.mixer.Sound('match%s.wav' % i))

    # Create pygame.Rect objects for each board space to
    # do board-coordinate-to-pixel-coordinate conversions.
    BOARDRECTS = []
    for x in range(BOARDWIDTH):
        BOARDRECTS.append([])
```

```
        for y in range(BOARDHEIGHT):
            r = pygame.Rect((XMARGIN + (x * GEMIMAGESIZE),
                             YMARGIN + (y * GEMIMAGESIZE),
                             GEMIMAGESIZE,
                             GEMIMAGESIZE))
            BOARDRECTS[x].append(r)

    while True:
        runGame()


def runGame():
    # Plays through a single game. When the game is over, this function returns.

    # initialize the board
    gameBoard = getBlankBoard()
    score = 0
    fillBoardAndAnimate(gameBoard, [], score) # Drop the initial gems.

    # initialize variables for the start of a new game
    firstSelectedGem = None
    lastMouseDownX = None
    lastMouseDownY = None
    gameIsOver = False
    lastScoreDeduction = time.time()
    clickContinueTextSurf = None

    while True: # main game loop
        clickedSpace = None
        for event in pygame.event.get(): # event handling loop
            if event.type == QUIT or (event.type == KEYUP and event.key == K_ESCAPE):
                pygame.quit()
                sys.exit()
            elif event.type == KEYUP and event.key == K_BACKSPACE:
                return # start a new game

            elif event.type == MOUSEBUTTONUP:
                if gameIsOver:
                    return # after games ends, click to start a new game

                if event.pos == (lastMouseDownX, lastMouseDownY):
                    # This event is a mouse click, not the end of a mouse drag.
                    clickedSpace = checkForGemClick(event.pos)
                else:
                    # this is the end of a mouse drag
                    firstSelectedGem = checkForGemClick((lastMouseDownX, lastMouseDownY))
                    clickedSpace = checkForGemClick(event.pos)
                    if not firstSelectedGem or not clickedSpace:
                        # if not part of a valid drag, deselect both
                        firstSelectedGem = None
                        clickedSpace = None
```

```
            elif event.type == MOUSEBUTTONDOWN:
                # this is the start of a mouse click or mouse drag
                lastMouseDownX, lastMouseDownY = event.pos

        if clickedSpace and not firstSelectedGem:
            # This was the first gem clicked on.
            firstSelectedGem = clickedSpace
        elif clickedSpace and firstSelectedGem:
            # Two gems have been clicked on and selected. Swap the gems.
            firstSwappingGem, secondSwappingGem = getSwappingGems(gameBoard, firstSelectedGem, clickedSpace)
            if firstSwappingGem == None and secondSwappingGem == None:
                # If both are None, then the gems were not adjacent
                firstSelectedGem = None # deselect the first gem
                continue

            # Show the swap animation on the screen.
            boardCopy = getBoardCopyMinusGems(gameBoard, (firstSwappingGem, secondSwappingGem))
            animateMovingGems(boardCopy, [firstSwappingGem, secondSwappingGem], [], score)

            # Swap the gems in the board data structure.
            gameBoard[firstSwappingGem['x']][firstSwappingGem['y']] = secondSwappingGem['imageNum']
            gameBoard[secondSwappingGem['x']][secondSwappingGem['y']] = firstSwappingGem['imageNum']

            # See if this is a matching move.
            matchedGems = findMatchingGems(gameBoard)
            if matchedGems == []:
                # Was not a matching move; swap the gems back
                GAMESOUNDS['bad swap'].play()
                animateMovingGems(boardCopy, [firstSwappingGem, secondSwappingGem], [], score)
                gameBoard[firstSwappingGem['x']][firstSwappingGem['y']] = firstSwappingGem['imageNum']
                gameBoard[secondSwappingGem['x']][secondSwappingGem['y']] = secondSwappingGem['imageNum']
            else:
                # This was a matching move.
                scoreAdd = 0
                while matchedGems != []:
                    # Remove matched gems, then pull down the board.

```

```
                    # points is a list of dicts that tells fillBoardAndAnimate()
                    # where on the screen to display text to show how many
                    # points the player got. points is a list because if
                    # the player gets multiple matches, then multiple points text should appear.
                    points = []
                    for gemSet in matchedGems:
                        scoreAdd += (10 + (len(gemSet) - 3) * 10)
                        for gem in gemSet:
                            gameBoard[gem[0]][gem[1]] = EMPTY_SPACE
                        points.append({'points': scoreAdd,
                                       'x': gem[0] * GEMIMAGESIZE + XMARGIN,
                                       'y': gem[1] * GEMIMAGESIZE + YMARGIN})
                    random.choice(GAMESOUNDS['match']).play()
                    score += scoreAdd

                    # Drop the new gems.
                    fillBoardAndAnimate(gameBoard, points, score)

                    # Check if there are any new matches.
                    matchedGems = findMatchingGems(gameBoard)
                firstSelectedGem = None

                if not canMakeMove(gameBoard):
                    gameIsOver = True

        # Draw the board.
        DISPLAYSURF.fill(BGCOLOR)
        drawBoard(gameBoard)
        if firstSelectedGem != None:
            highlightSpace(firstSelectedGem['x'], firstSelectedGem['y'])
        if gameIsOver:
            if clickContinueTextSurf == None:
                # Only render the text once. In future iterations, just
                # use the Surface object already in clickContinueTextSurf
                clickContinueTextSurf = BASICFONT.render('Final Score: %s (Click to continue)' % (score), 1, GAMEOVERCOLOR, GAMEOVERBGCOLOR)
                clickContinueTextRect = clickContinueTextSurf.get_rect()
                clickContinueTextRect.center = int(WINDOWWIDTH / 2), int(WINDOWHEIGHT / 2)
            DISPLAYSURF.blit(clickContinueTextSurf, clickContinueTextRect)
        elif score > 0 and time.time() - lastScoreDeduction > DEDUCTSPEED:
            # score drops over time
```

```
            score -= 1
            lastScoreDeduction = time.time()
        drawScore(score)
        pygame.display.update()
        FPSCLOCK.tick(FPS)


def getSwappingGems(board, firstXY, secondXY):
    # If the gems at the (X, Y) coordinates of the two gems are adjacent,
    # then their 'direction' keys are set to the appropriate direction
    # value to be swapped with each other.
    # Otherwise, (None, None) is returned.
    firstGem = {'imageNum': board[firstXY['x']][firstXY['y']],
                'x': firstXY['x'],
                'y': firstXY['y']}
    secondGem = {'imageNum': board[secondXY['x']][secondXY['y']],
                 'x': secondXY['x'],
                 'y': secondXY['y']}
    highlightedGem = None
    if firstGem['x'] == secondGem['x'] + 1 and firstGem['y'] == secondGem['y']:
        firstGem['direction'] = LEFT
        secondGem['direction'] = RIGHT
    elif firstGem['x'] == secondGem['x'] - 1 and firstGem['y'] == secondGem['y']:
        firstGem['direction'] = RIGHT
        secondGem['direction'] = LEFT
    elif firstGem['y'] == secondGem['y'] + 1 and firstGem['x'] == secondGem['x']:
        firstGem['direction'] = UP
        secondGem['direction'] = DOWN
    elif firstGem['y'] == secondGem['y'] - 1 and firstGem['x'] == secondGem['x']:
        firstGem['direction'] = DOWN
        secondGem['direction'] = UP
    else:
        # These gems are not adjacent and can't be swapped.
        return None, None
    return firstGem, secondGem


def getBlankBoard():
    # Create and return a blank board data structure.
    board = []
    for x in range(BOARDWIDTH):
        board.append([EMPTY_SPACE] * BOARDHEIGHT)
```

```
    return board


def canMakeMove(board):
    # Return True if the board is in a state where a matching
    # move can be made on it. Otherwise return False.

    # The patterns in oneOffPatterns represent gems that are configured
    # in a way where it only takes one move to make a triplet.
    oneOffPatterns = (((0,1), (1,0), (2,0)),
                      ((0,1), (1,1), (2,0)),
                      ((0,0), (1,1), (2,0)),
                      ((0,1), (1,0), (2,1)),
                      ((0,0), (1,0), (2,1)),
                      ((0,0), (1,1), (2,1)),
                      ((0,0), (0,2), (0,3)),
                      ((0,0), (0,1), (0,3)))

    # The x and y variables iterate over each space on the board.
    # If we use + to represent the currently iterated space on the
    # board, then this pattern: ((0,1), (1,0), (2,0))refers to identical
    # gems being set up like this:
    #
    #     +A
    #     B
    #     C
    #
    # That is, gem A is offset from the + by (0,1), gem B is offset
    # by (1,0), and gem C is offset by (2,0). In this case, gem A can
    # be swapped to the left to form a vertical three-in-a-row triplet.
    #
    # There are eight possible ways for the gems to be one move
    # away from forming a triple, hence oneOffPattern has 8 patterns.

    for x in range(BOARDWIDTH):
        for y in range(BOARDHEIGHT):
            for pat in oneOffPatterns:
                # check each possible pattern of "match in next move" to
                # see if a possible move can be made.
                if (getGemAt(board, x+pat[0][0], y+pat[0][1]) == \
                    getGemAt(board, x+pat[1][0], y+pat[1][1]) == \
                    getGemAt(board, x+pat[2][0], y+pat[2][1]) != None) or \
                   (getGemAt(board, x+pat[0][1], y+pat[0][0]) == \
                    getGemAt(board, x+pat[1][1], y+pat[1][0]) == \
                    getGemAt(board, x+pat[2][1], y+pat[2][0]) != None):
```

```
                    return True # return True the first time you find a pattern
    return False


def drawMovingGem(gem, progress):
    # Draw a gem sliding in the direction that its 'direction' key
    # indicates. The progress parameter is a number from 0 (just
    # starting) to 100 (slide complete).
    movex = 0
    movey = 0
    progress *= 0.01

    if gem['direction'] == UP:
        movey = -int(progress * GEMIMAGESIZE)
    elif gem['direction'] == DOWN:
        movey = int(progress * GEMIMAGESIZE)
    elif gem['direction'] == RIGHT:
        movex = int(progress * GEMIMAGESIZE)
    elif gem['direction'] == LEFT:
        movex = -int(progress * GEMIMAGESIZE)

    basex = gem['x']
    basey = gem['y']
    if basey == ROWABOVEBOARD:
        basey = -1

    pixelx = XMARGIN + (basex * GEMIMAGESIZE)
    pixely = YMARGIN + (basey * GEMIMAGESIZE)
    r = pygame.Rect( (pixelx + movex, pixely + movey, GEMIMAGESIZE, GEMIMAGESIZE) )
    DISPLAYSURF.blit(GEMIMAGES[gem['imageNum']], r)


def pullDownAllGems(board):
    # pulls down gems on the board to the bottom to fill in any gaps
    for x in range(BOARDWIDTH):
        gemsInColumn = []
        for y in range(BOARDHEIGHT):
            if board[x][y] != EMPTY_SPACE:
                gemsInColumn.append(board[x][y])
        board[x] = ([EMPTY_SPACE] * (BOARDHEIGHT - len(gemsInColumn))) + gemsInColumn


def getGemAt(board, x, y):
```

```
    if x < 0 or y < 0 or x >= BOARDWIDTH or y >= BOARDHEIGHT:
        return None
    else:
        return board[x][y]


def getDropSlots(board):
    # Creates a "drop slot" for each column and fills the slot with a
    # number of gems that that column is lacking. This function assumes
    # that the gems have been gravity dropped already.
    boardCopy = copy.deepcopy(board)
    pullDownAllGems(boardCopy)

    dropSlots = []
    for i in range(BOARDWIDTH):
        dropSlots.append([])

    # count the number of empty spaces in each column on the board
    for x in range(BOARDWIDTH):
        for y in range(BOARDHEIGHT-1, -1, -1): # start from bottom, going up
            if boardCopy[x][y] == EMPTY_SPACE:
                possibleGems = list(range(len(GEMIMAGES)))
                for offsetX, offsetY in ((0, -1), (1, 0), (0, 1), (-1, 0)):
                    # Narrow down the possible gems we should put in the
                    # blank space so we don't end up putting an two of
                    # the same gems next to each other when they drop.
                    neighborGem = getGemAt(boardCopy, x + offsetX, y + offsetY)
                    if neighborGem != None and neighborGem in possibleGems:
                        possibleGems.remove(neighborGem)

                newGem = random.choice(possibleGems)
                boardCopy[x][y] = newGem
                dropSlots[x].append(newGem)
    return dropSlots


def findMatchingGems(board):
    gemsToRemove = [] # a list of lists of gems in matching triplets that should be removed
    boardCopy = copy.deepcopy(board)

    # loop through each space, checking for 3 adjacent identical gems
```

```
    for x in range(BOARDWIDTH):
        for y in range(BOARDHEIGHT):
            # look for horizontal matches
            if getGemAt(boardCopy, x, y) == getGemAt(boardCopy, x + 1, y) == getGemAt(boardCopy, x + 2, y) and getGemAt(boardCopy, x, y) != EMPTY_SPACE:
                targetGem = boardCopy[x][y]
                offset = 0
                removeSet = []
                while getGemAt(boardCopy, x + offset, y) == targetGem:
                    # keep checking, in case there's more than 3 gems in a row
                    removeSet.append((x + offset, y))
                    boardCopy[x + offset][y] = EMPTY_SPACE
                    offset += 1
                gemsToRemove.append(removeSet)

            # look for vertical matches
            if getGemAt(boardCopy, x, y) == getGemAt(boardCopy, x, y + 1) == getGemAt(boardCopy, x, y + 2) and getGemAt(boardCopy, x, y) != EMPTY_SPACE:
                targetGem = boardCopy[x][y]
                offset = 0
                removeSet = []
                while getGemAt(boardCopy, x, y + offset) == targetGem:
                    # keep checking if there's more than 3 gems in a row
                    removeSet.append((x, y + offset))
                    boardCopy[x][y + offset] = EMPTY_SPACE
                    offset += 1
                gemsToRemove.append(removeSet)

    return gemsToRemove


def highlightSpace(x, y):
    pygame.draw.rect(DISPLAYSURF, HIGHLIGHTCOLOR, BOARDRECTS[x][y], 4)


def getDroppingGems(board):
    # Find all the gems that have an empty space below them
    boardCopy = copy.deepcopy(board)
    droppingGems = []
    for x in range(BOARDWIDTH):
        for y in range(BOARDHEIGHT - 2, -1, -1):
            if boardCopy[x][y + 1] == EMPTY_SPACE and boardCopy[x][y] != EMPTY_SPACE:
                # This space drops if not empty but the space below it is
```

```
                dropingGems.append( {'imageNum': boardCopy[x][y], 'x': x, 'y': y, 'direction': DOWN} )
                boardCopy[x][y] = EMPTY_SPACE
    return droppingGems


def animateMovingGems(board, gems, pointsText, score):
    # pointsText is a dictionary with keys 'x', 'y', and 'points'
    progress = 0 # progress at 0 represents beginning, 100 means finished.
    while progress < 100: # animation loop
        DISPLAYSURF.fill(BGCOLOR)
        drawBoard(board)
        for gem in gems: # Draw each gem.
            drawMovingGem(gem, progress)
        drawScore(score)
        for pointText in pointsText:
            pointsSurf = BASICFONT.render(str(pointText['points']), 1, SCORECOLOR)
            pointsRect = pointsSurf.get_rect()
            pointsRect.center = (pointText['x'], pointText['y'])
            DISPLAYSURF.blit(pointsSurf, pointsRect)

        pygame.display.update()
        FPSCLOCK.tick(FPS)
        progress += MOVERATE # progress the animation a little bit more for the next frame


def moveGems(board, movingGems):
    # movingGems is a list of dicts with keys x, y, direction, imageNum
    for gem in movingGems:
        if gem['y'] != ROWABOVEBOARD:
            board[gem['x']][gem['y']] = EMPTY_SPACE
            movex = 0
            movey = 0
            if gem['direction'] == LEFT:
                movex = -1
            elif gem['direction'] == RIGHT:
                movex = 1
            elif gem['direction'] == DOWN:
                movey = 1
            elif gem['direction'] == UP:
                movey = -1
            board[gem['x'] + movex][gem['y'] + movey] = gem['imageNum']
        else:
            # gem is located above the board (where new gems come from)
```

```
            board[gem['x']][0] = gem['imageNum'] # move to top row


def fillBoardAndAnimate(board, points, score):
    dropSlots = getDropSlots(board)
    while dropSlots != [[]] * BOARDWIDTH:
        # do the dropping animation as long as there are more gems to drop
        movingGems = getDroppingGems(board)
        for x in range(len(dropSlots)):
            if len(dropSlots[x]) != 0:
                # cause the lowest gem in each slot to begin moving in the DOWN direction
                movingGems.append({'imageNum': dropSlots[x][0], 'x': x, 'y': ROWABOVEBOARD, 'direction': DOWN})

        boardCopy = getBoardCopyMinusGems(board, movingGems)
        animateMovingGems(boardCopy, movingGems, points, score)
        moveGems(board, movingGems)

        # Make the next row of gems from the drop slots
        # the lowest by deleting the previous lowest gems.
        for x in range(len(dropSlots)):
            if len(dropSlots[x]) == 0:
                continue
            board[x][0] = dropSlots[x][0]
            del dropSlots[x][0]


def checkForGemClick(pos):
    # See if the mouse click was on the board
    for x in range(BOARDWIDTH):
        for y in range(BOARDHEIGHT):
            if BOARDRECTS[x][y].collidepoint(pos[0], pos[1]):
                return {'x': x, 'y': y}
    return None # Click was not on the board.


def drawBoard(board):
    for x in range(BOARDWIDTH):
        for y in range(BOARDHEIGHT):
            pygame.draw.rect(DISPLAYSURF, GRIDCOLOR, BOARDRECTS[x][y], 1)
            gemToDraw = board[x][y]
            if gemToDraw != EMPTY_SPACE:
                DISPLAYSURF.blit(GEMIMAGES[gemToDraw], BOARDRECTS[x][y])
```

```
def getBoardCopyMinusGems(board, gems):
    # Creates and returns a copy of the passed board data structure,
    # with the gems in the "gems" list removed from it.
    #
    # Gems is a list of dicts, with keys x, y, direction, imageNum

    boardCopy = copy.deepcopy(board)

    # Remove some of the gems from this board data structure copy.
    for gem in gems:
        if gem['y'] != ROWABOVEBOARD:
            boardCopy[gem['x']][gem['y']] = EMPTY_SPACE
    return boardCopy


def drawScore(score):
    scoreImg = BASICFONT.render(str(score), 1, SCORECOLOR)
    scoreRect = scoreImg.get_rect()
    scoreRect.bottomleft = (10, WINDOWHEIGHT - 6)
    DISPLAYSURF.blit(scoreImg, scoreRect)


if __name__ == '__main__':
    main()
```

SUMMARY

I hope these game programs have given you your own ideas about what games you'd like to make and how you can write the code for them. Even if you don't have any ideas of your own, it's great practice to try to program clones of other games you've played.

INDEX

www.ingramcontent.com/pod-product-compliance
Lightning Source LLC
LaVergne TN
LVHW062114200926
848484LV00007B/1666
* 9 7 8 1 7 8 7 1 5 3 7 9 0 *